P9-DGU-933

AN ESSAY CONCERNING HUMAN UNDERSTANDING

JOHN LOCKE

AN ESSAY CONCERNING HUMAN UNDERSTANDING

Abridged and Edited,
with an Introduction and Notes, by
KENNETH P. WINKLER

Hackett Publishing Company, Inc.
Indianapolis / Cambridge

John Locke: 1632–1704

An Essay Concerning Human Understanding
was first published in 1689

Abridgment copyright © 1996 by Kenneth P. Winkler

All rights reserved
Printed in the United States of America

22 21 20 19 6 7 8 9 10

For further information, please address

Hackett Publishing Company, Inc.
P.O. Box 44937
Indianapolis, Indiana 46244-0937
www.hackettpublishing.com

Cover design by Listenberger Design & Associates

Text design by Dan Kirklin

Library of Congress Cataloging-in-Publication Data

Locke, John, 1632–1704
[Essay concerning human understanding. Selections
An essay concerning human understanding: abridged,
with introduction and notes/by Kenneth P. Winkler.
p. cm.
Includes bibliographical references and index.
ISBN 0-87220-217-8 (cloth). ISBN 0-87220-216-X (pbk.)
1. Knowledge, Theory of—Early works to 1800. I. Winkler
Kenneth P. II. Title.
B1291.L63 1996
121—dc20 96-26935
CIP

ISBN-13: 978-0-87220-217-7 (cloth)
ISBN-13: 978-0-87220-216-0 (pbk.)

Contents

Editor's Introduction ix
Chronology xxvii
Bibliography xix

An Essay Concerning Human Understanding

Bracketed chapters have been omitted from this abridgment.

The Epistle to the Reader 1

BOOK I. Of innate notions

i *Introduction* 4
ii *No innate principles in the mind* 7
iii *No innate practical principles* 15
iv *Other considerations concerning innate principles, both speculative and practical* 23

BOOK II. Of ideas

i *Of* ideas *in general, and their original* 33
ii *Of simple* ideas 40
iii *Of* ideas *of one sense* 41
iv *Of solidity* 42
v *Of simple* ideas *of divers senses* 44
vi *Of simple* ideas *of reflection* 44
vii *Of simple* ideas *of both sensation and reflection* 45
viii *Some farther considerations concerning our simple* ideas primary/secondary qualities 47
ix *Of perception* 56
x *Of retention* 60
xi *Of discerning, and other operations of the mind* 63
xii *Of complex* ideas 66
xiii *Of simple modes; and first, of the simple modes of space* 69
xiv *Of duration, and its simple modes* 79
xv *Of duration and expansion, considered together* 83
xvi *Of number* 84
xvii *Of infinity* 85

xviii [*Of other simple modes*]
xix *Of the modes of thinking* 90
xx *Of modes of pleasure and pain* 90
xxi *Of power* 93
xxii *Of mixed modes* 114
xxiii *Of our complex* ideas *of substances* 117
xxiv *Of collective* ideas *of substances* 129
xxv *Of relation* 129
xxvi *Of cause and effect, and other relations* 132
xxvii *Of identity and diversity* 133
xxviii *Of other relations* 150
xxix *Of clear and distinct, obscure and confused* ideas 154
xxx *Of real and fantastical* ideas 157
xxxi *Of adequate and inadequate* ideas 160
xxxii *Of true and false* ideas 166
xxxiii *Of the association of* ideas 172

BOOK III. Of words

i *Of words or language in general* 176
ii *Of the signification of words* 178
iii *Of general terms* 180
iv *Of the names of simple* ideas 187
v *Of the names of mixed modes and relations* 189
vi *Of the names of substances* 192
vii *Of particles* 203
viii [*Of abstract and concrete terms*]
ix *Of the imperfection of words* 204
x *Of the abuse of words* 208
xi *Of the remedies of the foregoing imperfections and abuses* 215

BOOK IV. Of knowledge and opinion

i *Of knowledge in general* 224
ii *Of the degrees of our knowledge* 228
iii *Of the extent of human knowledge* 235
iv *Of the reality of knowledge* 250
v *Of truth in general* 254
vi *Of universal propositions, their truth and certainty* 257

vii *Of maxims* 264
viii *Of trifling propositions* 270
ix *Of our knowledge of existence* 274
x *Of our knowledge of the existence of a GOD* 275
xi *Of our knowledge of the existence of other things* 284
xii *Of the improvement of our knowledge* 292
xiii *Some farther considerations concerning our knowledge* 300
xiv *Of judgment* 301
xv *Of probability* 302
xvi *Of the degrees of assent* 305
xvii *Of reason* 312
xviii *Of faith and reason, and their distinct provinces* 323
xix [*Of enthusiasm*]
xx *Of wrong assent or error* 329
xxi *Of the division of the sciences* 336

The Stillingfleet Correspondence 339
Glossary 358

Index 365

Editor's Introduction

An Essay Concerning Human Understanding is an unusual book: it is one of the largest, richest, and most ambitious works in the history of philosophy, but it became recommended reading for students almost as soon as it first appeared in print. John Locke published the *Essay* late in 1689 (the title page of the first edition carries the year 1690); by the end of 1692, the Provost of Trinity College Dublin was so "wonderfully pleased and satisfyd" with the book that he "Orderd it to be read by the Batchelors" at his college [that is, candidates for the bachelor's degree, or perhaps recent recipients], who were then "strictly" examined—by the Provost himself—in their progress.[1]

The most obvious obstacle to the *Essay*'s success as a textbook was its length: the generous folio pages of the fourth edition of 1700, the last one to appear in Locke's lifetime (and the basis of the present abridgment) contain over three hundred thousand words.[2] Locke himself worried about the length or "prolixity" of the *Essay,* even before he thought seriously about its being used by students. As he admits in "The Epistle to the Reader," "*possibly . . . some parts of* [the book] *might be contracted: the way it has been writ in, by catches, and many long intervals of interruption, being apt to cause some repetitions.*" He adds that he is now "*too lazy, or too busy to make it shorter,*" but in 1692, when he went to work on the second edition (to appear in 1694), he asked his friend William Molyneux, the leading Irish scientist of his day, whether he should condense it. Molyneux in turn asked two "very Ingenious" friends to read the book with Locke's concern in mind; all three found it "in all its Parts . . . so wonderfully Curious, and Instructive; that they would not venture to alter anything in it."[3] Locke was relieved. He had been "of a mind to contract it," out of fear that some of its "explications" were "too long, though turn'd several ways, to make those abstract notions the easier sink into minds prejudiced in the ordinary way of

1. Molyneux to Locke, letter 1579 in *The Correspondence of John Locke,* volume 4, edited by E. S. De Beer (Oxford: Clarendon Press, 1979). University authorities were not unanimous in their approval of the *Essay,* however. In Oxford in the 1690s, for example, there was a brief (but ultimately unsuccessful) campaign to block tutors from reading the book with their students.

2. A folio page is one half of a full printed sheet. The pages of the fourth edition are more than a foot tall and about eight inches wide.

3. Molyneux to Locke, letter 1579.

education." But finding that others "judge[d] the redundancy in it a pardonable fault," he decided he would take "very little pains to reform it."[4]

Molyneux may have been happy with the *Essay,* but he thought Locke should write *another* book, in a form more suitable for students. "Your next [book]," he told Locke, "should be of a Model wholy New, and that is by Way of Logick, something accommodated to the Usual Forms, together with the Consideration of Extension, Solidity, Mobility, Thinking, Existence, Duration, Number, etc. and of the Mind of Man, and its Powers, as may make up a Compleat Body of what the Schooles [that is, the universities] call Logicks and Metaphisicks."[5] (I hope the archaic spelling of Locke and his correspondents is not too distracting. I preserve the spelling here in my introduction, because I am quoting from the standard scholarly edition of Locke's correspondence. In the abridgment itself, Locke's spelling and capitalization have been modernized, as I explain below.) "A Large Discourse in the way of a Logick," Molyneux continued, "would be much more taking [that is, more captivating or attractive] in the Universitys, wherein Youths do not satisfy themselves to have the Breeding or Busines of the Place, unles they are ingaged in something that bears the name and Form of Logick."[6] Locke wrote back to say that he had no interest in the project: he thought that the topics listed by Molyneux had been dealt with in the *Essay,* and if the *Essay* already contained the "matter" of logic and metaphysics, he wondered, what would be gained by adopting the "method" of the textbooks? "I like the method [the *Essay*] is in better than that of the schools," where doctrines are set down as if they can't be questioned or revised.[7] "I am fully convinced," Molyneux wrote in reply, "by the Arguments you give me for not turning your Book into the . . . form of a Logick and Metaphysicks; and I had no other reason to advice the other, but meerly to get it promoted the easier in our Universitys; One of the Businesses of which Places is to Learn according to the Old Forms."[8] These forms aside, he thought, there was no better logic than the *Essay*. "I know no Logick that Deserves to be Named [as reading for students]," he wrote several months later, "but the Essay of Humane Understanding."[9]

4. Locke to Molyneux, letter 1592, in volume 4 of the *Correspondence*.

5. Letter 1579.

6. Letter 1579.

7. Letter 1592.

8. Letter 1609, in volume 4 of the *Correspondence*.

9. Molyneux to Locke, letter 1652, in volume 4 of the *Correspondence*. Molyneux's *Dioptrica*

Despite his refusal to recast the *Essay* for student use, three years later Locke told Molyneux that a younger scholar was at work on a related task: "an abridgment [of the *Essay*] is now making (if it be not already done) by one of the university of Oxford, for the use of young scholars, in the place of an ordinary system of logick."[10] The Oxford scholar was John Wynne, who had told Locke that "Tho [the abridgment] will in all respects come far short of the Perfection of the Essay at large, yet I am perswaded that It will, even in this Form, far exceed, and be of much more real use, then what commonly we learn and teach, under the Name of Logick."[11] Wynne's *Abridgment of Mr. Locke's Essay concerning Humane Understanding* appeared, with Locke's approval, in 1696.

Why all this fuss over "logic"? A large part of the reason is that Locke himself viewed the *Essay* as a contribution to logic, and his conception of logic, which was widely shared, made its study—or a sensitivity to its concerns—vitally important for anyone claiming to be educated.

In the closing chapter of the *Essay* (Book IV, chapter xxi), Locke presents what he takes to be an exhaustive "division" or catalogue of the "sciences" or forms of inquiry: some, he explains, are concerned with the nature of things (physics is one example, but a science of the soul would be another); others are concerned with how things ought to be (ethics, for example, or the systematic study of law); and the rest are concerned with *signs,* whether words or ideas. Words are signs because they express ideas. And ideas, "the object[s] of the understanding when a man thinks" (Book I, chapter i, § 8), are signs of the things the mind contemplates (IV xxi 14).[12] The third branch of inquiry, Locke explains, though it can be called σημειωτική (or "the doctrine of signs"), is "aptly enough termed also λογική, logic," whose

---

Nova, the first book in English on the theory of vision, was published in London by Benjamin Tooke in 1692. Molyneux dedicated the book to the Royal Society. On the fourth unnumbered page he tells members of the Society that it is now "*full time . . . to begin a Reformation of our Human Literature, by establishing more useful Methods of Education, especially for the Employment of our more tender years.*" "Logick," he continues, "*has put on a Countenance clearly different from what it appeared in formerly,*" an observation he supports by citing *The Port-Royal Logic,* Malebranche's *Search after Truth,* and Locke's *Essay.*

10. Locke to Molyneux, letter 1887, in volume 5 of the *Correspondence,* edited by E. S. De Beer (Oxford: Clarendon Press, 1979).

11. Wynne to Locke, letter 1869, in volume 5 of the *Correspondence.*

12. Locke's *Essay* is divided into four "books." The books are divided into chapters, which are then divided into numbered sections. Throughout this volume I use uppercase roman numerals for books, lowercase roman numerals for chapters, and arabic numerals for sections. Thus "IV xxi 14" refers to Book IV, chapter xxi, section (or "§") 14.

business is "to consider the nature of signs, the mind makes use of for the understanding of things, or conveying its knowledge to others" (§ 4).

Locke does not say where in this division the *Essay* itself falls, but it clearly belongs to logic, because ideas and words are the very stuff of Locke's concern there. This is made plain by the titles of the *Essay*'s four main parts, or "books." Book II, the longest of the four, is "Of ideas." Book III is "Of words." Book IV, "Of knowledge and opinion," is perhaps not so obviously part of logic as Locke defines it, but as Locke explains there, the vehicles of knowledge and opinion are "propositions," and according to IV iv 2, every proposition is "the *joining* or *separating* of signs."[13] Book I, "Of innate notions," is an argument that no notions are present in the mind before experience, and the two kinds of "notions" under discussion there are ideas and propositions (or, as Locke often calls them, "principles," which are propositions alleged to be more basic or better known than others).

Locke's definition of logic as the science of signs may sound odd to a student enrolled in what we now call logic, because the main task of the present-day student is to internalize rules for deriving conclusions from premisses. Rules of derivation are certainly *part* of logic as Locke understands it (they are applied, after all, to what Locke calls propositions), and in *Essay* IV xvii, Locke takes up some of the claims made for the rules that prevailed in the seventeenth century. But Locke's broader conception of logic was not an idiosyncratic one. We have already seen that it was shared by Molyneux and Wynne, and it was also accepted by some of the leading textbooks of the day. One example is *The Art of Thinking* (also known as *The Port-Royal Logic*), by the French philosophers Antoine Arnauld and Pierre Nicole, a book used widely in Europe and North America from its publication in 1662 until the nineteenth century. Part I of the book, which is devoted to conception (or thinking-of, the "first" or most basic operation of the understanding), opens with the following words:[14]

> As we can have no Knowledge of what is without us, but by the Help of the Ideas which are within us; the Reflections that may be made upon our Ideas are perhaps the most important Part of Logic, because it is the Foundation of the Rest.

13. The joining or separating of ideas (or its upshot) is what Locke calls a *mental* proposition; the joining or separating of words (or its upshot) is a *verbal* one.

14. *Logic: Or, the Art of Thinking*, translated by John Ozell (London: William Taylor, 1723), p. 32.

Part I of *The Art of Thinking* corresponds in many ways to Book II of the *Essay*. In each case, an inquiry that at first seems confined or narrow swells to include almost everything. The logic of Arnauld and Nicole, for example, comes to include what was traditionally known as "general ontology," the part of traditional metaphysics that aims to identify the fundamental kinds or "categories" into which all the world's objects fall. Aristotle was the founder of systematic general ontology, and in his book *Categories,* he contends that there are ten such kinds. He argues that the category of substance—occupied by independently existing individuals, such as the human being Socrates and the horse Bucephalus—is the most basic of all, because the items in other categories (qualities, relations, and positions, for example) exist only because of the substances that "have" them. (The quality of equine shape, for example, exists only because there are horses like Bucephalus or other substances—a statue, for example—that resemble them.) Arnauld and Nicole interpret Aristotle's *Categories* as a contribution to logic. It is, they say, a classification of "all the Objects of our Thoughts" (p. 46). It is therefore a classification of what they call our ideas, and, at the same time, a classification of the world's objects—a classification of objects, that is, *insofar as we think or speak of them*. Book II of Locke's *Essay* is also a classification—and clarification—of our ideas, and therefore a classification—and clarification—of the world's objects insofar as they can be thought of or understood. This is one reason why Locke felt free to ask Molyneux whether there were any topics in metaphysics neglected in the first edition of the *Essay* that should be dealt with in the second.[15] Almost any topic in metaphysics could rightly find its way into the *Essay,* because logic, as the science of signs, bears on everything.

There is a second reason for the importance of logic to Locke, Molyneux, and Wynne. Locke describes his second branch of inquiry, the one concerned with how things ought to be, as inquiry into "the skill of right applying our own powers and actions, for the attainment of things good and useful." The end of such an inquiry is not "bare speculation," he says, but right conduct (IV xxi 3). Here Locke is describing what philosophers now call *normative* inquiry, inquiry into the "norms" or standards of conduct. And logic as Locke understands it, despite his neat threefold division, has a normative component, or at any rate a normative upshot. We can see this more clearly if we turn to Locke's aims in the *Essay*.

15. Molyneux suggested the *principle of individuation,* whatever it is in things that accounts for their distinction from other things and their self-identity over time. Locke responded by writing the present II xxvii ("Of identity and diversity").

1. *THE OVERALL SHAPE OF THE* ESSAY

In his prefatory letter, or "Epistle to the Reader," Locke explains what moved him to write the *Essay:*

> *Were it fit to trouble thee with the history of this essay, I should tell thee that five or six friends meeting at my chamber, and discoursing on a subject very remote from this, found themselves quickly at a stand, by the difficulties that rose on every side. After we had a while puzzled ourselves, without coming any nearer a resolution of those doubts which perplexed us, it came into my thoughts, that we took a wrong course; and that, before we set ourselves upon inquiries of this nature, it was necessary to examine our own abilities, and see, what objects our understandings were, or were not fitted to deal with.*

Locke's friend James Tyrrell was at the meeting in Locke's chamber; he reports that the topic was "the principles of morality and revealed religion."[16] As Locke suggests in the quoted passage, his aim in the *Essay* is to prepare his readers to conduct, with some hope of success, the kind of ambitious inquiry that brought Locke and his friends to a standstill. He is not interested merely in classifying (or even in clarifying) our ideas; he hopes besides, as he writes at I i 2, to assess the "original [or origin], certainty, and extent of human knowledge; together with the grounds and degrees of belief, opinion, and assent." Aristotle's logical writings were traditionally known as "the *Organon,*" from the Greek word ὄργανον, meaning "instrument." Locke's *Essay* is also an *organon,* an instrument designed to serve those seeking truth (or reasonable belief). And Locke's logic is at the same time an ethics—an ethics of conception and belief. Its aim is not bare speculation, but the reform of conduct.[17]

In Laurence Sterne's comic novel *The Life and Opinions of Tristram Shandy, Gentleman,* Tristram describes Locke's *Essay* as "a history-book"—a history, he adds, "of what passes in a man's own mind." Tristram promises the reader that "if you will say so much of the book, and no more,

16. In a note in his own copy of the *Essay,* now in the British Library; see Maurice Cranston, *John Locke: A Biography* (New York: Macmillan, 1957), pp. 140–41.

17. Locke's interest in the ethics of belief is especially prominent in his unfinished (and posthumously published) *Of the Conduct of the Understanding.* (It can be found in volume 3 of *The Works of John Locke* [London: Thomas Tegg, 1823].) When Locke began writing the *Conduct* he expected to include it, as a new chapter, in the fourth edition of the *Essay.*

believe me, you will cut no contemptible figure in a metaphysic circle."[18] Tristram's description is, as I will argue in a moment (and as he comes close to admitting), incomplete, but its truth, at least up to a point, is confirmed by Locke, who describes his own method as "historical" and "plain" (I i 2). "I shall not meddle," Locke writes, "with the physical consideration of the mind [that is, with its inner nature]; or trouble myself to examine, wherein its essence consists, or by what motions of our spirits, or alterations of our bodies, we come to have any sensation by our organs, or any *ideas* in our understandings; and whether those *ideas* do in their formation, any, or all of them, depend on matter, or no" (I i 2). He will instead confine himself to reporting what he observes. The *Essay* is, at least in part, a "natural history" of the understanding, akin to what we even now describe (following seventeenth-century usage) as the natural history of an animal or plant. Locke's natural history describes and classifies the objects and operations of the understanding, and like the natural history of, say, a robin, which may trace a bird's life from its birth in summer to its nesting in the following spring, Locke's history of the understanding has a temporal (and sometimes even a narrative) dimension. The narrative begins with an understanding that enters the world as "white paper, void of characters" (II i 2), and beginning in Book II, Locke shows how it comes to be "furnished" with ideas. He begins with what he calls *simple* ideas, "the materials of all our knowledge" (II ii 2), each containing "nothing but *one uniform appearance,* or conception in the mind" (II ii 1). These ideas are furnished to the mind by experience: either by *sensation,* our experience of external, sensible objects, or by *reflection,* our experience of our own inner lives. In the later chapters of Book II Locke shows how, by various operations, our *complex* ideas (including ideas that seem to be very distant from experience, such as our ideas of God and the infinite) are derived from simple ones.

To describe the *Essay* simply as a history, however, is to deny its standing as a logic. The historian's task is descriptive, narrative, or classificatory; the task of the logician is normative or evaluative. Matters of evaluation or assessment occupy Locke in some of the closing chapters of Book II, where he takes up the clarity, adequacy, and truth of our ideas, and throughout Book IV, where he considers the extent and reality of knowledge, the forms of assent that fall short of knowledge, and the boundary between faith and reason.

18. Volume 2, chapter 2, p. 85 in the edition prepared by James Aiken Work (New York: Odyssey Press, 1940). I am grateful to Edwin McCann for bringing this passage to my attention.

Tristram's description is incomplete for a second reason: its emphasis on what passes in one's *own* mind suggests that the subject of the *Essay* is a solitary individual who owes little or nothing to others. In Book III, however, the subject of the *Essay* emerges as a member of a linguistic community. Though a person's words are, immediately, signs of his or her "*internal conceptions*"—signs of conceptions locked, as Locke says, "within [one's] own mind" (III i 1)—they are used to communicate thoughts to others, so that human beings can achieve the sociability God intends for them. There are other ways in which the speaker of Book III is a social subject, and Locke's interest in our sociability carries over into Book IV, where our success in inquiry is shown to depend, at least at times, on the support of others.

2. *THE ESSAYIST IN THE* ESSAY

We now use the word "essay" for any piece of short expository writing. In the seventeenth century the word had a narrower meaning, one worth recalling as you begin to read the *Essay*. In this narrower sense, an essay is a literary *venture,* an attempt to understand or clarify its subject. Its humane and modest author does not pretend to have the last word; he or she addresses the reader not as a pupil to be instructed but as an equal, perhaps even as a friend, but at the very least as a fellow seeker after wisdom or understanding. Often, instead of pushing single-mindedly toward a definite conclusion, the essay moves off in various directions, one after the other, following questions wherever they lead. As a result, an essay can be very long. One mark of the essayist is to admit this, but to refuse to do anything about it, as if the book, rendered lean and efficient, would no longer be an essay but a more impersonal treatise.[19]

Experiments and Considerations Touching Colours, a book by Locke's friend, the chemist Robert Boyle, is an example of such an essay. It was, as its title page announces, "*First Occasionally Written, among Some Other* Essays, *to a Friend.*"[20] In the preface Boyle insists that it is not "*an accurate Treatise of Colours.*" It is merely "*an Occasional Essay*"—"occasional" because it responds to a friend's request for help or information (the book was

19. For more on the themes of this paragraph see Rosalie Colie, "The Essayist in his *Essay,*" in John W. Yolton (ed.), *John Locke: Problems and Perspectives* (Cambridge: Cambridge University Press, 1969), pp. 234–61.

20. *Experiments and Considerations Touching Colours, First Occasionally Written, among Some Other* Essays, *to a Friend* (London: Henry Herringman, 1664). The passages quoted appear in the preface, on the ninth and second of its unnumbered pages.

written, Boyle explains, "*to acquaint a private friend*" with his thoughts), an "essay" because it makes an attempt at clarification, without claiming final truth for its contentions or suggestions. The book could have been made shorter, Boyle admits, but it was written "*by snatches, at several times, and places.*"

In introducing the *Essay* to the reader, Locke makes use of many of the same devices. He calls his book an essay, and he explains that it was occasioned by a conversation with friends. He admits, as we saw, that it is longer than it needs to be; it was written, he explains, (not by Boyle's "snatches" but) by "catches," and he is now too lazy or busy to abridge it. "I pretend not to teach," he writes at II xi 17, "but to inquire." The mottos displayed on Locke's title page (but not included in this abridgment) convey the same open-mindedness and modesty. A Latin motto from Cicero's *On the Nature of the Gods* says how fine it is to admit one's ignorance, instead of causing disgust with the kind of uninformed chatter that in the end leaves everyone dissatisfied, even the speaker. And a quotation from Ecclesiastes 11:5, added to the title page in the fourth edition, says that "*as thou knowest not what is the way of the Spirit, nor how the bones do grow in the Womb of her that is with Child: even so thou knowest not the works of God, who maketh all things.*"

In the *Essay,* Locke is inculcating attitudes more than doctrines. He is trying to make the reader more like him: judicious, modest, reasonable, cautious, independent, skeptical, demanding of clarity, respectful of experience, sensitive to competing considerations, unwilling to accept anything on authority or tradition. Some of these qualities emerge in the very cadence of his sentences. He explores possibilities, some of them extreme, and then retreats to more modest and secure conclusions. *This* seems to be so, he says, but on the other hand one might say *that,* or even *that.* But be that as it may, he concludes, *this much* is certain.

All this, of course, is a matter of literary form; the author of the *Essay* was not always as diffident as he appears to be. But the form has had a powerful effect on many of the book's readers, friend as well as foe. James Lowde, for example, tempers his criticism of the *Essay* by reminding himself that it is offered "only by way of Essay."[21] And Locke's friend Nicolas Toinard, after seeing Locke's own abstract of the *Essay,* wrote that his only objection was to the book's title: such a masterpiece, he said, should not be called an essay.[22]

21. *Moral Essays* (York: Fra. Hildyard, 1699), p. 32. Note that Lowde's title claims the same protection he extends to Locke.

22. Toinard to Locke, letter 1072, in volume 3 of the *Correspondence,* edited by E. S. De Beer (Oxford: Clarendon Press, 1978).

The form of the *Essay* tells us something important about the effect Locke hoped for, and about what he expected from his readers. The *Essay,* like other essays, demands time (even in an abridgment), patience, and a kind of readerly collaboration: the willingness to think along with the author, to share the burden of his difficulties, to feel the full force of competing considerations. Knowing this helps us understand how to profit most from a reading of the book.

It can also teach us a bit about the subsequent history of philosophy. The titles of the great works of early modern British philosophy are, at first glance, bewildering combinations of apparently interchangeable elements. Each one is a "Treatise" or "Essay" or "Enquiry" "of" or "concerning" . . . "Human Understanding" or "Human Knowledge" or "Human Nature." But their titles are worth pausing over and remembering, because they are actually quite revealing. When David Hume, for example, published his first book, he called it *A Treatise of Human Nature*. The reference to Locke is unmistakable. Hume described his subject as "Human Nature" because he was taking on *more* than Locke had taken on: "Of Understanding" was the subtitle of Book I of the *Treatise,* but Hume went on to consider both the passions (in Book II) and morals (in Book III). And he described his book as a "Treatise" because he was, at least as the book began, making no display of modesty: he was establishing a new "science of man" whose results, he thought, would be quite firm. Later he became less confident, and the reworked version of Book I of the *Treatise* carried the more Lockean title *Philosophical Essays Concerning Human Understanding*.[23]

In the next four sections of this introduction I provide a brief account of some of the main themes of the four books of the *Essay*. (It may be helpful to read each section as you begin the corresponding book.) In the closing section I explain how this abridgment was prepared and describe the aids to the reader that are included in the volume.

3. *BOOK I*, "OF INNATE NOTIONS"

Chapter i of Book I is an introduction to the *Essay* as a whole, but the bulk of Book I is an attack on a view now known as *nativism:* the belief that certain ideas or beliefs (or pieces of knowledge) are planted in the mind before experience. Locke writes that "it would be sufficient to convince unprejudiced readers of the falseness of this supposition, if I should only show (as I

23. It was later retitled *An Enquiry Concerning Human Understanding*, which paired the book with *An Enquiry Concerning Morals*, a reworking of Book III of the *Treatise*.

hope I shall in the following parts of this discourse) how men, barely by the use of their natural faculties, may attain to all the knowledge they have, without the help of any innate impressions; and may arrive at certainty, without any such original notions or principles" (I ii 1); for this reason, neither Locke's own abstract of the *Essay* nor Wynne's abridgment includes the attack on nativism.

But Book I is very important to the rest of the book. Like the arguments of Descartes's First Meditation, the arguments of Book I are a kind of ground-clearing operation. Locke is preparing the way for a naturalistic investigation of the mind and its capacities, one in which attainments ascribed by others to the hand of God will be traced to our "natural" faculties, and to what Locke calls "things themselves." Our faculties are, in Locke's view, both innate and God-given, but Locke attaches great importance to the contrast between *their* creation (or our creation as beings in whom those faculties are, as he says, "inherent") and the special act of encoding or inscription called for by nativism.

Locke's main strategy in his attack on nativism is to offer interpretations of the doctrine and to show that, on each interpretation, the doctrine is either clearly false, or true in a way that must leave its defenders dissatisfied. If, for example, the doctrine means that certain beliefs are "universally agreed upon by all mankind" (I i 2), then it is clearly false: children, for example, are unaware of such allegedly innate truths as *it is impossible for the same thing to be, or not to be*. It can be argued, of course, that such truths can be present even when the mind is unaware of them, but Locke insists that "to be in the understanding, and, not to be understood; to be in the mind, and, never to be perceived, is all one, as to say, anything is, and is not, in the mind or understanding" (§ 5). Nativists may try to escape this refutation by reinterpreting the doctrine: it may become the view that innate beliefs are those that are assented to as soon as they are proposed or understood. But on this interpretation, Locke argues, there will be "legions" of innate beliefs, one for every proposition that is self-evidently true. And on the plausible assumption that "no proposition can be innate, unless the *ideas*, about which it is, be innate" (I ii 18), it follows that *every* idea will be innate, since every idea figures in at least one self-evident proposition, if only the proposition asserting that the idea is the same as itself.

The mind, according to Locke, is a blank tablet, or *tabula rasa*; it is filled or inscribed only by experience. Its knowledge of particular truths (such as *white is not red*) does not depend on a grasp of the general truths of which the particulars are "instances"; knowledge of the particular truth comes before knowledge of the general. And particular ideas come before their general counterparts, which are derived from particular ideas by abstraction.

Book I ends with an appeal to "men's own unprejudiced *experience*, and observation" (I iv 25). Like Descartes's First Meditation, Book I is designed to relieve the mind of prejudice or preconceived opinion, to prepare it for an impartial response to the evidence of experience and the compelling power of argument.

4. *BOOK II*, "OF IDEAS"

In Book II Locke traces many of our ideas to their sources in sensation and reflection, and examines their clarity, adequacy, and reality. This part of the *Essay* contains some of its most famous passages. Locke is trying to show how ideas derive their content from experience, so he must say what the content of those ideas *is*. It is here that an essay on understanding becomes an essay on almost everything. In his chapter (xxi) on our idea of power, for example, Locke argues that liberty is compatible with causal determination.

All ideas, as we saw above, originate in sensation or reflection. Some simple ideas arise from a single sense: solidity, for example, is conveyed to the mind only by the sense of touch. Others are furnished by both sight and touch: extension, for example, as well as figure, rest, and motion. Others arise only from reflection (thinking and willing, for example), and still others enter the mind "by all the ways of sensation and reflection" (II vii 1), among them pleasure, pain, power, existence, and unity.

Locke distinguishes between our ideas and the corresponding qualities in the object:

> Whatsoever the mind perceives in itself, or is the immediate object of perception, thought, or understanding, that I call *idea*; and the power to produce any *idea* in our mind, I call *quality* of the subject wherein that power is. (II viii 8)

According to II viii, these qualities are of two kinds. Objects retain their *primary* qualities no matter what happens to them; we find them in every particle of matter large enough to be perceived, and we cannot suppose that dividing the smallest sensible particles into even smaller parts would drive these qualities away. They include solidity, extension, figure, motion or rest, and number. The *secondary* qualities are merely powers to produce sensations, powers the object owes to the primary qualities of its insensible parts (and their "texture" or arrangement). The secondary qualities include colors, sounds, and tastes. There is nothing in the object that resembles the sensation of color, sound, or taste that it stimulates, but there is something in the object that resembles our ideas of solidity, extension, figure, and the other primary qualities.

There are, Locke explains, three kinds of complex ideas. Ideas of *substances* are combinations of simple ideas taken to represent a thing existing independently of other things. Ideas of *modes* are complex ideas whose objects are considered "as dependences on, or affections of substances" (II xii 4). The idea of gratitude, for example, is a mode, because gratitude is taken to exist not on its own, but in (say) a grateful person. A *relation* "consists in the consideration and comparing one *idea* with another" (II xii 7).

Locke claims that the idea of any particular substance includes the idea of "some *substratum*" in which the qualities of the substance "subsist, and from which they do result" (II xxiii 1). Our idea of this substratum is, Locke argues, hopelessly obscure: we conceive of it as a something, "we know not what," that upholds—in a way we cannot clarify—the qualities of the object. Our ideas of mind and body are, Locke argues, equally obscure, in part because both involve the obscure idea of substance or substratum.

In II xxvii, which first appeared in the second edition of the *Essay*, Locke argues that, despite our ignorance of substance, we can make confident—and practically important—judgments of identity over time. Here Locke develops his influential account of personal identity. Personal identity, he claims, consists in consciousness: "as far as this consciousness can be extended backwards to any past action or thought, so far reaches the identity of that *person;* it is the same *self* now it was then; and 'tis by the same *self* with this present one that now reflects on it, that that action was done" (§ 9).

5. *BOOK III*, "OF WORDS"

Book III was not part of Locke's original plan for the *Essay*. He intended at first to move directly from ideas (the "instruments, or materials, of our knowledge") to the "use the understanding makes of them, and what knowledge we have by them" (II xxxiii 19).[24] But he discovered that because there is "so close a connection between *ideas* and words," and because

24. II xxxiii was added to the *Essay* in the fourth edition, but § 19 appeared in all earlier editions as the concluding section of the concluding chapter of Book II.

abstract ideas, in particular, have "so constant a relation" to general words, "it is impossible to speak clearly and distinctly of our knowledge, which all consists in propositions, without considering, first, the nature, use, and signification of language."

One purpose of Book III, as Locke explains at III v 16, is to combat the disorder triggered by "the careless, and confused use and application of words." The "first and most palpable" abuse of words is using them "without clear and distinct *ideas;* or, which is worse, signs without anything signified" (III x 2). "I shall imagine I have done some service to truth, peace, and learning," Locke writes, "if, by any enlargement on this subject, I can make men reflect on their own use of language; and give them reason to suspect, that since it is frequent for others, it may also be possible for them, to have sometimes very good and approved words in their mouths, and writings, with very uncertain, little, or no signification" (III v 16).

According to Locke, most words, "*in their primary or immediate signification,*" stand for ideas in the mind of the person who uses them (III ii 2). The exceptions are "particles" such as *is* and *is not*, which signify some action or "intimation" of the mind, and "negative" or "privative" words such as *barrenness* or *ignorance*, which "relate" to ideas but do not signify them. (They instead signify the absence of the ideas to which they relate.) General words stand for general ideas, so Locke offers an account of how ideas (which enter the mind as particulars) become general. He appeals to a process of abstraction, in which the mind attends selectively to features that one idea shares with others.

Words also signify ideas in the minds of others, as well as things themselves. This is another source of abuse, because people too often apply words to ideas different from those in common use, or to ideas that disagree with the nature of things. It is also a source of imperfection. The common names of substances, for example, signify a complex idea "wherein several particular substances do, or might agree" (III vi 1). The complex idea signified by the common name *gold*, for example, is the idea of a body of a certain color and weight, which is also malleable, fusible, and "fixed" (i.e., able to preserve its weight in fire). This is the *nominal essence* of gold, or the abstract idea the word stands for. Locke distinguishes the nominal essence from the *real essence* of the metal, which is the "real constitution" (or those aspects of the real constitution) on which the properties in the nominal essence depend. "The *real essence,*" he writes at III vi 2, "is the constitution of those insensible [or imperceptible] parts of that body, on which those qualities, and all the other properties of *gold* [for example, its solubility in *aqua regia*] depend." The real essence, in other words, is the *foundation* of the properties in the nominal essence and of the properties found to coexist with it. The nominal essence is assembled by us; it determines the boundary of a sort or species. The real essence is generally unknown. *We* range things into sorts, and we cannot do it by means of an essence we do not know. In framing ideas of substances we follow nature, or at least we aspire to do so. Names of substances are therefore imperfect, because they refer to standards that cannot be known at all, or can be known only imperfectly.

6. *BOOK IV*, "OF KNOWLEDGE AND OPINION"

The final book of the *Essay* is concerned primarily with matters of assessment: the reality, scope, and limits of knowledge; the nature and grounds of reasonable belief falling short of knowledge; and the relation between reason and faith.

Locke defines knowledge as "nothing but *the perception of the connection and agreement, or disagreement and repugnancy of any of our ideas*" (IV i 2). It comes, he says, in three degrees: *intuitive* knowledge (our knowledge of the self-evident axioms of geometry, for example), *demonstrative* knowledge (our knowledge of the theorems of geometry, which are not self-evident, but are derived from the axioms by self-evidently acceptable steps), and *sensitive* knowledge (our knowledge of external objects, at the moment we are perceiving them, which "puts us past doubting" [IV ii 14], even though it is less clear and certain than the other two).

Our knowledge of existence exhibits all three degrees. Knowledge of our own existence is intuitive; here Locke's treatment (IV x 3) recalls Descartes's discovery, in the Second Meditation, that his own existence is indubitable. Our knowledge of God's existence is demonstrative; in IV xi, Locke offers a demonstrative proof that there is an eternal, omniscient, and omnipotent being. Our knowledge of the existence of other things, at the very moment we perceive them, is (as we saw above) sensitive. Locke does not take skepticism about the external world very seriously. He jokes that anyone who suspects that all we experience "is but the series and deluding appearances of a long dream, whereof there is no reality" should be told "that if all be a dream, then he does but dream, that he makes the question; and so it is not much matter, that a waking man should answer him" (IV xi 8). Anyone who puts his or her hand into a furnace, thinking it a dream or fancy, will soon learn that "our evidence [of its reality] is as great, as we can desire, being as certain to us, as our pleasure or pain" (IV xi 8).

Knowledge of existence is only one of four kinds of knowledge: the others are knowledge of identity or diversity (for example, *white is white* and *white is not red*); knowledge of relation (for example, *equals taken from equals, the remainder will be equals*); and knowledge of coexistence (or necessary connection) or exclusion (for example, *two bodies cannot be in the same place*). Our knowledge, Locke insists, reaches no farther than our ideas. Our knowledge of coexistence is particularly scanty, partly because we are ignorant of the real essences of substances. To improve our knowledge we must consult experience. Much of what we achieve in "improving" our knowledge turns out not to be knowledge strictly so called. There is no necessary connection—or no necessary connection we can perceive—between the nominal essence of gold and solubility in *aqua regia*. In such a case we must consult experience, and our knowledge reaches no farther than the samples of gold we have encountered. If we conclude that gold is *always* soluble in *aqua regia*, this is "but judgment and opinion, not knowledge and certainty" (IV xii 10).

Locke defines judgment as "the putting *ideas* together, or separating them one from another in the mind, when their certain agreement or disagreement is not perceived, but *presumed* to be so" (IV xiv 4). Probability is the appearance of agreement or disagreement of ideas whose connection is not perceived to be constant and immutable (IV xv 1). It is "likeness to be true" (§ 3), and in "natural philosophy" (what we now call natural science) probability is, for the most part, the best that we can hope for. Locke surveys the grounds of probability in chapter xv, and in chapter xvi he explains how, as the grounds vary in strength, the "degrees of assent" vary with them.

In his chapter on reason (xviii), Locke observes that the word "reason" can be defined in several ways. According to one especially important definition, reason is "the discovery of the certainty or probability of such propositions or truths, which the mind arrives at by deductions made from *ideas*, which it has got by the use of its natural faculties" (IV xviii 2). Faith, by contrast, is the assent to a proposition "not . . . made out by the deductions of reason," but "upon the credit of the proposer, as coming from GOD, in some extraordinary way of communication" known as revelation (§ 2). But "it still belongs to *reason*," Locke argues, "to judge of the truth of its being a revelation, and of the signification of the words, wherein it is delivered." No doubt can be made of what God has revealed, Locke insists, but it is the role of reason to determine whether revelation is genuine.

7. *ABOUT THIS ABRIDGMENT*

The text of this abridgement is based on the fourth edition of the *Essay*, the last one published in Locke's lifetime. Locke prepared a fifth edition for the press, but he did not live to see it printed. Because of the importance Locke attached to the substantive revisions in II xxi ("Of Power"), I have incorporated them into this edition.[25] I have modernized spelling and capitalization, but I have retained Locke's punctuation and italics. I found that I could not modernize the punctuation without making what amounted to compositional decisions.

This abridgment amounts to roughly forty percent of the *Essay*—about one hundred forty thousand words. I have achieved this mainly by sacrificing sections, but I have also eliminated certain chapters. The titles of omitted chapters appear, in brackets, in the table of contents. Because every section is numbered, the omission of a section can be inferred from the section numbers surrounding it. I have also removed sentences (and parts of sentences) from within sections. These are indicated by ellipses. Locke's section headings are placed at the beginning of sections, rather than in the margin; some have been edited to conform to the abridgment. Unlike Wynne (whose abridgment came to only ninety thousand words, partly because he eliminated chapters ii, iii, and iv of Book I), I have not rewritten Locke's sentences.

This volume includes a number of aids for the reader: explanatory footnotes in the abridgment itself; a chronology of Locke's life; a bibliography; a glossary of unfamiliar terms; and an index whose entries are taken from Locke's own index to the *Essay*. I have also included excerpts, arranged by topic, from Locke's replies to criticisms of the *Essay* made by Edward Stillingfleet, the Bishop of Worcester. Locke's replies to Stillingfleet clarify some of the most important themes in the *Essay*.[26]

For the 2005 reprinting, I have updated the bibliography and (at the urging of Jonathan Adler with regard to IV xvii 24 and of Marian David with regard to II xi 1) made two changes to the text of the abridgment.

25. Locke calls attention to the revisions in a codicil to his will, as well as in the closing paragraph of the fifth edition Epistole to the Reader, where he writes that "*in this fifth Edition, there is very little added or altered, the greater part of what is new, is contained in the* 21 *Chapter of the second Book, which any one, if he thinks it worth the while, may, with a very little Labour, transcribe into the Margent of the former edition.*"

26. I thank the Houghton Library of Harvard University for allowing me to microfilm and print its copy of the fourth edition of the *Essay*. I am grateful to James Hullett and Deborah Wilkes of Hackett Publishing Company for their support and patience, and to Susan Meyer for her comments on a draft of my introduction. I am especially indebted to Vere Chappell for his very generous and helpful advice on every aspect of the volume.

Chronology

1632 Born 29 August in Somerset, England

1647 Enters Westminster School

1652 Enters Christ Church, Oxford. He becomes Bachelor of Arts in 1656, Master of Arts in 1658, Bachelor of Medicine in 1675.

1660 Tutor at Christ Church. Soon afterwards he begins the study of medicine.

1665 Leaves Christ Church for a diplomatic assignment to Cleves

1666 Meets Lord Ashley, a leading Whig politician

1667 Moves to London to live with Ashley, serving him as physician, secretary, and political advisor

1668 Supervises an operation that saves Ashley's life

1671 Begins work on a draft of the *Essay*

1672 Ashley (now the Earl of Shaftesbury) named Lord High Chancellor, the king's highest minister

1673 Locke serves (until 1675) as Secretary to the Council of Trade and Plantations.

1675 Returns briefly to Oxford after Shaftesbury's fall from power; elected to a medical fellowship at Christ Church

Leaves England for France

1679 Returns from France

1681 Begins writing the *Two Treatises of Government*

1681 Shaftesbury arrested and charged with treason. He is released after a few months, but in 1682 he is forced into hiding in London. He later escapes to Holland, where he dies in 1683.

1683 Locke, himself in danger of arrest, leaves for Holland.

1684 Expelled (by the express command of the king) from Christ Church

1687 Completes the *Essay*

1688 An abstract of the *Essay* appears in the *Bibliothèque Universelle.*

1689 William of Orange and his forces drive King James II from the throne.

Locke returns to England, in the convoy carrying Mary of Orange.

William and Mary become king and queen.

Epistola de Tolerantia published (anonymously) in Holland; it appears, again anonymously, in English translation as *A Letter concerning Toleration*

1689 *Two Treatises of Government* published (anonymously)
The first edition of the *Essay* appears.

1691 Moves to Oates, the country home of his friend Lady Masham (Damaris Cudworth) in North Essex, about twenty miles from London
Publishes *Some Considerations of the Consequences of the Lowering of Interest, and Raising the Value of Money*

1693 Publishes *Some Thoughts concerning Education*

1695 *The Reasonableness of Christianity* published (anonymously)

1696 Begins commuting to London to serve (until 1700) as Commissioner of Trade

1704 Dies 28 October at Oates; in a codicil to his will he acknowledges authorship of *Epistola de Tolerantia, Two Treatises of Government,* and *The Reasonableness of Christianity*

Bibliography

EDITIONS OF LOCKE'S WORKS

The Works of John Locke. 10 volumes. London: Thomas Tegg, 1823. Reprinted at Aalen, Germany by Scientia Verlag in 1963.

The Clarendon Edition of the Works of John Locke, edited by Peter H. Nidditch, John Yolton, and others. Approximately 30 volumes. Oxford: Clarendon Press, 1975– .

Philosophical Works and Selected Correspondence of John Locke is an electronic edition available on disk and CD-ROM from the InteLex Corporation of Charlottesville, Virginia. This edition is based largely on the 1823 edition of the *Works*, but some important material has been added, and some of the 1823 texts have been compared to other editions and revised.

LOCKE'S CORRESPONDENCE

The Correspondence of John Locke, edited by E. S. De Beer. 9 volumes. Oxford: Clarendon Press, 1976– .

EDITIONS OF THE *ESSAY*

An Essay concerning Humane Understanding, first edition. London: Thomas Basset, 1690.

An Essay concerning Humane Understanding, second edition. London: Awnsham and John Churchil, S. Manship, 1694.

An Essay concerning Humane Understanding, third edition. London: Awnsham and John Churchil, S. Manship, 1695.

An Essay concerning Humane Understanding, fourth edition. London: Awnsham and John Churchil, S. Manship, 1700.

An Essay concerning Humane Understanding, fifth edition. London: Awnsham and John Churchill, S. Manship, 1706.

An Essay concerning Human Understanding, edited by Peter H. Nidditch. Oxford: Clarendon Press, 1975.

DRAFTS OF THE *ESSAY*

There are three surviving drafts of (or for) the *Essay*, known to scholars as "A" (written in 1671), "B" (written later in the same year), and "C" (1685).

An Early Draft of Locke's Essay [Draft A], edited by R. I. Aaron and Jocelyn Gibb. Oxford: Clarendon Press, 1936.

Drafts for the Essay concerning Human Understanding, and Other Philosophical Writings, edited by P. H. Nidditch and G. A. J. Rogers. 3 volumes. Oxford: Clarendon Press 1990– .

ABSTRACTS AND ABRIDGMENTS OF THE *ESSAY*

"Abstract of the Essay," in Peter King (ed.), *The Life and Letters of John Locke*, new edition, pp. 365–98. London: Henry Bohn, 1858. This is the basis of the French abstract published in *Bibliothèque Universelle* (8) 1688, pp. 49–162. The French abstract was published separately in 1688, and later translated into English as *An Extract of a Book, Entituled*, A Philosophical Essay upon Human Understanding (London: J. Dunton, 1692).

An Abridgment of Mr. Locke's Essay concerning Humane Understanding, edited by John Wynne. London: A. and J. Churchil, Edward Castle, 1696.

THE STILLINGFLEET CORRESPONDENCE

John Locke, *A Letter to the Right Reverend Edward, Ld Bishop of Worcester.* London: A. and J. Churchill, E. Castle, 1697.

Edward Stillingfleet, *The Bishop of Worcester's Answer to Mr. Locke's Letter.* London: Henry Mortlock, 1697.

Locke, *Mr. Locke's Reply to the . . . Bishop of Worcester's Answer to His Letter.* London: A. and J. Churchill, E. Castle, 1697.

Stillingfleet, *The Bishop of Worcester's Answer to Mr. Locke's Second Letter.* London: Henry Mortlock, 1698.

Locke, *Mr. Locke's Reply to the . . . Bishop of Worcester's Answer to His Second Letter.* London: A. and J. Churchill, C. Castle, 1699.

Locke's letters to Stillingfleet appear in volume 4 of the 1823 edition of Locke's *Works*. Stillingfleet's letters to Locke appear with selections from his *A Discourse in Vindication of the Doctrine of the Trinity* (London: Henry Mortlock, 1697), the book that initiated the controversy, in *Three Criticisms of Locke* (Hildesheim and New York: Georg Olms, 1987).

LOCKE'S LIFE

Richard Ashcraft, *Revolutionary Politics and Locke's* Two Treatises of Government. Princeton: Princeton University Press, 1986. Not a biography, but Locke's political activities are recounted and interpreted in chapters 3 and 7–10.

Maurice Cranston, *John Locke: A Biography*. New York: Macmillan, 1957.

H. R. Fox-Bourne, *The Life of John Locke*. Two volumes. New York: Harper, 1876.

John Marshall, *John Locke: Resistance, Religion, and Responsibility*. Cambridge: Cambridge University Press, 1994. A study of the development of Locke's political, religious, moral, and social thought. Marshall refines or revises some of Ashcraft's conclusions.

Roger Woolhouse, *Locke: A Biography*. New York: Cambridge University Press, 2007.

REFERENCE TOOLS

John C. Attig, *The Works of John Locke: A Comprehensive Bibliography from the Seventeenth Century to the Present*. Westport, Connecticut: Greenwood Press, 1975.

Roland Hall and Roger Woolhouse, *80 Years of Locke Scholarship: A Bibliographical Guide*. Edinburgh: Edinburgh University Press, 1983.

Jean S. Yolton, *John Locke: A Descriptive Bibliography*. Bristol: Thoemmes Press, 1998.

Jean S. Yolton and John W. Yolton, *John Locke: A Reference Guide*. Boston: G. K. Hall, 1985.

John W. Yolton, *A Locke Dictionary*. Oxford: Blackwell, 1993.

Each issue of *The Locke Newsletter*, an annual periodical renamed *Locke Studies* in 2001, includes a list of recent publications on Locke.

BOOKS DISCUSSING THE *ESSAY*

R. I. Aaron, *John Locke*, third edition. Oxford: Clarendon Press, 1971.

Peter Alexander, *Ideas, Qualities, and Corpuscles: Locke and Boyle on the External World*. Cambridge: Cambridge University Press, 1985.

Michael Ayers, *Locke*. Two volumes. London: Routledge, 1991.

Jonathan Bennett, *Learning from Six Philosophers: Descartes, Spinoza, Leibniz, Locke, Berkeley, Hume*, volume 2. Oxford: Clarendon Press, 2001.

Bennett, *Locke, Berkeley, Hume: Central Themes*. Oxford: Clarendon Press, 1971.

Gerd Buchdahl, *Metaphysics and the Philosophy of Science: The Classical Origins, Descartes to Kant.* Oxford: Blackwell, 1969. Locke is discussed in chapter 4.

Christopher Hughes Conn, *Locke on Essence and Identity*. Dordrecht: Kluwer, 2003.

John Dunn, *Locke.* Oxford: Oxford University Press, 1984.

James Gibson, *Locke's Theory of Knowledge and its Historical Relations.* Cambridge: Cambridge University Press, 1917.

Nicholas Jolley, *Locke: His Philosophical Thought.* Oxford: Oxford University Press, 1999.

G. W. Leibniz, *New Essays on Human Understanding,* translated by Peter Remnant and Jonathan Bennett. Cambridge: Cambridge University Press, 1981. A dialogue on main themes of the *Essay* between Philalethes (a representative of Locke) and Theophilus (a representative of Leibniz). Nicholas Jolley's *Leibniz and Locke* (Oxford: Clarendon Press, 1984) is a study of the *New Essays.*

Thomas Lennon, *The Battle of the Gods and Giants: The Legacies of Descartes and Gassendi, 1655–1715.* Princeton: Princeton University Press, 1993.

E. J. Lowe, *Locke.* London: Routledge, 2005.

Lowe, *Routledge Philosophy Guidebook to Locke on Human Understanding.* London: Routledge, 1995.

J. D. Mabbott, *John Locke.* London: Macmillan, 1973.

J. L. Mackie, *Problems from Locke.* Oxford: Clarendon Press, 1976.

Maurice Mandelbaum, *Philosophy, Science, and Sense Perception.* Baltimore: Johns Hopkins Press, 1964. Locke is discussed in chapter 1.

D. J. O'Connor, *John Locke.* Harmondsworth: Penguin, 1952.

Walter Ott, *Locke's Philosophy of Language.* Cambridge: Cambridge University Press, 2004.

G. A. J. Rogers, *Locke's Enlightenment: Aspects of the Origin, Nature and Impact of his Philosophy.* Hildesheim: George Olms Verlag, 1988.

Peter A. Schouls, *Reasoned Freedom: John Locke and Enlightenment.* Ithaca: Cornell University Press, 1992.

Ian Tipton, *Locke.* Milton Keynes: The Open University Press, 1983.

Nicholas Wolterstorff, *John Locke and the Ethics of Belief.* Cambridge: Cambridge University Press, 1996.

Neal Wood, *The Politics of Locke's Philosophy: A Social Study of* "An Essay Concerning Human Understanding." Berkeley: University of California Press, 1983.

Roger Woolhouse, *Locke.* Brighton: Harvester, 1983.

Woolhouse, *Locke's Philosophy of Science and Knowledge.* Oxford: Blackwell, 1971.

Gideon Yaffe, *Liberty Worth the Name: Locke on Free Agency.* Princeton: Princeton University Press, 2000.

John W. Yolton, *John Locke and the Way of Ideas.* Oxford: Clarendon Press, 1956.

Yolton, *Locke and the Compass of Human Understanding: A Selective Commentary on the* Essay. Cambridge: Cambridge University Press, 1970.

Yolton, *Locke: An Introduction.* Oxford: Blackwell, 1985.

ANTHOLOGIES RELATING TO THE *ESSAY*

Peter R. Anstey (ed.), *The Philosophy of John Locke: New Perspectives.* London: Routledge, 2003.

Richard Ashcraft (ed.), *John Locke: Critical Assessments.* 4 volumes. London: Routledge, 1991.

Reinhard Brandt (ed.), *John Locke: Symposium Wolfenbüttel 1979.* Berlin: Walter de Gruyter, 1981.

Vere Chappell (ed.), *The Cambridge Companion to Locke.* Cambridge: Cambridge University Press, 1994.

Chappell (ed.), *John Locke—Theory of Knowledge. Essays on Early Modern Philosophers,* volume 8. Hamden, Connecticut: Garland Publishing Company, 1992.

Chappell (ed.), *Locke.* Oxford: Oxford University Press, 1998.

Chappell (ed.), "Symposium on Locke and the Veil of Perception," *Pacific Philosophical Quarterly* 85 (2004), 243–363.

C. B. Martin and David Armstrong (eds.), *Locke and Berkeley.* Garden City, New York: Doubleday, 1968.

G. A. J. Rogers (ed.), *Locke's Philosophy: Content and Context.* Oxford: Clarendon Press, 1994.

Ian Tipton (ed.), *Locke on Human Understanding.* Oxford: Oxford University Press, 1977.

John W. Yolton (ed.), *John Locke: Problems and Perspectives.* Cambridge: Cambridge University Press, 1969.

AN ESSAY CONCERNING HUMAN UNDERSTANDING

The EPISTLE TO THE READER.

Reader,

I here put into thy hands, what has been the diversion of some of my idle and heavy hours: if it has the good luck to prove so of any of thine, and thou hast but half so much pleasure in reading, as I had in writing it, thou wilt as little think thy money, as I do my pains, ill bestowed. Mistake not this, for a commendation of my work; nor conclude, because I was pleased with the doing of it, that therefore I am fondly taken with it now it is done. He that hawks at larks and sparrows, has no less sport, though a much less considerable quarry, than he that flies at nobler game: and he is little acquainted with the subject of this treatise, the UNDERSTANDING, *who does not know, that as it is the most elevated faculty of the soul, so it is employed with a greater, and more constant delight than any of the other. Its searches after truth, are a sort of hawking and hunting, wherein the very pursuit makes a great part of the pleasure. Every step the mind takes in its progress towards knowledge, makes some discovery, which is not only new, but the best too, for the time at least.*

. . . .

. . . . Though it be certain, that there is nothing in this treatise of the truth whereof I am not fully persuaded; yet I consider myself as liable to mistakes, as I can think thee; and know, that this book must stand or fall with thee, not by any opinion I have of it, but by thy own. If thou findest little in it new or instructive to thee, thou art not to blame me for it. It was not meant for those, that had already mastered this subject, and made a thorough acquaintance with their own understandings; but for my own information, and the satisfaction of a few friends, who acknowledged themselves not to have sufficiently considered it. Were it fit to trouble thee with the history of this essay, I should tell thee that five or six friends meeting at my chamber, and discoursing on a subject very remote from this, found themselves quickly at a stand, by the difficulties that rose on every side. After we

had a while puzzled ourselves, without coming any nearer a resolution of those doubts which perplexed us, it came into my thoughts, that we took a wrong course; and that, before we set ourselves upon inquiries of that nature, it was necessary to examine our own abilities, and see, what objects our understandings were, or were not fitted to deal with. This I proposed to the company, who all readily assented; and thereupon it was agreed, that this should be our first inquiry. Some hasty and undigested thoughts, on a subject I had never before considered, which I set down against our next meeting, gave the first entrance into this discourse, which having been thus begun with chance, was continued by entreaty; written by incoherent parcels; and, after long intervals of neglect, resumed again, as my humor or occasions permitted; and at last, in a retirement, where an attendance on my health gave me leisure, it was brought into that order, thou now seest it.

This discontinued way of writing may have occasioned, besides others, two-contrary faults, viz. *that too little, and too much may be said in it. If thou findest anything wanting, I shall be glad, that what I have writ, gives thee any desire, that I should have gone farther: if it seems too much to thee, thou must blame the subject; for when I first put pen to paper, I thought all I should have to say on this matter, would have been contained in one sheet of paper; but the farther I went, the larger prospect I had: new discoveries led me still on, and so it grew insensibly to the bulk it now appears in. I will not deny, but possibly it might be reduced to a narrower compass than it is; and that some parts of it might be contracted: the way it has been writ in, by catches, and many long intervals of interruption, being apt to cause some repetitions. But to confess the truth, I am now too lazy, or too busy to make it shorter.*

. . . . I have so little affection to be in print, that if I were not flattered, this essay might be of some use to others, as I think, it has been to me, I should have confined it to the view of some friends, who gave the first occasion to it. My appearing therefore in print, being on purpose to be as useful as I may, I think it necessary to make, what I have to say, as easy and intelligible to all sorts of readers as I can. And I had much rather the speculative and quick-sighted should complain of my being in some parts tedious, than anyone, not accustomed to abstract speculations, or prepossessed with different notions, should mistake, or not comprehend my meaning.

. . . . If I have not the good luck to please, yet nobody ought to be offended with me. I plainly tell all my readers, except half a dozen, this treatise was not at first intended for them; and therefore they need not be at the trouble to be of that number. But yet if anyone thinks fit to be angry, and rail at it, he may do it securely: for I shall find some better way of spending my time, than in such kind of conversation. I shall always have the satisfaction to have aimed sincerely at truth and usefulness, though in one of the meanest ways. The commonwealth of

learning, is not at this time without master-builders, whose mighty designs, in advancing the sciences, will leave lasting monuments to the admiration of posterity; but everyone must not hope to be a Boyle, *or a* Sydenham; *and in an age that produces such masters, as the great*——Huygenius, *and the incomparable Mr.* Newton, *with some other of that strain; 'tis ambition enough to be employed as an under-laborer in clearing ground a little, and removing some of the rubbish, that lies in the way to knowledge; which certainly had been very much more advanced in the world, if the endeavors of ingenious and industrious men had not been much cumbered with the learned but frivolous use of uncouth, affected, or unintelligible terms, introduced into the sciences, and there made an art of, to that degree, that philosophy, which is nothing but the true knowledge of things, was thought unfit, or uncapable to be brought into well-bred company, and polite conversation.*[1] *Vague and insignificant forms of speech, and abuse of language, have so long passed for mysteries of science; and hard or misapplied words, with little or no meaning, have, by prescription, such a right to be mistaken for deep learning, and height of speculation, that it will not be easy to persuade either those who speak, or those who hear them, that they are but the covers of ignorance, and hindrance of true knowledge. . . .*

. . . .

1. Robert Boyle (1627–1691), British scientist; Thomas Sydenham (1624–1689), British physician; Christiaan Huygens (1629–1695), Dutch scientist, author of *Treatise on Light* (1678); Isaac Newton (1642–1727), British scientist, author of *Mathematical Principles of Natural Philosophy* (1687). Locke, who was himself a physician, knew all four of these men; he assisted Boyle in his laboratory and collaborated with Sydenham.

BOOK I.

CHAP. I

Introduction.

1. *An inquiry into the understanding pleasant and useful.* Since it is the *understanding* that sets man above the rest of sensible beings, and gives him all the advantage and dominion, which he has over them; it is certainly a subject, even for its nobleness, worth our labor to inquire into. The understanding, like the eye, whilst it makes us see, and perceive all other things, takes no notice of itself: and it requires art and pains to set it at a distance, and make it its own object. But whatever be the difficulties, that lie in the way of this inquiry; whatever it be, that keeps us so much in the dark to ourselves; sure I am, that all the light we can let in upon our own minds; all the acquaintance we can make with our own understandings, will not only be very pleasant; but bring us great advantage, in directing our thoughts in the search of other things.

2. *Design.* This, therefore, being my *purpose* to inquire into the original, certainty, and extent of human knowledge; together, with the grounds and degrees of belief, opinion, and assent; I shall not at present meddle with the physical consideration of the mind; or trouble myself to examine, wherein its essence consists, or by what motions of our spirits, or alterations of our bodies, we come to have any sensation by our organs, or any *ideas* in our understandings; and whether those *ideas* do in their formation, any, or all of them, depend on matter, or no. These are speculations, which, however curious and entertaining, I shall decline, as lying out of my way, in the design I am now upon. It shall suffice to my present purpose, to consider the discerning faculties of a man, as they are employed about the objects, which they have to do with: and I shall imagine that I have not wholly misemployed myself in the thoughts I shall have on this occasion, if, in this historical, plain method, I can give any account of the ways, whereby our understandings come to attain those notions of things we have, and can set down any measures of the certainty of our knowledge, or the grounds of those persuasions, which are to be found amongst men, so various, differ-

ent, and wholly contradictory; and yet asserted somewhere or other with such assurance and confidence, that he that shall take a view of the opinions of mankind, observe their oppositions, and at the same time, consider the fondness, and devotion wherewith they are embraced; the resolution, and eagerness, wherewith they are maintained, may perhaps have reason to suspect, that either there is no such thing as truth at all; or that mankind has no sufficient means to attain a certain knowledge of it.

3. *Method.* It is therefore worthwhile, to search out the *bounds* between opinion and knowledge; and examine by what measures, in things, whereof we have no certain knowledge, we ought to regulate our assent, and moderate our persuasions. In order whereunto, I shall pursue this following method.

First, I shall inquire into the *original* of those *ideas*, notions, or whatever else you please to call them, which a man observes, and is conscious to himself he has in his mind; and the ways whereby the understanding comes to be furnished with them.

Secondly, I shall endeavor to show, what *knowledge* the understanding has by those *ideas;* and the certainty, evidence, and extent of it.

Thirdly, I shall make some inquiry into the nature and grounds of *faith*, or *opinion:* whereby I mean that assent, which we give to any proposition as true, of whose truth yet we have no certain knowledge: and here we shall have occasion to examine the reasons and degrees of *assent*.

4. *Useful to know the extent of our comprehension.* If by this inquiry into the nature of the understanding, I can discover the powers thereof; *how far* they reach; to what things they are in any degree proportionate; and where they fail us, I suppose it may be of use, to prevail with the busy mind of man, to be more cautious in meddling with things exceeding its comprehension; to stop, when it is at the utmost extent of its tether; and to sit down in a quiet ignorance of those things, which, upon examination, are found to be beyond the reach of our capacities. We should not then perhaps be so forward, out of an affectation of an universal knowledge, to raise questions, and perplex ourselves and others with disputes about things, to which our understandings are not suited; and of which we cannot frame in our minds any clear or distinct perceptions, or whereof (as it has perhaps too often happened) we have not any notions at all. . . .

. . . .

6. *Knowledge of our capacity a cure of skepticism and idleness*. . . . 'Tis of great use to the sailor to know the length of his line, though he cannot with it fathom all the depths of the ocean. 'Tis well he knows, that it is long enough to reach the bottom, at such places, as are necessary to direct his voyage, and caution him against running upon shoals, that may ruin him. Our business here is not to know all things, but those which concern our conduct. If we can find out those measures, whereby a rational creature put into that state, which man is in, in this world, may, and ought to govern his opinions, and actions depending thereon, we need not be troubled, that some other things escape our knowledge.

7. *Occasion of this essay*. This was that which gave the first *rise* to this essay concerning the understanding. For I thought that the first step towards satisfying several inquiries, the mind of man was very apt to run into, was, to take a survey of our own understandings, examine our own powers, and see to what things they were adapted. Till that was done I suspected we began at the wrong end, and in vain sought for satisfaction in a quiet and secure possession of truths, that most concerned us, whilst we let loose our thoughts into the vast ocean of *being*, as if all that boundless extent, were the natural, and undoubted possession of our understandings, wherein there was nothing exempt from its decisions, or that escaped its comprehension. Thus men, extending their inquiries beyond their capacities, and letting their thoughts wander into those depths, where they can find no sure footing; 'tis no wonder, that they raise questions, and multiply disputes, which never coming to any clear resolution, are proper only to continue and increase their doubts, and to confirm them at last in perfect skepticism. Whereas were the capacities of our understandings well considered, the extent of our knowledge once discovered, and the horizon found, which sets the bounds between the enlightened and dark parts of things; between what is, and what is not comprehensible by us, men would perhaps with less scruple acquiesce in the avowed ignorance of the one, and employ their thoughts and discourse, with more advantage and satisfaction in the other.

8. *What* idea *stands for*. Thus much I thought necessary to say concerning the occasion of this inquiry into human understanding. But, before I proceed on to what I have thought on this subject, I must here in the entrance beg pardon of my reader, for the frequent use of the word *idea*, which he will find in the following treatise. It being that term, which, I think, serves best to stand for whatsoever is the object of the understanding when a man thinks, I have used is to express whatever is meant by *phantasm*,

notion, species, or whatever it is, which the mind can be employed about in thinking; and I could not avoid frequently using it.

I presume it will be easily granted me, that there are such *ideas* in men's minds; everyone is conscious of them in himself, and men's words and actions will satisfy him, that they are in others.

Our first inquiry then shall be, how they come into the mind.

CHAP. II

No innate principles in the mind.

1. *The way shown how we come by any knowledge, sufficient to prove it not innate.* It is an established opinion amongst some men, that there are in the understanding certain *innate principles;* some primary notions, κοιναὶ ἔννοιαι, characters, as it were stamped upon the mind of man, which the soul receives in its very first being; and brings into the world with it.[2] It would be sufficient to convince unprejudiced readers of the falseness of this supposition, if I should only show (as I hope I shall in the following parts of this discourse) how men, barely by the use of their natural faculties, may attain to all the knowledge they have, without the help of any innate impressions; and may arrive at certainty, without any such original notions or principles. For I imagine anyone will easily grant, that it would be impertinent to suppose, the *ideas* of colors innate in a creature, to whom God has given sight, and a power to receive them by the eyes from external objects: and no less unreasonable would it be to attribute several truths, to the impressions of nature, and innate characters, when we may observe in ourselves faculties, fit to attain as easy and certain knowledge of them, as if they were originally imprinted on the mind.

But because a man is not permitted without censure to follow his own thoughts in the search of truth, when they lead him ever so little out of the common road: I shall set down the reasons, that made me doubt of the truth of that opinion, as an excuse for my mistake, if I be in one, which I leave to be considered by those, who, with me, dispose themselves to embrace truth, wherever they find it.

2. *General assent the great argument.* There is nothing more commonly taken for granted, than that there are certain principles both *speculative* and

2. κοιναὶ ἔννοιαι, common notions.

practical (for they speak of both) universally agreed upon by all mankind: which therefore they argue, must needs be the constant impressions, which the souls of men receive in their first beings, and which they bring into the world with them, as necessarily and really as they do any of their inherent faculties.

3. *Universal consent proves nothing innate*. This argument, drawn from *universal consent*, has this misfortune in it, that if it were true in matter of fact, that there were certain truths, wherein all mankind agreed, it would not prove them innate, if there can be any other way shown, how men may come to that universal agreement, in the things they do consent in; which I presume may be done.

4. What is, is; *and* it is impossible for the same thing to be, and not to be, *not universally assented to*. But, which is worse, this argument of universal consent, which is made use of, to prove innate principles, seems to me a demonstration that there are none such: because there are none to which all mankind give an universal assent. I shall begin with the speculative, and instance in those magnified principles of demonstration, *whatsoever is, is;* and *'tis impossible for the same thing to be, and not to be*, which of all others I think have the most allowed title to innate. These have so settled a reputation of maxims universally received, that 'twill, no doubt, be thought strange, if anyone should seem to question it. But yet I take liberty to say, that these propositions are so far from having an universal assent, that there are a great part of mankind, to whom they are not so much as known.

5. *Not on the mind naturally imprinted, because not known to children, idiots, &c*. For, first 'tis evident, that all *children*, and *idiots*, have not the least apprehension or thought of them: and the want of that is enough to destroy that universal assent, which must needs be the necessary concomitant of all innate truths: it seeming to me near a contradiction, to say, that there are truths imprinted on the soul, which it perceives or understands not; imprinting, if it signify anything, being nothing else, but the making certain truths to be perceived. For to imprint anything on the mind without the mind's perceiving it, seems to me hardly intelligible. If therefore children and *idiots* have souls, have minds, with those impressions upon them, they must unavoidably perceive them, and necessarily know and assent to these truths, which since they do not, it is evident that there are no such impressions. For if they are not notions naturally imprinted, how can they be innate? And if they are notions imprinted, how can they be unknown? To say a notion is imprinted on the mind, and yet at the same time to say, that

the mind is ignorant of it, and never yet took notice of it, is to make this impression nothing. No proposition can be said to be in the mind, which it never yet knew, which it was never yet conscious of. For if any one may; then, by the same reason, all propositions that are true, and the mind is capable ever of assenting to, may be said to be in the mind, and to be imprinted: since if any one can be said to be in the mind, which it never yet knew, it must be only because it is capable of knowing it; and so the mind is of all truths it ever shall know. Nay, thus truths may be imprinted on the mind, which it never did, nor ever shall know: for a man may live long, and die at last in ignorance of many truths, which his mind was capable of knowing, and that with certainty. So that if the capacity of knowing be the natural impression contended for, all the truths a man ever comes to know, will, by this account, be, every one of them, innate; and this great point will amount to no more, but only to a very improper way of speaking; which whilst it pretends to assert the contrary, says nothing different from those, who deny innate principles. For nobody, I think, ever denied, that the mind was capable of knowing several truths. The capacity, they say, is innate, the knowledge acquired. But then to what end such contest for certain innate maxims? If truths can be imprinted on the understanding without being perceived, I can see no difference there can be, between any truths the mind is capable of knowing in respect of their original: they must all be innate, or all adventitious: in vain shall a man go about to distinguish them. He therefore that talks of innate notions in the understanding, cannot (if he intend thereby any distinct sort of truths) mean such truths to be in the understanding, as it never perceived, and is yet wholly ignorant of. For if these words (*to be in the understanding*) have any propriety, they signify to be understood. So that, to be in the understanding, and, not to be understood; to be in the mind, and, never to be perceived, is all one, as to say, anything is, and is not, in the mind or understanding. If therefore these two propositions, *whatsoever is, is;* and *it is impossible for the same thing to be, and not to be*, are by nature imprinted, children cannot be ignorant of them: infants, and all that have souls must necessarily have them in their understandings, know the truth of them, and assent to it.

6. *That men know them when they come to the use of reason, answered.* To avoid this, 'tis usually answered, that all men know and *assent* to them, *when they come to the use of reason*, and this is enough to prove them innate. I answer,

7. Doubtful expressions, that have scarce any signification, go for clear reasons to those, who being prepossessed, take not the pains to examine

even what they themselves say. For to apply this answer with any tolerable sense to our present purpose, it must signify one of these two things; either, that as soon as men come to the use of reason, these supposed native inscriptions come to be known, and observed by them: or else, that the use and exercise of men's reasons assists them in the discovery of these principles, and certainly makes them known to be true.

8. *If reason discovered them, that would not prove them innate*. If they mean that by the *use of reason* men may discover these principles; and that this is sufficient to prove them innate; their way of arguing will stand thus, (*viz.*) that whatever truths reason can certainly discover to us, and make us firmly assent to, those are all naturally imprinted on the mind; since that universal assent, which is made the mark of them, amounts to no more but this; that by the use of reason, we are capable to come to a certain knowledge of, and assent to them; and by this means there will be no difference between the maxims of the mathematicians, and theorems they deduce from them: all must equally be allowed innate, they being all discoveries made by the use of reason, and truths that a rational creature may certainly come to know, if he apply his thoughts rightly that way.

9. *'Tis false that reason discovers them*. But how can these men think the *use of reason* necessary to discover principles that are supposed innate, when reason (if we may believe them) is nothing else, but the faculty of deducing unknown truths from principles or propositions, that are already known? That certainly can never be thought innate, which we have need of reason to discover, unless as I have said, we will have all the certain truths, that reason ever teaches us, to be innate. . . .

. . . .

12. *The coming to the use of reason, not the time we come to know these maxims*. If by knowing and assenting to them, *when we come to the use of reason* be meant, that this is the time, when they come to be taken notice of by the mind; and that as soon as children come to the use of reason, they come also to know and assent to these maxims; this also is false, and frivolous. *First*, it is false. Because it is evident, these maxims are not in the mind so early as the use of reason: and therefore the coming to the use of reason is falsely assigned, as the time of their discovery. How many instances of the use of reason may we observe in children, a long time before they have any knowledge of this maxim, *that it is impossible for the same thing to be, and not*

to be? and a great part of illiterate people, and savages, pass many years, even of their rational age, without ever thinking on this, and the like general propositions. I grant men come not to knowledge of these general and more abstract truths, which are thought innate, till they come to the use of reason; and I add, nor then neither. Which is so, because till after they come to the use of reason, those general abstract *ideas* are not framed in the mind, about which those general maxims are, which are mistaken for innate principles, but are indeed discoveries made, and verities introduced, and brought into the mind by the same way, and discovered by the same steps, as several other propositions, which nobody was ever so extravagant as to suppose innate. . . .

. . . .

14. *If coming to the use of reason were the time of their discovery, it would not prove them innate*. But *secondly*, were it true, that the precise time of their being known, and assented to, were, when men come to the *use of reason;* neither would that prove them innate. This way of arguing is as frivolous, as the supposition of itself is false. For by what kind of logic will it appear, that any notion is originally by nature imprinted in the mind in its first constitution, because it comes first to be observed, and assented to, when a faculty of the mind, which has quite a distinct province, begins to exert itself? And therefore, the coming to the use of speech, if it were supposed the time, that these maxims are first assented to (which it may be with as much truth, as the time when men come to the use of reason) would be as good a proof that they were innate, as to say, they are innate because men assent to them, when they come to the use of reason. I agree then with these men of innate principles, that there is no knowledge of these general and self-evident maxims in the mind, till it comes to the exercise of reason: but I deny that the coming to the use of reason, is the precise time when they are first taken notice of; and, if that were the precise time, I deny that it would prove them innate. . . .

15. *The steps by which the mind attains several truths*. The senses at first let in particular *ideas*, and furnish the yet empty cabinet: and the mind by degrees growing familiar with some of them, they are lodged in the memory, and names got to them. Afterwards the mind proceeding farther, abstracts them, and by degrees learns the use of general names. In this manner the mind comes to be furnished with *ideas* and language, the materials about which to exercise its discursive faculty: and the use of reason becomes daily

more visible, as these materials, that give it employment, increase. But though the having of general *ideas*, and the use of general words and reason usually grow together; yet, I see not, how this any way proves them innate. The knowledge of some truths, I confess, is very early in the mind; but in a way that shows them not to be innate. For, if we will observe, we shall find it still to be about *ideas*, not innate, but acquired: it being about those first, which are imprinted by external things, with which infants have earliest to do, and which make the most frequent impressions on their senses. In *ideas* thus got, the mind discovers, that some agree, and others differ, probably as soon as it has any use of memory; as soon as it is able, to retain and receive distinct *ideas*. But whether it be then, or no, this is certain, it does so long before it has the use of words; or comes to that, which we commonly call the *use of reason*. For a child knows as certainly, before it can speak, the difference between the *ideas* of sweet and bitter (*i. e.* that sweet is not bitter) as it knows afterwards (when it comes to speak) that wormwood and sugarplums, are not the same thing.

. . . .

17. *Assenting as soon as proposed and understood, proves them not innate*. This evasion therefore of general assent, when men come to the use of reason, failing as it does, and leaving no difference between those supposed-innate, and other truths, that are afterwards acquired and learned, men have endeavored to secure an universal assent to those they call maxims, by saying, they are generally *assented to, as soon as proposed*, and the terms they are proposed in, understood. . . .

18. *If such an assent be a mark of innate, then that one and two are equal to three; that sweetness is not bitterness; and a thousand the like must be innate*. In answer to this, I demand whether ready *assent*, given to a proposition *upon first hearing*, and understanding the terms, be a certain mark of an innate principle? If it be not, such a general assent is in vain urged as a proof of them: if it be said, that it is a mark of innate, they must then allow all such propositions to be innate, which are generally assented to as soon as heard, whereby they will find themselves plentifully stored with innate principles. For upon the same ground (*viz.*) of assent at first hearing and understanding the terms, that men would have those maxims pass for innate, they must also admit several propositions about numbers, to be innate: and thus, *that one and two are equal to three, that two and two are equal to four*, and a multitude of other the like propositions in numbers, that everybody assents

to, at first hearing, and understanding the terms, must have a place amongst these innate axioms. Nor is this the prerogative of numbers alone, and propositions made about several of them: but even natural philosophy, and all the other sciences afford propositions, which are sure to meet with assent, as soon as they are understood. *That two bodies cannot be in the same place*, is a truth, that nobody any more sticks at, than at this maxim, *that it is impossible for the same thing to be, and not to be; that white is not black, that a square is not a circle, that yellowness is not sweetness:* these, and a million of other such propositions, as many at least, as we have distinct *ideas*, every man in his wits, at first hearing, and knowing what the names stand for, must necessarily assent to. If then these men will be true to their own rule, and have *assent at first hearing and understanding the terms*, to be a mark of innate, they must allow, not only as many innate propositions, as men have distinct *ideas;* but as many as men can make propositions, wherein different *ideas* are denied one of another. . . . But since no proposition can be innate, unless the *ideas*, about which it is, be innate, this will be, to suppose all our *ideas* of colors, sounds, tastes, figures, *&c.* innate; than which there cannot be anything more opposite to reason and experience. Universal and ready assent, upon hearing and understanding the terms, is (I grant) a mark of self-evidence: but self-evidence, depending not on innate impressions, but on something else (as we shall show hereafter) belongs to several propositions, which nobody was yet so extravagant, as to pretend to be innate.

19. *Such less general propositions known before these universal maxims.* Nor let it be said, that those more particular self-evident propositions, which are assented to at first hearing, as, *that one and two are equal to three; that green is not red*, &c. are received as the consequences of those more universal propositions, which are looked on as innate principles: since anyone, who will but take the pains to observe what passes in the understanding, will certainly find, that these, and the like less general propositions, are certainly known and firmly assented to, by those, who are utterly ignorant of those more general maxims; and so, being earlier in the mind than those (as they are called) first principles, cannot owe to them the assent, wherewith they are received at first hearing.

. . . .

21. *These maxims not being known sometimes till proposed, proves them not innate.* But we have not yet done with *assenting to propositions at first hearing*

and understanding their terms; 'tis fit we first take notice, that this, instead of being a mark, that they are innate, is a proof of the contrary: since it supposes, that several, who understand and know other things, are ignorant of these principles, till they are proposed to them; and that one may be unacquainted with these truths, till he hears them from others. For if they were innate, what need they be proposed, in order to gaining assent; when, by being in the understanding, by a natural and original impression (if there were any such) they could not but be known before? . . .

22. *Implicitly known before proposing, signifies that the mind is capable of understanding them, or else signifies nothing.* If it be said, the understanding has an *implicit knowledge* of these principles, but not an explicit, before this first hearing, (as they must, who will say, that they are in the understanding before they are known) it will be hard to conceive what is meant by a principle imprinted on the understanding implicitly; unless it be this, that the mind is capable of understanding and assenting firmly to such propositions. And thus all mathematical demonstrations, as well as first principles, must be received as native impressions on the mind: which, I fear they will scarce allow them to be, who find it harder to demonstrate a proposition, than assent to it, when demonstrated. . . .

. . . .

24. *Not innate, because not universally assented to.* To conclude this argument of universal consent, I agree with these defenders of innate principles, that if they are *innate,* they must needs *have universal assent.* For that a truth should be innate, and yet not assented to, is to me as unintelligible, as for a man to know a truth, and be ignorant of it at the same time. But then, by these men's own confession, they cannot be innate; since they are not assented to, by those who understand not the terms, nor by a great part of those who do understand them, but have yet never heard, nor thought of those propositions; which, I think, is at least half of mankind. But were the number far less, it would be enough to destroy universal assent, and thereby show these propositions not to be innate, if children alone were ignorant of them.

. . . .

CHAP. III.

No innate practical principles.

1. *No moral principles so clear and so generally received, as the forementioned speculative maxims.* If those speculative maxims, whereof we discoursed in the foregoing chapter, have not an actual universal assent from all mankind, as we there proved, it is much more visible concerning *practical* principles that they *come short of an universal reception:* and I think it will be hard to instance any one moral rule, which can pretend to so general and ready an assent as, *what is, is,* or to be so manifest a truth as this, *that it is impossible for the same thing to be, and not to be.* Whereby it is evident, that they are farther removed from a title to be innate; and the doubt of their being native impressions on the mind, is stronger against these moral principles than the other. Not that it brings their truth at all in question. They are equally true, though not equally evident. Those speculative maxims carry their own evidence with them: but moral principles require reasoning and discourse, and some exercise of the mind, to discover the certainty of their truth. They lie not open as natural characters engraven on the mind; which if any such were, they must needs be visible by themselves, and by their own light be certain and known to everybody. But this is no derogation to their truth and certainty, no more than it is to the truth or certainty, of the three angles of a triangle being equal to two right ones, because it is not so evident, as *the whole is bigger than a part;* nor so apt to be assented to at first hearing. It may suffice, that these moral rules are capable of demonstration: and therefore it is our own faults, if we come not to a certain knowledge of them. But the ignorance wherein many men are of them, and the slowness of assent, wherewith others receive them, are manifest proofs, that they are not innate, and such as offer themselves to their view without searching.

2. *Faith and justice not owned as principles by all men.* Whether there be any such moral principles, wherein all men do agree, I appeal to any, who have been but moderately conversant in the history of mankind, and looked abroad beyond the smoke of their own chimneys. Where is that practical truth, that is universally received without doubt or question, as it must be if innate? *Justice,* and keeping of contracts, is that which *most men seem to agree in.* This is a principle, which is thought to extend itself to the dens of thieves, and the confederacies of the greatest villains; and they who have

gone farthest towards the putting off of humanity itself, keep faith and rules of justice one with another. I grant that outlaws themselves do this one amongst another: but 'tis without receiving these as the innate laws of nature. They practice them as rules of convenience within their own communities: but it is impossible to conceive, that he embraces justice as a practical principle, who acts fairly with his fellow highwaymen, and at the same time plunders, or kills the next honest man he meets with. Justice and truth are the common ties of society; and therefore, even outlaws and robbers, who break with all the world besides, must keep faith and rules of equity amongst themselves, or else they cannot hold together. But will anyone say, that those that live by fraud and rapine, have innate principles of truth and justice which they allow and assent to?

3. Obj. *Though men deny them in their practice, yet they admit them in their thoughts, answered.* Perhaps it will be urged, that the *tacit assent of their minds agrees to what their practice contradicts.* I answer, *first,* I have always thought the actions of men the best interpreters of their thoughts. But since it is certain, that most men's practice, and some men's open professions, have either questioned or denied these principles, it is impossible to establish an universal consent (though we should look for it only amongst grown men) without which, it is impossible to conclude them innate. *Secondly,* 'tis very strange and unreasonable, to suppose innate practical principles, that terminate only in contemplation. Practical principles derived from nature, are there for operation, and must produce conformity of action, not barely speculative assent to their truth, or else they are in vain distinguished from speculative maxims. Nature, I confess, has put into man a desire of happiness, and an aversion to misery: these indeed are innate practical principles, which (as practical principles ought) do continue constantly to operate and influence all our actions, without ceasing: these may be observed in all persons and all ages, steady and universal; but these are inclinations of the appetite to good, not impressions of truth on the understanding. I deny not, that there are natural tendencies imprinted on the minds of men; and that, from the very first instances of sense and perception, there are some things, that are grateful, and others unwelcome to them; some things that they incline to, and others that they fly: but this makes nothing for innate characters on the mind, which are to be the principles of knowledge, regulating our practice. . . .

4. *Moral rules need a proof,* ergo *not innate.* Another reason that makes me doubt of any innate practical principles, is, that I think, *there cannot any one*

moral rule be proposed, whereof a man may not justly demand a reason: which would be perfectly ridiculous and absurd, if they were innate, or so much as self-evident; which every innate principle must needs be, and not need any proof to ascertain its truth, nor want any reason to gain it approbation. He would be thought void of common sense, who asked on the one side, or on the other side went about to give a reason, *why it is impossible for the same thing to be, or not to be*. It carries its own light and evidence with it, and needs no other proof: he that understands the terms, assents to it for its own sake, or else nothing will ever be able to prevail with him to do it. But should that most unshaken rule of morality, and foundation of all social virtue, *that one should do as he would be done unto*, be proposed to one, who never heard it before, but yet is of capacity to understand its meaning; might he not without any absurdity ask a reason why? And were not he that proposed it, bound to make out the truth and reasonableness of it to him? Which plainly shows it not to be innate; for if it were, it could neither want nor receive any proof; but must needs (at least, as soon as heard and understood) be received and assented to, as an unquestionable truth, which a man can by no means doubt of. So that the truth of all these moral rules, plainly depends upon some other antecedent to them, and from which they must be deduced, which could not be, if they were innate, or so much as self-evident.

5. *Instance in keeping compacts.* That men should keep their compacts, is certainly a great and undeniable rule in morality: but yet, if a Christian, who has the view of happiness and misery in another life, be asked why a man must keep his word, he will *give* this as a *reason:* because God, who has the power of eternal life and death, requires it of us. But if an *Hobbist* be asked why; he will answer: because the public requires it, and the *Leviathan* will punish you, if you do not.[3] And if one of the old *heathen* philosophers had been asked, he would have answered: because it was dishonest, below the dignity of man, and opposite to virtue, the highest perfection of human nature, to do otherwise.

6. *Virtue generally approved, not because innate, but because profitable.* Hence naturally flows the great variety of opinions, concerning moral rules, which are to be found amongst men, according to the different sorts of happiness, they have a prospect of, or propose to themselves: which could not be, if

3. A Hobbist is a follower of Thomas Hobbes (1588–1679), author of *Leviathan* (1651), where Hobbes argues that to avoid a state of war in which life is "solitary, poor, nasty, brutish, and short," we must transfer virtually all of our natural rights and powers, including the power to punish, to a sovereign—an "earthly God" or Leviathan—who will govern in our name.

practical principles were innate, and imprinted in our minds immediately by the hand of God. I grant the existence of God, is so many ways manifest, and the obedience we owe him, so congruous to the light of reason, that a great part of mankind give testimony to the law of nature: but yet I think it must be allowed, that several moral rules, may receive, from mankind, a very general approbation, without either knowing, or admitting the true ground of morality; which can only be the will and law of a God, who sees men in the dark, has in his hand rewards and punishments, and power enough to call to account the proudest offender. For God, having, by an inseparable connection, joined *virtue* and public happiness together; and made the practice thereof, necessary to the preservation of society, and visibly *beneficial* to all, with whom the virtuous man has to do; it is no wonder, that everyone should, not only allow, but recommend, and magnify those rules to others, from whose observance of them, he is sure to reap advantage to himself. . . .

. . . .

9. *Instances of enormities practiced without remorse.* . . . I cannot see how any *men,* should ever *transgress* those *moral rules, with confidence,* and *serenity,* were they innate, and stamped upon their minds. View but an army at the sacking of a town, and see what observation, or sense of moral principles, or what touch of conscience, for all the outrages they do. *Robberies, murders, rapes,* are the sports of men set at liberty from punishment and censure. Have there not been whole nations, and those of the most civilized people, amongst whom, the exposing their children, and leaving them in the fields, to perish by want or wild beasts, has been the practice, as little condemned or scrupled, as the begetting them? Do they not still, in some countries, put them into the same graves with their mothers, if they die in childbirth; or dispatch them, if a pretended astrologer declares them to have unhappy stars? And are there not places, where at a certain age, they kill, or expose their parents without any remorse at all? . . . Where then are those innate principles, of justice, piety, gratitude, equity, chastity? Or, where is that universal consent, that assures us there are such inbred rules? Murders in duels, when fashion has made them honorable, are committed without remorse of conscience: nay, in many places, innocence in this case is the greatest ignominy. And if we will look abroad, to take a view of men, as they are, we shall find, that they have remorse in one place, for doing or omitting that, which others, in another place, think they merit by.

10. *Men have contrary practical principles.* He that will carefully peruse the history of mankind, and look abroad into the several tribes of men, and with indifferency survey their actions, will be able to satisfy himself, that there is scarce that principle of morality to be named, or *rule* of *virtue* to be thought on (those only excepted, that are absolutely necessary to hold society together, which commonly too are neglected betwixt distinct societies) which is not, somewhere or other, *slighted* and condemned by the general fashion of *whole societies* of men, governed by practical opinions, and rules of living quite opposite to others.

11. *Whole nations reject several moral rules.* Here, perhaps, 'twill be objected, that it is no argument, that the *rule* is *not known, because* it is *broken.* I grant the objection good, where men, though they transgress, yet disown not the law. . . . But it is impossible to conceive, that a *whole nation* of men should all *publicly reject* and renounce, what everyone of them, certainly and infallibly, knew to be a law. . . . Whatever practical principle is innate, cannot but be known to everyone, to be just and good. It is therefore little less than a contradiction, to suppose, that whole nations of men should both in their professions, and practice unanimously and universally give the lie to what, by the most invincible evidence, every one of them knew to be true, right, and good. This is enough to satisfy us, that no practical rule; which is anywhere universally, and with public approbation, or allowance, transgressed, can be supposed innate. But I have something farther to add, in answer to this objection.

12. The breaking of a rule, say you, is no argument, that it is unknown. I grant it: but the *generally allowed breach of it anywhere,* I say, *is a proof, that it is not innate.* For example, let us take any of these rules, which being the most obvious deductions of human reason, and conformable to the natural inclination of the greatest part of men, fewest people have had the impudence to deny, or inconsideration to doubt of. If any can be thought to be naturally imprinted, none, I think can have a fairer pretense to be innate, than this; *parents preserve and cherish your children.* When therefore you say, that this is an innate rule, what do you mean? Either, that it is an innate principle; which upon all occasions, excites and directs the actions of all men: or else, that it is a truth, which all men have imprinted on their minds, and which therefore they know, and assent to. But in neither of these senses is it innate. *First,* that it is not a principle, which influences all men's actions, is, what I have proved by the examples before cited: nor need we seek so far as *Mingrelia* or *Peru,* to find instances of such as neglect, abuse,

nay and destroy their children. . . .[4] It was a familiar, and uncondemned practice amongst the *Greeks* and *Romans,* to expose, without pity or remorse, their innocent infants. *Secondly,* that it is an innate truth, known to all men, is also false. For, *parents preserve your children,* is so far from an innate truth, that it is no truth at all; it being a command, and not a proposition, and so not capable of truth or falsehood. To make it capable of being assented to as true, it must be reduced to some such proposition as this: *it is the duty of parents to preserve their children.* But what duty is, cannot be understood without a law; nor a law be known, or supposed without a lawmaker, or without reward and punishment: so that it is impossible, that this, or any other practical principle should be innate; *i.e.* be imprinted on the mind as a duty, without supposing the *ideas* of God, of law, of obligation, of punishment, of a life after this, innate. For that punishment follows not, in this life, the breach of this rule; and consequently, that it is has not the force of a law in countries, where the generally allowed practice runs counter to it, is in itself evident. But these *ideas* (which must be all of them innate, if anything as a duty be so) are so far from being innate, that 'tis not every studious or thinking man, much less everyone that is born, in whom they are to be found clear and distinct: and that one of them, which of all others seems most likely to be innate, is not so, (I mean the *idea* of God) I think, in the next chapter, will appear very evident to any considering man.

13. . . . Principles of actions indeed there are lodged in men's appetites, but these are so far from being innate moral principles, that if they were left to their full swing, they would carry men to the overturning of all morality. . . . I would not be here mistaken, as if, because I deny an innate law, I thought there were none but positive laws. There is a great deal of difference between an innate law, and a law of nature; between something imprinted on our minds in this very original, and something that we being ignorant of may attain to the knowledge of, by the use and due application of our natural faculties. And I think they equally forsake the truth, who running into the contrary extremes, either affirm an innate law, or deny that there is a law, knowable by the light of nature; *i.e.* without the help of positive revelation.

14. *Those who maintain innate practical principles, tell us not what they are.* The difference there is amongst men in their practical principles, is so evident, that, I think, I need say no more to evince, that it will be impossible

4. Mingrelia is a region between the Black Sea and the Caucasus.

to find any innate moral rules, by this mark of general assent. . . . In truth, were there any such innate principles, there would be no need to teach them. Did men find such innate propositions stamped on their minds, they would easily be able to distinguish them from other truths, that they afterwards learned, and deduced from them; and there would be nothing more easy, than to know what, and how many they were. There could be no more doubt about their number, than there is about the number of our fingers. . . . But since nobody, that I know, has ventured yet to give a catalogue of them, they cannot blame those who doubt of these innate principles; since even they who require men to believe, that there are such innate propositions, do not tell us what they are. . . . A great part of men are so far from finding any such innate moral principles in themselves, that by denying freedom to mankind; and thereby making men no other than bare machines, they take away not only innate, but all moral rules whatsoever, and leave not a possibility to believe any such, to those who cannot conceive, how anything can be capable of law, that is not a free agent: and upon that ground, they must necessarily reject all principles of virtue, who cannot *put morality and mechanism together;* which are not very easy to be reconciled, or made consistent.

. . . .

20. Obj. *Innate principles may be corrupted, answered.* Nor will it be of much moment here, to offer that very ready, but not very material answer, (*viz.*) that the *innate principles* of morality, *may, by education, and custom,* and the general opinion of those, amongst whom we converse, *be darkened,* and at last *quite worn out* of the minds of men. Which assertion of theirs, if true, quite takes away the argument of universal consent, by which this opinion of innate ideas is endeavored to be proved. . . . I desire these men to say, whether they can, or cannot, by education and custom, be blurred and blotted out: if they cannot, we must find them in all mankind alike, and they must be clear in everybody: and if they may suffer variation from adventitious notions, we must then find them clearest and most perspicuous, nearest the fountain, in children and illiterate people, who have received least impression from foreign opinions. Let them take which side they please, they will certainly find it inconsistent with visible matter of fact, and daily observation.

. . . .

22. *How men commonly come by their principles. . . . Doctrines,* that have been derived from no better original, than the superstition of a nurse, or the authority of an old woman; may, by length of time, and consent of neighbors, *grow up to the dignity of principles* in religion and morality. For such, who are careful (as they call it) to principle children well, . . . instill into the unwary, and, as yet, unprejudiced understanding, (for white paper receives any characters) those doctrines they would have them retain and profess. These being taught them as soon as they have any apprehension; and still as they grow up, confirmed to them, either by the open profession, or tacit consent, of all they have to do with; or at least by those, of whose wisdom, knowledge, and piety, they have an opinion, who never suffer those propositions to be otherwise mentioned, but as the basis and foundation, on which they build either their religion or manners, come, by these means, to have the reputation of unquestionable, self-evident, and innate truths.

. . . .

24. This will appear very likely, and almost unavoidable to come to pass, if we consider the nature of mankind, and the constitution of human affairs; wherein *most men cannot live, without employing their time in the daily labors of their callings; nor be at quiet in their minds, without some foundation or principles to rest their thoughts on.* There is scarce anyone so floating and superficial in his understanding, who has not some reverenced propositions, which are to him the principles on which he bottoms his reasonings; and by which he judges of truth and falsehood, right and wrong; which some, wanting skill and leisure, and others the inclination, and some being taught, that they ought not, to examine; there are few to be found, who are not exposed by their ignorance, laziness, education, or precipitancy, to *take them upon trust.*

25. This is evidently the case of all children and young folk; and custom, a greater power than nature, seldom failing to make them worship for divine, what she has inured them to bow their minds, and submit their understandings to, it is no wonder, that grown *men,* either perplexed in the necessary affairs of life, or hot in the pursuit of pleasures, should *not* seriously sit down to *examine their own tenets;* especially when one of their principles is, that principles ought not to be questioned. . . .

. . . .

27. *Principles must be examined.* . . . If it be the privilege of innate principles, to be received upon their own authority, without examination, I know not what may not be believed, or how anyone's *principles* can be questioned. If they may, and *ought to be examined,* and tried, I desire to know how first and innate principles can be tried; or at least it is reasonable to demand the marks and characters, whereby the genuine, innate principles, may be distinguished from others. . . . When this is done, I shall be ready to embrace such welcome, and useful, propositions; and till then I may with modesty doubt, since I fear universal consent, which is the only one produced, will scarce prove a sufficient mark to direct my choice, and assure me of any innate principles. From what has been said, I think it is past doubt, that there are no practical principles wherein all mean agree; and therefore none innate.

Chap. IV.

Other considerations concerning innate principles, both speculative and practical.

1. *Principles not innate, unless their* ideas *be innate.* Had those, who would persuade us, that there are innate principles, not taken them together in gross; but considered, separately, the parts, out of which those propositions are made, they would not, perhaps, have been so forward to believe they were innate. Since, if the *ideas,* which made up those truths, were not, it was impossible, that the propositions, made up of them, should be *innate,* or our knowledge of them be born with us. For if the *ideas* be not *innate,* there was a time, when the mind was without those principles; and then, they will not be innate, but be derived from some other original. For, where the *ideas* themselves are not, there can be no knowledge, no assent, no mental, or verbal propositions about them.

2. Ideas, *especially those belonging to principles, not born with children.* If we will attentively consider newborn *children,* we shall have little reason, to think, that they bring many *ideas* into the world with them. For, bating, perhaps, some faint *ideas,* of hunger, and thirst, and warmth, and some pains, which they may *have* felt in the womb, there is *not* the least

appearance of any settled *ideas* at all in them; especially of *ideas, answering the terms, which make up those universal propositions,* that are esteemed innate principles. One may perceive how, by degrees, afterwards, *ideas* come into their minds; and that they get no more, nor no other, than what experience, and the observation of things, that come in their way, furnish them with; which might be enough to satisfy us, that they are not original characters, stamped on the mind.

3. *It is impossible for the same thing to be, and not to be,* is certainly (if there be any such) an innate principle. But can anyone think, or will anyone say, that *impossibility* and *identity,* are too innate *ideas*? Are they such as all mankind have, and bring into the world with them? And are they those, that are the first in children, and antecedent to all acquired ones? If they are innate, they must needs be so. Has a child an *idea* of *impossibility* and *identity,* before it has of *white* or *black; sweet* or *bitter*? And is it from knowledge of this principle, that it concludes, that wormwood rubbed on the nipple, has not the same taste, that it used to receive from thence? Is it the actual knowledge of *impossibile est idem esse, & non esse,* that makes a child distinguish between its mother and a stranger; or, that makes it fond of the one, and fly the other?[5]. . .

4. *Identity an* idea *not innate.* If *identity* (to instance in that alone) be a native impression; and consequently so clear and obvious to us, that we must needs know it even from our cradles; I would gladly be resolved, by one of seven, or seventy years old, whether a man, being a creature, consisting of soul and body, be the same man, when his body is changed? Whether *Euphorbus* and *Pythagoras,* having had the same soul, were the same man, though they lived several ages asunder? Nay, whether the cock too, which had the same soul, were not the same with both of them? Whereby, perhaps it will appear, that our *idea of sameness,* is *not* so settled and clear, as to deserve to be thought *innate* in us. For if those innate *ideas,* are not clear and distinct, so as to be universally known, and naturally agreed on, they cannot be the subjects of universal, and undoubted truths; but will be the unavoidable occasion of perpetual uncertainty. For, I suppose, everyone's *idea* of *identity,* will not be the same, that *Pythagoras,* and thousands others of his followers, have: and which then shall be the true? Which innate? Or are there two different *ideas* of *identity,* both innate?

5. *impossibile est idem esse, & non esse:* it is impossible for the same thing to be, and not to be.

5. Nor let anyone think, that the questions, I have here proposed, about the *identity* of man, are bare, empty speculations; which if they were, would be enough to show, that there was in the understandings of men *no innate* idea *of* identity. He, that shall, with a little attention, reflect on the Resurrection, and consider, that divine justice shall bring to judgment, at the last day, the very same persons, to be happy or miserable in the other, who did well or ill in this life, will find it, perhaps, not easy to resolve with himself, what makes the same man, or wherein *identity* consists: and will not be forward to think he, and everyone, even children themselves, have naturally a clear *idea* of it.[6]

6. *Whole and part not innate* ideas. Let us examine that principle of mathematics, *viz. that the whole is bigger than a part*. This, I take it, is reckoned amongst innate principles. I am sure it has as good a title, as any, to be thought so; which yet, nobody can think it to be, when he considers the *ideas* it comprehends in it, *whole* and *part,* are perfectly relative; but the positive *ideas,* to which they properly and immediately belong, are extension and number, of which alone, *whole* and *part,* are relations. So that if *whole* and *part* are innate *ideas,* extension and number must be so too, it being impossible to have an *idea* of a relation, without having any at all of the thing to which it belongs, and in which it is founded. Now, whether the minds of men have naturally imprinted on them the *idea* of extension and number, I leave to be considered by those, who are the patrons of innate principles.

7. Idea *of worship not innate*. That *God is to be worshipped,* is, without doubt, as great a truth as any can enter into the mind of man, and deserves the first place amongst all practical principles. But yet, it can by no means be thought innate, unless the *ideas* of *God,* and *worship,* are innate. That the *idea,* the term *worship* stands for, is not in the understanding of children, and a character stamped on the mind in its first original, I think, will be easily granted, by anyone, that considers how few there be, amongst grown men, who have a clear and distinct notion of it. . . .

8. Idea *of* GOD *not innate*. If any *idea* can be imagined *innate,* the *idea of God* may, of all others, for many reasons, be thought so; since it is hard to conceive, how there should be innate moral principles, without an innate

6. The Resurrection is the raising of the dead promised by Jesus at (for example) John 6:40: "And this is the will of him that sent me, that every one who seeth the Son, and believeth in him, may have everlasting life: and I will raise him up at the last day."

idea of a *deity:* without a notion of a lawmaker, it is impossible to have a notion of a law, and an obligation to observe it. Besides the atheists, taken notice of amongst the ancients, and left branded upon the records of history, has not navigation discovered, in these latter ages, whole nations . . . amongst whom there was to be found no notion of a God, no religion. . . . There are instances of nations where uncultivated nature has been left to itself, without the help of letters, and discipline, and the improvement of arts and sciences. But there are others to be found, who have enjoyed these in a very great measure, who yet, for want of a due application of their thoughts this way, want the *idea,* and knowledge of God. . . . And, perhaps, if we should, with attention, mind the lives, and discourses of people not so far off, we should have too much reason to fear, that many, in more civilized countries, have no very strong, and clear impressions of a deity upon their minds; and that the complaints of atheism, made from the pulpit, are not without reason. . . .

9. But had all mankind, everywhere, a *notion of a God,* (whereof yet history tells us the contrary) it would *not* from thence follow, that the *idea* of him was *innate*. For, though no nation were to be found without a name, and some few dark notions of him; yet that would not prove them to be natural impressions on the mind, no more than the names of fire, or the sun, heat, or number, do prove the *ideas* they stand for, to be innate, because the names of those things, and the *ideas* of them, are so universally received, and known amongst mankind. Nor, on the contrary, is the want of such a name, or the absence of such a notion out of men's minds, any argument against the being of a God, any more, than it would be a proof, that there was no lodestone in the world, because a great part of mankind, had neither a notion of any such thing, nor a name for it. . . . Men . . . can scarce avoid having some kind of *ideas* of those things, whose names, those they converse with, have occasion frequently to mention to them: and if it carry with it the notion of excellency, greatness, or something extraordinary; if apprehension and concernment accompany it; if the fear of absolute and irresistible power set it on upon the mind, the *idea* is likely to sink the deeper, and spread the farther; especially if it be such an *idea,* as is agreeable to the common light of reason, and naturally deducible from every part of our knowledge, as that of God is. For the visible marks of extraordinary wisdom and power, appear so plainly in all the works of the creation, that a rational creature, who will but seriously reflect on them, cannot miss the discovery of a *deity*. . . .

10. The name of God being once mentioned in any part of the world, to express a superior, powerful, wise, invisible being, the suitableness of such a notion to the principles of common reason, and the interest men will always have to mention it often, must necessarily spread it far and wide; and continue it down to all generations: though yet the *general reception of this name, and some imperfect and unsteady notions, conveyed thereby* to the unthinking part of mankind, *prove not the* idea *to be innate;* but only that they, who made the discovery, had made a right use of their reason, thought maturely of the causes of things, and traced them to their original; from whom other less considering people, having once received so important a notion, it could not easily be lost again.

. . . .

12. *Suitable to* GOD'*s goodness, that all men should have an* idea *of him, therefore naturally imprinted by him; answered.* . . . Had you or I been born at the Bay of *Soldania,* possibly our thoughts, and notions, had not exceeded those brutish ones of the *Hotentots* that inhabit there: and had the *Virginia* King *Apochancana,* been educated in *England,* he had, perhaps, been as knowing a divine, and as good a mathematician, as any in it. The difference between him, and a more improved *English*-man, lying barely in this, that exercise of his faculties was bounded within the ways, modes, and notions of his own country, and never directed to any other, or farther inquiries: and if he had not any *idea* of a God, it was only because he pursued not those thoughts, that would have led him to it.

. . . .

14. *Ideas of* GOD *various in different men.* Can it be thought, that the *ideas* men have of God, are the characters, and marks of himself, engraven in their minds by his own finger, when we see, that in the same country, under one and the same name *men have far different,* nay, often *contrary and inconsistent ideas,* and conceptions *of him?* Their agreeing in a name, or sound, will scarce prove an innate notion of him.

15. What true or tolerable notion of a *deity,* could they have, who acknowledged, and worshipped hundreds? Every deity, that they owned above one, was an infallible evidence of their ignorance of him, and a proof, that they had no true notion of God, where unity, infinity, and eternity, were

excluded. To which if we add their gross conceptions of corporeity, expressed in their images, and representations of their deities; the amours, marriages, copulations, lusts, quarrels, and other mean qualities, attributed by to them to their gods; we shall have little reason to think, that the heathen world, *i.e.* the greatest part of mankind, had any such *ideas* of God in their minds, as he himself, out of care, that they should not be mistaken about him, was author of. . . .

15.[7] If it be said, that *wise men* of all nations came to *have true conceptions* of the unity and infinity *of the deity,* I grant it. But then this,

First, excludes universality of consent in anything, but the name, for those wise men being very few, perhaps one of a thousand, this universality is very narrow.

Secondly, it seems to me plainly to prove, that the truest and best notions men had of God, were not imprinted, but acquired by thought and meditation, and a right use of their faculties: since the wise and considerate men of the world, by a right and careful employment of their thoughts and reason, attained true notions in this, as well as other things; whilst the lazy and inconsiderate part of men, making the far greater number, took up their notions, by chance, from common tradition and vulgar conceptions without much beating their heads about them. And if it be a reason to think *the notion of God innate,* because all wise men had it, virtue too must be thought innate; for that also wise men have always had.

. . . .

17. *If the* idea *of* GOD *be not innate, no other can be supposed innate*. Since then though the knowledge of a *GOD,* be the most natural discovery of human reason, yet *the idea of him,* is *not innate,* as, I think, is evident from what has been said; I imagine there will be scarce any other *idea* found, that can pretend to it: since if God had set any impression, any character on the understanding of men, it is most reasonable to expect it should have been some clear and uniform *idea* of himself, as far as our weak capacities were capable to receive so incomprehensible and infinite an object. But our minds being, at first, void of that *idea,* which we are most concerned to have, it *is a strong presumption against all other innate characters*. I must own, as far as I can observe, I can find none, and would be glad to be informed by any other.

7. I have retained Locke's numbering, which assigns the number 15 to two successive sections.

18. Idea *of substance not innate*. I confess, there is another *idea,* which would be of general use for mankind to have, as it is of general talk as if they had it; and that is the *idea of substance,* which we neither have, nor can have, by *sensation* or *reflection*. If nature took care to provide us any *ideas,* we might well expect it should be such, as by our own faculties we cannot procure to ourselves: but we see on the contrary, that since by those ways, whereby others *ideas* are brought into our minds, this is not, we have no such *clear idea* at all, and therefore signify nothing by the word *substance,* but only an uncertain supposition of we know not what; (*i.e.* of something whereof we have no particular distinct positive) *idea,* which we take to be the *substratum,* or support, of those *ideas* we do know.

. . . .

20. *No innate* ideas *in the memory*. . . . If there be any innate *ideas,* any *ideas,* in the mind, which the mind does not actually think on; they must be lodged in the memory, and from thence must be brought into view by remembrance; *i.e.* must be known, when they are remembered, to have been perceptions in the mind before, unless remembrance can be without remembrance. For to remember is to perceive anything with memory, or with a consciousness, that it was known or perceived before: without this, whatever *idea* comes into the mind is new, and not remembered: this consciousness of its having been in the mind before, being that, which distinguishes remembering from all other ways of thinking. Whatever *idea* was never perceived by the mind, was never in the mind. Whatever *idea* is in the mind, is either an actual perception, or else having been an actual perception, is so in the mind, that by memory it can be made an actual perception. Whenever there is the actual perception of any *idea* without memory, the *idea* appears perfectly new and unknown before to the understanding: whenever the memory brings any *idea* into actual view, it is with a consciousness, that it had been there before, and was not wholly a stranger to the mind. Whether this be not so, I appeal to everyone's observation: and then I desire an instance of an *idea,* pretended to be innate, which (before any impression of it by ways hereafter to be mentioned) anyone could revive and remember as an *idea,* he had formerly known; without which consciousness of a former perception there is no remembrance; and whatever *idea* comes into the mind without that consciousness is not remembered, or comes not out of the memory, nor can be said to be in the mind before that appearance. For what is not either actually in view, or in the memory, is in the mind no way at all, and is all one as if it

never had been there. . . . If therefore there be any innate *ideas,* they must be in the memory, or else nowhere in the mind; and if they be in the memory, they can be revived without any impression from without, and whenever they are brought into the mind, they are remembered, *i.e.* they bring with them a perception of their not being wholly new to it. . . . By this it may be tried, whether there be any innate *ideas* in the mind before impression from *sensation* or *reflection.* I would fain meet with the man, who when he came to the use of reason, or at any other time remembered any of them: and to whom, after he was born, they were never new. If anyone will say, there are *ideas* in the mind, that are not in the memory; I desire him to explain himself, and make what he says intelligible.

. . . .

22. *Difference of men's discoveries depends upon the different application of their faculties.* To conclude, some *ideas* forwardly offer themselves to all men's understandings; and some sorts of truths result from any *ideas,* as soon as the mind puts them into propositions: other truths require a train of *ideas* placed in order, a due comparing of them, and deductions made with attention, before they can be discovered, and assented to. Some of the first sort, because of their general and easy reception, have been mistaken for innate: but the truth is, *ideas* and notions are no more born with us, than arts and sciences; though some of them, indeed, offer themselves to our faculties, more readily than others; and therefore are more generally received. . . . . How much our *knowledge depends upon the right use of those powers nature has bestowed on us,* and how little upon such innate principles, as are in vain supposed to be in all mankind for their direction. . . .

23. *Men must think and know for themselves.* What censure, doubting thus of innate principles, may deserve from men, who will be apt to call it, pulling up the old foundations of knowledge and certainty, I cannot tell: I persuade myself, at least, that the way I have pursued, being conformable to truth, lays those foundations surer. This I am certain, I have not made it my business, either to quit, or follow any authority in the ensuing discourse: truth has been my only aim; and wherever that has appeared to lead, my thoughts have impartially followed, without minding, whether the footsteps of any other lay that way, or no. Not that I want a due respect for other men's opinions; but after all, the *greatest reverence is due to truth;* and, I hope, it will not be thought arrogance, to say, that, perhaps, we should make greater progress in the discovery of rational and contemplative *knowledge,* if

we *sought* it in the fountain, *in the consideration of things themselves;* and made use rather of our own thoughts, than other men's to find it. . . . In the sciences, everyone has so much, as he really knows and comprehends: what he believes only, and takes upon trust, are but shreds; which however well in the whole piece, make no considerable addition to his stock, who gathers them. Such borrowed wealth, like fairy-money, though it were gold in the hand from which he received it, will be but leaves and dust when it comes to use.

24. *Whence the opinion of innate principles.* When men have found some general propositions that could not be doubted of, as soon as understood, it was, I know, *a short and easy way to conclude them innate.* This being once received, it eased the lazy from the pains of search, and stopped the inquiry of the doubtful, concerning all that was once styled innate: and it was of no small advantage to those who affected to be masters and teachers, to make this the principle of *principles,* that principles must not be questioned: for having once established this tenet, that there are innate principles, it put their followers upon a necessity of receiving some doctrines as such; which was to take them off from the use of their own reason and judgment, and put them upon believing and taking them upon trust, without farther examination: in which posture of blind credulity, they might be more easily governed by, and made useful to some sort of men, who had the skill and office to principle and guide them. Nor is it a small power it gives one man over another, to have the authority to be the dictator of principles, and teacher of unquestionable truths; and to make a man swallow that for an innate principle, which may serve to his purpose, who teaches them. Whereas had they examined the ways, whereby men came to the knowledge of many universal *truths,* they would have found them to result in the minds of men, from the being of things themselves, when duly considered; and that they were discovered by the application of those faculties, that were fitted by nature to receive and judge of them, when duly employed about them.

25. *Conclusion. To show how the understanding proceeds herein, is the design of the following discourse;* which I shall proceed to, when I have first premised, that hitherto to clear my way to those foundations, which, I conceive are the only true ones, whereon to establish those notions we can have of our own knowledge, it has been necessary for me to give an account of the reasons I had to doubt of innate principles: and since the arguments which are against them, do, some of them, rise from common received opinions, I have been forced to take several things for granted, which is hardly avoidable to anyone, whose task it is to show the falsehood, or improbability, of any tenet; it

happening in controversial discourses, as it does in assaulting of towns; where, if the ground be but firm, whereon the batteries are erected, there is no farther inquiry of whom it is borrowed, nor whom it belongs to, so it affords but a fit rise for the present purpose. But in the future part of this discourse, designing to raise an edifice uniform, and consistent with itself, as far as my own experience and observation will assist me, I hope, to erect it on such a basis, that I shall not need to shore it up with props and buttresses, leaning on borrowed or begged foundations: or at least, if mine prove a castle in the air, I will endeavor it shall be all of a piece, and hang together. Wherein I warn the reader not to expect undeniable cogent demonstrations, unless I may be allowed the privilege, not seldom assumed by others, to take my principles for granted; and then, I doubt not, but I can demonstrate too. All that I shall say for the principles I proceed on, is, that I can only *appeal* to men's own unprejudiced *experience*, and observation, whether they be true, or no; and this is enough for a man who professes no more, than to lay down candidly and freely his own conjectures, concerning a subject lying somewhat in the dark, without any other design, than an unbiased inquiry after truth.

BOOK II.

CHAP. I.

Of ideas *in general, and their original.*

1. Idea *is the object of thinking.* Every man being conscious to himself, that he thinks, and that which his mind is employed about whilst thinking being the *ideas,* that are there, 'tis past doubt, that men have in their minds several *ideas,* such as are those expressed by the words, *whiteness, hardness, sweetness, thinking, motion, man, elephant, army, drunkenness,* and others: it is in the first place then to be inquired, how he comes by them? I know it is a received doctrine, that men have native *ideas,* and original characters stamped upon their minds, in their very first being. This opinion I have at large examined already; and, I suppose, what I have said in the foregoing book, will be much more easily admitted, when I have shown, whence the understanding may get all the *ideas* it has, and by what ways and degrees they may come into the mind; for which I shall appeal to everyone's own observation and experience.

2. *All* ideas *come from sensation or reflection.* Let us then suppose the mind to be, as we say, white paper, void of all characters, without any *ideas;* how comes it to be furnished? Whence comes it by that vast store, which the busy and boundless fancy of man has painted on it, with an almost endless variety? Whence has it all the materials of reason and knowledge? To this I answer, in one word, from *experience:* in that, all our knowledge is founded; and from that it ultimately derives itself. Our observation employed either about *external, sensible objects; or about the internal operations of our minds, perceived and reflected on by ourselves, is that, which supplies our understandings with all the materials of thinking.* These two are the fountains of knowledge, from whence all the *ideas* we have, or can naturally have, do spring.

3. *The objects of sensation one source of* ideas. First, *our senses,* conversant about particular sensible objects, do *convey into the mind,* several distinct *perceptions* of things, according to those various ways, wherein those objects do affect them: and thus we come by those *ideas,* we have of *yellow, white,*

heat, cold, soft, hard, bitter, sweet, and all those which we call sensible qualities, which when I say the senses convey into the mind, I mean, they from external objects convey into the mind what produces there those *perceptions.* This great source, of most of the *ideas* we have, depending wholly upon our senses, and derived by them to the understanding, I call *SENSATION.*

4. *The operations of our minds, the other source of them.* Secondly, the other fountain, from which experience furnishes the understanding with *ideas,* is the *perception of the operations of our own minds* within us, as it is employed about the *ideas* it has got; which operations, when the soul comes to reflect on, and consider, do furnish the understanding with another set of *ideas,* which could not be had from things without: and such are, *perception, thinking, doubting, believing, reasoning, knowing, willing,* and all the different actings of our own minds; which we being conscious of, and observing in ourselves, do from these receive into our understandings, as distinct *ideas,* as we do from bodies affecting our senses. This source of *ideas,* every man has wholly in himself: and though it be not sense, as having nothing to do with external objects; yet it is very like it, and might properly enough be called internal sense. But as I call the other *sensation,* so I call this *REFLECTION,* the *ideas* it affords being such only, as the mind gets by reflecting on its own operations within itself. By *REFLECTION* then, in the following part of this discourse, I would be understood to mean, that notice which the mind takes of its own operations, and the manner of them, by reason whereof, there come to be *ideas* of these operations in the understanding. These two, I say, *viz.* external, material things, as the objects of *SENSATION;* and the operations of our own minds within, as the objects of *REFLECTION,* are, to me, the only originals, from whence all our *ideas* take their beginnings. The term *operations* here, I use in a large sense, as comprehending not barely the actions of the mind about its ideas, but some sort of passions arising sometimes from them, such as is the satisfaction or uneasiness arising from any thought.

5. *All our* ideas *are of the one or the other of these.* The understanding seems to me, not to have the least glimmering of any *ideas,* which it does not receive from one of these two. *External objects furnish the mind with the* ideas *of sensible qualities,* which are all those different perceptions they produce in us: and the *mind furnishes the understanding with* ideas *of its own operations.* These, when we have taken a full survey of them, and their several modes, combinations, and relations, we shall find to contain all our whole stock of

ideas; and that we have nothing in our minds, which did not come in, one of these two ways. Let anyone examine his own thoughts, and thoroughly search into his understanding, and then let him tell me, whether all the original *ideas* he has there, are any other than that of objects of his *senses;* or of the operations of his mind, considered as objects of his *reflection:* and how great a mass of knowledge soever he imagines to be lodged there, he will, upon taking a strict view, see, that he has *not any* idea *in his mind, but what one of these two have imprinted;* though, perhaps, with infinite variety compounded and enlarged by the understanding, as we shall see hereafter.

6. *Observable in children.* He that attentively considers the state of a *child,* at his first coming into the world, will have little reason to think him stored with plenty of *ideas,* that are to be the matter of his future knowledge. . . . If a child were kept in a place, where he never saw any other but black and white, till he were a man, he would have no more *ideas* of scarlet or green, than he that from his childhood never tasted an oyster, or a pineapple, has of those particular relishes.

7. *Men are differently furnished with these, according to the different objects they converse with.* Men then come to be furnished with fewer or more simple *ideas* from without, according as the *objects,* they converse with, afford greater or less variety; and from the operation of their minds within, according as they more or less *reflect* on them. For, though he that contemplates the operations of his mind, cannot but have plain and clear *ideas* of them; yet unless he turn his thoughts that way, and considers them *attentively,* he will no more have clear and distinct *ideas* of all the *operations of his mind,* and all that may be observed therein, than he will have all the particular *ideas* of any landscape, or of the parts and motion of a clock, who will not turn his eyes to it, and with attention heed all the parts of it. . . .

8. Ideas *of reflection later, because they need attention.* And hence we see the reason, why 'tis pretty late, before most children get *ideas* of the operations of their own minds; and some have not any very clear, or perfect *ideas* of the greatest part of them all their lives. Because, though they pass there continually; yet like floating visions, they make not deep impressions enough, to leave in the mind clear distinct lasting *ideas,* till the understanding turns inwards upon itself, *reflects* on its own *operations,* and makes them the object of its own contemplation. . . .

9. *The soul begins to have* ideas, *when it begins to perceive.* To ask, *at what time a man has first any* ideas, is to ask, when he begins to perceive, having *ideas* and perception being the same thing. I know it is an opinion, that the soul always thinks, and that it has the actual perception of *ideas* in itself constantly, as long as it exists; and that actual thinking is as inseparable from the soul, as actual extension is from the body; which if true, to inquire after the beginning of a man's *ideas,* is the same, as to inquire after the beginning of his soul. For by this account, soul and its *ideas,* as body and its extension, will begin to exist both at the same time.

10. *The soul thinks not always, for this wants proofs.* But whether the soul be supposed to exist antecedent to, or coeval with, or some time after the first rudiments of organization, or the beginnings of life in the body, I leave to be disputed by those, who have better thought of that matter. I confess myself, to have one of those dull souls, that does not perceive itself always to contemplate *ideas,* nor can it conceive it any more necessary for the *soul always to think,* that for the body always to move: the perception of *ideas* being (as I conceive) to the soul, what motion is to the body, not its essence, but one of its operations: and therefore, though thinking be supposed never so much the proper action of the soul; yet it is not necessary, to suppose, that it should be always thinking, always in action. That, perhaps, is the privilege of the infinite author and preserver of things, *who never slumbers or sleeps;* but is not competent to any finite being, at least not to the soul of man.[8] We know certainly by experience, that we sometimes think, and thence draw this infallible consequence, that there is something in us, that has a power to think: but whether that substance perpetually thinks, or no, we can be no farther assured, than experience informs us. . . .

11. *It is not always conscious of it.* I grant that the soul in a waking man is never without thought, because it is the condition of being awake: but whether sleeping without dreaming be not an affection of the whole man, mind as well as body, may be worth a waking man's consideration; it being hard to conceive, that anything should think, and not be conscious of it. If the *soul* does *think in a sleeping man,* without being conscious of it, I ask, whether, during such thinking, it has any pleasure or pain, or be capable of happiness or misery? I am sure the man is not, no more than the bed or earth he lies on. For to be happy or miserable without being conscious of it, seems to me utterly inconsistent and impossible. Or if it be possible, that

8. *who never slumbers or sleeps,* Psalms 121:4.

the soul can, whilst the body is sleeping, have its thinking, enjoyments, and concerns, its pleasure or pain apart, which the man is not conscious of, nor partakes in, it is certain that *Socrates* asleep, and *Socrates* awake, is not the same person; but his soul when he sleeps, and *Socrates* the man consisting of body and soul when he is waking, are two persons: since waking *Socrates,* has no knowledge of, or concernment for that happiness, or misery of his soul, which it enjoys alone by itself whilst he sleeps, without perceiving anything of it. . . . For if we take wholly away all consciousness of our actions and sensations, especially of pleasure and pain, and the concernment that accompanies it, it will be hard to know wherein to place personal identity.

12. *If a sleeping man thinks without knowing it, the sleeping and waking man are two persons.* The soul, during sound sleep, thinks, say these men. *Whilst it thinks* and perceives, it is capable certainly of those of delight or trouble, as well as any other perceptions; and *it must necessarily be conscious of its own perceptions.* But it has all this apart: the sleeping man, 'tis plain, is conscious of nothing of all this. Let us suppose then the soul of *Castor,* whilst he is sleeping, retired from his body, which is no impossible supposition for the men I have here to do with, who so liberally allow life, without a thinking soul to all other animals. These men cannot then judge it impossible, or a contradiction, that the body should live without the soul; nor that the soul should subsist and think, or have perception, even perception of happiness or misery, without the body. Let us then, as I say, suppose the soul of *Castor* separated, during his sleep, from his body, to think apart. Let us suppose too, that it chooses for its scene of thinking, the body of another man, *v.g. Pollux,* who is sleeping without a soul: for if *Castor*'s soul can think while *Castor* is asleep, what *Castor* is never conscious of, 'tis no matter what place it chooses to think in. We have here then the bodies of two men with only one soul between them, which we will suppose to sleep and wake by turns; and the soul still thinking in the waking man, whereof the sleeping man is never conscious, has never the least perception. I ask then, whether *Castor* and *Pollux,* thus, with only one soul between them, which thinks and perceives in one, what the other is never conscious of, nor is concerned for, are not two as distinct persons, as *Castor* and *Hercules;* or, as *Socrates* and *Plato* were? And whether one of them might not be very happy, and the other very miserable? Just by the same reason, they make the soul and the man two persons, who make the soul think apart, what the man is not conscious of. For, I suppose, nobody will make identity of persons, to consist in the soul's being united to the very same numerical particles of matter: for if that be necessary to identity, 'twill be impossible, in that

constant flux of the particles of our bodies, that any man should be the same person, two days, or two moments together.

13. *Impossible to convince those that sleep without dreaming, that they think.* Thus, methinks every drowsy nod shakes their doctrine, who teach, that the soul is always thinking. . . .

14. *That men dream without remembering it, in vain urged.* 'Twill perhaps be said, that the *soul thinks,* even *in* the soundest *sleep, but the memory retains it not.* That the soul in a sleeping man should be this moment busy athinking, and the next moment in a waking man, not remember, nor be able to recollect one jot of all those thoughts, is very hard to be conceived, and would need some better proof than bare assertion, to make it be believed. . . .

. . . .

19. *That a man should be busy in thinking, and yet not retain it the next moment, very improbable.* To suppose the soul to think, and the man not to perceive it, is, as has been said, to make two persons in one man: and if one considers well these men's way of speaking, one shall be led into a suspicion, that they do so. For they who tell us, that the soul always thinks, do never, that I remember, say, that a man always thinks. Can the soul think, and not the man? Or a man think, and not be conscious of it? This, perhaps, would be suspected of *jargon* in others. If they say, the man thinks always, but is not always conscious of it; they may as well say, his body is extended, without having parts. For 'tis altogether as intelligible to say, that a body is extended without parts, as that anything *thinks without being conscious of it,* or perceiving, that it does so. They who talk thus, may, with as much reason, if it be necessary to their hypothesis, say, that a man is always hungry, but that he does not always feel it: whereas hunger consists in that very sensation, as thinking consists in being conscious that one thinks. . . .

20. *No* ideas *but from sensation or reflection, evident, if we observe children.* I see no reason therefore to believe, that the *soul thinks before the senses have furnished it with ideas* to think on; and as those are increased, and retained; so it comes, by exercise, to improve its faculty of thinking in the several parts of it, as well as afterwards, by compounding those *ideas,* and reflecting on its own operations, it increases its stock as well as facility, in remembering, imagining, reasoning, and other modes of thinking.

. . . .

23. If it shall be demanded then, *when a man begins to have any ideas?* I think, the true answer is, when he first has any *sensation.* For since there appear not to be any *ideas* in the mind, before the senses have conveyed any in, I conceive that *ideas* in the understanding, are coeval with *sensation;* which is such an impression or motion, made in some part of the body, as produces some perception in the understanding.

24. *The original of all our knowledge.* The *impressions* then, that are made on our *senses* by outward objects, that are extrinsical to the mind, and *its own operations,* about the impressions, *reflected* on by itself, as proper objects to be contemplated by it, *are,* I conceive, *the original of all knowledge;* and the first capacity of human intellect, is, that the mind is fitted to receive the impressions made on it; either, through the *senses,* by outward objects; or by its own operations, when it *reflects* on them. This is the first step a man makes towards the discovery of anything, and the groundwork, whereon to build all those notions, which ever he shall have naturally in this world. All those sublime thoughts, which tower above the clouds, and reach as high as heaven itself, take their rise and footing here: in all that great extent wherein the mind wanders, in those remote speculations, it may seem to be elevated with, it stirs not one jot beyond those *ideas,* which *sense* or *reflection,* have offered for its contemplation.

25. *In the reception of simple* ideas, *the understanding is for the most part passive.* In this part, the *understanding* is merely *passive;* and whether or not, it will have these beginnings, and as it were materials of knowledge, is not in its own power. For the objects of our senses, do, many of them, obtrude their particular *ideas* upon our minds, whether we will or no: and the operations of our minds, will not let us be without, at least some obscure notions of them. No man, can be wholly ignorant of what he does, when he thinks. These *simple ideas,* when offered to the mind, *the understanding can* no more refuse to have, nor alter, when they are imprinted, nor blot them out, and make new ones in itself, than a mirror can refuse, alter, or obliterate the images or *ideas,* which, the objects set before it, do therein produce. As the bodies that surround us, do diversely affect our organs, the mind is forced to receive the impressions; and cannot avoid the perception of those *ideas* that are annexed to them.

CHAP. II
Of simple ideas.

1. *Uncompounded appearances.* The better to understand the nature, manner, and extent of our knowledge, one thing is carefully to be observed, concerning the *ideas* we have; and that is, that *some* of them are *simple,* and *some complex.*

Though the qualities that affect our senses, are, in the things themselves, so united and blended, that there is no separation, no distance between them; yet 'tis plain, the *ideas* they produce in the mind, enter by the senses simple and unmixed. For though the sight and touch often take in from the same object, at the same time, different *ideas;* as a man sees at once motion and color; the hand feels softness and warmth in the same piece of wax: yet the simple *ideas* thus united in the same object, are as perfectly distinct, as those that come in by different senses. The coldness and hardness, which a man feels in a piece of *ice,* being as distinct *ideas* in the mind, as the smell and whiteness of a lily; or as the taste of sugar, and smell of a rose: and there is nothing can be plainer to a man, than the clear and distinct perception he has of those simple *ideas;* which being each in itself uncompounded, contains in it nothing but *one uniform appearance,* or conception in the mind, and is not distinguishable into different ideas.

2. *The mind can neither make nor destroy them.* These simple ideas, the materials of all our knowledge, are suggested and furnished to the mind, only by those two ways above mentioned, *viz. sensation* and *reflection.* When the understanding is once stored with these simple *ideas,* it has the power to repeat, compare, and unite them even to an almost infinite variety, and so can make at pleasure new complex *ideas.* But it is not in the power of the most exalted wit, or enlarged understanding, by any quickness or variety of thought, to *invent or frame one new simple* idea in the mind, not taken in by the ways before mentioned: nor can any force of the understanding, *destroy* those that are there. . . .

3. This is the reason why, though we cannot believe it impossible to God, to make a creature with other organs, and more ways to convey into the understanding the notice of corporeal things, than those five, as they are usually counted, which he has given to man: yet I think, it is *not possible,* for

anyone *to imagine* any other *qualities* in bodies, howsoever constituted, whereby they can be taken notice of, besides sounds, tastes, smells, visible and tangible qualities. And had mankind been made with but four senses, the qualities then, which are the object of the fifth sense, had been as far from our notice, imagination, and conception, as now any *belonging to a sixth, seventh, or eighth sense,* can possibly be: which, whether yet some other creatures, in some other parts of this vast, and stupendous universe, may not have, will be a great presumption to deny. . . .

CHAP. III
Of ideas *of one sense.*

1. *Division of simple* ideas. Ideas *of one sense.* The better to conceive the *ideas,* we receive from sensation, it may not be amiss for us to consider them, in reference to the different ways, whereby they make their approaches to our minds, and make themselves perceivable by us.

First then, there are some, which come into our minds *by one sense* only.

Secondly, there are others, that convey themselves into the mind *by more senses than one.*

Thirdly, others that are had from *reflection* only.

Fourthly, there are some that make themselves way, and are suggested to the mind *by all the ways of sensation and reflection.*

We shall consider them apart under these several heads.

First, there are *some* ideas, *which have admittance only through one sense,* which is peculiarly adapted to receive them. Thus light and colors, as white, red, yellow, blue; with their several degrees or shades, and mixtures, as green, scarlet, purple, sea-green, and the rest, come in only by the eyes: all kinds of noises, sounds, and tones only by the ears: the several tastes and smells, by the nose and palate. And if these organs, or the nerves which are the conduits, to convey them from without to their audience in the brain, the mind's presence-room (as I may so call it) are any of them so disordered, as not to perform their functions, they have no postern to be admitted by; no other way to bring themselves into view, and be perceived by the understanding.

The most considerable of those, belonging to the touch, are heat and cold, and solidity; all the rest, consisting almost wholly in the sensible configuration, as smooth and rough; or else more, or less firm adhesion of the parts, as hard and soft, tough and brittle, are obvious enough.

2. *Few simple* ideas *have names.* I think, it will be needless to enumerate all the particular *simple ideas,* belonging to each sense. Nor indeed is it possible, if we would, there being a great many *more* of them belonging to most of the senses, *than we have names for.* . . . I shall therefore in the account of simple *ideas,* I am here giving, content myself to set down only such, as are most material to our present purpose, or are in themselves less apt to be taken notice of, though they are very frequently the ingredients of our complex *ideas,* amongst which, I think, I may well account solidity; which therefore I shall treat of in the next chapter.

CHAP. IV
Of solidity.

1. *We receive this* idea *from touch.* The *idea* of *solidity* we receive by our touch; and it arises from the resistance which we find in body, to the entrance of any other body into the place it possesses, till it has left it. There is no *idea,* which we receive more constantly from sensation, than *solidity.* Whether we move, or rest, in what posture soever we are, we always feel something under us, that supports us, and hinders our farther sinking downwards; and the bodies which we daily handle, make us perceive, that whilst they remain between them, they do by an insurmountable force, hinder the approach of the parts of our hands that press them. That which thus hinders the approach of two bodies, when they are moving towards one another, I call *solidity.* . . . But if anyone think it better to call it *impenetrability,* he has my consent. Only I have thought the term *solidity,* the more proper to express this *idea,* not only because of its vulgar use in that sense; but also, because it carries something more of positive in it, than *impenetrability,* which is negative; and is, perhaps, more a consequence of *solidity,* than *solidity* itself. This of all other, seems the *idea* most intimately connected with, and essential to body, so as nowhere else to be found or imagined, but only in matter: and though our senses take no notice of it, but in masses of matter, of a bulk sufficient to cause a sensation in us; yet the mind, having once got this *idea* from such grosser sensible bodies, traces it farther; and considers

it, as well as figure, in the minutest particle of matter, that can exist; and finds it inseparably inherent in body, wherever, or however modified.

2. *Solidity fills space.* This is the *idea* belongs to body, whereby we conceive it to *fill space.* The *idea* of which filling of space, is, that where we imagine any space taken up by a solid substance, we conceive it so to possess it, that it excludes all other solid substances; and, will forever hinder any two other bodies, that move towards one another in a straight line, from coming to touch one another, unless it removes from between them in a line, not parallel to that which they move in. . . .

3. *Distinct from space.* This resistance, whereby it keeps other bodies out of the space which it possesses, is so great, that no force, how great soever, can surmount it. All the bodies in the world, pressing a drop of water on all sides, will never be able to overcome the resistance, which it will make, as soft as it is, to their approaching one another, till it be removed out of their way; whereby our *idea* of *solidity* is *distinguished* both *from pure space,* which is capable neither of resistance nor motion; and from the ordinary *idea* of *hardness*. . . .

4. *From hardness. Solidity* is . . . *differenced from hardness,* in that solidity consists in repletion, and so an utter exclusion of other bodies out of the space it possesses; but hardness, in a firm cohesion of the parts of matter, making up masses of a sensible bulk, so that the whole does not easily change its figure. And indeed, hard and soft are names that we give to things, only in relation to the constitutions of our own bodies; that being generally called hard by us, which will put us to pain, sooner than change figure by the pressure of any part of our bodies; and that, on the contrary, soft, which changes the situation of its parts upon an easy, and unpainful touch.

. . . .

5. *On solidity depends impulse, resistance, and protrusion.* By this *idea* of solidity, is the extension of body distinguished from the extension of space. The extension of body being nothing, but the cohesion or continuity of solid, separable, movable parts; and the extension of space, the continuity of unsolid, inseparable, and immovable parts. *Upon the solidity of bodies* also *depends their mutual impulse, resistance, and protrusion*. . . .

6. *What it is.* If anyone asks me, *what this solidity is,* I send him to his senses to inform him: let him put a flint, or a football between his hands; and then endeavor to join them, and he will know. . . . The simple *ideas* we have are such, as experience teaches them us; but if beyond that, we endeavor, by words, to make them clearer in the mind, we shall succeed no better, than if we went about to clear up the darkness of a blind man's mind, by talking; and to discourse into him the *ideas* of light and colors. The reason of this, I shall show, in another place.

CHAP. V.
Of simple ideas *of divers senses.*

The *ideas* we get by more than one sense, are of *space,* or *extension, figure, rest,* and *motion:* for these make perceivable impressions, both on the eyes and touch; and we can receive and convey into our minds the *ideas* of the extension, figure, motion, and rest of bodies, both by seeing and feeling. But having occasion to speak more at large of these in another place, I here only enumerate them.

CHAP. VI.
Of simple ideas *of reflection.*

1. *Are the operations of the mind about its other* ideas. The mind receiving the *ideas,* mentioned in the foregoing chapters, from without, when it turns its view, inward upon itself, and observes its own actions about those *ideas* it has, takes from thence other *ideas,* which are as capable to be the objects of its contemplation, as any of those it received from foreign things.

2. *The* idea *of perception, and* idea *of willing, we have from reflection.* The two great and principal actions of the mind . . . are these two:

Perception, or *thinking,* and
Volition, or *willing.*

The power of thinking is called the *understanding,* and the power of volition is called the *will,* and these two powers or abilities in the mind are denominated *faculties.* Of some of the modes of the simple *ideas* of reflection, such as are *remembrance, discerning, reasoning, judging, knowledge, faith, &c.* I shall have occasion to speak hereafter.

CHAP. VII.

Of simple ideas *of both sensation and reflection.*

1. *Pleasure and pain.* There be other simple *ideas,* which convey themselves into the mind, by all the ways of sensation and reflection, *viz.*

Pleasure, or *delight,* and its opposite.
Pain, or *uneasiness.*
Power.
Existence.
Unity.

2. *Delight,* or *uneasiness,* one or other of them join themselves to almost all our *ideas,* both of sensation and reflection: and there is scarce any affection of our senses from without, any retired thought of our mind within, which is not able to produce in us *pleasure* or *pain.* By *pleasure* and *pain,* I would be understood to signify, whatsoever delights or molests us; whether it arises from the thoughts of our minds, or anything operating on our bodies. . . .

. . . .

7. *Existence and unity. Existence* and *unity,* are two other *ideas,* that are suggested to the understanding, by every object without, and every *Idea* within. When *ideas* are in our minds, we consider them as being actually there, as well as we consider things to be actually without us; which is, that they exist, or have *existence:* and whatever we can consider as one thing, whether a real being, or *idea,* suggests to the understanding, the *idea* of *unity.*

8. *Power. Power* also is another of those simple *ideas,* which we receive from *sensation and reflection.* For observing in ourselves, that we do, and can think; and that we can, at pleasure, move several parts of our bodies, which were at rest; the effects also, that natural bodies are able to produce in one another, occurring every moment to our senses, we both these ways get the *idea* of *power.*

9. *Succession.* Besides these, there is another *idea,* which though suggested by our senses, yet is more constantly offered us, by what passes in our own minds; and that is the *idea* of *succession.* For if we look immediately into ourselves, and reflect on what is observable there, we shall find our *ideas* always, whilst we are awake, or have any thought, passing in train, one going, and another coming, without intermission.

10. *Simple* ideas *the materials of all our knowledge.* These, if they are not all, are at least (as I think) the most considerable of those *simple ideas* which the mind has, and out of which is made all its other knowledge; all which it receives only by the two forementioned ways of *sensation* and *reflection.*

Nor let anyone think these too narrow bounds for the capacious mind of man to expatiate in, which takes its flight farther than the stars, and cannot be confined by the limits of the world; that extends its thoughts often, even beyond the utmost expansion of matter, and makes excursions into that incomprehensible *inane.* I grant all this, but desire anyone to assign any *simple idea,* which is not *received from* one of *those inlets* before-mentioned, or any *complex idea* not *made out of those simple ones.* Nor will it be so strange, to think these few simple *ideas* sufficient to employ the quickest thought, or largest capacity; and to furnish the materials of all that various knowledge, and more various fancies and opinions of all mankind, if we consider how many words may be made out of the various composition of 24 letters; or if going one step farther, we will but reflect on the variety of combinations may be made, with barely one of the above-mentioned *ideas, viz.* number, whose stock is inexhaustible, and truly infinite: and what a large and immense field, does extension alone afford the mathematicians?

CHAP. VIII.

Some farther considerations concerning our simple ideas.

1. *Positive* ideas *from privative causes.* Concerning the simple *ideas* of sensation 'tis to be considered, that whatsoever is so constituted in nature, as to be able, by affecting our senses, to cause any perception in the mind, does thereby produce in the understanding a simple *idea;* which, whatever be the external cause of it, when it comes to be taken notice of, by our discerning faculty, it is by the mind looked on and considered there, to be a real *positive idea* in the understanding, as much as any other whatsoever; though, perhaps, the cause of it be but a privation in the subject.

2. Thus the *ideas* of heat and cold, light and darkness, white and black, motion or rest, are equally clear and *positive ideas* in the mind; though, perhaps, some of *the causes* which produce them, are barely *privations* in those subjects, from whence our senses derives those *ideas.* These the understanding, in its view of them, considers all as distinct positive *ideas,* without taking notice of the causes that produce them: which is an inquiry not belonging to the *idea,* as it is in the understanding; but to the nature of the things existing without us. These are two very different things, and carefully to be distinguished; it being one thing to perceive, and know the *idea* of white or black, and quite another to examine what kind of particles they must be, and how ranged in the superficies, to make any object appear white or black.

3. A painter or dyer, who never inquired into their causes, has the *ideas* of white and black, and other colors, as clearly, perfectly, and distinctly in his understanding, and perhaps more distinctly, than the philosopher, who has busied himself in considering their natures, and thinks he knows how far either of them is in its cause positive or privative; and the *idea of black* is no less *positive* in his mind, than that of white, *however the cause* of that color in the external object, may *be only a privation.*

4. If it were the design of my present undertaking, to inquire into the natural causes and manner of perception, I should offer this as a reason *why*

a privative cause might, in some cases at least, *produce a positive idea, viz.* that all sensation being produced in us, only by different degrees and modes of motion in our animal spirits, variously agitated by external objects, the abatement of any former motion, must as necessarily produce a new sensation, as the variation or increase of it; and so introduces a new *idea,* which depends only on a different motion of the animal spirits in that organ.

5. But whether this be so, or no, I will not here determine, but appeal to everyone's own experience, whether the shadow of a man, though it consists of nothing but the absence of light (and the more the absence of light is, the more discernible is the shadow) does not, when a man looks on it, cause as clear and positive an *idea* in his mind, as a man himself, though covered over with clear sunshine? And the picture of a shadow, is a positive thing. Indeed, we have *negative names,* which stand not directly for positive *ideas,* but for their absence, such as *insipid, silence, nihil,* &c. which words denote positive *ideas; v.g. taste, sound, being,* with a signification of their absence.

6. And thus one may truly be said to see darkness. For supposing a hole perfectly dark, from whence no light is reflected, 'tis certain one may see the figure of it, or it may be painted; or whether the ink, I write with, makes any other *idea,* is a question. The privative causes I have here assigned of positive *ideas,* are according to the common opinion; but in truth it will be hard to determine, whether there be really any *ideas* from a privative cause, till it be determined, *whether rest be any more a privation than motion.*

7. Ideas *in the mind, qualities in bodies.* To discover the nature of our *ideas* the better, and to discourse of them intelligibly, it will be convenient to distinguish them, as they are *ideas* or perceptions in our minds; and as they are modifications of matter in the bodies that cause such perceptions in us: that so we *may not* think (as perhaps usually is done) that they are exactly the images, and *resemblances* of something inherent in the subject; most of those of sensation being in the mind no more the likeness of something existing without us, than the names, that stand for them are the likeness of our *ideas,* which yet upon hearing, they are apt to excite in us.

8. Whatsoever the mind perceives in itself, or is the immediate object of perception, thought, or understanding, that I call *idea;* and the power to produce any *idea* in our mind, I call *quality* of the subject wherein that

power is. Thus a snowball having the power to produce in us the *ideas* of *white, cold,* and *round,* the powers to produce those *ideas* in us, as they are in the snowball, I call *qualities;* and as they are sensations, or perceptions, in our understandings, I call them *ideas:* which *ideas,* if I speak of sometimes, as in the things themselves, I would be understood to mean those qualities in the objects which produce them in us.

9. *Primary and secondary qualities.* Qualities thus considered in bodies are, first such as are utterly inseparable from the body, in what estate soever it be; such as in all the alterations and changes it suffers, all the force can be used upon it, it constantly keeps; and such as sense constantly finds in every particle of matter, which has bulk enough to be perceived, and the mind finds inseparable from every particle of matter, though less than to make itself singly be perceived by our senses. *v.g.* Take a grain of wheat, divide it into two parts, each part has still *solidity, extension, figure,* and *mobility;* divide it again, and it retains still the same qualities; and so divide it on, till the parts become insensible, they must retain still each of them all those qualities. For division (which is all that a mill, or pestle, or any other body, does upon another, in reducing it to insensible parts) can never take away either solidity, extension, figure, or mobility from any body, but only makes two, or more distinct separate masses of matter, of that which was but one before, all which distinct masses, reckoned as so many distinct bodies, after division make a certain number. These I call *original* or *primary qualities* of body, which I think we may observe to produce simple *ideas* in us, *viz.* solidity, extension, motion, or rest and number.

10. 2*dly.* Such *qualities,* which in truth are nothing in the objects themselves, but powers to produce various sensations in us by their *primary qualities, i.e.* by the bulk, figure, texture, and motion of their insensible parts, as colors, sounds, tastes, *&c.* These I call *secondary qualities.* To these might be added a third sort which are allowed to be barely powers though they are as much real qualities in the subject, as those which I to comply with the common way of speaking call *qualities,* but for distinction *secondary qualities.* For the power in fire to produce a new color, or consistency in wax or clay by its primary qualities, is as much a quality in fire, as the power it has to produce in me a new *idea* or sensation of warmth or burning, which I felt not before, by the same primary qualities, *viz.* the bulk, texture and motion of its insensible parts.

11. *How primary qualities produce their* ideas. The next thing to be considered, is how *bodies* produce *ideas* in us, and that is manifestly *by impulse,* the only way which we can conceive bodies operate in.[9]

12. If then external objects be not united to our minds, when they produce *ideas* in it; and yet we perceive *these original qualities* in such of them as singly fall under our senses, 'tis evident, that some motion must be thence continued by our nerves, or animal spirits, by some parts of our bodies, to the brains or the seat of sensation, there to *produce in our minds the particular* ideas *we have of them.* And since the extension, figure, number, and motion of bodies of an observable bigness, may be perceived at a distance *by* the sight, 'tis evident some singly imperceptible bodies must come from them to the eyes, and thereby convey to the brain some *motion,* which produces these *ideas,* which we have of them in us.

13. *How secondary.* After the same manner, that the *ideas* of these original qualities are produced in us, we may conceive, that the *ideas of secondary qualities* are also *produced,* viz. *by the operation of insensible particles on our senses.* For it being manifest, that there are bodies, and good store of bodies, each whereof is so small, that we cannot, by any of our senses discover either their bulk, figure, or motion, as is evident in the particles of the air and water, and other extremely smaller than those, perhaps, as much smaller than the particles of air, or water, as the particles of air or water, are smaller than peas or hail-stones. Let us suppose at present, that the different motions and figures, bulk and number of such particles, affecting the several organs of our senses, produce in us those different sensations, which we have from the colors and smells of bodies, *v.g.* that a violet, by the impulse of such insensible particles of matter of peculiar figures, and bulks, and in different degrees and modifications of their motions, causes the *ideas* of the blue color, and sweet scent of that flower to be produced in our minds. It being no more impossible, to conceive, that God should annex such *ideas* to such motions, with which they have no similitude; than

9. This sentence replaces the following passage in the first edition: "The next thing to be considered, is how *bodies operate* one upon another, and that is manifestly *by impulse,* and nothing else. It being impossible to conceive, that body should operate on what it does not touch, (which is all one as to imagine it can operate where it is not) or when it does touch, operate any other way than by motion." In the second and third editions Locke revised the second sentence to say that it is impossible to conceive that a body should "operate any way without motion." For Locke's explanation of the more significant changes made in the fourth edition, see the passage on "Gravity and Impulse" in the selections from the Stillingfleet correspondence (p. 354 in this volume).

that he should annex the *idea* of pain to the motion of a piece of steel dividing our flesh, with which that *idea* has no resemblance.

14. What I have said concerning *colors* and *smells,* may be understood also of *tastes* and *sounds, and other the like sensible qualities;* which, whatever reality we, by mistake, attribute to them, are in truth nothing in the objects themselves, but powers to produce various sensations in us, and depend *on those primary qualities, viz.* bulk, figure, texture and motion of parts; as I have said.

15. Ideas *of primary qualities are resemblances; of secondary, not.* From whence I think it is easy to draw this observation, that the *ideas of primary qualities* of bodies, *are resemblances* of them, and their patterns do really exist in the bodies themselves; but the *ideas, produced* in us *by* these *secondary qualities, have no resemblance* of them at all. There is nothing like our *ideas,* existing in the bodies themselves. They are in the bodies, we denominate from them, only a power to produce those sensations in us: and what is sweet, blue, or warm in *idea,* is but the certain bulk, figure, and motion of the insensible parts in the bodies themselves, which we call so.

16. *Flame* is denominated *hot* and *light; snow white* and *cold;* and *manna white* and *sweet,* from the *ideas* they produce in us. Which qualities are commonly thought to be the same in those bodies, that those *ideas* are in us, the one the perfect resemblance of the other, as they are in a mirror; and it would by most men be judged very extravagant, if one should say otherwise. And yet he, that will consider, that *the same fire,* that at one distance *produces* in us the sensation of *warmth,* does at a nearer approach, produce in us the far different sensation of *pain,* ought to bethink himself, what reason he has to say, that his *idea* of *warmth,* which was produced in him by the fire, is actually *in the fire;* and his *idea* of *pain,* which the same fire produced in him in the same way, is *not* in the *fire.* Why is whiteness and coldness in snow, and pain not, when it produces the one and the other *idea* in us; and can do neither, but by the bulk, figure, number, and motion of its solid parts?

17. The particular *bulk, number, figure, and motion of the parts of fire, or snow, are really in them,* whether anyone's senses perceive them or no: and therefore they may be called *real qualities,* because they really exist in those bodies. But *light, heat, whiteness,* or *coldness, are no more really in them, than sickness or pain is in* manna. Take away the sensation of them; let not the eyes see light, or colors, nor the ears hear sounds; let the palate not taste, nor the

nose smell, and all colors, tastes, odors, and sounds, as they are such particular *ideas,* vanish and cease, and are reduced to their causes, *i.e.* bulk, figure, and motion of parts.

18. A piece of *manna* of a sensible bulk, is able to produce in us the *idea* of a round or square figure; and, by being removed from one place to another, the *idea* of motion. This *idea* of motion represents it, as it really is in the *manna* moving: a circle or square are the same, whether in *idea* or existence; in the mind, or in the *manna:* and this, both *motion and figure are really in the manna,* whether we take notice of them or no: this everybody is ready to agree to. Besides, *manna* by the bulk, figure, texture, and motion of its parts, has a power to produce the sensations of sickness, and sometimes of acute pains, or gripings in us. That these *ideas* of *sickness and pain are not in the* manna, but effects of its operations on us, and are nowhere when we feel them not: this also everyone readily agrees to. And yet men are hardly to be brought to think, that *sweetness and whiteness are not really in manna;* which are but the effects of the operations of *manna,* by the motion, size, and figure of its particles on the eyes and palate; as the pain and sickness caused by *manna,* are confessedly nothing, but the effects of its operations on the stomach and guts, by the size, motion, and figure of its insensible parts; (for by nothing else can a body operate, as has been proved:) as if it could not operate on the eyes and palate, and thereby produce in the mind particular distinct *ideas,* which in itself it has not, as well as we allow it can operate on the guts and stomach, and thereby produce distinct *ideas,* which in itself it has not. These *ideas* being all effects of the operations of *manna,* on several parts of our bodies, by the size, figure, number, and motion of its parts, why those produced by the eyes and palate, should rather be thought to be really in the *manna,* than those produced by the stomach and guts; or why the pain and sickness, *ideas* that are the effects of *manna,* should be thought to be nowhere, when they are not felt; and yet the sweetness and whiteness, effects of the same *manna* on other parts of the body, by ways equally as unknown, should be thought to exist in the *manna,* when they are not seen nor tasted, would need some reason to explain.

19. Let us consider the red and white colors in *porphyry:* hinder light but from striking on it, and its colors vanish; it no longer produces any such *ideas* in us: upon the return of light, it produces these appearances on us again. Can anyone think any real alterations are made in the *porphyry,* by the presence or absence of light; and that those *ideas* of whiteness and

redness, are really in *porphyry* in the light, when 'tis plain *it has no color in the dark?* It has, indeed, such a configuration of particles, both night and day, as are apt by the rays of light rebounding from some parts of that hard stone, to produce in us the *idea* of redness, and from others the *idea* of whiteness: but whiteness or redness are not in it at any time, but such a texture, that has the power to produce such a sensation in us.

20. Pound an almond, and the clear white *color* will be altered into a dirty one, and the sweet *taste* into an oily one. What real alteration can the beating of the pestle make in any body, but an alteration of the *texture* of it?

21. *Ideas* being thus distinguished and understood, we may be able to give an account, how the same water, at the same time, may produce the *idea* of cold by one hand, and of heat by the other: whereas it is impossible, that the same water, if those *ideas* were really in it, should at the same time be both hot and cold. For if we imagine *warmth,* as it is *in our hands,* to be *nothing but a certain sort and degree of motion in the minute particles of our nerves, or animal spirits,* we may understand, how it is possible, that the same water may at the same time produce the sensation of heat in one hand, and cold in the other; which yet figure never does, that never producing the *idea* of a square by one hand, which has produced the *idea* of globe by another. But if the sensation of heat and cold, be nothing but the increase or diminution of the motion of the minute parts of our bodies, caused by the corpuscles of any other body, it is easy to be understood, that if that motion be greater in one hand, than in the other; if a body be applied to the two hands, which has in its minute particles a greater motion, than in those of one of the hands, and a less, than in those of the other, it will increase the motion of the one hand, and lessen it in the other, and so cause the different sensations of heat and cold, that depend thereon.

22. I have in what just goes before, been engaged in physical inquiries a little farther than, perhaps, I intended. But it being necessary, to make the nature of sensation a little understood, and to make the *difference between the qualities in bodies, and the* ideas *produced by them in the mind,* to be distinctly conceived, without which it were impossible to discourse intelligibly of them; I hope, I shall be pardoned this little excursion into natural philosophy, it being necessary in our present inquiry, to distinguish the *primary,* and *real qualities* of bodies, which are always in them, (*viz.* solidity, extension, figure, number, and motion, or rest; and are sometimes perceived by us, *viz.* when the bodies they are in, are big enough singly to be

discerned) from those *secondary* and *imputed qualities,* which are but the powers of several combinations of those primary ones, when they operate, without being distinctly discerned; whereby we also may come to know what *ideas* are, and what are not resemblances of something really existing in the bodies, we denominate from them.

23. *Three sorts of qualities in bodies.* The *qualities* then that are in *bodies* rightly considered, are of *three sorts.*

First, the *bulk, figure, number, situation,* and *motion, or rest* of their solid parts; those are in them, whether we perceive them or no; and when they are of that size, that we can discover them, we have by these an *idea* of the thing, as it is in itself, as is plain in artificial things. These I call *primary qualities.*

Secondly, the *power* that is in any body, by reason of *its* insensible *primary qualities,* to operate after a peculiar manner on any of our senses, and thereby *produce in us* the *different ideas* of several colors, sounds, smells, tastes, *&c.* These are usually called sensible qualities.

Thirdly, the *power* that is in any body, *by* reason of the particular constitution of *its primary qualities, to* make such a *change* in the *bulk, figure, texture, and motion of another body,* as to make it operate on our senses, differently from what it did before. Thus the sun has a power to make wax white, and fire to make lead fluid. These *are* usually called powers.

The first of these, as has been said, I think, may be properly called *real original,* or *primary qualities,* because they are in the things themselves, whether they are perceived or no: and upon their different modifications it is, that the secondary qualities depend.

The other two, are only powers to act differently upon other things, which powers result from the different modifications of those primary qualities.

24. *The* 1st *are resemblances. The* 2d *thought resemblances, but are not. The* 3d *neither are nor are thought so.* But though *these two later sorts of qualities are powers barely,* and nothing but powers, relating to several other bodies, and resulting from the different modifications of the original qualities; yet they are generally otherwise thought of. For *the second sort, viz.* the powers to produce several *ideas* in us by our senses, *are looked upon as real qualities, in the things* thus affecting us: but *the third sort are called, and esteemed barely powers, v.g.* the *idea* of heat, or light, which we receive by our eyes, or touch from the sun, are commonly thought *real qualities,*

existing in the sun, and something more than mere powers in it. But when we consider the sun, in reference to wax, which it melts or blanches, we look upon the whiteness and softness produced in the wax, not as qualities in the sun, but effects produced by *powers* in it: whereas, if rightly considered, these qualities of light and warmth, which are perceptions in me when I am warmed, or enlightened by the sun, are no otherwise in the sun, than the changes made in the wax, when it is blanched or melted, are in the sun. They are all of them equally powers in the sun, depending on its primary qualities; whereby it is able in the one case, so to alter the bulk, figure, texture, or motion of some of the insensible parts of my eyes, or hands, as thereby to produce in me the *ideas* of light or heat; and in the other, it is able so to alter the bulk, figure, texture, or motion of the insensible parts of the wax, as to make them fit to produce in me the distinct *ideas* of white and fluid.

25. The reason, *why the one are ordinarily taken for real qualities, and the other only for bare powers,* seems to be, because the *ideas* we have of distinct colors, sounds, *&c.* containing nothing at all in them, of bulk, figure, or motion, we are not apt to think them the effects of these primary qualities, which appear not to our senses to operate in their production; and with which, they have not any apparent congruity, or conceivable connection. Hence it is, that we are so forward to imagine, that those *ideas* are the resemblances of something really existing in the objects themselves: since sensation discovers nothing of bulk, figure, or motion of parts in their production; nor can reason show, how bodies by their bulk, figure, and motion, should produce in the mind the *ideas* of blue, or yellow, *&c.* But in the other case, in the operations of bodies, changing the qualities one of another, we plainly discover, that the quality produced, has commonly no resemblance with anything in the thing producing it; wherefore we look on it as a bare effect of power. For though receiving the *idea* of heat, or light, from the sun, we are apt to think, 'tis a perception and resemblance of such a quality in the sun: yet when we see wax, or a fair face, receive change of color from the sun, we cannot imagine, that to be the reception or resemblance of anything in the sun, because we find not those different colors in the sun itself. For our senses, being able to observe a likeness, or unlikeness of sensible qualities in two different external objects, we forwardly enough conclude the production of any sensible quality in any subject, to be an effect of bare power, and not the communication of any quality, which was really in the efficient, when we find no such sensible quality in the thing that produced it. But

our senses, not being able to discover any unlikeness between the *idea* produced in us, and the quality of the object producing it, we are apt to imagine, that our *ideas* are resemblances of something in the objects, and not the effects of certain powers, placed in the modification of their primary qualities, with which primary qualities the *ideas* produced in us have no resemblance.

26. *Secondary qualities twofold; first, immediately perceivable; secondly, mediately perceivable.* To conclude, beside those before mentioned *primary qualities* in bodies, *viz.* bulk, figure, extension, number, and motion of their solid parts; all the rest, whereby we take notice of bodies, and distinguish them one from another, are nothing else, but several powers in them, depending on those primary qualities; whereby they are fitted, either by immediately operating on our bodies, to produce several different *ideas* in us; or else by operating on other bodies, so to change their primary qualities, as to render them capable of producing *ideas* in us, different from what before they did. The former of these, I think may be called *secondary qualities, immediately perceivable:* the latter, *secondary qualities, mediately perceivable.*

CHAP. IX.

Of perception.

1. *It is the first simple* idea *of reflection. Perception,* as it is the first faculty of the mind, exercised about our *ideas;* so it is the first and simplest *idea* we have from reflection, and is by some called thinking in general. Though thinking, in the propriety of the *English* tongue, signifies that sort of operation of the mind about its *ideas,* wherein the mind is active; where it with some degree of voluntary attention, considers anything. For in bare naked *perception,* the mind is, for the most part, only passive; and what it perceives, it cannot avoid perceiving.

2. *Perception is only when the mind receives the impression. What perception is,* everyone will know better by reflecting on what he does himself, when he sees, hears, feels, *&c.* or thinks, than by any discourse of mine. Whoever reflects on what passes in his own mind, cannot miss it: and if he does not reflect, all the words in the world, cannot make him have any notion of it.

3. This is certain, that whatever alterations are made in the body, if they reach not the mind; whatever impressions are made on the outward parts, if they are not taken notice of within, there is no perception. Fire may burn our bodies, with no other effect, than it does a billet, unless the motion be continued to the brain, and there the sense of heat, or *idea* of pain, be produced in the mind, wherein consists *actual perception.*

4. How often may a man observe in himself, that whilst his mind is intently employed in the contemplation of some objects; and curiously surveying some *ideas* that are there, it takes no notice of impressions of sounding bodies, made upon the organ of hearing, with the same alteration, that uses to be for the producing the *idea* of a sound? A sufficient impulse there may be on one organ; but it not reaching the observation of the mind, there follows no perception. . . . Want of sensation in this case, is not through any defect in the organ, or that the man's ears are less affected, than at other times, when he does hear: but that which uses to produce the *idea,* though conveyed in by the usual organ, not being taken notice of in the understanding, and so imprinting no *idea* on the mind, there follows no sensation. *So that wherever there is sense,* or *perception, there some* idea *is actually produced, and present in the understanding.*

5. *Children, though they have* Ideas, *in the womb, have none innate.* Therefore I doubt not but *children,* by the exercise of their senses about objects, that affect them *in the womb, receive some few ideas,* before they are born, as the unavoidable effects, either of the bodies that environ them, or else of those wants or diseases they suffer; amongst which, (if one may conjecture concerning things not very capable of examination) I think the *ideas* of hunger and warmth are two: which probably are some of the first that children have, and which they scarce ever part with again.

6. But though it be reasonable to imagine, that *children* receive some *ideas* before they come into the world, yet these simple *ideas* are *far from* those *innate principles,* which some contend for, and we above have rejected. These here mentioned, being the effects of sensation, are only from some affections of the body, which happen to them there, and so depend on something exterior to the mind; no otherwise differing in their manner of production from other *ideas* derived from sense, but only in the precedency of time: whereas those innate principles are supposed to be of quite another nature; not coming into the mind by any accidental alterations in, or

operations on the body; but, as it were, original characters impressed upon it, in the very first moment of its being and constitution.

. . . .

8. Ideas *of sensation changed by judgment*. We are farther to consider concerning perception, that the *ideas we receive by sensation, are often* in grown people *altered by the judgment*, without our taking notice of it. When we set before our eyes a round globe, of any uniform color, *v.g.* gold, alabaster, or jet, 'tis certain, that the *idea* thereby imprinted in our mind, is of a flat circle variously shadowed, with several degrees of light and brightness coming to our eyes. But we having by use been accustomed to perceive, what kind of appearance convex bodies are wont to make in us; what alterations are made in the reflections of light, by the difference of the sensible figures of bodies, the judgment presently, by an habitual custom, alters the appearances into their causes: so that from that, which truly is variety of shadow or color, collecting the figure, it makes it pass for a mark of figure, and frames to itself the perception of a convex figure, and an uniform color; when the *idea* we receive from thence, is only a plane variously colored, as is evident in painting. To which purpose I shall here insert a problem of that very ingenious and studious promoter of real knowledge, the learned and worthy Mr. *Molyneux*, which he was pleased to send me in a letter some months since; and it is this: *Suppose a man born blind, and now adult, and taught by his touch to distinguish between a cube, and a sphere of the same metal, and nighly of the same bigness, so as to tell, when he felt one and t'other, which is the cube, which the sphere.*[10] *Suppose then the cube and sphere placed on a table, and the blind man to be made to see. Quære, whether by his sight, before he touched them, he could now distinguish, and tell, which is the globe, which the cube.* To which the acute and judicious proposer answers: *Not. For though he has obtained the experience of, how a globe, how a cube affects his touch; yet he has not yet attained the experience, that what afflicts his touch so or so, must affect his sight so or so; or that a protuberant angle in the cube, that pressed his hand unequally, shall appear to his eye, as it does in the cube.* I agree with this thinking gent. whom I am proud to call my friend, in his answer to this his problem; and am of opinion, that the blind man, at first sight, would not be able with certainty to say, which was the globe, which the cube, whilst

10. William Molyneux (1656-1698), Irish scientist, author of *Dioptrica Nova* (1692). Molyneux first proposed his problem to Locke in a 1688 letter sent to the editor of *Bibliothèque universelle*, where a French abridgment of Locke's *Essay* had appeared. Locke ignored the problem until Molyneux repeated it in a private letter dated 2 March 1693.

he only saw them: though he could unerringly name them by his touch, and certainly distinguish them by the difference of their figures felt. This I have set down, and leave with my reader, as an occasion for him to consider, how much he may be beholden to experience, improvement, and acquired notions, where he thinks, he has not the least use of, or help from them: and the rather, because this observing gent. farther adds, that *having upon the occasion of my book, proposed this to divers very ingenious men, he hardly ever met with one, that at first gave the answer to it, which he thinks true, till by hearing his reasons they were convinced.*

9. But this is not, I think, usual in any of our *ideas,* but those received by *sight:* because sight, the most comprehensive of all our senses, conveying to our minds the *ideas* of light and colors, which are peculiar only to that sense; and also the far different *ideas* of space, figure, and motion, the several varieties whereof change the appearances of its proper object, *viz.* light and colors, we bring ourselves by use, to judge of the one by the other. This in many cases, by a settled habit, in things whereof we have frequent experience, is performed so constantly, and so quick, that we take that for the perception of our sensation, which is an *idea* formed by our judgment; so that one, *viz.* that of sensation, serves only to excite the other, and is scarce taken notice of itself; as a man who reads or hears with attention and understanding, takes little notice of the characters, or sounds, but of the *ideas,* that are excited in him by them.

. . . .

11. *Perception puts the difference between animals and inferior beings.* This faculty of *perception,* seems to me to be that, which *puts the distinction betwixt the animal kingdom, and the inferior parts of nature.* For however vegetables have, many of them, some degrees of motion, and upon the different application of other bodies to them, do very briskly alter their figures and motions, and so have obtained the name of sensitive plants, from a motion, which has some resemblance to that, which in animals follows upon sensation: yet, I suppose, it is all bare mechanism; and no otherwise produced, than the turning of a wild oat-beard, by the insinuation of the particles of moisture; or the shortening of a rope, by the affusion of water. All which is done without any sensation in the subject, or the having or receiving any *ideas.*

12. *Perception,* I believe, is, in some degree, *in all sorts of animals;* though in some, possibly, the avenues, provided by nature for the reception of

sensations are so few, and the perception, they are received with, so obscure and dull, that it comes extremely short of the quickness and variety of sensations, which is in other animals. . . .

. . . .

CHAP. X.

Of retention.

1. *Contemplation.* The next faculty of mind, whereby it makes a farther progress towards knowledge, is that which I call *retention,* or the keeping of those simple *ideas,* which from sensation or reflection it has received. This is done two ways. First, by keeping the *idea,* which is brought into it, for some time actually in view, which is called *contemplation.*

2. *Memory.* The other way of retention is the power to revive again in our minds those *ideas,* which after imprinting have disappeared, or have been as it were laid out of sight: and thus we do, when we conceive heat or light, yellow or sweet, the object being removed. This is *memory,* which is as it were the storehouse of our *ideas.* For the narrow mind of man, not being capable of having many *ideas* under view and consideration at once, it was necessary to have a repository, to lay up those *ideas,* which at another time it might have use of. But our *ideas* being nothing, but actual perceptions in the mind, which cease to be anything, when there is no perception of them, this *laying up* of our *ideas* in the repository of the memory, signifies no more but this, that the mind has a power, in many cases, to revive perceptions, which it has once had, with this additional perception annexed to them, that it has had them before. And in this sense it is, that our *ideas* are said to be in our memories, when indeed, they are actually nowhere, but only there is an ability in the mind, when it will, to revive them again; and as it were paint them anew on itself, though some with more, some with less difficulty; some more lively, and others more obscurely. And thus it is, by the assistance of this faculty, that we are said to have all those *ideas* in our understandings, which though we do not actually contemplate, yet we can bring in sight, and make appear again, and be the objects of our thoughts, without the help of those sensible qualities, which first imprinted them there.

. . . .

5. Ideas *fade in the memory. . . . The pictures drawn in our minds, are laid in fading colors;* and if not sometimes refreshed, vanish and disappear. How much the constitution of our bodies, and the make of our animal spirits, are concerned in this; and whether the temper of the brain make this difference, that in some it retains the characters drawn on it like marble, in others like freestone, and in others little better than sand, I shall not here inquire, though it may seem probable, that the constitution of the body does sometimes influence the memory; since we oftentimes find a disease quite strip the mind of all its *ideas,* and the flames of a fever, in a few days, calcine all those images to dust and confusion, which seemed to be as lasting, as if carved in marble.

6. *Constantly repeated* ideas *can scarce be lost.* But concerning the ideas themselves, it is easy to remark, that those that are *oftenest refreshed* (amongst which are those that are conveyed into the mind by more ways than one) by a frequent return of the objects or actions that produce them, *fix themselves best in the memory,* and remain clearest and longest there: and therefore those, which are the original qualities of bodies, *viz. solidity, extension, figure, motion,* and *rest,* and those that almost constantly affect our bodies, as *heat* and *cold;* and those which are the affections of all kinds of beings, as *existence, duration,* and *number,* which almost every object that affects our senses, every thought which employs our minds, bring along with them: these, I say, and the like *ideas,* are seldom quite lost, whilst the mind retains any *ideas* at all.

7. *In remembering the mind is often active.* In this secondary perception, as I may so call it, or viewing again of ideas, that are lodged *in* the *memory, the mind is oftentimes more than barely passive,* the appearance of those dormant pictures, depending sometimes on the will. The mind very often sets itself on working in search of some hidden *idea,* and turns, as it were, the eye of the soul upon it; though sometimes too they start up in our minds of their own accord, and offer themselves to the understanding; and very often are roused and tumbled out of their dark cells, into open daylight, by some turbulent and tempestuous passion; our affections bringing *ideas* to our memory, which had otherwise lain quiet and unregarded. This farther is to be observed, concerning *ideas* lodged in the memory, and upon occasion revived by the mind, that they are not only (as the word *revive* imports) none of them new ones; but also that the mind takes notice of them, as of a

former impression, and renews its acquaintance with them, as with *ideas* it had known before. So that though *ideas* formerly imprinted are not all constantly in view, yet in remembrance they are constantly known to be such, as have been formerly imprinted, *i.e.* in view, and taken notice of before by the understanding.

8. *Two defects in the memory, oblivion and slowness. Memory*, in an intellectual creature, is necessary in the next degree to perception. It is of so great moment, that where it is wanting, all the rest of our faculties are in great measure useless: and we in our thoughts, reasonings, and knowledge, could not proceed beyond present objects, were it not for the assistance of our memories, wherein there may be *two defects*.

First, that it *loses the idea* quite, and so far it produces perfect ignorance. For since we can know nothing farther, than we have the *idea* of it, when that is gone, we are in perfect *ignorance*.

Second, that it moves slowly, and *retrieves not the ideas*, that it has, and are laid up in store, *quick enough* to serve the mind upon occasions. . . .

. . . .

10. *Brutes have memory.* This faculty of laying up, and retaining the *ideas*, that are brought into the mind, several *other animals* seems to have, to a great degree, as well as man. For to pass by other instances, birds learning of tunes, and the endeavors one may observe in them, to hit the notes right, put it past doubt with me, that they have perception, and retain *ideas* in their memories, and use them for patterns. For it seems to me impossible, that they should endeavor to conform their voices to notes (as 'tis plain they do) of which they had *ideas*. For though I should grant sound may mechanically cause a certain motion of the animal spirits, in the brains of those birds, whilst the tune is actually playing; and that motion may be continued on to the muscles of the wings, and so the bird mechanically be driven away by certain noises, because this may tend to the bird's preservation: yet that can never be supposed a reason, why it should cause mechanically, either whilst the tune was playing, much less after it has ceased, such a motion in the organs of the bird's voice, as should conform it to the notes of a foreign sound, which imitation can be of no use to the bird's preservation. But which is more, it cannot with any appearance of reason, be supposed (much less proved) that birds, without sense and memory, can approach their notes, nearer and nearer by degrees, to a tune played yesterday; which if they have no *idea* of in their memory, is now nowhere, nor can be a pattern

for them to imitate, or which any repeated essays can bring them nearer to. Since there is no reason why the sound of a pipe should leave traces in their brains, which not at first, but by their after-endeavors, should produce the like sounds; and why the sounds they make themselves, should not make traces which they should follow, as well as those of the pipe, is impossible to conceive.

CHAP. XI.

Of discerning, and other operations of the mind.

1. *No knowledge without it.* Another faculty, we may take notice of in our minds, is that of *discerning* and distinguishing between the several *ideas* it has. . . . On this faculty of distinguishing one thing from another, depends the *evidence and certainty* of several even very general propositions, which have passed for innate truths; because men over-looking the true cause, why those propositions find universal assent, impute it wholly to native uniform impressions; whereas it in truth *depends on this clear discerning faculty*. . . .

. . . .

4. *Comparing.* The *COMPARING* them one with another, in respect of extent, degrees, time, place, or any other circumstances, is another operation of the mind about its *ideas,* and is that upon which depends all that large tribe of *ideas,* comprehended under *relation;* which of how vast an extent it is, I shall have occasion to consider hereafter.

. . . .

6. *Compounding.* The next operation we may observe in the mind about its *ideas,* is *COMPOSITION;* whereby it puts together several of those simple ones it has received from sensation and reflection, and combines them into complex ones. Under this of composition, may be reckoned also that of *ENLARGING;* wherein though the composition does not so much appear as in more complex ones, yet it is nevertheless a putting several *ideas* together, though of the same kind. . . .

. . . .

8. *Naming.* When children have, by repeated sensations, got *ideas* fixed in their memories, they begin, by degrees, to learn the use of signs. And when they have got the skill to apply the organs of speech to the framing of articulate sounds, they begin to make *use of words,* to signify their *ideas* to others: these verbal signs they sometimes borrow from others, and sometimes make themselves, as one may observe among the new and unusual names children often give to things in their first use of language.

9. *Abstraction.* The use of words then being to stand as outward marks of our internal *ideas,* and those *ideas* being taken from particular things, if every particular *idea* that we take in, should have a distinct name, names must be endless. To prevent this, the mind makes the particular *ideas,* received from particular objects, to become general; which is done by considering them as they are in the mind such appearances, separate from all other existences, and the circumstances of real existence, as time, place, or any other concomitant *ideas.* This is called *ABSTRACTION,* whereby *ideas* taken from particular beings, become general representatives of all of the same kind; and their names general names, applicable to whatever exists conformable to such abstract *ideas.* Such precise, naked appearances in the mind, without considering, how, whence, or with what others they came there, the understanding lays up (with names commonly annexed to them) as the standards to rank real existences into sorts, as they agree with those patterns, and to *denominate* them accordingly. Thus the same color being observed today in chalk or snow, which the mind yesterday received from milk, it considers that appearance alone, makes it a representative of all of that kind; and having given it the name *whiteness,* it by that sound signifies the same quality wheresoever to be imagined or met with; and thus universals, whether *ideas* or terms, are made.

10. *Brutes abstract not.* If it may be doubted, whether *beasts* compound and enlarge their *ideas* that way, to any degree: this, I think, I may be positive in, that the power of *abstracting* is not at all in them; and that the having of general *ideas,* is that which puts a perfect distinction betwixt man and brutes; and is an excellency which the faculties of brutes do by no means attain to. For it is evident, we observe no footsteps in them, of making use of general signs for universal *ideas;* from which we have reason to imagine, that they have not the faculty of abstracting, or making general *ideas,* since they have no use of words, or any other general signs.

11. Nor can it be imputed to their want of fit organs, to frame articulate sounds, that they have no use, or knowledge of general words; since many of them, we find, can fashion such sounds, and pronounce words distinctly enough, but never with any such application. And on the other side, men, who through some defect in the organs, want words, yet fail not to express their universal *ideas* by signs, which serve them instead of general words, a faculty which we see beasts come short in. And therefore I think we may suppose, that 'tis in this, that the species of *brutes* are discriminated from man; and 'tis that proper difference wherein they are wholly separated, and which at last widens to so vast a distance. For if they have any *ideas* at all, and are not bare machines (as some would have them) we cannot deny them to have some reason. It seems as evident to me, that they do some of them in certain instances reason, as that they have sense; but it is only in particular *ideas,* just as they received them from their senses. They are the best of them tied up within those narrow bounds, and *have not* (as I think) the faculty to enlarge them by any kind of *abstraction.*

. . . .

15. *These are the beginnings of human knowledge.* And thus I have given a short, and, I think, true *history of the first beginnings of human knowledge;* whence the mind has its first objects, and by what steps it makes its progress to the laying in, and storing up those *ideas,* out of which is to be framed all the knowledge it is capable of; wherein I must appeal to experience and observation, whether I am in the right: the best way to come to truth, being to examine things as they really are, and not to conclude they are, as we fancy of ourselves, or have been taught by others to imagine.

. . . .

17. *Dark room.* I pretend not to teach, but to inquire; and therefore cannot but confess here again, that external and internal sensation, are the only passages that I can find, of knowledge, to the understanding. These alone, as far as I can discover, are the windows by which light is let into this *dark room.* For, methinks, the *understanding* is not much unlike a closet wholly shut from light, with only some little opening left, to let in external visible resemblances, or *ideas* of things without; would the pictures coming into such a dark room but stay there, and lie so orderly as to be found upon occasion, it would very much resemble the understanding of a man, in reference to all objects of sight, and the *ideas* of them.

These are my guesses concerning the minds whereby the understanding comes to have, and retain simple *ideas,* and the modes of them, with some other operations about them. I proceed now to examine some of these simple *ideas,* and their modes, a little more particularly.

CHAP. XII.

Of complex ideas.

1. *Made by the mind out of simple ones.* We have hitherto considered those *ideas,* in the reception whereof, the mind is only passive, which are those simple ones received from *sensation* and *reflection* before-mentioned, whereof the mind cannot make any one to itself, nor have any *idea* which does not wholly consist of them. But as the mind is wholly passive in the reception of all its simple *ideas,* so it exerts several acts of its own, whereby out of its simple *ideas,* as the materials and foundations of the rest, the other are framed. The acts of the mind wherein it exerts its power over its simple *ideas* are chiefly these three, 1. Combining several simple *ideas* into one compound one, and thus all complex *ideas* are made. 2. The 2*d.* is bring two *ideas,* whether simple or complex, together; and setting them by one another, so as to take a view of them at once, without uniting them into one; by which way it gets all its *ideas* of relations. 3. The 3*d.* is separating them from all other *ideas* that accompany them in their real existence; this is called *abstraction:* and thus all its general *ideas* are made. This shows man's power and its ways of operation to be muchwhat the same in the material and intellectual world. For the materials in both being such as he has no power over, either to make or destroy, all that man can do is either to unite them together, or to set them by one another or wholly separate them. I shall here begin with the first of these in the consideration of complex *ideas,* and come to the other two in their due places. As simple *ideas* are observed to exist in several combinations united together; so the mind has a power to consider several of them united together, as one *idea;* and that not only as they are united in external objects, but as itself has joined them. *Ideas* thus made up of several simple ones put together, I call *complex;* such as are *beauty, gratitude, a man, an army, the universe;* which though complicated of various simple *ideas,* or *complex ideas* made up of simple ones, yet are, when the mind pleases, considered each by itself, as one entire thing, and signified by one name.

2. *Made voluntarily.* In this faculty of repeating and joining together its *ideas,* the mind has great power in varying and multiplying the objects of its thoughts, infinitely beyond what *sensation* or *reflection* furnished it with: but all this still confined to those simple *ideas,* which it received from those two sources, and which are the ultimate materials of all its compositions. For simple *ideas* are all from things themselves; and of these *the mind can* have no more, nor other than what are suggested to it. It can have no other *ideas* of sensible qualities, than what come from without by the senses; nor any *ideas* of other kind of operations of a thinking substance, than what it finds in itself: but when it has once got these simple *ideas,* it is not confined barely to observation, and what offers itself from without; it can, by its own power, put together those *ideas* it has, and *make new complex ones,* which it never received so united.

3. *Are either modes, substances, or relations. Complex ideas,* however compounded and decompounded, though their number be infinite, and the variety endless, wherewith they fill, and entertain the thoughts of men; yet, I think, they may be all reduced under these three heads.

1. *Modes.*
2. *Substances.*
3. *Relations.*

4. *Modes.* First, *modes* I call such complex *ideas,* which however compounded, contain not in them the supposition of subsisting by themselves, but are considered as dependences on, or affections of substances; such are the *ideas* signified by the words *triangle, gratitude, murder, &c.* And if in this I use the word *mode,* in somewhat a different sense from its ordinary signification, I beg pardon; it being unavoidable in discourses, differing from the ordinary received notions, either to make new words, or to use old words in somewhat a new signification, the latter whereof, in our present case, is perhaps the more tolerable of the two.

5. *Simple and mixed modes.* Of these *modes,* there are two sorts, which deserve distinct consideration. First, there are some which are only variations, or different combinations of the same simple *idea,* without the mixture of any other, as a dozen, or score; which are nothing but the *ideas* of so many distinct units added together, and these I call *simple modes,* as being contained within the bounds of one simple *idea.* Secondly, there are others compounded of simple *ideas* of several kinds, put together to make one

complex one; *v. g. beauty,* consisting of a certain composition of color and figure, causing delight in the beholder; *theft,* which being the concealed change of the possession of anything, without the consent of the proprietor, contains, as is visible, a combination of several *ideas* of several kinds; and these I call *mixed modes.*

6. *Substances single or collective.* Secondly, the *ideas* of *substances* are such combinations of simple *ideas,* as are taken to represent distinct particular things subsisting by themselves; in which the supposed, or confused *idea* of substance, such as it is, is always the first and chief. Thus if to substance be joined the simple *idea* of a certain dull whitish color, with certain degrees of weight, hardness, ductility, and fusibility, we have the *idea* of *lead;* and a combination of the *ideas* of a certain sort of figure, with the powers of motion, thought, and reasoning, joined to substance, make the ordinary *idea* of *a man.* Now of substances also, there are two sorts of *ideas;* one of single substances, as they exist separately, as of *a man,* or *a sheep;* the other of several of those put together, as an *army* of men, or *flock* of sheep; which *collective* ideas *of* several *substances* thus put together, are as much each of them one single *idea,* as that of a man, or an unit.

7. *Relation.* Thirdly, the last sort of complex *idea,* is that we call *relation,* which consists in the consideration and comparing one *idea* with another: of these several kinds we shall treat in their order.

8. *The abstrusest* ideas *from the two sources.* If we will trace the progress of our minds, and with attention observe how it repeats, adds together, and unites its simple *ideas* received from sensation or reflection, it will lead us farther than at first, perhaps, we should have imagined. And, I believe, we shall find, if we warily observe the originals of our notions, that even *the most abstruse* ideas, how remote soever they may seem from sense, or from any operation of our own minds, are yet only such, as the understanding frames to itself, by repeating and joining together *ideas,* that it had either from objects of sense, or from its own operations about them: so that those even large *and abstract* ideas *are derived from sensation, or reflection,* being no other than what the mind, by the ordinary use of its own faculties, employed about *ideas,* received from objects of sense, or from the operations it observes in itself about them, may, and does attain unto. This I shall endeavor to show in the *ideas* we have of *space, time,* and *infinity,* and some few other, that seem the most remote from those originals.

CHAP. XIII.

Of simple modes; and first, of the simple modes of space.

1. *Simple modes.* Though in the foregoing part, I have often mentioned simple *ideas,* which are truly the materials of all our knowledge; yet having treated of them there, rather in the way that they come into the mind, than as distinguished from others more compounded, it will not be, perhaps, amiss to take a view of some of them again under this consideration, and examine those different *modifications of the same* idea; which the mind either finds in things existing, or is able to make within itself, without the help of any extrinsical object, or any foreign suggestion.

Those *modifications of any one simple* idea, (which, as has been said, *I call simple modes*) are as perfectly different and distinct *ideas* in the mind, as those of the greatest distance or contrariety. For the *idea* of *two,* is as distinct from that of *one,* as *blueness* from *heat,* or either of them from any number: and yet it is made up only of that simple *idea* of an unit repeated; and repetitions of this kind joined together, make those distinct *simple modes,* of a *dozen,* a *gross,* a *million.*

2. Idea *of space.* I shall begin with the *simple idea of space.* I have showed above, *Chap.* iv. that we get the *idea* of space, both by our sight, and touch; which, I think, is so evident, that it would be as needless, to go to prove, that men perceive, by their sight, a distance between bodies of different colors, or between the parts of the same body; as that they see colors themselves: nor is it less obvious, that they can do so in the dark by feeling and touch.

3. *Space and extension.* This space considered barely in length between any two beings, without considering anything else between them, is called *distance:* if considered in length, breadth, and thickness, I think, it may be called *capacity:* the term extension is usually applied to it, in what manner soever considered.

4. *Immensity.* Each different distance is a different modification of space, and *each* idea *of any different distance, or space, is a simple mode of this* idea. Men for the use, and by the custom of measuring, settle in their minds

the *ideas* of certain stated lengths, such as are an *inch, foot, yard, fathom, mile, diameter of the earth,* &c. which are so many distinct *ideas* made up only of space. When any such stated lengths or measures of space are made familiar to men's thoughts, they can, in their minds, repeat them as often as they will, without mixing or joining to them the *idea* of body, or anything else; and frame to themselves the *ideas* of long, square, or cubic, *feet, yards,* or *fathoms,* here amongst the bodies of the universe, or else beyond the utmost bounds of all bodies; and by adding these still one to another, enlarge their *idea* of space as much as they please. This power of repeating, or doubling any *idea* we have of any distance, and adding it to the former as often as we will, without ever being able to come to any stop or stint, let us enlarge it as much as we will, is that, which gives us the *idea* of *immensity*.

5. *Figure.* There is another modification of this *idea,* which is nothing but the relation which the parts of the termination of extension, or circumscribed space have amongst themselves. This the touch discovers in sensible bodies, whose extremities come within our reach; and the eye takes both from bodies and colors, whose boundaries are within its view: where observing how the extremities terminate, either in straight lines, which meet at discernible angles; or in crooked lines, wherein no angles can be perceived, by considering these as they relate to one another, in all parts of the extremities of any body or space, it has that *idea* we call *figure,* which affords to the mind infinite variety. For besides the vast number of different figures, that do really exist in the coherent masses of matter, the stock, that the mind has in its power, by varying the *idea* of space; and thereby making still new compositions, by repeating its own *ideas,* and joining them as it pleases, is perfectly inexhaustible: and so it can multiply figures *in infinitum*.

. . . .

11. *Extension and body not the same.* There are some that would persuade us, that *body and extension are the same thing;* who either change the signification of words, which I would not suspect them of, they having so severely condemned the philosophy of others, because it has been too much placed in the uncertain meaning, or deceitful obscurity of doubtful or insignificant terms. If therefore they mean by *body and extension the same,* that other people do, *viz.* by *body* something that is solid, and extended, whose parts are separable and movable different ways; and by extension, only the space

that lies between the extremities of those solid coherent parts, and which is possessed by them, they confound very different *ideas* one with another. For I appeal to every man's own thoughts, whether the *idea* of space be not as distinct from that of solidity, as it is from the *idea* of scarlet-color? 'Tis true, solidity cannot exist without extension, neither can scarlet-color exist without extension; but this hinders not, but that they are distinct ideas. Many *ideas* require others as necessary to their existence or conception, which yet are very distinct *ideas.* Motion can neither be, nor be conceived without space; and yet motion is not space, nor space motion: space can exist without it, and they are very distinct *ideas;* and so, I think, are those of space and solidity. Solidity is so inseparable an *idea* from body, that upon that depends its filling of space, its contact, impulse, and communication of motion upon impulse. And if it be a reason to prove, that spirit is different from body, because thinking includes not the *idea* of extension in it; the same reason will be as valid, I suppose, to prove, that *space is not body,* because it includes not the *idea* of solidity in it; *space and solidity* being *as distinct ideas,* as thinking and extension, and as wholly separable in the mind one from another. *Body* then and *extension,* 'tis evident, are two distinct *ideas.* For,

12. *First, extension* includes no solidity, nor resistance to the motion of *body,* as body does.

13. *Secondly,* the parts of pure space are inseparable one from the other; so that the continuity cannot be separated, neither really, nor mentally. For I demand of anyone, to remove any part of it from another, with which it is continued, even so much as in thought. To divide and separate actually, is, as I think, by removing the parts one from another, two make two superficies, where before there was a continuity: and to divide mentally, is to make in the mind two superficies, where before there was a continuity, and consider them as removed one from the other; which can only be done in things considered by the mind, as capable of being separated; and by separation, of acquiring new distinct superficies, which they then have not, but are capable of: but neither of these ways of separation, whether real or mental, is, as I think, compatible to pure *space.*

'Tis true, a man may consider so much of such a *space,* as is answerable or commensurate to a foot, without considering the rest; which is indeed a partial consideration, but not so much as mental separation, or division; since a man can no more mentally divide, without considering two superficies, separate one from the other, than he can actually divide, without making two superficies disjoined one from the other: but a partial consideration is not separating. A man may consider light in the sun, without its heat; or mobility in body without its extension, without thinking of their separation. One is only a partial consideration, terminating in one alone; and the other is a consideration of both, as existing separately.

14. *Thirdly,* the parts of pure *space,* are immovable, which follows from their inseparability; *motion* being nothing but change of distance between any two things; but this cannot be between parts that are inseparable; which therefore must needs be at perpetual rest one amongst another.

Thus the determined *idea* of simple *space* distinguishes it plainly, and sufficiently from *body;* since its parts are inseparable, immovable, and without resistance to the motion of body.

. . . .

16. *Division of beings into bodies and spirits proves not space and body the same.* Those who contend that *space and body* are *the same,* bring this *dilemma.* Either this *space* is something or nothing; if nothing be between two bodies, they must necessarily touch; if it be allowed to be something, they ask, whether it be body or spirit? To which I answer by another question, who told them, that there was, or could be nothing, but solid beings, which could not think; and thinking beings that were not extended? Which is all they mean by the terms *body* and *spirit.*

17. *Substance which we know not, no proof against space without body.* If it be demanded (as usually it is) whether this *space* void of *body,* be *substance* or *accident,* I shall readily answer, I know not: nor shall be ashamed to own my ignorance, till they that ask, show me a clear distinct *idea* of *substance.*

18. I endeavor, as much as I can, to deliver myself from those fallacies, which we are apt to put upon ourselves, by taking words for things. It helps not our ignorance to feign a knowledge, where we have none, by making a noise with sounds, without clear and distinct significations. Names made at pleasure, neither alter the nature of things, nor make us understand them, but as they are signs of, and stand for determined *ideas.* And I desire those who lay so much stress on the sound of these two syllables, *substance,* to consider, whether applying it, as they do, to the infinite incomprehensible GOD, to finite spirits, and to body it be in the same sense; and whether it stands for the same *idea,* when each of those three so different beings are

called *substances*? If so, whether it will not thence follow, that God, spirits, and body, agreeing in the same common nature of *substance,* differ not any otherwise than in a bare different modification of that *substance;* as a tree and a pebble, being in the same sense body, and agreeing in the common nature of body, different only in a bare modification of that common matter; which will be a very harsh doctrine. If they say, that they apply it to God, finite spirits, and matter, in three different significations, and that it stands for one *idea,* when GOD is said to be a *substance;* for another when the soul is called *substance;* and for a third, when a body is called so. If the name *substance,* stands for three several distinct *ideas,* they would do well to make known those distinct *ideas,* or at least to give three distinct names to them, to prevent in so important a notion, the confusion and errors, that will naturally follow from the promiscuous use of so doubtful a term; which is so far from being suspected to have three distinct, that in ordinary use it has scarce one clear distinct signification: and if they can thus make three distinct *ideas* of *substance,* what hinders, why another may not make a fourth?

19. *Substance and accidents of little use in philosophy.* They who first ran into the notion of *accidents,* as a sort of real beings, that needed something to inhere in, were forced to find out the word *substance,* to support them. Had the poor *Indian* philosopher (who imagined that the earth also wanted something to bear it up) but thought of this word *substance,* he needed not to have been at the trouble to find an elephant to support it, and a tortoise to support his elephant: the word *substance* would have done it effectually. And he that inquired, might have taken it for as good an answer from an *Indian* philosopher, that *substance,* without knowing what it is, is that which supports the earth, as we take it for a sufficient answer, and good doctrine, from our *European* philosophers, that *substance* without knowing what it is, is that which supports *accidents.* So that of *substance,* we have no *idea* of what it is, but only a confused obscure one of what it does.

20. Whatever a learned man may do here, an intelligent *American,* who inquired into the nature of things, would scarce take it for a satisfactory account, if desiring to learn our architecture, he should be told, that a pillar was a thing supported by a *basis,* and a *basis* something that supported a pillar. Would he not think himself mocked, instead of taught, with such an account as this? And a stranger to them would be very liberally instructed in the nature of books, and the things they contained, if he should be told, that all learned books consisted of paper and letters, and that letters were

things inhering in paper, and paper a thing that held forth letters; a notable way of having clear *ideas* of letters and paper. But were the Latin words *inha erentia* and *substantia,* put into the plain English ones that answer them, and were called *sticking on,* and *under-propping,* they would better discover to us the very great clearness there is in the doctrine of *substance and accidents,* and show of what use they are in deciding of questions in philosophy.

21. *A* vacuum *beyond the utmost bounds of body.* But to return to our *idea* of *space.* If *body* be not supposed infinite, which, I think, no one will affirm, I would ask, whether, if God placed a man at the extremity of corporeal beings, he could not stretch his hand beyond his body? If he could, then he would put his arm, where there was before *space* without *body;* and if there he spread his fingers, there would still be *space* between them without *body:* if he could not stretch out his hand, it must be because of some external hindrance; (for we suppose him alive, with such a power of moving the parts of his body, that he has now, which is not in itself impossible, if God so pleased to have it; or at least it is not impossible for God so to move him:) and then I ask, whether that which hinders his hand from moving outwards, be substance or accident, something or nothing? And when they have resolved that, they will be able to resolve themselves, what that is, which is or may be between two bodies at a distance, that is not body, has no solidity. In the meantime, the argument is at least as good, that where nothing hinders, (as beyond the utmost bounds of all bodies) a *body* put in motion may move on, as where there is nothing between, there two bodies must necessarily touch. For pure *space* between, is sufficient to take away the necessity of mutual contact; but bare *space* in the way, is not sufficient to stop motion. The truth is, these men must either own, that they think body infinite, though they are loathe to speak it out, or else affirm, that *space* is not *body.* For I would fain meet with that thinking man, that can, in his thoughts, set any bounds to space, more than he can to duration; or by thinking, hope to arrive at the end of either: and therefore if his *idea* of eternity be infinite, so is his *idea* of immensity; they are both finite or infinite alike.

21.[11] *The power of annihilation proves a* vacuum. Farther, those who assert the impossibility of *space* existing without *matter,* must not only make body infinite, but must also deny a power in God to annihilate any part of matter.

11. I have retained Locke's numbering, which assigns the number 21 to two successive sections.

No one, I suppose, will deny, that God can put an end to all motion that is in matter, and fix all the bodies of the universe in a perfect quiet and rest, and continue them so as long as he pleases. Whoever then will allow, that God can, during such a general rest, annihilate either this book, or the body of him that reads it, must necessarily admit the possibility of a *vacuum.* For it is evident, that the space, that was filled by the parts of the annihilated body, will still remain, and be a space without body. For the circumambient bodies being in perfect rest, are a wall of adamant, and in that state make it a perfect impossibility for any other body to get into that space. And indeed the necessary motion of one particle of matter, into the place from whence another particle of matter is removed, is but a consequence from the supposition of plenitude; which will therefore need some better proof, than a supposed matter of fact, which experiment can never make out; our own clear and distinct *ideas* plainly satisfying us, that there is no necessary connection between *space* and *solidity,* since we can conceive the one without the other. And those who dispute for or against a *vacuum,* do thereby confess, they have distinct *ideas* of *vacuum* and *plenum,* i.e. that they have an *idea* of extension void of solidity, though they deny its existence; or else they dispute about nothing at all. For they who so much alter the signification of words, as to call *extension body,* and consequently make the whole essence of body, to be nothing but pure extension without solidity, must talk absurdly, whenever they speak of *vacuum,* since it is impossible for extension to be without extension. For *vacuum,* whether we affirm or deny its existence, signifies space without body, whose very existence no one can deny to be possible, who will not make matter infinite, and take from God a power to annihilate any particle of it.

22. *Motion proves a* vacuum. But not to go so far as beyond the utmost bounds of body in the universe, nor appeal to God's omnipotency to find a *vacuum,* the *motion* of bodies, that are in our view and neighborhood, seems to me plainly to evince it. For I desire anyone so to divide a solid body, of any dimension he pleases, as to make it possible for the solid parts to move up and down freely every way within the bounds of that superficies, if there be not left in it a void space, as big as the least part into which he has divided the said solid body. And if where the least particle of the body divided, is as big as a mustard-seed, a void space equal to the bulk of a mustard-seed, be requisite to make room for the free motion of the parts of the divided body within the bounds of its superficies, where the particles of matter are 100,000,000 less than a mustard-seed, there must also be a space void of

solid matter, as big as 100,000,000 part of a mustard-seed; for if it holds in the one, it will hold in the other, and so on *in infinitum.* And let this void space be as little as it will, it destroys the hypothesis of *plenitude.* For if there can be a space void of body, equal to the smallest separate particle of matter now existing in nature, 'tis still space without body; and makes as great a difference between space and body, as if it were μέγα χάσμα, a distance as wide as any in nature.[12] And therefore if we suppose not the void space necessary to motion, equal to the least parcel of the divided solid matter, but to 1/10 or 1/1000 of it, the same consequence will always follow of space without matter.

23. *The* ideas *of space and body distinct.* But the question being here, whether the *idea of space* or *extension,* be *the same with the idea of body,* it is not necessary to prove the real existence of a *vacuum,* but the *idea* of it; which 'tis plain men have, when they inquire and dispute, whether there be a *vacuum* or no? For if they had not the *idea* of space without body, they could not make a question about its existence: and if their *idea* of body did not include in it something more than the bare *idea* of space, they could have no doubt about the plenitude of the world; and 'twould be as absurd to demand, whether there were space without body, as whether there were space without space, or body without body, since these were but different names of the same *idea.*

24. *Extension being inseparable from body, proves it not the same.* 'Tis true, the *idea* of *extension* joins itself so inseparably with all visible, and most tangible qualities, that it suffers us to see no one, or feel very few external objects, without taking in impressions of extension too. This readiness of extension to make itself be taken notice of so constantly with other *ideas,* has been the occasion, I guess, that some have made the whole essence of *body,* to consist in extension; which is not much to be wondered at, since some have had their minds, by their eyes and touch, (the busiest of all our senses) so filled with the *idea* of extension, and as it were wholly possessed with it, that they allowed no existence to anything, that had not extension. I shall not now argue with those men, who take the measure and possibility of all being, only from their narrow and gross imaginations: but having here to do only with those who conclude the essence of body to be *extension,* because, they say, they cannot imagine any sensible quality of any body without exten-

12. μέγα χάσμα, "mighty chasm" or great gulf. At *Theogony* 740, Hesiod (eighth century B.C.) describes the lower world (or the world of the dead) as the μέγα χάσμα of Tartaros.

sion, I shall desire them to consider, that had they reflected on their *ideas* of tastes and smells, as much as on those of sight and touch; nay, had they examined their *ideas* of hunger and thirst, and several other pains, they would have found, that they included in them no *idea* of extension at all, which is but an affection of body, as well as the rest discoverable by our senses, which are scarce acute enough to look into the pure essences of things.

25. If those *ideas,* which are constantly joined to all others, must therefore be concluded to be the essence of those things, which have constantly those *ideas* joined to them, and are inseparable from them; then unity is without doubt the essence of everything. For there is not any object of sensation or reflection, which does not carry with it the *idea* of one: but the weakness of this kind of argument, we have already shown sufficiently.

26. Ideas *of space and solidity distinct.* To conclude, whatever men shall think concerning the existence of a *vacuum,* this is plain to me, that we have as clear an *idea of space distinct from solidity,* as we have of solidity distinct from motion, or motion from space. We have not any two more distinct *ideas,* and we can as easily conceive space without solidity, as we can conceive body or space without motion, though it be never so certain, that neither body nor motion can exist without space. But whether anyone will take space to be only a relation resulting from the existence of other beings at a distance; or whether they will think the words of the most knowing King *Solomon, the heaven, and the heaven of heavens, cannot contain thee,* or those more emphatical ones of the inspired philosopher St. *Paul, in him we live, move, and have our being,* are to be understood in a literal sense, I leave everyone to consider; only our *idea* of *space* is, I think, such as I have mentioned, and distinct from that of *body.*[13] For whether we consider in matter itself, the distance of its coherent solid parts, and call it, in respect of those solid parts, *extension;* or whether considering it, as lying between the extremities of any body in its several dimensions, we call it *length, breadth,* and *thickness;* or else considering it as lying between any two bodies, or positive beings, without any consideration, whether there be any matter or no between, we call it *distance.* However named or considered, it is always the same uniform simple *idea* of *space,* taken from objects, about which our senses have been conversant, whereof having settled *ideas* in our minds, we can revive,

13. *the heaven . . . cannot contain thee,* 1 Kings 8:27; *in him we live, move, and have our being,* Acts 17:28.

repeat, and add them one to another as often as we will, and consider the space or distance so imagined, either as filled with solid parts, so that another body cannot come there, without displacing and thrusting out the body that was there before; or else as void of solidity, so that a body of equal dimensions to that empty or pure space, may be placed in it without the removing or expulsion of anything that was there. But to avoid confusion in discourses concerning this matter, it were possibly to be wished that the name *extension* were applied only to matter, or the distance of the extremities of particular bodies, and the term *expansion* to space in general, with or without solid matter possessing it, so as to say *space* is *expanded,* and *body extended.* But in this everyone has his liberty; I propose it only for the more clear and distinct way of speaking.

27. *Men differ little in clear simple* ideas. The knowing precisely what our words stand for, would, I imagine, in this, as well as a great many other cases, quickly end the dispute. For I am apt to think, that men, when they come to examine them, find their simple *ideas* all generally to agree, though in discourse with one another, they perhaps confound one another with different names. I imagine, that men who abstract their thoughts, and do well examine the *ideas* of their own minds, *cannot much differ in thinking;* however, they may perplex themselves with words, according to the way of speaking of the several schools, or sects, they have been bred up in: though amongst unthinking men, who examine not scrupulously and carefully their own *ideas,* and strip them not from the marks men use for them, but confound them with words, there must be endless dispute, wrangling, and jargon; especially if they be learned bookish men, devoted to some sect, and accustomed to the language of it; and have learned to talk after others. But if it should happen, that any two thinking men should really have different *ideas,* I do not see how they could discourse or argue one with another. Here I must not be mistaken, to think that every floating imagination in men's brains, is presently of that sort of *ideas* I speak of. 'Tis not easy for the mind to put off those confused notions and prejudices it has imbibed from custom, inadvertency, and common conversation: it requires pains and assiduity to examine its *ideas,* till it resolves them into those clear and distinct simple ones, out of which they are compounded; and to see which, amongst its simple ones, have or have not a necessary connection and dependence one upon another: till a man does this in the primary and original notions of things, he builds upon floating and uncertain principles, and will often find himself at a loss.

CHAP. XIV.

Of duration, and its simple modes.

1. *Duration is fleeting extension.* There is another sort of distance, or length, the *idea* whereof we get not from the permanent parts of space, but from the fleeting and perpetually perishing parts of succession. This we call *duration,* the simple modes whereof are any different lengths of it, whereof we have distinct *ideas,* as *hours, days, years,* &c. *time,* and *eternity.*

2. *Its* idea *from reflection on the train of our* ideas. The answer of a great man, to one who asked what time was *si non rogas intelligo* (which amounts to this; the more I set myself to think of it, the less I understand it;) might perhaps persuade one, that *time,* which reveals all other things, is itself not to be discovered.[14] *Duration, time,* and *eternity,* are, not without reason, thought to have something very abstruse in their nature. But however remote these may seem from our comprehension, yet if we trace them right to their originals, I doubt not but one of those sources of all our knowledge, *viz. sensation* and *reflection,* will be able to furnish us with these *ideas,* as clear and distinct as many other, which are thought much less obscure; and we shall find, that the *idea* of eternity itself is derived from the same common original with the rest of our ideas.

3. To understand *time* and *eternity* aright, we ought with attention to consider what *idea* it is we have of *duration,* and how we came by it. 'Tis evident to anyone who will but observe what passes in his own mind, that there is a train of *ideas,* which constantly succeed one another in his understanding, as long as he is awake. *Reflection* on these appearances of several *ideas* one after another in our minds, is that which furnishes us with the *idea* of *succession:* and the distance between any parts of that succession, or between the appearance of any two *ideas* in our minds, is that we call *duration.* For whilst we are thinking, or whilst we receive successively several *ideas* in our minds, we know that we do exist; and so we call the existence, or the continuation of the existence of ourselves, or anything

14. *si non rogas intelligo,* if you do not ask, I understand (from St. Augustine, [354–430] *Confessions* XI xiv).

else, commensurate to the succession of any *ideas* in our minds, the *duration* of ourselves, or any such other thing coexisting with our thinking.

. . . .

13. *The mind cannot fix long on one invariable idea.* If it be so, that the *ideas* of our minds, whilst we have any there, do constantly change, and shift in a continual succession, it would be impossible, may anyone say, for a man to think long of any one thing: by which if it be meant, that a man may *have one self-same single* idea *a long time alone in his mind, without any variation at all,* I think, in matter of fact it is *not possible,* for which (not knowing how the *ideas* of our minds are framed, of what materials they are made, whence they have their light, and how they come to make their appearances,) I can give no other reason but experience: and I would have anyone try, whether he can keep one unvaried single *idea* in his mind, without any other, for any considerable time together.

14. For trial, let him take any figure, any degree of light or whiteness, or what other he pleases; and he will, I suppose, find it difficult to keep all other *ideas* out of his mind: but that some, either of another kind, or various considerations of that *idea* (each of which considerations is a new *idea*) will constantly succeed one another in his thoughts, let him be as wary as he can.

. . . .

17. *Time is duration set out by measures.* Having thus got the *idea* of duration, the next thing natural for the mind to do, is to get some *measure of* this common *duration,* whereby it might judge of its different lengths, and consider the distinct order, wherein several things exist, without which a great part of our knowledge would be confused, and a great part of history be rendered very useless. This consideration of duration, as set out by certain periods, and marked by certain measures or *epochs,* is that, I think, which most properly we call *time.*

. . . .

19. *The revolutions of the sun and moon the properest measures of time.* The diurnal, and annual *revolutions of the sun,* as having been from the beginning of nature, constant, regular, and universally observable by all mankind, and

supposed equal to one another, have been with reason *made use of for the measure of duration*. . . .

. . . .

23. *Minutes, hours, and years, not necessary measures of duration. Minutes, hours, days, and years,* are . . . *no* more *necessary to time* or duration, than inches, feet, yards, and miles, marked out in any manner, are to extension. For though we in this part of the universe, by the constant use of them, as of periods set out by the revolutions of the sun, or as known parts of such periods, have fixed the *ideas* of such lengths of duration in our minds, which we apply to all parts of time, whose length we would consider; yet there may be other parts of the universe, where they no more use these measures of ours, than in *Japan* they do our inches, feet, or miles: but yet something analogous to them, there must be. . . .

. . . .

25. *Our measure of* time *applicable to duration before time.* The mind having once got such a measure of time, as the annual revolution of the sun, can apply that measure to duration, wherein that measure itself did not exist, and with which in the reality of its being, it had nothing to do. . . . The *idea of duration equal to an annual revolution of the sun,* is as easily *applicable* in our thoughts to *duration, where no sun nor motion was,* as the *idea* of a foot or yard taken from bodies here, can be applied in our thoughts to distances, beyond the confines of the world, where are no bodies at all.

. . . .

28. *Eternity.* By the same means . . . and from the same original that we come to have *the idea of* time, we have also that *idea* which we call *eternity; viz.* having got the *idea* of succession and duration, by reflecting on the train of our own *ideas,* caused in us either by the natural appearances of those *ideas* coming constantly of themselves into our waking thoughts, or else caused by external objects successively affecting our senses; and having from the revolutions of the sun got the *ideas* of certain lengths of duration, we can, in our thoughts, add such lengths of duration to one another, as often as we please, and apply them, so added, to durations past or to come: and this we can continue to do on, without bounds or limits, and proceed *in infinitum,* and apply thus the length of the annual motion of the sun to

duration, supposed before the sun's, or any other motion had its being; which is no more difficult or absurd, than to apply the notion I have of the moving of a shadow, one hour today upon the sun-dial, to the duration of something last night; *v.g.* the burning of a candle, which is now absolutely separate from all actual motion, and it is as impossible for the duration of that flame for an hour last night, to coexist with any motion that now is, or forever shall be, as for any part of duration, that was before the beginning of the world, to coexist with the motion of the sun now. But yet this hinders not, but that having the *idea* of the length of the motion of the shadow on a dial between the marks of two hours, I can as distinctly measure in my thoughts the duration of that candlelight last night, as I can the duration of anything, that does now exist: and it is no more than to think, that had the sun shone then on the dial, and moved after the same rate it does now, the shadow on the dial would have passed from one hour-line to another, whilst that flame of the candle lasted.

. . . .

32. And thus I think it is plain, that *from* those two fountains of all knowledge before mentioned, *(viz.) reflection and sensation, we get the ideas of duration,* and the measures of it.

For *first,* by observing what passes in our minds, how our *ideas* there in train constantly some vanish, and others begin to appear, we come by the *idea* of *succession.*

Secondly, by observing a distance in the parts of this succession, we get the *idea* of *duration.*

Thirdly, by sensation observing certain appearances, at certain regular and seeming equidistant periods, we get the *ideas* of certain lengths or *measures of duration,* as minutes, hours, days, years, *&c.*

Fourthly, by being able to repeat those measures of time, or *ideas* of stated length of duration in our minds, as often as we will, we can come to *imagine duration, where nothing does really endure or exist;* and thus we imagine tomorrow, next year, or seven years hence.

Fifthly, by being able to repeat any such *idea* of any length of time, as of a minute, a year, or an age, as often as we will in our own thoughts, and add them one to another, without ever coming to the end of such addition, any nearer than we can to the end of number, to which we can always add, we come by the *idea* of *eternity,* as the future eternal duration of our souls, as well as the eternity of that infinite being, which must necessarily have always existed.

Sixthly, by considering any part of infinite duration, as set out by periodical measures, we come by the *idea* of what we call *time* in general.

. . . .

CHAP. XV.

Of duration and expansion, considered together.

9. *All the parts of extension are extension; and all the parts of duration, are duration.* . . . One thing . . . wherein *space and duration* have a great conformity, . . . is, though they are justly reckoned amongst our *simple ideas:* yet none of the distinct *ideas* we have of either is without all manner of *composition,* it is the very nature of both of them to consist of parts: but their parts being all of the same kind, and without the mixture of any other *idea,* hinder them not from having a place amongst simple *ideas.* Could the mind, as in number, come to so small a part of extension or duration, as excluded divisibility, that would be, as it were, the indivisible unit, or *idea;* by repetition of which, it would make its more enlarged *ideas* of extension and duration. But since the mind is not able to frame an *idea* of any space, without parts; instead thereof it makes use of the common measures, which by familiar use, in each country, have imprinted themselves on the memory (as inches, and feet; or cubits, and parasangs; and so seconds, minutes, hours, days, and years in duration:) the mind makes use, I say, of such *ideas* as these, as simple ones; and these are the component parts of larger *ideas,* which the mind, upon occasion, makes by the addition of such known lengths, which it is acquainted with. On the other side, the ordinary smallest measure we have of either, is looked on as an unit in number, when the mind by division would reduce them into less fractions. Though on both sides, both in addition and division, either of space or duration, when the *idea* under consideration becomes very big, or very small, its precise bulk becomes very obscure and confused; and it is the number of its repeated additions, or divisions, that alone remains clear and distinct, as will easily appear to anyone, who will let his thoughts loose in the vast expansion of space, or divisibility of matter. Every part of duration is

duration too; and every part of extension is extension, both of them capable of addition or division *in infinitum.* But the least portions of either of them, whereof we have clear and distinct *ideas,* may perhaps be fittest to be considered by us, as the simple *ideas* of that kind, out of which our complex modes of space, extension, and duration, are made up, and into which they can again be distinctly resolved. Such a small part in duration, may be called a *moment,* and is the time of one *idea* in our minds, in the train of their ordinary succession there. The other, wanting a proper name, I know not whether I may be allowed to call *a sensible point,* meaning thereby the least particle of matter or space we can discern, which is ordinarily about a minute, and to the sharpest eyes seldom less than thirty seconds of a circle, whereof the eye is the center.

. . . .

CHAP. XVI.
Of number.

1. *Number the simplest and most universal* idea. Amongst all the *ideas* we have, as there is none suggested to the mind by more ways, so there is none more simple, than that *of unity,* or one: it has no shadow of variety or composition in it: every object our senses are employed about; every *idea* in our understandings; every thought of our minds brings this *idea* along with it. And therefore it is the most intimate to our thoughts, as well as it is, in its agreement to all other things, the most universal *idea* we have. For number applies itself to men, angels, actions, thoughts, everything that either does exist, or can be imagined.

2. *Its modes made by addition.* By repeating this *idea* in our minds, and adding the repetitions together, we come by the *complex* ideas *of the modes of it.* Thus by adding one to one, we have the complex *idea* of two; by putting twelve units together, we have the complex *idea* of a dozen; and so of a score, or a million, or any other number.

3. *Each mode distinct. The simplest modes of number are of all other the most distinct;* every the least variation, which is an unit, making each combina-

tion, as clearly different from that, which approaches nearest to it, as the most remote; two being as distinct from one, as two hundred; and the *idea* of two, as distinct from the *idea* of three, as the magnitude of the whole earth, is from that of a mite. This is not so in other simple modes, in which it is not so easy, nor, perhaps, possible for us to distinguish betwixt two approaching *ideas,* which yet are really different. For who will undertake to find a difference between the white of this paper, and that of the next degree to it: or can form distinct *ideas* of every the least excess in extension?

. . . .

8. *Number measures all measurables.* This farther is observable in *number,* that it is that, which the mind makes use of in *measuring all things,* that by us are measurable, which principally are *expansion and duration;* and our *idea* of infinity, even when applied to those, seems to be nothing, but the infinity of number. For what else are our *ideas* of eternity and immensity, but the repeated additions of certain *ideas* of imagined parts of duration, and expansion with the infinity of number, in which we can come to no end of addition? For such an inexhaustible stock, number, of all other our *ideas,* most clearly furnishes us with, as is obvious to everyone. For let a man collect into one sum, as great a number as he pleases, this multitude, how great soever, lessens not one jot the power of adding to it, or brings him any nearer the end of the inexhaustible stock of number, where still there remains as much to be added, as if none were taken out. And this endless *addition* or *addibility* (if anyone like the word better) of numbers, so apparent to the mind, is that, I think, which gives us the clearest and most distinct *idea* of infinity: of which more in the following chapter.

CHAP. XVII.

Of infinity.

1. *Infinity, in its original intention, attributed to space, duration, and number.* He that would know what kind of *idea* it is to which we give the name of *infinity,* cannot do it better, than by considering to what infinity is by the mind more immediately attributed, and then how the mind comes to frame it.

Finite, and *infinite,* seem to me to be looked upon by the mind, as the *modes of quantity,* and to be attributed primarily in their first designation only to those things, which have parts, and are capable of increase or diminution, by the addition or subtraction of any the least part: and such are the *ideas* of space, duration, and number, which we have considered in the foregoing chapters. 'Tis true, that we cannot but be assured, that the great GOD, of whom, and from whom are all things, is incomprehensibly infinite: but yet, when we apply to that first and supreme being, our *idea* of infinite, in our weak and narrow thoughts, we do it primarily in respect of his duration and ubiquity; and, I think, more figuratively to his power, wisdom, and goodness, and other attributes, which are properly inexhaustible and incomprehensible, *&c.* For when we call them infinite, we have no other *idea* of this infinity, but what carries with it some reflection on, and intimation of that number or extent of the acts or objects of God's power, wisdom, and goodness, which can never be supposed so great, or so many, which these attributes will not always surmount and exceed, let us multiply them in our thoughts with all the infinity of endless number. I do not pretend to say how these attributes are in GOD, who is infinitely beyond the reach of our narrow capacities: they do, without doubt, contain in them all possible perfection: but this, I say, is our way of conceiving them, and these our *ideas* of their infinity.

2. *The* idea *of finite easily got.* Finite then, and infinite, being by the mind looked on as modifications of expansion and duration, the next things to be considered is, *how the mind comes by* them. As for the *idea of finite,* there is no great difficulty. The obvious portions of extension, that affect our senses, carry with them into the mind the *idea* of finite: and the ordinary periods of succession, whereby we measure time and duration, as hours, days, and years, are bounded lengths. The difficulty is, how we come by those boundless *ideas* of *eternity* and *immensity,* since the objects, which we converse with, come so much short of any approach or proportion to that largeness.

3. *How we come by the* idea *of infinity.* Everyone, that has any *idea* of any stated lengths of space, as a foot, finds, that he can repeat that *idea;* and joining it to the former, make the *idea* of two foot; and by the addition of a third, three foot; and so on, without ever coming to an end of his additions, whether of the same *idea* of a foot, or if he pleases of doubling it, or any other *idea* he has of length, as a mile, or diameter of the earth, or of the *orbis magnus:* for whichever of these he takes, and how often soever he doubles, or any otherwise multiplies it, he finds, that after he has continued this doubling in his thoughts, and enlarged his *idea,* as much as he pleases, he has

no more reason to stop, nor is one jot nearer to the end of such addition, than he was at first setting out; the power of enlarging his *idea* of space by farther additions, remaining still the same, he hence takes *the idea of infinite space*.[15]

. . . .

5. *And so of duration.* As, by the power we find in ourselves of repeating, as often as we will, any *idea* of space, we get the *idea* of immensity; so, by being able to repeat the *idea* of any length of duration, we have in our minds, with all the endless addition of number, we come by the *idea* of *eternity*. . . .

. . . .

7. *Difference between infinity of space, and space infinite. . . . Our idea of infinity* being, as I think, *an endless growing idea,* but the *idea* of any quantity the mind has, being at that time terminated in that *idea,* (for be it as great as it will, it can be no greater than it is,) to join infinity to it is to adjust a standing measure to a growing bulk; and therefore I think it is not an insignificant subtlety, if I say, that we are carefully to distinguish between the *idea* of the infinity of space, and the *idea* of a space infinite: the first is nothing but a supposed endless progression of the mind, over what repeated *ideas* of space it pleases; but to have actually in the mind an *idea* of a space infinite, is to suppose the mind already passed over, and actually to have a view of all those repeated *ideas* of space, which an endless repetition can never totally represent to it, which carries in it a plain contradiction.

8. *We have no* idea *of infinite space.* This, perhaps, will be a little plainer, if we consider it in numbers. The infinity of numbers, to the end of whose addition everyone perceives there is no approach, easily appears to anyone that reflects on it: but how clear soever this *idea* of the infinity of number be, there is nothing yet more evident, than the absurdity of the actual *idea* of an infinite number. Whatsoever positive *ideas* we have in our minds of any space, duration, or number, let them be never so great, they are still finite; but when we suppose an inexhaustible remainder, from which we remove all bounds, and wherein we allow the mind an endless progression of thought, without ever completing the *idea,* there we have our *idea* of infinity; which though it seems to be pretty clear, when we consider nothing else in it, but the negation of an end, yet when we would frame in our minds

15. *orbis magnus,* "great circle" or great disk, the path of the earth's annual orbit around the sun.

the *idea* of an infinite space or duration, that *idea* is very obscure, and confused, because it is made up of two parts, very different, if not inconsistent. For let a man frame in his mind an *idea* of any space or number, as great as he will; 'tis plain, the mind rests and terminates in that *idea,* which is contrary to the *idea of infinity,* which *consists in a supposed endless progression.* And therefore, I think, it is, that we are so easily confounded, when we come to argue, and reason about infinite space or duration, *&c.* Because the parts of such an *idea,* not being perceived to be, as they are, inconsistent, the one side or other always perplexes, whatever consequences we draw from the other, as an *idea* of motion not passing on, would perplex anyone, who should argue from such an *idea,* which is not better than an *idea* of motion at rest; and such another seems to me to be the *idea* of a space, or (which is the same thing) a number infinite, *i.e.* of a space or number, which the mind actually has, and so views, and terminates in; and of a space or number, which in a constant and endless enlarging, and progression, it can in thought never attain to. For how large soever an *idea* of space I have in my mind, it is no larger than it is that instant, that I have it, though I be capable the next instant to double it; and so on *in infinitum:* for that alone is infinite, which has no bounds; and that the *idea* of infinity, in which our thoughts can find none.

9. *Number affords us the clearest* idea *of infinity.* But of all other *ideas,* it is *number,* as I have said, which, I think, *furnishes us with the clearest and most distinct* idea *of infinity,* we are capable of. For even in space and duration, when the mind pursues the *idea* of infinity, it there makes use of the *ideas* and repetitions of numbers. . . .

. . . .

12. *Infinite divisibility.* And since in any bulk of matter, our thoughts can never arrive at the utmost *divisibility,* therefore there is an apparent infinity to us also in that, which has the infinity also of number, but with this difference, that in the former considerations of the infinity of space and duration, we only use addition of numbers; whereas this is like the division of an unit into its fractions, wherein the mind can also proceed *in infinitum,* as well as in the former additions, it being indeed but the addition still of new numbers: though in the addition of the one, we can have no more the positive *idea* of a space infinitely great, than in the division of the other, we can have the *idea* of a body infinitely little; our *idea* of infinity being, as I may so say, a growing and fugitive *idea,* still in a boundless progression, that can stop nowhere.

13. *No positive* idea *of infinite.* Though it be hard, I think, to find anyone so absurd, as to say, he has the positive *idea* of an actual infinite number; the infinity whereof lies only in a power of still adding any combination of units to any former number, and that as long, and as much as one will; the like also being in the infinity of space and duration, which power leaves always to the mind room for endless additions; yet there be those, who imagine they have *positive* ideas *of infinite* duration and space. It would, I think, be enough to destroy any such positive *idea* of infinite, to ask him that has it, whether he could add to it or no; which would easily show the mistake of such a positive *idea.* We can, I think, have no positive *idea* of any space or duration, which is not made up of, and commensurate to repeated numbers of feet or yards, or days and years. . . . And therefore, since an *idea* of infinite space or duration must needs be made up of infinite parts, it can have no other infinity, than that of number capable still of farther addition; but not an actual positive *idea* of a number infinite. For, I think, it is evident, that the addition of finite things together (as are all lengths, whereof we have the positive *ideas*) can never otherwise produce the *idea* of infinite, than as number does; which consisting of additions of finite units one to another, suggests the *idea* of infinite, only by a power, we find we have of still increasing the sum, and adding more of the same kind, without coming one jot nearer the end of such progression.

. . . .

22. *All these* ideas *from sensation and reflection.* If I have dwelt pretty long on the considerations of duration, space, and number; and what arises from the contemplation of them, infinity, 'tis possibly no more, than the matter requires, there being few simple *ideas,* whose modes give more exercise to the thoughts of man, than these do. I pretend not to treat of them in their full latitude: it suffices to my design, to show, how the mind receives them, such as they are, from *sensation* and *reflection;* and how even the *idea* we have of *infinity,* how remote soever it may seem to be from any object of sense, or operation of our mind, has nevertheless, as all our other *ideas,* its original there. Some mathematicians, perhaps, of advanced speculations, may have other ways to introduce into their minds *ideas* of infinity: but this hinders not, but that they themselves, as well as all other men, got the first *ideas,* which they had of infinity, from sensation and reflection, in the method we have here set down.

. . . .

CHAP. XIX.

Of the modes of thinking.

1. *Sensation, remembrance, contemplation, &c.* When the mind turns its view inwards upon itself, and contemplates its own actions, *thinking* is the first that occurs. In it the mind observes a great variety of modifications, and from thence receives distinct *ideas.* Thus the perception, which actually accompanies, and is annexed to any impression on the body, made by an external object, being distinct from all other modifications of *thinking,* furnishes the mind with a distinct *idea,* which we call *sensation;* which is, as it were, the actual entrance of any *idea* into the understanding by the senses. The same *idea,* when it again recurs without the operation of the like object on the external sensory, is *remembrance:* if it be sought after by the mind, and with pain and endeavor found, and brought again in view, 'tis *recollection:* if it be held there long under attentive consideration, 'tis *contemplation:* when *ideas* float in our mind, without any reflection or regard of the understanding, it is that, which the *French* call *reverie;* our language has scarce a name for it: when the *ideas* that offer themselves, . . . are taken notice of, and, as it were, registered in the memory, it is *attention* . . . .

. . . .

CHAP. XX.

Of modes of pleasure and pain.

1. *Pleasure and pain simple* ideas. Amongst the simple *ideas,* which we receive both from *sensation* and *reflection, pain* and *pleasure* are two very considerable ones. For as in the body, there is sensation barely in itself, or accompanied with *pain* or *pleasure;* so the thought, or perception of the mind is simply so, or else accompanied also with *pleasure* or *pain,* delight or trouble, call it how you please. These like other simple *ideas* cannot be described, nor their names defined; the way of knowing them is, as of the simple *ideas* of the senses, only by experience. For to define them by the

presence of good or evil, is no otherwise to make them known to us, than by making us reflect on what we feel in ourselves, upon the several and various operations of good and evil upon our minds, as they are differently applied to, or considered by us.

2. *Good and evil what.* Things then are good or evil, only in reference to pleasure or pain. That we call *good,* which *is apt to cause or increase pleasure, or diminish pain in us; or else to procure, or preserve us the possession of any other good, or absence of an evil.* And on the contrary we name that *evil,* which *is apt to produce or increase any pain, or diminish any pleasure in us; or else to procure us any evil, or deprive us of any good.* By pleasure and pain, I must be understood to mean of body or mind, as they are commonly distinguished; though in truth, they be only different constitutions of the mind, sometimes occasioned by disorder in the body, sometimes by thoughts of the mind.

3. *Our passions moved by good and evil. Pleasure* and *pain,* and that which causes them, good and evil, are the hinges on which our *passions* turn: and if we reflect on ourselves, and observe how these, under various considerations, operate in us; what modifications or tempers of mind, what internal sensations, (if I may so call them,) they produce in us, we may thence form to ourselves the *ideas* of our *passions.*

4. *Love.* Thus anyone reflecting upon the thought he has of the delight, which any present, or absent thing is apt to produce in him, has the *idea* we call *love*. . . .

. . . .

6. *Desire.* The uneasiness a man finds in himself upon the absence of anything, whose present enjoyment carries the *idea* of delight with it, is that we call *desire,* which is greater or less, as that uneasiness is more or less vehement. Where by the by it may perhaps be of some use to remark, that the chief if not only spur to human industry and action is uneasiness. For whatever good is proposed, if its absence carries no displeasure nor pain with it; if a man be easy and content without it, there is no desire of it, nor endeavor after it; there is no more but a bare *velleity,* the term used to signify the lowest degree of desire, and that which is next to none at all, when there is so little uneasiness in the absence of anything, that it carries a man no farther than some faint wishes for it, without any more effectual or

vigorous use of the means to attain it. *Desire* also is stopped or abated by the opinion of the impossibility or unattainableness of the good proposed, as far as the uneasiness is cured or allayed by that consideration. This might carry our thoughts farther were it seasonable in this place.

. . . .

12. *Anger. Anger* is uneasiness or discomposure of the mind, upon the receipt of any injury, with a present purpose of revenge.

13. *Envy. Envy* is an uneasiness of mind, caused by the consideration of a good we desire, obtained by one, we think should not have had it before us.

14. *What passions all men have.* These two last, *envy* and *anger,* not being caused by pain and pleasure simply in themselves, but having in them some mixed considerations of ourselves and others, are not therefore to be found in all men, because those other parts of valuing their merits, or intending revenge, is wanting in them: but all the rest terminated purely in pain and pleasure, are, I think, to be found in all men. . . .

15. *Pleasure and pain what.* By *pleasure* and *pain,* delight and uneasiness, I must all along be understood (as I have above intimated) to mean, not only bodily pain and pleasure, but whatsoever *delight* or *uneasiness* is felt by us, whether arising from any grateful, or unacceptable sensation or reflection.

. . . .

18. *These instances to show how our* ideas *of the passions are got from sensation, and reflection.* I would not be mistaken here, as if I meant this as a discourse of the *passions;* they are *many more than those* I have here named: and those I have taken notice of, would each of them require a much larger, and more accurate discourse. I have only mentioned these here, as so many instances of modes of pleasure and pain resulting in our minds, from various considerations of good and evil. I might, perhaps, have instanced in other modes of pleasure and pain more simple than these, as the pain of *hunger* and *thirst,* and the pleasure of eating and drinking to remove them; the pain of tender eyes, and the pleasure of music; pain from captious uninstructive wrangling, and the pleasure of rational conversation with a friend, or of well directed study in the search and discovery of truth. But the passions being of much more concernment to us, I rather made choice to instance in them, and show how the *ideas* we have of them, are derived from sensation and reflection.

CHAP. XXI.

Of power.

1. *This* idea *how got.* The mind, being every day informed, by the senses, of the alteration of those simple *ideas,* it observes in things without; and taking notice how one comes to an end, and ceases to be, and another begins to exist, which was not before; reflecting also on what passes within itself, and observing a constant change of its *ideas,* sometimes by the impression of outward objects on the senses, and sometimes by the determination of its own choice; and concluding from what it has so constantly observed to have been, that the like changes will for the future be made, in the same things, by like agents, and by the like ways, considers in one thing the possibility of having any of its simple *ideas* changed, and in another the possibility of making that change; and so comes by that *idea* which we call *power.* Thus we say, fire has a *power* to melt gold, *i.e.* to destroy the consistency of its insensible parts, and consequently its hardness, and make it fluid; and gold has a *power* to be melted; that the sun has a *power* to blanch wax, and wax a *power* to be blanched by the sun, whereby the yellowness is destroyed, and whiteness made to exist in its room. In which, and the like cases, the *power* we consider is in reference to the change of perceivable *ideas.* For we cannot observe any alteration to be made in, or operation upon anything, but by the observable change of its sensible *ideas;* nor conceive any alteration to be made, but by conceiving a change of some of its *ideas.*

2. *Power active and passive. Power* thus considered is twofold, *viz.* as able to make, or able to receive any change: the one may be called *active,* and the other *passive power.* Whether matter be not wholly destitute of *active power,* as its author GOD is truly above all *passive power;* and whether the intermediate state of created spirits be not that alone, which is capable of both *active* and *passive power,* may be worth consideration. I shall not now enter into that inquiry, my present business being not to search into the original of power, but how we come by the *idea* of it. But since *active powers* make so great a part of our complex *ideas* of natural substances, (as we shall see hereafter,) and I mention them as such, according to common apprehension; yet they being not, perhaps, so truly *active powers,* as our hasty thoughts are apt to represent them, I judge it not amiss, by this intimation, to direct our minds to the consideration of GOD and spirits, for the clearest *idea* of *active power.*

3. *Power includes relation.* I confess *power includes in it some kind of relation,* (a relation to action or change,) as indeed which of our *ideas,* of what kind soever, when attentively considered, does not? For our *ideas* of extension, duration, and number, do they not all contain in them a secret relation of the parts? Figure and motion have something relative in them much more visibly: and sensible qualities, as colors and smells, *&c.* what are they but the *powers* of different bodies, in relation to our perception, *&c.* And if considered in the things themselves, do they not depend on the bulk, figure, texture, and motion of the parts? All which include some kind of relation in them. Our *idea* therefore of *power,* I think, may well have a place amongst other simple *ideas,* and be considered as one of them, being one of those, that make a principal ingredient in our complex *ideas* of substances, as we shall hereafter have occasion to observe.

4. *The clearest* idea *of active power had from spirit.* We are abundantly furnished with the *idea* of *passive power,* by almost all sorts of sensible things. . . . Nor have we of *active power* (which is the more proper signification of the word *power*) fewer instances. Since whatever change is observed, the mind must collect a power somewhere, able to make that change, as well as a possibility in the thing itself to receive it. But yet, if we will consider it attentively, bodies, by our senses, do not afford us so clear and distinct an *idea* of *active power,* as we have from the reflection on the operations of our minds. For all *power* relating to action, and there being but two sorts of action, whereof we have any *idea, viz.* thinking and motion, let us consider whence we have the clearest *ideas* of the *powers,* which produce these actions. 1. Of thinking, body affords us no *idea* at all, it is only from reflection that we have that: 2. Neither have we from body any *idea* of the beginning of motion. A body at rest affords us no *idea* of any *active power* to move; and when it is set in motion itself, that motion is rather a passion, than an action in it. For when the ball obeys the stroke of a billiard-stick, it is not any action of the ball, but bare passion: also when by impulse it sets another ball in motion, that lay in its way, it only communicates the motion it had received from another, and loses in itself so much, as the other received; which gives us but a very obscure *idea* of an *active power* of moving in body, whilst we observe it only to transfer, but not produce any motion. For it is but a very obscure *idea* of *power,* which reaches not the production of the action, but the continuation of the passion. . . . The *idea* of the beginning of motion, we have only from reflection on what passes in ourselves, where we find by experience, that barely by willing it, barely by a thought of the mind, we can move the parts of our bodies, which were before at rest. . . .

5. *Will and understanding, two powers.* This at least I think evident, that we find in ourselves a *power* to begin or forbear, continue or end several actions of our minds, and motions of our bodies, barely by a thought or preference of the mind ordering, or as it were commanding the doing or not doing such or such a particular action. This *power* which the mind has, thus to order the consideration of any *idea,* or the forbearing to consider it; or to prefer the motion of any part of the body to its rest, and *vice versa* in any particular instance is that which we call the *will.* The actual exercise of this power, by directing any particular action, or its forbearance is that which we call *volition* or *willing.* The forbearance or performance of that action, consequent to such order or command of the mind is called *voluntary.* And whatsoever action is performed without such a thought of the mind is called *involuntary.* The power of perception is that which we call the *understanding.* Perception, which we make the act of the understanding, is of three sorts: 1. The perception of *ideas* in our minds. 2. The perception of the signification of signs. 3. The perception of the connection or repugnancy, agreement or disagreement, that there is between any of our ideas. All these are attributed to the *understanding,* or perceptive power, though it be the two latter only that use allows us to say we understand.

. . . .

7. *Whence the* ideas *of liberty and necessity.* Everyone, I think, finds in himself a *power* to begin or forbear, continue or put an end to several actions in himself. From the consideration of the extent of this power of the mind over the actions of the man, which everyone finds in himself, arise the *ideas* of *liberty* and *necessity.*

8. *Liberty what.* . . . So far as a man has a power to think, or not to think; to move, or not to move, according to the preference or direction of his own mind, so far is a man *free.* Wherever any performance or forbearance are not equally in a man's power; wherever doing or not doing, will not equally follow upon the preference of his mind directing it, there he is not *free,* though perhaps the action may be voluntary. So that the *idea* of *liberty,* is the *idea* of a power in any agent to do or forbear any particular action, according to the determination or thought of the mind, whereby either of them is preferred to the other; where either of them is not in the power of the agent to be produced by him according to his *volition,* there he is not at *liberty,* that agent is under *necessity.* So that *liberty* cannot be, where there is no thought, no volition, no will; but there may be thought, there may be will,

there may be volition, where there is no *liberty.* A little consideration of an obvious instance or two may make this clear.

9. *Supposes the understanding, and will.* A tennis ball, whether in motion by the stroke of a racket, or lying still at rest, is not by anyone taken to be a *free agent.* If we inquire into the reason, we shall find it is, because we conceive not a tennis ball to think, and consequently not to have any volition, or preference of motion to rest, or *vice versa;* and therefore has not *liberty,* is not a free agent; but all its motion and rest, come under our *idea* of *necessary,* and are so called. Likewise a man falling into the water, (a bridge breaking under him,) has not therein liberty, is not a free agent. For though he has volition, though he prefers his not falling to falling; yet the forbearance of that motion not being in his power, the stop or cessation of that motion follows not upon his volition; and therefore therein he is not *free.* So a man striking himself, or his friend, by a convulsive motion of his arm, which it is not in his power, by volition or the direction of his mind to stop, or forbear; nobody thinks he has in this *liberty;* everyone pities him, as acting by necessity and constraint.

10. *Belongs not to volition.* Again, suppose a man be carried, whilst fast asleep, into a room, where is a person he longs to see and speak with; and be there locked fast in, beyond his power to get out: he awakes, and is glad to find himself in so desireable company, which he stays willingly in, *i.e.* prefers his stay to going away. I ask, is not this stay voluntary? I think, nobody will doubt it: and yet being locked fast in, 'tis evident he is not at liberty not to stay, he has not freedom to be gone. So that *liberty is not an* idea *belonging to volition,* or preferring; but to the person having the power of doing, or forbearing to do, according as the mind shall choose or direct. Our *idea* of liberty reaches as far as that power, and no farther. For wherever restraint comes to check that power, or compulsion takes away that indifferency of ability on either side to act, or to forbear acting, there *liberty,* and our notion of it, presently ceases.

11. *Voluntary opposed to involuntary, not to necessary. . . . Voluntary* then *is not opposed to necessary; but to involuntary.* For a man may prefer what he can do, to what he cannot do; the state he is in, to its absence or change, though necessity has made it in itself unalterable.

. . . .

13. *Necessity what.* Wherever thought is wholly wanting, or the power to act or forbear according to the direction of thought, there *necessity* takes place. This in an agent capable of volition, when the beginning or continuation of any action is contrary to that preference of his mind, is called *compulsion;* when the hindering or stopping any action is contrary to his volition, it is called *restraint*. . . .

14. *Liberty belongs not to the will.* If this be so, (as I imagine it is,) I leave it to be considered, whether it may not help to put an end to that long agitated, and, I think, unreasonable, because unintelligible, question, *viz. whether man's will be free, or no.* For if I mistake not, it follows, from what I have said, that the question itself is altogether improper; and it is as insignificant to ask, whether man's *will* be free, as to ask, whether his sleep be swift, or his virtue square: *liberty* being as little applicable to the *will,* as swiftness of motion is to sleep, or squareness to virtue. . . . *Liberty,* which is but a power, belongs only to agents, and cannot be an attribute or modification of the *will,* which is also but a power.

15. *Volition*. . . . *Volition,* 'tis plain, is an act of the mind knowingly exerting that dominion it takes itself to have over any part of the man, by employing it in, or withholding it from any particular action. And what is the *will,* but the faculty to do this? And is that faculty anything more in effect, than a power, the power of the mind to determine its thought, to the producing, continuing, or stopping any action, as far as it depends on us? For can it be denied, that whatever agent has a power to think on its own actions, and to prefer their doing or omission either to other, has that faculty called *will. Will* then is nothing but such a power. *Liberty,* on the other side, is the power a man has to do or forbear doing any particular action, according as its doing or forbearance has the actual preference in the mind, which is the same thing as to say, according as he himself *wills* it.

16. *Powers belong to agents.* 'Tis plain, then, that the *will* is nothing but one power or ability, and *freedom* another power or ability: so that to ask, whether the *will has freedom,* is to ask, whether one power has another power, one ability another ability; a question at first sight too grossly absurd to make a dispute, or need an answer. For who is it that sees not, that *powers* belong only to *agents,* and *are attributes only of substances, and not of powers* themselves? . . .

17. However the *name faculty,* which men have given to this power called the *will,* and whereby they have been led into a way of talking of the will as

acting, may, by an appropriation that disguises its true sense, serve a little to palliate the absurdity; yet the *will* in truth, signifies nothing but a power, or ability, to prefer or choose: and when the *will*, under the name of a *faculty*, is considered, as it is, barely as an ability to do something, the absurdity, in saying it is free, or not free, will easily discover itself. . . .

. . . .

19. I grant, that this or that actual thought may be the occasion of volition, or exercising the power a man has to choose. . . . But . . . it is not one *power* that operates on another: but it is the mind that operates, and exerts these powers; it is the man that does the action, it is the agent that has power, or is able to do. For *powers* are relations, not agents: and *that which has the power, or not the power to operate, is that alone, which is, or is not free,* and not the power itself: for freedom, or not freedom, can belong to nothing, but what has, or has not a power to act.

20. *Liberty belongs not to the will.* . . . Not that I deny there are *faculties* both in the body and mind: they both of them have their *powers* of operating, else neither the one nor the other could operate. . . . But the fault has been, that faculties have been spoken of, and represented, as so many distinct agents. . . .

21. *But to the agent or man.* To return then to the inquiry about liberty, I think *the question is not proper, whether the will be free, but whether a man be free.* Thus, I think,

1. That so far as anyone can, by the direction or choice of his mind, preferring the existence of any action, to the non-existence of that action, and *vice versa,* make it to exist, or not exist, so far he is *free.* . . . For such a preferring of action to its absence, is the *willing* of it; and we can scarce tell how to imagine any *being* freer, than to be able to do what he *wills.* . . .

22. *In respect of willing, a man is not free.* But the inquisitive mind of man, willing to shift off from himself, as far as he can, all thoughts of guilt, though it be by putting himself into a worse state, than that of fatal necessity, is not content with this: freedom, unless it reaches farther than this, will not serve the turn: and it passes for a good plea, that a man is not free at all, if he be not as free to will, as he is to act, what he wills. Concerning a man's liberty there yet therefore is raised this farther question, *whether a man be free to will;* which, I think, is what is meant, when it is disputed, whether the *will* be free. And as to that I imagine,

23. 2. That *willing,* or *volition* being an action, and freedom consisting in a power of acting, or not acting, *a man in respect of willing, or the act of volition, when any action in his power is once proposed to his thoughts, as presently to be done, cannot be free.* The reason whereof is very manifest: for it being unavoidable that the action depending on his *will,* should exist, or not exist; and its existence, or not existence, following perfectly the determination, and preference of his will, he cannot avoid willing the existence, or not existence, of that action; it is absolutely necessary that he *will* the one, or the other, *i.e. prefer* the one to the other: since one of them must necessarily follow; and that which does follow, follows by the choice and determination of his mind, that is, by his *willing it:* for if he did not *will* it, it would not be. So that in respect of the act of *willing,* a man in such a case is not free: liberty consisting in a power to act, or not to act, which, in regard of volition, a man, upon such a proposal, has not. For it is unavoidably necessary to prefer the doing, or forbearance, of an action in a man's power, which is once so proposed to his thoughts; a man must necessarily *will* the one, or the other of them, upon which preference, or volition, the action, or its forbearance, certainly follows, and is truly voluntary: but the act of volition, or preferring one of the two, being that which he cannot avoid, a man in respect of that act of *willing* is under a necessity, and so cannot be free; unless necessity and freedom can consist together, and a man can be free and bound at once.

24. This then is evident, that in all proposals of present action, *a man is not at liberty to will, or not to will, because he cannot forbear willing:* liberty consisting in a power to act, or to forbear acting, and in that only. . . . A man that is walking, to whom it is proposed to give off walking, is not at liberty, whether he *will* determine himself to walk, or give off walking, or no: he must necessarily prefer one, or t'other of them; walking or not walking: and so it is in regard of all other actions in our power so proposed, which are the far greater number. For considering the vast number of voluntary actions, that succeed one another every moment that we are awake, in the course of our lives, there are but few of them that are thought on or proposed to the *will,* till the time they are to be done: and in all such actions, as I have shown, the mind in respect of *willing* has not a power to act, or not to act, wherein consists liberty: the mind in that case has not a power to forbear *willing;* it cannot avoid some determination concerning them, let the consideration be as short, the thought as quick, as it will, it either leaves the man in the state he was before thinking, or changes it; continues the action, or puts an end to it. Whereby it is manifest, that it orders and directs one in preference to, or with neglect

of the other, and thereby either the continuation, or change becomes unavoidably voluntary.

25. *The will determined by something without it.* Since then it is plain, that in most cases a man is not at liberty, whether he will *will,* or no; the next thing demanded is, *whether a man be at liberty to will which of the two he pleases, motion or rest.* This question carries the absurdity of it so manifestly in itself, that one might thereby sufficiently be convinced, that liberty concerns not the will. For to ask, whether a man be at liberty to will either motion, or rest; speaking, or silence; which he pleases, is to ask, whether a man can *will,* what he *wills;* or be pleased with what he is pleased with. A question, which, I think, needs no answer: and they, who can make a question of it, must suppose one will to determine the acts of another, and another to determine that; and so on *in infinitum.*

26. To avoid these, and the like absurdities, nothing can be of greater use, than to establish in our minds determined *ideas* of the things under consideration. . . .

27. *Freedom. First* then, it is carefully to be remembered, that *freedom consists in the dependence of the existence, or not existence of any action, upon our volition of it, and not in the dependence of any action, or its contrary, on our preference. . . .*

28. *Volition what. Secondly,* we must remember, that *volition,* or *willing,* is an act of the mind directing its thought to the production of any action, and thereby exerting its power to produce it. . . .

29. *What determines the will. Thirdly,* the *will* being nothing but a power in the mind to direct the operative faculties of a man to motion or rest, as far as they depend on such direction. To the question, what is it determines the will? The true and proper answer is, the mind. For that which determines the general power of directing, to this or that particular direction, is nothing but the agent itself exercising the power it has, that particular way. If this answer satisfies not, 'tis plain the meaning of the question, *what determines the will?* is this, what moves the mind, in every particular instance, to determine its general power of directing, to this or that particular motion or rest? And to this I answer, the motive, for continuing in the same state or action, is only the present satisfaction in it; the motive to change, is always some *uneasiness:* nothing setting us upon the change of

state, or upon any new action, but some *uneasiness.* This is the great motive that works on the mind to put it upon action, which for shortness sake we will call *determining of the will,* which I shall more at large explain.

30. *Will and desire must not be confounded.* . . . I find the will often confounded with several of the affections, especially *desire;* and one put for the other. . . . This, I imagine, has been no small occasion of obscurity and mistake in this matter; and therefore is, as much as may be, to be avoided. For he, that shall turn his thoughts inwards upon what passes in his mind, when he *wills,* shall see, that the *will* or power of *volition* is conversant about nothing, but our own actions; terminates there; and reaches no farther; and that *volition* is nothing, but that particular determination of the mind, whereby, barely by a thought, the mind endeavors to give rise, continuation, or stop to any action, which it takes to be in its power. This well considered plainly shows, that the *will* is perfectly distinguished from *desire,* which in the very same action may have a quite contrary tendency from that which our *wills* set us upon. A man, whom I cannot deny, may oblige me to use persuasions to another, which at the same time I am speaking, I may wish may not prevail on him. In this case, 'tis plain the *will* and *desire* run counter. I will the action, that tends one way, whilst my desire tends another, and that the directly contrary. . . .

31. *Uneasiness determines the will.* To return then to the inquiry, *what is it that determines the will in regard to our actions?* And that . . . is not, as is generally supposed, the greater good in view: but some (and for the most part the most pressing) *uneasiness* a man is at present under. This is that which successively determines the *will,* and sets us upon those actions, we perform. This *uneasiness* we may call, as it is, *desire;* which is an uneasiness of the mind for want of some absent good. . . .

32. *Desire is uneasiness.* That *desire* is a state of uneasiness, everyone who reflects on himself, will quickly find. . . .

33. *The uneasiness of desire determines the will.* Good and evil, present and absent, 'tis true, work upon the mind: but that which immediately determines the *will,* from time to time, to every voluntary action, is the *uneasiness* of *desire,* fixed on some absent good, either negative, as indolency to one in pain; or positive, as enjoyment of pleasure. That it is this *uneasiness,* that determines the *will* to the successive voluntary actions, whereof the greatest part of our lives is made up, and by which we are

conducted through different courses to different ends, I shall endeavor to show both from experience, and the reason of the thing.

34. *This the spring of action.* When a man is perfectly content with the state he is in, which is when he is perfectly without any *uneasiness,* what industry, what action, what *will* is there left, but to continue in it? Of this every man's observation will satisfy him. And thus we see our all-wise maker, suitable to our constitution and frame, and knowing what it is that determines the *will,* has put into man the *uneasiness* of hunger and thirst, and other natural desires, that return at their seasons, to move and determine their *wills,* for the preservation of themselves, and the continuation of their species. For I think we may conclude, that, if the bare contemplation of these good ends, to which we are carried by these several *uneasinesses,* had been sufficient to determine the *will,* and set us on work, we should have had none of these natural pains, and perhaps in this world, little or no pain at all. *It is better to marry than to burn,* says St. *Paul;* where we may see, what it is, that chiefly drives men into the enjoyments of a conjugal life.[16] A little burning felt pushes us more powerfully, than greater pleasures in prospect draw or allure.

35. *The greatest positive good determines not the will, but uneasiness.* It seems so established and settled a maxim by the general consent of all mankind, that good, the greater good, determines the will, that I do not at all wonder, that when I first published my thoughts on this subject, I took it for granted; and I imagine, that by a great many I shall be thought more excusable, for having then done so, than that now I have ventured to recede from so received an opinion. But yet upon a stricter inquiry, I am forced to conclude, that *good,* the *greater good,* though apprehended and acknowledged to be so, does not determine the *will,* until our desire, raised proportionably to it, makes us *uneasy* in the want of it. Convince a man never so much, that plenty has its advantages over poverty; make him see and own, that the handsome conveniences of life are better than nasty penury: yet as long as he is content with the latter, and finds no *uneasiness* in it, he moves not. . . . Let a drunkard see, that his health decays, his estate wastes; discredit and diseases, and the want of all things, even of his beloved drink, attends him in the course he follows: yet the returns of *uneasiness* to miss his companions; the habitual thirst after his cups, at the usual time, drives him to the tavern, though he has in his view the loss of

16. *it is better to marry than to burn,* I Corinthians 7:9.

health and plenty, and perhaps of the joys of another life. . . . 'Tis not for want to viewing the greater good: for he sees, and acknowledges it, and in the intervals of his drinking hours, will take resolutions to pursue the greater good; but when the *uneasiness* to miss his accustomed delight returns, the greater acknowledged good loses its hold, and the present *uneasiness* determines the *will* to its accustomed action. . . . And thus he is, from time to time, in the state of that unhappy complainer, *video meliora proboque, deteriora sequor:* which sentence, allowed for true, and made good by constant experience, may this, and possibly no other, way be easily made intelligible.[17]

36. *Because the removal of uneasiness is the first step to happiness.* If we inquire into the reason of what experience makes so evident in fact, and examine why 'tis *uneasiness* alone operates on the *will*, and determines it in its choice, we shall find, that we being capable of but one determination of the will to one action at once, the present *uneasiness*, that we are under, does naturally determine the will, in order to that happiness which we all aim at in all our actions: for as much as whilst we are under any *uneasiness*, we cannot apprehend ourselves happy, or in the way to it. . . .

37. *Because uneasiness alone is present.* Another reason why 'tis *uneasiness* alone determines the will, may be this. Because that alone is present, and 'tis against the nature of things, that what is absent should operate, where it is not. It may be said, that absent good may by contemplation be brought home to the mind, and made present. The *idea* of it indeed may be in the mind, and viewed as present there: but nothing will be in the mind as a present good, able to counterbalance the removal of any *uneasiness*, which we are under, till it raises our desire, and the *uneasiness* of that has the prevalency in determining the *will*. . . .

38. *Because all who allow the joys of heaven possible, pursue them not.* Were the *will* determined by the views of good, as it appears in contemplation greater or less to the understanding, which is the state of all absent good, and that, which in the received opinion the *will* is supposed to move to, and to be moved by, I do not see how it could ever get loose from the infinite eternal joys of heaven, once proposed and considered as possible. . . .

17. *video meliora proboque, deteriora sequor*, I see the better [way] and approve it, but I follow the worse (from Ovid (43 B.C.–17 or 18 A.D.), *Metamorphoses* VII, 20–21).

But any great uneasiness is never neglected. This would be the state of mind, and regular tendency of the *will* in all its determinations, were it determined by that, which is considered, and in view the greater good: but that it is not so is visible in experience. . . .

. . . .

40. *The most pressing uneasiness naturally determines the will.* But we being in this world beset with sundry *uneasinesses,* distracted with different *desires,* the next inquiry will naturally be, which of them has the precedency in determining the *will* to the next action? And to that the answer is, that ordinarily, which is the most pressing of those, that are judged capable of being then removed. . . .

41. *All desire happiness.* If it be farther asked, what 'tis moves *desire*? I answer happiness and that alone. . . .

42. *Happiness what. Happiness* . . . in its full extent is the utmost pleasure we are capable of, and *misery* the utmost pain: and the lowest degree of what can be called *happiness,* is so much ease from all pain, and so much present pleasure, as without which anyone cannot be content. Now because pleasure and pain are produced in us, by the operation of certain objects, either on our minds or our bodies; and in different degrees: therefore what has an aptness to produce pleasure in us, is that we call *good,* and what is apt to produce pain in us, we call *evil,* for no other reason, but for its aptness to produce pleasure and pain in us, wherein consists our *happiness* and *misery.* . . .

43. *What good is desired, what not?* Though this be that, which is called *good* and *evil;* and all good be the proper object of *desire* in general; yet all good, even seen, and confessed to be so, does not necessarily move every particular man's *desire;* but only that part, or so much of it, as is considered, and taken to be a necessary part of his happiness. All other good however great in reality, or appearance, excites not a man's *desires,* who looks not on it to make a part of that happiness, wherewith he, in his present thoughts, can satisfy himself. . . .

44. *Why the greatest good is not always desired.* This, I think, anyone may observe in himself, and others, that the *greater visible good* does not always raise men's *desires* in proportion to the greatness, it appears, and is acknowledged to have: though every little trouble moves us, and sets us on

work to get rid of it. The reason whereof is evident from the nature of our *happiness* and *misery* itself. All present pain, whatever it be, makes a part of our present *misery;* but all absent good does not at any time make a necessary part of our present *happiness,* nor the absence of it make a part of our *misery.* If it did, we should be constantly and infinitely miserable; there being infinite degrees of happiness, which are not in our possession. . . .

45. *Why not being desired, it moves not the will.* . . . We are seldom at ease, and free enough from the solicitation of our natural or adopted desires, but a constant succession of *uneasinesses* out of that stock, which natural wants, or acquired habits have heaped up, take the *will* in their turns; and no sooner is one action dispatched, which by such a determination of the *will* we are set upon, but another *uneasiness* is ready to set us on work. For the removing of pains we feel, and are at present pressed with, being the getting out of misery, and consequently the first thing to be done in order to happiness, absent good, though thought on, confessed, and appearing to be good, not making any part of this unhappiness in its absence, is jostled out, to make way for the removal of those *uneasinesses* we feel, till due, and repeated contemplation has brought it nearer to our mind, given some relish of it, and raised in us some desire; which then beginning to make a part of our present *uneasiness,* stands upon fair terms with the rest, to be satisfied, and so according to its greatness, and pressure, comes in its turn to determine the *will.*

46. *Due consideration raises desire.* And thus, by a due consideration and examining any good proposed, it is in our power, to raise our desires, in a due proportion to the value of that good, whereby in its turn, and place, it may come to work upon the *will,* and be pursued. . . .

47. *The power to suspend the prosecution of any desire makes way for consideration.* There being in us a great many *uneasinesses* always soliciting, and ready to determine the *will,* it is natural, as I have said, that the greatest and most pressing should determine the *will* to the next action; and so it does for the most part, but not always. For the mind having in most cases, as is evident in experience, a power to *suspend* the execution and satisfaction of any of its desires, and so all, one after another, is at liberty to consider the objects of them; examine them on all sides, and weigh them with others. In this lies the liberty man has; and from the not using it right comes all that variety of mistakes, errors, and faults which we run into, in the conduct of our lives, and our endeavors after happiness; whilst we precipitate the determination of our *wills,* and engage too soon before due *examination.* To

prevent this we have a power to *suspend* the prosecution of this or that desire, as everyone daily may experiment in himself. This seems to me the source of all liberty; in this seems to consist that, which is (as I think improperly) called *free will.* For during this *suspension* of any desire, before the *will* be determined to action, and the action (which follows that determination) done, we have opportunity to examine, view, and judge, of the good or evil of what we are going to do; and when, upon due *examination,* we have judged, we have done our duty, all that we can, or ought to do, in pursuit of our happiness; and 'tis not a fault, but a perfection of our nature to desire, will, and act according to the last result of a fair *examination.*

48. *To be determined by our own judgment is no restraint to liberty.* This is so far from being a restraint or diminution of *freedom,* that it is the very improvement and benefit of it; 'tis not an abridgment, 'tis the end and use of our *liberty;* and the farther we are removed from such determination, the nearer we are to misery and slavery. A perfect indifferency in the mind, not determinable by its last judgment of the good or evil, that is thought to attend its choice, would be so far from being an advantage and excellency of any intellectual nature, that it would be as great an imperfection, as the want of indifferency to act, or not to act, till determined by the *will,* would be an imperfection on the other side. A man is at liberty to lift up his hand to his head, or let it rest quiet: he is perfectly indifferent in either; and it would be an imperfection in him, if he wanted that power, if he were deprived of that indifferency. But it would be as great an imperfection, if he had the same indifferency, whether he would prefer the lifting up his hand, or its remaining in rest, when it would save his head or eyes from a blow he sees coming: *'tis* as much *a perfection, that desire or the power of preferring should be determined by good,* as that the power of acting should be determined by the *will,* and the certainer such determination is, the greater is the perfection. Nay were we determined by anything but the last result of our own minds, judging of the good or evil of any action, we were not free, the very end of our freedom being, that we might attain the good we choose. And therefore every man is put under a necessity by his constitution, as an intelligent being, to be determined in *willing* by his own thought and judgment, what is best for him to do: else he would be under the determination of some other than himself, which is want of liberty. And to deny, that a man's *will,* in every determination, follows his own judgment, is to say, that a man *wills* and acts for an end that he would not have at the time that he *wills* and acts for it. For if he prefers it in his present thoughts before

any other, 'tis plain he then thinks better of it, and would have it before any other, unless he can have, and not have it; *will* and not *will* it at the same time; a contradiction too manifest to be admitted.

49. *The freest agents are so determined.* If we look upon those *superior beings* above us, who enjoy perfect happiness, we shall have reason to judge that they are more steadily *determined in their choice of good* than we; and yet we have no reason to think they are less happy, or less free, than we are. And if it were fit for such poor finite creatures as we are, to pronounce what infinite wisdom and goodness could do, I think, we might say, that God himself cannot choose what is not good; the freedom of the almighty hinders not his being determined by what is best.

50. *A constant determination to a pursuit of happiness no abridgment of liberty.* But to give a right view of this mistaken part of liberty, let me ask, would anyone be a changeling, because he is less determined, by wise considerations, than a wise man? Is it worth the name of *freedom* to be at liberty to play the fool, and draw shame and misery upon a man's self? If to break loose from the conduct of reason, and to want that restraint of examination and judgment, which keeps us from choosing or doing the worse, be *liberty,* true liberty, madmen and fools are the only freemen: but yet, I think, nobody would choose to be mad for the sake of such *liberty,* but he that is mad already. The constant desire of happiness, and the constraint it puts upon us to act for it, nobody, I think, accounts an abridgment of *liberty,* or at least an abridgment of *liberty* to be complained of. God almighty himself is under the necessity of being happy; and the more any intelligent being is so, the nearer is its approach to infinite perfection and happiness. That in this state of ignorance we short-sighted creatures might not mistake true felicity, we are endowed with a power to suspend any particular desire, and keep it from determining the *will,* and engaging us in action. This is *standing still,* where we are not sufficiently assured of the way: examination is *consulting a guide.* The determination of the *will* upon inquiry is *following the direction of that guide:* and he that has a power to act, or not to act according as such determination directs, is a *free agent;* such determination abridges not that power wherein liberty consists. He that has his chains knocked off, and the prison-doors set open to him, is perfectly at *liberty,* because he may either go or stay, as he best likes; though his preference be determined to stay, by the darkness of the night, or illness of the weather, or want of other lodging. He ceases not to be free; though the desire of some

convenience to be had there, absolutely determines his preference, and makes him stay in his prison.

51. *The necessity of pursuing true happiness the foundation of liberty.* As therefore the highest perfection of intellectual nature, lies in a careful and constant pursuit of true and solid happiness; so the care of ourselves, that we mistake not imaginary for real happiness, is the necessary foundation of our *liberty.* The stronger ties, we have, to an unalterable pursuit of happiness in general, which is our greatest good, and which as such our desires always follow, the more we are free from any necessary determination of our *will* to any particular action, and from a necessary compliance with our desire, set upon any particular, and then appearing preferable good, till we have duly examined, whether it has a tendency to, or be inconsistent with our real happiness; and therefore till we are as much informed upon this inquiry, as the weight of the matter, and the nature of the case demands, we are by the necessity of preferring and pursuing true happiness as our greatest good, obliged to suspend the satisfaction of our desire in particular cases.

52. *The reason of this.* This is the hinge on which turns the *liberty* of intellectual beings in their constant endeavors after, and a steady prosecution of true felicity, since they can *suspend* this prosecution in particular cases, till they have looked before them, and informed themselves, whether that particular thing, which is then proposed, or desired, lie in the way to their main end, and make a real part of that which is their greatest good. For the inclination, and tendency of their nature to happiness is an obligation, and motive to them, to take care not to mistake, or miss it; and so necessarily puts them upon caution, deliberation, and wariness, in the direction of their particular actions, which are the means to obtain it. Whatever necessity determines the pursuit of real bliss, the same necessity, with the same force establishes *suspense, deliberation,* and scrutiny of each successive desire, whether the satisfaction of it, does not interfere with our true happiness, and mislead us from it. This as seems to me is the great privilege of finite intellectual beings; and I desire it may be well considered, whether the great inlet, and exercise of all the *liberty* men have, are capable of, or can be useful to them, and that whereon depends the turn of their actions, does not lie in this, that they can *suspend* their desires, and stop them from determining their *wills* to any action, till they have duly and fairly *examined* the good and evil of it, as far forth as the weight of the thing requires. This we are able to do; and when we have done it, we have done

our duty, and all that is in our power; and indeed all that needs. For, since the *will* supposes knowledge to guide its choice, all that we can do, is to hold our *wills* undetermined, till we have *examined* the good and evil of what we desire. What follows after that, follows in a chain of consequences linked one to another, all depending on the last determination of the judgment, which whether it shall be upon an hasty and precipitate view, or upon a due and mature *examination,* is in our power; experience showing us, that in most cases we are able to suspend the present satisfaction of any desire.

53. *Government of our passions the right improvement of liberty.* But if any extreme disturbance (as sometimes it happens) possess our whole mind, as when the pain of the rack, an impetuous *uneasiness,* as of love, anger, or any other violent passion, running away with us, allows us not the liberty of thought, and we are not masters enough of our own minds to consider thoroughly, and examine fairly; God, who knows our frailty, pities our weakness, and requires of us no more than we are able to do, and sees what was, and what was not in our power, will judge as a kind and merciful father. But the forbearance of a too hasty compliance with our desires, the moderation and restraint of our passions, so that our understandings may be *free* to examine, and reason unbiased give its judgment, being that, whereon a right direction of our conduct to true happiness depends; 'tis in this we should employ our chief care and endeavors. In this we should take pains to suit the relish of our minds to the intrinsic good or ill, that is in things; and not permit an allowed or supposed possible great and weighty good to slip out of our thoughts, without leaving any relish, any desire of itself there, till, by a due consideration of its true worth, we have formed appetites in our minds suitable to it, and made ourselves uneasy in the want of it, or in the fear of losing it. And how much this is in everyone's power, everyone by making resolutions to himself, such as he may keep, is easy for everyone to try. Nor let anyone say, he cannot govern his passions, nor hinder them from breaking out, and carrying him into action; for what he can do before a prince, or a great man, he can do alone, or in the presence of God, if he will.

54. *How men come to pursue different courses.* From what has been said, it is easy to give an account, how it comes to pass, that though all men desire happiness, yet their *wills carry them so contrarily,* and consequently some of them to what is evil. And to this I say, that the various and contrary choices, that men make in this world, do not argue, that they do not all pursue good; but that the same thing is not good to every man alike. This variety of

pursuits shows, that everyone does not place his happiness in the same thing, or choose the same way to it. . . .

. . . .

56. *How men come to choose ill.* These things duly weighed, will give us, as I think, a clear view into the state of human liberty. Liberty 'tis plain consists in a power to do, or not to do; to do, or forbear doing as we *will.* This cannot be denied. But this seeming to comprehend only the actions of a man consecutive to volition, it is farther inquired, whether he be at liberty to *will,* or no? And to this it has been answered, that in most cases a man is not at liberty to forbear the act of volition; he must exert an act of his *will,* whereby the action proposed, is made to exist, or not to exist. But yet there is a case wherein a man is at liberty in respect of *willing,* and that is the choosing of a remote good as an end to be pursued. Here a man may suspend the act of his choice from being determined for or against the thing proposed, till he has examined, whether it be really of a nature in itself and consequences to make him happy, or no. For when he has once chosen it, and thereby it is become a part of his happiness, it raises desire, and that proportionably gives him uneasiness, which determines his *will,* and sets him at work in pursuit of his choice on all occasions that offer. And here we may see how it comes to pass, that a man may justly incur punishment, though it be certain that in all the particular actions that he *wills,* he does, and necessarily does will that, which he then judges to be good. For though his *will* be always determined by that, which is judged good by his understanding, yet it excuses him not: because, by a too hasty choice of his own making, he has imposed on himself wrong measures of good and evil; which however false and fallacious, have the same influence on all his future conduct, as if they were true and right. He has vitiated his own palate, and must be answerable to himself for the sickness and death that follows from it. The eternal law and nature of things must be not altered to comply with his ill-ordered choice. If the neglect or abuse of the liberty he had, to examine what would really and truly make for his happiness, misleads him, the miscarriages that follow on it, must be imputed to his own election. He had a power to suspend his determination: it was given him, that he might examine, and take care of his own happiness, and look that he were not deceived. And he could never judge, that it was better to be deceived, than not, in a matter of so great and near concernment.

What has been said, may also discover to us the reason, why men in this world prefer different things, and pursue happiness by contrary courses.

But yet since men are always constant, and in earnest, in matter of happiness and misery, the question still remains, *how men come often to prefer the worse to the better;* and to choose that, which, by their own confession, has made them miserable.

57. To account for the various and contrary ways men take, though all aim at being happy, we must consider, whence the various *uneasinesses,* that determine the will in the preference of each voluntary action, have their rise.

1. *From bodily pains.* Some of them come from causes not in our power, such as are often the pains of the body from want, disease, or outward injuries, as the rack, *etc.* which when present, and violent, operate for the most part forcibly on the *will,* and turn the courses of men's lives from virtue, piety, and religion, and what before they judged to lead to happiness; everyone not endeavoring, or through disuse, not being able by the contemplation of remote, and future good, to raise in himself desires of them strong enough to counter-balance the uneasiness, he feels in those bodily torments; and to keep his *will* steady in the choice of those actions, which lead to future happiness. . . .

2. *From wrong desires arising from wrong judgment.* Other *uneasinesses* arise from our desires of absent good; which desires always bear proportion to, and depend on the judgment we make, and the relish we have of any absent good; in both which we are apt to be variously misled, and that by our own fault.

. . . .

69. *We can change the agreeableness or disagreeableness in things.* The last inquiry therefore concerning this matter is, whether it be in a man's power to change the pleasantness, and unpleasantness, that accompanies any sort of action? And to that, it is plain in many cases he can. Men may and should correct their palates, and give a relish to what either has, or they suppose has none. The relish of the mind is as various as that of the body, and like that too may be altered; and 'tis a mistake to think, that men cannot change the displeasingness, or indifferency, that is in actions, into pleasure and desire, if they will do but what is in their power. A due consideration will do it in some cases; and practice, application, and custom in most. Bread or tobacco may be neglected, where they are shown to be useful to health, because of an indifferency or disrelish to them; reason and consideration at first recommends, and begins their trial, and use finds, or custom makes

them pleasant. That this is so in virtue too, is very certain. . . . Trials often reconcile us to that, which at a distance we looked on with aversion; and by repetition wears us into a liking, of what possibly, in the first essay, displeased us. Habits have powerful charms, and put so strong attractions of easiness and pleasure into what we accustom ourselves to, that we cannot forbear to do, or at least be easy in the omission of acts, which habitual practice has suited, and thereby recommends to us. Though this be very visible, and everyone's experience shows him he can do; yet it is a part, in the conduct of men towards their happiness, neglected to a degree, that it will be possibly entertained as a paradox, if it be said, that men can make things or actions more or less pleasing to themselves; and thereby remedy that, to which one may justly impute a great deal of their wandering. Fashion and the common opinion have settled wrong notions, and education and custom ill habits, the just values of things are misplaced, and the palates of men corrupted. Pains should be taken to rectify these; and contrary habits change our pleasures, and give a relish to that, which is necessary, or conducive to our happiness. This everyone must confess he can do, and when happiness is lost, and misery overtakes him, he will confess, he did amiss in neglecting it; and condemn himself for it: and I ask everyone whether he has not often done so?

. . . .

71. *Recapitulation.* To conclude this inquiry into human liberty, . . . *liberty* is a power to act or not to act according as the mind directs. A power to direct the operative faculties to motion or rest in particular instances, is that which we call the *will.* That which in the train of our voluntary actions determines the *will* to any change of operation, is some present uneasiness, which is, or at least is always accompanied with that of *desire.* Desire is always moved by evil, to fly it: because a total freedom from pain always makes a necessary part of our happiness: but every *good,* nay every *greater good* does not constantly move *desire,* because it may not make, or may not be taken to make any necessary part of our happiness. For all that we desire is only to be happy. But though this general *desire* of happiness operates constantly and invariably, yet the satisfaction of any particular *desire* can be suspended from determining the *will* to any subservient action, till we have maturely examined, whether the particular apparent good, which we then desire, makes a part of our real happiness, or be consistent or inconsistent with it. The result of our judgment upon that examination is what ultimately determines the man, who could not be *free* if his *will* were determined by anything, but his own *desire* guided by his own *judgment.* . . .

72. . . . Before I close this chapter, it may perhaps be to our purpose, and help to give us clearer conceptions about *power,* if we make our thoughts take a little more exact survey of *action.* I have said above, that we have *ideas* but of two sorts of *action,* viz. *motion* and *thinking.* These, in truth, though called and counted *actions,* yet, if nearly considered, will not be found to be always perfectly so. For, if I mistake not, there are instances of both kinds, which, upon due consideration, will be found rather *passions* than *actions,* and consequently so far the effects barely of passive powers in those subjects, which yet on their account are thought *agents.* For in these instances, the substance that has motion, or thought, receives the impression whereby it is put into that *action* purely from without, and so acts merely by the capacity it has to receive such an impression from some external agent; and such a *power* is not properly an *active power,* but a mere passive capacity in the subject. Sometimes the substance, or agent, puts itself into *action* by its own power, and this is properly *active power.* Whatsoever modification a substance has, whereby it produces any effect, that is called *action; v. g.* a solid substance by motion operates on, or alters the sensible *ideas* of another substance, and therefore this modification of motion we call action. But yet this motion in that solid substance is, when rightly considered, but a passion, if it received it only from some external agent. So that the *active power* of motion is in no substance which cannot begin motion in itself, or in another substance when at rest. So likewise in *thinking,* a power to receive *ideas,* or thoughts, from the operation of any external substance, is called a *power* of thinking: but this is but a *passive power,* or capacity. . . .

73. And thus I have, in a short draft, given a view of our *original ideas,* from whence all the rest are derived, and of which they are made up; which if I would consider, as a philosopher, and examine on what causes they depend, and of what they are made, I believe they all might be reduced to these very few primary, and original ones, *viz.*

extension,
solidity,
mobility, or the power of being moved;

which by our senses we receive from body:

perceptivity, or the power of perception, or thinking;
motivity, or the power of moving;

which by reflection we receive from our minds. I crave leave to make use of these two new words, to avoid the danger of being mistaken in the use of those which are equivocal. To which if we add

existence,
duration,
number;

which belong both to the one, and the other, we have, perhaps, all the original *ideas* on which the rest depend. For by these, I imagine, might be explained the nature of colors, sounds, tastes, smells, and all other *ideas* we have, if we had but faculties acute enough to perceive the severally modified extensions, and motions, of these minute bodies, which produce those several sensations in us. But my present purpose being only to inquire into the knowledge the mind has of things, by those *ideas,* and appearances, which *God* has fitted it to receive from them, and how the mind comes by that knowledge; rather than into their causes, or manner of production, I shall not, contrary to the design of this essay, set myself to inquire philosophically into the peculiar constitution of bodies, and the configuration of parts, whereby they have the power to produce in us the *ideas* of their sensible qualities: I shall not enter any farther into that disquisition; it sufficing to my purpose to observe, that gold, or saffron, has a power to produce in us the *idea* of yellow; and snow, or milk, the *idea* of white; which we can only have by our sight, without examining the texture of the parts of those bodies, or the particular figures, or motion of the particles, which rebound from them, to cause in us that particular sensation: though when we go beyond the bare *ideas* in our minds, and would inquire into their causes, we cannot conceive anything else, to be in any sensible object, whereby it produces different *ideas* in us, but the different bulk, figure, number, texture, and motion of its insensible parts.

Chap. XXII.
Of mixed modes.

1. *Mixed modes what.* Having treated of *simple ideas* in the foregoing chapters, and given several instances of some of the most considerable of them, to show what they are, and how we come by them; we are now in the

next place to consider those we call *mixed modes,* such are the complex *ideas,* we mark by the names *obligation, drunkenness,* a *lie,* &c. which consisting of several combinations of simple *ideas* of different kinds, I have called *mixed modes,* to distinguish them from the more simple modes, which consist only of simple *ideas* of the same kind. These mixed modes being also such combinations of simple *ideas,* as are not looked upon to be the characteristical marks of any real beings that have a steady existence, but scattered and independent *ideas,* put together by the mind, are thereby distinguished from the complex *ideas* of substances.

2. *Made by the mind.* That the mind, in respect of its simple *ideas,* is wholly passive, and receives them all from the existence and operations of things, such as sensation or reflection offers them, without being able to make any one *idea,* experience shows us. But if we attentively consider these *ideas* I call *mixed modes,* . . . we shall find their original quite different. *The mind* often *exercises an active power in the making these* several *combinations.* For it being once furnished with simple *ideas,* it can put them together in several compositions, and so make variety of complex *ideas,* without examining whether they exist so together in nature. And hence, I think, it is, that these *ideas* are called *notions:* as if they had their original, and constant existence, more in the thoughts of men, than in the reality of things; and to form such *ideas,* it sufficed, that the mind put the parts of them together, and that they were consistent in the understanding, without considering whether they had any real being: though I do not deny, but several of them might be taken from observation, and the existence of several simple *ideas* so combined, as they are put together in the understanding. For the man who first framed the *idea* of *hypocrisy,* might have either taken it at first from the observation of one, who make show of good qualities which he had not; or else have framed that *idea* in his mind, without having any such pattern to fashion it by. For it is evident, that in the beginning of languages and societies of men, several of those complex *ideas,* which were consequent to the constitutions established amongst them, must needs have been in the minds of men, before they existed anywhere else; and that many names that stood for such complex *ideas,* were in use, and so those *ideas* framed, before the combinations they stood for, ever existed.

3. *Sometimes got by the explication of their names.* Indeed, now that languages are made, and abound with words standing for such combinations, *an usual way of getting these complex* ideas, *is by the explication of those terms that stand for them.* . . .

4. *The name ties the parts of the mixed modes into one* idea. Every *mixed mode* consisting of many distinct simple *ideas,* it seems reasonable to inquire, *whence it has its unity;* and how such a precise multitude comes to make but one *idea,* since that combination does not always exist together in nature. To which I answer it is plain, it has its unity from an act of the mind combining those several simple *ideas* together, and considering them as one complex one, consisting of those parts; and the mark of this union, or that which is looked on generally to complete it, is one name given to that combination. For 'tis by their names, that men commonly regulate their account of their distinct species of mixed modes, seldom allowing or considering any number of simple *ideas,* to make one complex one, but such collections as there be names for. . . .

5. *The cause of making mixed modes.* If we should inquire a little farther, to see *what* it is, that *occasions men to make several combinations of simple* ideas into distinct, and, as it were, settled *modes,* and neglect others, . . . we shall find the reason of it to be the end of language; which being to mark, or communicate men's thoughts to one another, with all the dispatch that may be, they usually make such collections of ideas into complex modes, and affix names to them, as they have frequent use of in their way of living and conversation. . . .

. . . .

9. *How we get the* ideas *of mixed modes.* There are . . . *three ways whereby we get these complex* ideas *of mixed modes.* 1. By experience and *observation* of things themselves. Thus by seeing two men wrestle, or fence, we get the *idea* of wrestling or fencing. 2. By *invention,* or voluntary putting together of several simple *ideas* in our own minds: so that he who first invented printing, or etching, had an *idea* of it in his mind, before it ever existed. 3. Which is the most usual way, by *explaining the names of* actions we never saw, or notions we cannot see; and by enumerating, and thereby, as it were, setting before our imaginations all those *ideas* which go to the making them up, and are the constituent parts of them. For having by *sensation* and *reflection* stored our minds with simple *ideas,* and by use got the names, that stand for them, we can by those names represent to another any complex *idea,* we would have him conceive; so that it has in it no simple *idea,* but what he knows, and has, with us, the same name for. For all our complex *ideas* are ultimately resolvable into simple *ideas,* of which they are compounded, and originally made up, though perhaps their immediate ingredients, as I may so say, are also complex *ideas.* . . .

10. *Motion, thinking and power, have been most modified.* It is worth our observing *which of all our simple* ideas *have been most modified, and had most mixed modes made out of them, with names given to them:* and those have been these three; thinking, and motion, (which are the two *ideas* which comprehend in them all action,) and power, from whence these actions are conceived to flow. . . .

11. *Several words seeming to signify action, signify but the effect. Power* being the source from whence all action proceeds, the substances wherein these powers are, when they exert this power into act, are called *causes,* and the substances which thereupon are produced, or the simple *ideas* which are introduced into any subject by the exerting of that power, are called *effects.* The *efficacy* whereby the new substance or *idea* is produced, is called, in the subject exerting that power, *action;* but in the subject, wherein any simple *idea* is changed or produced, it is called *passion:* which efficacy however various, and the effects almost infinite; yet we can, I think, conceive it, in intellectual agents, to be nothing else but modes of thinking, and willing; in corporeal agents, nothing else but modifications of motion. . . . And . . . *many words, which seem to express some action,* signify nothing of the action, or *modus operandi* at all, *but* barely *the effect,* with some circumstances of the subject wrought on, or cause operating; *v.g.* creation, annihilation, contain in them no *idea* of the action or manner, whereby they are produced, but barely of the cause, and the thing done.[18] And when a country-man says, the cold freezes water, though the word freezing seems to import some *action,* yet truly it signifies nothing, but the effect, *viz.* that water, that was before fluid, is become hard and consistent, without containing any *idea* of the action whereby it is done.

. . . .

CHAP. XXIII.

Of our complex ideas of substances.

1. Ideas *of substances how made.* The mind being, as I have declared, furnished with a great number of the simple *ideas,* conveyed in by the *senses,* as they are found in exterior things, or by *reflection* on its own operations,

18. *modus operandi,* way of operating.

takes notice also, that a certain number of these simple *ideas* go constantly together; which being presumed to belong to one thing, and words being suited to common apprehensions, and made use of for quick dispatch, are called so united in one subject, by one name; which by inadvertency we are apt afterward to talk of and consider as one simple *idea,* which indeed is a complication of many *ideas* together; because, as I have said, not imagining how these simple *ideas* can subsist by themselves, we accustom ourselves, to suppose some *substratum,* wherein they do subsist, and from which they do result, which therefore we call *substance.*

2. *Our* idea *of substance in general.* So that if anyone will examine himself concerning his *notion of pure substance in general,* he will find he has no other *idea* of it at all, but only a supposition of he knows not what support of such qualities, which are capable of producing simple *ideas* in us; which qualities are commonly called accidents. If anyone should be asked, what is the subject wherein color or weight inheres, he would have nothing to say, but the solid extended parts: and if he were demanded, what is it, that solidity and extension inhere in, he would not be in a much better case, than the *Indian* before mentioned; who, saying that the world was supported by a great elephant, was asked, what the elephant rested on; to which his answer was a great tortoise: but being again pressed to know what gave support to the broad-backed tortoise, replied, something, he knew not what. And thus here, as in all other cases, where we use words without having clear and distinct *ideas,* we talk like children; who, being questioned, what such a thing is, which they know not, readily give this satisfactory answer, that it is *something;* which in truth signifies no more, when so used, either by children or men, but that they know not what; and that the thing they pretend to know, and talk of, is what they have no distinct *idea* of at all, and so are perfectly ignorant of it, and in the dark. The *idea* then we have, to which we give the general name substance, being nothing, but the supposed, but unknown support of those qualities, we find existing, which we imagine cannot subsist, *sine re substante,* without something to support them, we call that support *substantia;* which, according to the true import of the word, is in plain *English, standing under,* or *upholding.*[19]

3. *Of the sorts of substances.* An obscure and relative *idea* of substance in general being thus made, we come to have the *ideas of particular sorts of substances,* by collecting such combinations of simple *ideas,* as are by

19. *sine re substante*, without a thing supporting [it]; *substantia*, substance.

experience and observation of men's senses taken notice of to exist together, and are therefore supposed to flow from the particular internal constitution, or unknown essence of that substance. Thus we come to have the *ideas* of a man, horse, gold, water, *&c.* of which substances, whether anyone has any other clear *idea,* farther than of certain simple *ideas* coexisting together, I appeal to everyone's own experience. . . . Only we must take notice, that our complex *ideas* of substances, besides all these simple *ideas* they are made up of, have always the confused *idea* of *something* to which they belong, and in which they subsist: and therefore when we speak of any sort of substance, we say it is a *thing* having such or such qualities, as body is a *thing* that is extended, figured, and capable of motion; a spirit a *thing* capable of thinking; and so hardness, friability, and power to draw iron, we say, are qualities to be found in a lodestone. These, and the like fashions of speaking intimate, that the substance is supposed always *something* besides the extension, figure, solidity, motion, thinking, or other observable *ideas,* though we know not what it is.

4. *No clear* idea *of substance in general.* Hence when we talk or think of any particular sort of corporeal substances, as *horse, stone, &c.* though the *idea,* we have of either of them, be but the complication, or collection of those several simple *ideas* of sensible qualities, which we use to find united in the thing called *horse* or *stone,* yet because we cannot conceive, how they should subsist alone, nor one in another, we suppose them existing in, and supported by some common subject; *which support we denote by the name substance,* though it be certain, we have no clear, or distinct *idea* of that *thing* we suppose a support.

5. *As clear an* idea *of spirit, as body.* The same happens concerning the operations of the mind, *viz.* thinking, reasoning, fearing, *&c.* which we concluding not to subsist of themselves, nor apprehending how they can belong to body, or be produced by it, we are apt to think these the actions of some other *substance,* which we call *spirit;* whereby yet it is evident, that having no other *idea* or notion, of matter, but *something* wherein those many sensible qualities, which affect our senses, do subsist; by supposing a substance, wherein *thinking, knowing, doubting,* and a power of moving, *&c.* do subsist, *we have as clear a notion of the substance of spirit, as we have of body;* the one being supposed to be (without knowing what it is) the *substratum* to those simple *ideas* we have from without; and the other supposed (with a like ignorance of what it is) to be the *substratum* to those operations, which

we experiment in ourselves within. 'Tis plain then, that the *idea* of corporeal *substance* in matter is as remote from our conceptions, and apprehensions, as that of spiritual *substance,* or *spirit;* and therefore from our not having any notion of the *substance* of spirit, we can no more conclude its non-existence, than we can, for the same reason, deny the existence of body: it being as rational to affirm, there is no body, because we have no clear and distinct *idea* of the *substance* of matter; as to say, there is no spirit, because we have no clear and distinct *idea* of the *substance* of a spirit.

6. *Of the sorts of substances.* Whatever therefore be the secret and abstract nature of *substance* in general, all *the* ideas *we have of particular distinct sorts of substances,* are nothing but several combinations of simple *ideas,* co-existing in such, though unknown, cause of their union, as makes the whole subsist of itself. . . .

7. *Powers a great part of our complex* ideas *of substances.* . . . He has the perfectest *idea* of any of the particular sorts of *substance,* who has gathered, and put together, most of those simple *ideas,* which do exist in it, among which are to be reckoned its active powers, and passive capacities; which though not simple *ideas,* yet, in this respect, for brevity's sake, may conveniently enough be reckoned amongst them. Thus the power of drawing iron, is one of the *ideas* of the complex one of that substance we call a *lodestone,* and a power to be so drawn is a part of the complex one we call *iron;* which powers pass for inherent qualities in those subjects. . . .

8. *And why.* Nor are we to wonder, that *powers make a great part of our complex* ideas *of substances;* since their secondary qualities are those, which in most of them serve principally to distinguish substances one from another, and commonly make a considerable part of the complex *idea* of the several sorts of them. For our senses failing us, in the discovery of the bulk, texture, and figure of the minute parts of bodies, on which their real constitutions and differences depend, we are fain to make use of their secondary qualities, as the characteristical notes and marks, whereby to frame *ideas* of them in our minds, and distinguish them one from another. All which secondary qualities, as has been shown, are nothing but bare powers. . . .

9. *Three sorts of* ideas *make our complex ones of substance. The* ideas *that make our complex ones of corporeal substances,* are of these three sorts. *First,* the *ideas* of the primary qualities of things, which are discovered by our senses,

and are in them even when we perceive them not, such are the bulk, figure, number, situation, and motion of the parts of bodies, which are really in them, whether we take notice of them or no. *Secondly,* the sensible secondary qualities, which depending on these, are nothing but the powers, those substances have to produce several *ideas* in us by our senses; which *ideas* are not in the things themselves, otherwise than as anything is in its cause. *Thirdly,* the aptness we consider in any substance, to give or receive alterations of primary qualities, as that the substance so altered, should produce in us different *ideas* from what it did before, these are called active and passive powers: all which powers, as far as we have any notice or notion of them, terminate only in sensible simple *ideas*. . . .

10. *Powers make a great part of our complex* ideas *of substances. Powers,* therefore, justly *make a great part of our complex* ideas *of substances.* He, that will examine his complex *idea* of gold, will find several of its *ideas,* that make it up, to be only powers, as the power of being melted, but of not spending itself in the fire; of being dissolved in *aqua regia,* are *ideas,* as necessary to make up our complex *idea* of gold, as its color and weight: which if duly considered, are also nothing but different powers. . . .

11. *The now secondary qualities of bodies would disappear, if we could discover the primary ones of their minute parts.* Had we senses acute enough to discern the minute particles of bodies, and the real constitution on which their sensible qualities depend, I doubt not but that they would produce quite different *ideas* in us; and that which is now the yellow color of gold, would then disappear, and instead of it we should see an admirable texture of parts of a certain size and figure. This microscopes plainly discover to us: for what to our naked eyes produces a certain color, is by thus augmenting the acuteness of our senses, discovered to be quite a different thing; and the thus altering, as it were, the proportion of the bulk of the minute parts of a colored object to our usual sight, produces different *ideas,* from what it did before. . . .

12. *Our faculties of discovery suited to our state.* The infinite wise contriver of us, and all things about us, has fitted our senses, faculties, and organs, to the conveniences of life, and the business we have to do here. . . . We are furnished with faculties (dull and weak as they are) to discover enough in the creatures, to lead us to the knowledge of the creator, and the knowledge of our duty; and we are fitted well enough with abilities, to provide for the conveniences of living: these are our business in this world. But were our

senses altered, and made much quicker and acuter, the appearance and outward scheme of things would have quite another face to us; and I am apt to think, would be inconsistent with our being, or at least well-being in this part of the universe, which we inhabit. . . . If our sense of hearing were but 1000 times quicker than it is, how would a perpetual noise distract us. . . . Nay, if that most instructive of our senses, seeing, were in any man 1000 or 100000 times more acute than it is now by the best microscope, things several millions of times less than the smallest object of his sight now, would then be visible to his naked eyes, and so he would come nearer the discovery of the texture and motion of the minute parts of corporeal things; and in many of them, probably get *ideas* of their internal constitutions: but then he would be in a quite different world from other people: nothing would appear the same to him, and others: the visible *ideas* of everything would be different. So that I doubt, whether he, and the rest of men, could discourse concerning the objects of sight; or have any communication about colors, their appearances being so wholly different. And, perhaps, such a quickness and tenderness of sight could not endure bright sunshine, or so much as open daylight; nor take in but a very small part of any object at once, and that too only at a very near distance. And if by the help of such microscopical eyes, (if I may so call them,) a man could penetrate farther than ordinary into the secret composition, and radical texture of bodies, he would not make any great advantage by the change, if such an acute sight would not serve to conduct him to the market and exchange; if he could not see things, he was to avoid, at a convenient distance; nor distinguish things he had to do with, by those sensible qualities others do. . . .

. . . .

14. *Complex* ideas *of substances.* But to return to the matter in hand, the *ideas* we have of substances, and the ways we come by them, I say *our specific* ideas *of substances* are nothing else but *a collection of a certain number of simple* ideas, *considered as united in one thing.* . . .

15. Ideas *of spiritual substances, as clear as of bodily substances.* Besides the complex *ideas* we have of material sensible substances, of which I have last spoken, by the simple *ideas* we have taken from those operations of our own minds, which we experiment daily in our own selves, as thinking, understanding, willing, knowing, and power of beginning motion, *&c.* co-existing in some substance, we are able to frame *the complex* idea *of an immaterial spirit.* And thus by putting together the *ideas* of thinking, perceiving, liberty, and power of moving themselves and other things, we have as clear a perception,

and notion of immaterial substances, as we have of material. . . . For our *idea* of substance, is equally obscure, or none at all, in both; it is but a supposed, I know not what, to support those *ideas,* we call accidents. . . .

16. *No* idea *of abstract substance.* By the complex *idea* of extended, figured, colored, and all other sensible qualities, which is all that we know if it, we are as far from the *idea* of the substance of body, as if we knew nothing at all: *nor* after all the acquaintance and familiarity, which we imagine we *have* with matter, and the many qualities *men* assure themselves they perceive and know in bodies, will it, perhaps, upon examination be found, that they have any *more, or clearer, primary* ideas *belonging to body, than they have belonging to immaterial spirit.*

17. *The cohesion of solid parts, and impulse, the primary* ideas *of body. The primary* ideas *we have peculiar to body,* as contradistinguished to spirit, *are the cohesion of solid,* and consequently separable *parts, and a power of communicating motion by impulse.* These, I think, are the original *ideas* proper and peculiar to body: for figure is but the consequence of finite extension.

18. *Thinking and motivity, the primary* ideas *of spirit. The* ideas *we have* belonging, and *peculiar to spirit, are thinking, and will,* or a power of putting body into motion by thought, and, which is consequent to it, liberty. For as body cannot but communicate its motion by impulse, to another body, which it meets with at rest; so the mind can put bodies into motion, or forbear to do so, as it pleases. The *ideas* of existence, duration, and mobility, are common to them both.

19. *Spirits capable of motion.* There is no reason why it should be thought strange, that I make *mobility belong to spirit:* for having no other *idea* of motion, but change of distance, with other beings, that are considered as at rest; and finding that spirits, as well as bodies, cannot operate, but where they are; and that spirits do operate at several times in several places, I cannot but attribute change of place to all finite spirits: (for of the infinite spirit, I speak not here). . . .

20. Everyone finds in himself, that his soul can think, will, and operate on his body, in the place where that is; but cannot operate on a body, or in a place, an hundred miles distant from it. . . .

. . . .

22. Idea *of soul and body compared.* Let us *compare* then our complex *idea* of an immaterial spirit, with our complex *idea* of body, and see whether there be any more obscurity in one, than in the other, and in which most. Our *idea* of body, as I think, is an extended solid substance, capable of communicating motion by impulse: and our *idea* of our soul, as a immaterial spirit, is of a substance that thinks, and has a power of exciting motion in body, by will, or thought. These, I think, are *our complex* ideas *of soul and body, as contradistinguished;* and now let us examine which has most obscurity in it, and difficulty to be apprehended. I know that people, whose thoughts are immersed in matter, and have so subjected their minds to their senses, that they seldom reflect on anything beyond them, are apt to say, they cannot comprehend a thinking thing, which, perhaps, is true; but I affirm, when they consider it well, they can no more comprehend an extended thing.

23. *Cohesion of solid parts in body, as hard to be conceived as thinking in a soul.* If anyone say, he knows not what 'tis thinks in him; he means he knows not what the substance is of that thinking thing: no more, say I, knows he what the substance is of that solid thing. Farther, if he says he knows not how he thinks; I answer, neither knows he how he is extended; how the solid parts of body are united, or cohere together to make extension. For though the pressure of the particles of air, may account for the *cohesion of several parts of matter,* that are grosser than the particles of air, and have pores less than the corpuscles of air; yet the weight, or pressure of the air, will not explain, nor can be a cause of the coherence of the particles of air themselves. And if the pressure of the æther, or any subtler matter than the air, may unite, and hold fast together the parts of a particle of air, as well as other bodies; yet it cannot make bonds for itself, and hold together the parts, that make up every the least corpuscle of that *materia subtilis.*[20] . . .

. . . .

25. I allow, it is usual for most people to wonder, how anyone should find a difficulty in what they think, they every day observe. Do we not see, will they be ready to say, the parts of bodies stick firmly together? Is there anything more common? And what doubt can there be made of it? And the like, I say, concerning *thinking,* and *voluntary motion:* do we not every moment experiment it in ourselves; and therefore can it be doubted? The matter of fact is clear, I confess; but when we would a little nearer look into

20. *materia subtilis*, subtle (i.e., thin or rarified) matter.

it, and consider how it is done, there, I think, we are at a loss, both in the one, and the other; and can as little understand how the parts of body cohere, as how we ourselves perceive, or move. . . .

. . . .

28. *Communication of motion by impulse, or by thought, equally intelligible.* Another *idea* we have of body, is the power of *communication of motion by impulse;* and of our souls, the power of *exciting motion by thought.* These *ideas,* the one of body, the other of our minds, every day's experience clearly furnishes us with: but if here again we inquire how this is done, we *are equally in the dark.* For in the communication of motion by impulse, wherein as much motion is lost to one body, as is got to the other, which is the ordinariest case, we can have no other conception, but of the passing of motion out of one body into another; which, I think, is as obscure and unconceivable, as how our minds move or stop our bodies by thought; which we every moment find they do. . . . And if we consider the active power of moving, or, as I may call it, *motivity,* it is much clearer in spirit than body; since two bodies, placed by one another at rest, will never afford us the *idea* of a power in the one to move the other, but by a borrowed motion: whereas the mind, every day, affords us *ideas* of an active power of moving of bodies; and therefore it is worth our consideration, whether active power be not the proper attribute of spirits, and passive power of matter. Hence may be conjectured, that created spirits are not totally separate from matter, because they are both active and passive. Pure spirit, *viz.* God, is only active; pure matter is only passive; those beings that are both active and passive we may judge to partake of both. But be that as it will, I think, we have as many, and as clear *ideas* belonging to spirit, as we have belonging to body, the substance of each being equally unknown to us; and the *idea* of thinking in spirit, as clear as of extension in body; and the communication of motion by thought, which we attribute to spirit, is as evident, as that by impulse, which we ascribe to body. . . .

. . . .

30. Ideas *of body and spirit compared.* So that, in short, *the idea* we have *of spirit, compared with the idea* we have *of body,* stands thus: the substance of spirit is unknown to us; and so is the substance of body, equally unknown to us: two primary qualities or properties of body, *viz.* solid coherent parts, and impulse we have distinct clear *ideas* of: so likewise we know, and have distinct clear *ideas* of two primary qualities, or properties of spirit, *viz.*

thinking, and a power of action; *i.e.* a power of beginning, or stopping several thoughts or motions. We have also the *ideas* of several qualities inherent in bodies, and have the clear distinct *ideas* of them: which qualities, are but the various modifications of the extension of cohering solid parts, and their motion. We have likewise the *ideas* of several modes of thinking, *viz.* believing, doubting, intending, fearing, hoping; all which, are but the several modes of thinking. We have also the *ideas* of willing, and moving the body consequent to it, and with the body itself too; for, as has been showed, spirit is capable of motion.

31. *The notion of spirit involves no more difficulty in it, than that of body.* Lastly, if this notion of immaterial spirit may have, perhaps, some difficulties in it, not easy to be explained, we have therefore no more reason to deny, or doubt the existence of such spirits, than we have to deny, or doubt the existence of body; because the notion of body is cumbered with some difficulties very hard, and, perhaps, impossible to be explained, or understood by us. For I would fain have instanced anything in our notion of spirit more perplexed, or nearer a contradiction, than the very notion of body includes in it; the divisibility *in infinitum* of any finite extension, involving us, whether we grant or deny it, in consequences impossible to be explicated, or made in our apprehensions consistent; consequences that carry greater difficulty, and more apparent absurdity, than anything can follow from the notion of an immaterial knowing substance.

32. *We know nothing beyond our simple* ideas. Which we are not at all to wonder at, since we having but some few superficial *ideas* of things, discovered to us only by the senses from without, or by the mind, reflecting on what it experiments in itself within, have no knowledge beyond that, much less of the internal constitution, and true nature of things, being destitute of faculties to attain it. And therefore experimenting and discovering in ourselves knowledge, and the power of voluntary motion, as certainly as we experiment, or discover in things without us, the cohesion and separation of solid parts, which is the extension and motion of bodies; *we have as much reason to be satisfied with our notion of immaterial spirit, as with our notion of body; and the existence of the one, as well as the other.* For it being no more a contradiction, that thinking should exist, separate, and independent from solidity; than it is a contradiction, that solidity should exist, separate, and independent from thinking, they being both but simple *ideas,* independent one from another; and having as clear and distinct *ideas* in us of thinking, as of solidity, I know not, why we may not as well allow a

thinking thing without solidity, *i.e. immaterial* to exist; as a solid thing without thinking, *i.e matter,* to exist; especially since it is no harder to conceive how thinking should exist without matter, than how matter should think. For whensoever we would proceed beyond these simple *ideas,* we have from sensation and reflection, and dive farther into the nature of things, we fall presently into darkness and obscurity, perplexedness and difficulties; and can discover nothing farther, but our own blindness and ignorance. But whichever of these complex *ideas* be clearest, that of body, or immaterial spirit, this is evident, that the simple *ideas* that make them up, are no other than what we have received from sensation or reflection; and so is it of all our other *ideas* of substance, even of God himself.

33. Idea *of God.* For if we examine the *idea* we have of the incomprehensible supreme being, we shall find, that we come by it the same way; and that the complex *ideas* we have both of God, and separate spirits, are made up of the simple *ideas* we receive from *reflection, v.g.* having from what we experiment in ourselves, got the *ideas* of existence and duration; of knowledge and power; of pleasure and happiness, and of several other qualities and powers, which it is better to have, than to be without; when we would frame an *idea* the most suitable we can to the supreme being, we enlarge every one of these with our *idea* of infinity; and so putting them together, make our complex *idea of God.* For that the mind has such a power of enlarging some of its *ideas,* received from sensation and reflection, has been already showed.

34. If I find, that I know some few things, and some of them, or all, perhaps, imperfectly, I can frame an *idea* of knowing twice as many; which I can double again, as often as I can add to number, and thus enlarge my *idea* of knowledge, by extending its comprehension to all things existing, or possible: the same also I can do of knowing them more perfectly; *i.e.* all their qualities, powers, causes, consequences, and relations, *&c.* till all be perfectly known, that is in them, or can any way relate to them, and thus frame the *idea* of infinite or boundless knowledge: the same may also be done of power, till we come to that we call infinite; and also of the duration of existence, without beginning or end; and so frame the *idea* of an eternal being: the degrees or extent, wherein we ascribe existence, power, wisdom, and all other perfection, (which we can have any *ideas* of) to that sovereign being, which we call God, being all boundless and infinite, we frame the best *idea* of him our minds are capable of; all which is done, I say, by enlarging those simple ideas, we have taken from the operations of our own

minds, by reflection; or by our senses, from exterior things, to that vastness, to which infinity can extend them.

35. For it is infinity, which, joined to our *ideas* of existence, power, knowledge, *&c.* makes that complex *idea,* whereby we represent to ourselves the best we can, the supreme being. For though in his own essence, (which certainly we do not know, not knowing the real essence of a pebble, or a fly, or of our own selves,) God be simple and uncompounded; yet, I think, I may say we have no other *idea* of him, but a complex one of existence, knowledge, power, happiness, *&c.* infinite and eternal: which are all distinct *ideas,* and some of them being relative, are again compounded of others; all which being, as has been shown, originally got from *sensation* and *reflection,* go to make up the *idea* or notion we have of God.

36. *No* ideas *in our complex one of spirits, but those got from sensation or reflection.* This farther is to be observed, that there is no *idea* we attribute to God, bating infinity, which is not also a part of our complex *idea* of other spirits. . . .

37. *Recapitulation.* And thus we have seen, *what kind of* ideas *we have of substances of all kinds,* wherein they consist, and how we come by them. From whence, I think, it is very evident.

First, that all our *ideas* of the several sorts of substances, are nothing but collections of simple *ideas,* with a supposition of something, to which they belong, and in which they subsist; though of this supposed something, we have no clear distinct *idea* at all.

Secondly, that all the simple *ideas,* that thus united in one common *substratum* make up our complex *ideas* of several sorts of substances, are no other but such, as we have received from *sensation* or *reflection.* So that even in those, which we think, we are most intimately acquainted with, and come nearest the comprehension of, our most enlarged conceptions, cannot reach beyond those simple *ideas.* . . .

Thirdly, that most of the simple *ideas* , that make up our complex *ideas* of substances, when truly considered, are only powers, however we are apt to take them for positive qualities; *v.g.* the greatest part of the *ideas,* that make our complex *idea* of *gold,* are yellowness, great weight, ductility, fusibility, and solubility, in *aqua regia, &c.* all united together in an unknown *substratum;* all which *ideas,* are nothing else, but so many relations to other substances; and are not really in the gold, considered barely in itself, though they depend on those real, and primary qualities of its internal constitution, whereby it has a fitness, differently to operate, and be operated on by several other substances.

CHAP. XXIV.

Of collective ideas *of substances.*

1. *One* idea. Besides these complex *ideas* of several single substances, as of man, horse, gold, violet, apple, *&c.* the mind has also *complex collective ideas* of substances; which I so call, because such *ideas* are made up of many particular substances considered together, as united into one *idea,* and which so joined, are looked on as one; *v.g.* the *idea* of such a collection of men as make an army, though consisting of a great number of distinct substances, is as much one *idea,* as the *idea* of a man: and the great collective *idea* of all bodies whatsoever signified by the name world, is as much one *idea,* as the *idea* of any the least particle of matter in it; it sufficing, to the unity of any *idea* that it be considered as one representation, or picture, though made up of never so many particulars.

2. *Made by the power of composing in the mind.* These collective *ideas* of substances, the mind makes by its power of composition, and uniting severally either simple or complex *ideas* into one, as it does, by the same faculty make the complex *ideas* of particular substances, consisting of an aggregate of divers simple *ideas,* united in one substance. . . .

. . . .

CHAP. XXV.

Of relation.

1. *Relation what.* Besides the *ideas,* whether simple or complex, that the mind has of things, as they are in themselves, there are others it gets from their comparison one with another. The understanding, in the consideration of anything, is not confined to that precise object: it can carry any *idea,*

as it were, beyond itself, or, at least, look beyond it, to see how it stands in conformity to any other. When the mind so considers one thing, that it does, as it were, bring it to, and set it by another, and carry its view from one to t'other: this is, as the words import, *relation* and *respect;* and the denominations given to positive things, intimating that respect, and serving as marks to lead the thoughts beyond the subject itself denominated, to something distinct from it, are what we call *relatives,* and the things so brought together, *related.* . . .

2. *Relations without correlative terms, not easily perceived.* These, and the like *relations, expressed by relative terms, that have others answering them, with a reciprocal intimation,* as father, and son; bigger, and less; cause, and effect, *are very obvious* to everyone, and everybody, at first sight, perceives the relation. For father, and son; husband and wife, and such other correlative terms, seem so nearly to belong one to another, and, through custom, do so readily chime, and answer one another in people's memories, that upon the naming of either of them, the thoughts are presently carried beyond the thing so named; and nobody overlooks, or doubts of a relation, where it is so plainly intimated. But where languages have failed to give correlative names, there the relation is not always so easily taken notice of. . . . Hence it is, that many of those names, which duly considered, do include evident relations, have been called external denominations. . . .

3. *Some seemingly absolute terms contain relations.* Another sort of *relative terms* there is, which are not looked on to be either relative, or so much as external denominations: *which* yet, under the form and appearance of signifying something absolute in the subject do conceal a tacit, though less observable, relation. Such are the *seemingly positive* terms of *old, great, imperfect,* &c. whereof I shall have occasion to speak more at large in the following chapters.

4. *Relation different from the things related.* This farther may be observed, that the *ideas* of relation, may be the same in men, who have far different *ideas* of the things that are related, or that are thus compared. *v.g.* Those who have far different *ideas* of a *man,* may yet agree in the notion of *father:* which is a notion superinduced to the substance, or man, and refers only to an act of that thing called man; whereby he contributed to the generation of one of his own kind, let man be what it will.

. . . .

7. *All things capable of relation.* Concerning relation in general, these things may be considered:

First, that there is *no one thing,* whether simple *idea,* substance, mode, or relation, or name of either of them, *which is not capable of almost an infinite number* of considerations, in reference to other things: and therefore this makes no small part of men's thoughts and words. . . .

8. *The* ideas *of relations clearer often, than of the subjects related. Secondly,* this farther may be considered concerning *relation,* that though it be not contained in the real existence of things, but something extraneous, and superinduced: yet the *ideas* which relative words stand for, are often clearer, and more distinct, than those of substances to which they do belong. The notion we have of a father, or brother, is a great deal clearer, and more distinct, than we have of a man: or, if you will, *paternity* is a thing whereof 'tis easier to have a clear *idea,* than of *humanity:* and I can much easier conceive what a friend is, then what GOD. . . . The *ideas* then of *relations are capable* at least *of being more perfect and distinct in our minds, than those of substances.* . . . Thus having the notion, that one laid the egg, out of which the other was hatched, I have a clear *idea* of the relation of *dam* and *chick,* between the two cassowaries in *St. James*'s Park; though, perhaps, I have but a very obscure and imperfect *idea* of those birds themselves.

9. *Relations all terminate in simple ideas. Thirdly,* though there be a great number of considerations, wherein things may be compared one with another, and so a multitude of *relations:* yet they *all terminate in,* and are concerned about those *simple ideas,* either of sensation or reflection, which I think to be the whole materials of all our knowledge. To clear this, I shall show it in the most considerable relations, that we have any notion of; and in some that seem to be the most remote from *sense* or *reflection:* which yet will appear to have their *ideas* from thence, and leave it past doubt, that the notions we have of them, are but certain simple *ideas,* and so originally derived from sense or reflection.

10. *Terms leading the mind beyond the subject denominated, are relative. Fourthly,* that *relation* being the considering of one thing with another, which is extrinsical to it, it is evident, that all words, that necessarily lead the mind to any other *ideas,* than are supposed really to exist in that thing, to which the world is applied, are *relative words.* . . .

11. *Conclusion.* Having laid down these premises concerning *relation* in general, I shall now proceed to show, in some instances, how all the *ideas* we have of *relation,* are made up, as the others are, only of simple *ideas;* and that they all, how refined, or remote from sense soever they seem, terminate at last in simple *ideas.* . . .

CHAP. XXVI.

Of cause and effect, and other relations.

1. *Whence their* ideas *got.* In the notice, that our senses take of the constant vicissitude of things, we cannot but observe, that several particular, both qualities, and substances begin to exist; and that they receive this their existence, from the due application and operation of some other being. From this observation, we get our *ideas* of *cause* and *effect.* That which produces any simple or complex *idea,* we denote by the general name *cause;* and that which is produced, *effect.* . . . So that whatever is considered by us, to conduce or operate, to the producing any particular simple *idea,* or collection of simple *ideas,* whether substance, or mode, which did not before exist, has thereby in our minds the relation of a cause, and so is denominated by us.

2. *Creation, generation, making alteration.* Having thus, from what our senses are able to discover, in the operations of bodies on one another, got the notion of *cause* and *effect; viz.* that a *cause* is that which makes any other thing, either simple *idea,* substance, or mode, begin to be; and an *effect* is that, which had its beginning from some other thing. The mind finds no great difficulty, to distinguish the several originals of things into two sorts.

First, when the thing is wholly made new, so that no part thereof did ever exist before; as when a new particle of matter does begin to exist, *in rerum natura,* which had before no being, and this we call *creation.*[21]

Secondly, when a thing is made up of particles, which did all of them before exist, but that very thing, so constituted of pre-existing particles, which considered together make up such a collection of simple *ideas,* had not any *existence* before, as this man, this egg, rose, or cherry, *&c.* And this, when referred to a substance, produced in the ordinary course of nature, by an internal principle, but set on work by, and received from some external agent, or cause, and working by insensible ways, which we perceive not, we

21. *in rerum natura*, in the nature of things.

call *generation;* when the cause is extrinsical, and the effect produced by a sensible separation, or *juxta*position of discernible parts, we call it *making;* and such are all artificial things. When any simple *idea* is produced, which was not in that subject before, we call it *alteration*. . . .

3. *Relations of time. Time* and *place* are also the foundations of very large relations, and all finite beings at least are concerned in them. But having already shown in another place, how we get these *ideas,* it may suffice here to intimate, that most of the denominations of things, received from time, are only relations; thus, when anyone says, that Queen *Elizabeth* lived sixty nine, and reigned forty five years; these words import only the relation of that duration to some other, and means no more but this, that the duration of her existence was equal to sixty nine, and the duration of her government to forty five annual revolutions of the sun; and so are all words, answering, *how long*. . . .

. . . .

5. *Relations of place and extension.* The *relation* also that things have to one another, in their *places* and distances, is very obvious to observe; as above, below, a mile distant from *Charing-cross,* in *England,* and in *London.* But as in duration, so in *extension* and bulk, there are some *ideas* that are relative, which we signify by names, that are thought positive; as *great, and little, are* truly *relations.* For here also having, by observation, settled in our minds the *ideas* of the bigness of several species of things, from those we have been most accustomed to, we make them, as it were, the standards whereby to denominate the bulk of others. Thus we call a great apple, such a one as is bigger than the ordinary sort of those we have been used to. . . .

6. *Absolute terms often stand for relations.* So likewise *weak and strong, are* but *relative denominations* of power, compared to some *idea* we have, at that time, of greater or less power. . . .

CHAP. XXVII.

Of identity and diversity.

1. *Wherein identity consists.* Another occasion, the mind often takes of comparing, is the very being of things, when considering anything as existing at any determined time and place, we compare it with itself existing

at another time, and thereon form the *ideas* of *identity* and *diversity*. When we see anything to be in any place in any instant of time, we are sure, (be it what it will) that it is that very thing, and not another, which at that same time exists in another place, how like and undistinguishable soever it may be in all other respects: and in this consists *identity,* when the *ideas* it is attributed to vary not at all from what they were at that moment, wherein we consider their former existence, and to which we compare the present. For we never finding, nor conceiving it possible, that two things of the same kind should exist in the same place at the same time, we rightly conclude, that whatever exists anywhere at any time, excludes all of the same kind, and is there itself alone. When therefore we demand, whether anything be the same or no, it refers always to something that existed such a time in such a place, which 'twas certain, at that instant, was the same with itself and no other: from whence it follows, that one thing cannot have two beginnings of existence, nor two things one beginning, it being impossible for two things of the same kind, to be or exist in the same instant, in the very same place; or one and the same thing in different places. That therefore that had one beginning is the same thing, and that which had a different beginning in time and place from that, is not the same but divers. That which has made the difficulty about this relation, has been the little care and attention used in having precise notions of the things to which it is attributed.

2. *Identity of substances. Identity of modes.* We have the *ideas* but of three sorts of substances; 1. God. 2. Finite intelligences. 3. *Bodies*. First, God is without beginning, eternal, unalterable, and everywhere; and therefore concerning his identity, there can be no doubt. Secondly, finite spirits having had each its determinate time and place of beginning to exist, the relation to that time and place will always determine to each of them its identity as long as it exists.

Thirdly, the same will hold of every particle of matter, to which no addition or subtraction of matter being made, it is the same. For though these three sorts of substances, as we term them, do not exclude one another out of the same place; yet we cannot conceive but that they must necessarily each of them exclude any of the same kind out of the same place: or else the notions and names of identity and diversity would be in vain, and there could be no such distinction of substances, or anything else one from another. For example, could two bodies be in the same place at the same time; then those two parcels of matter must be one and the same, take them great or little; nay, all bodies must be one and the same. For by the same reason that two particles of matter may be in one place, all bodies may be in one place: which, when it can be supposed, takes away the distinction of identity and diversity, of one and more, and renders it ridiculous. But it being a contradiction, that two or more should be one, identity and diversity are relations and ways of comparing well founded, and of use to the understanding. All other things being but modes or relations ultimately terminated in substances, the identity and diversity of each particular existence of them too will be by the same way determined: only as to things whose existence is in succession, such as are the actions of finite beings, *v.g. motion* and *thought,* both which consist in a continued train of succession, concerning their diversity there can be no question: because each perishing the moment it begins, they cannot exist in different times, or in different places, as permanent beings can at different times exist in distant places; and therefore no motion or thought considered as at different times can be the same, each part thereof having a different beginning of existence.

3. Principium individuationis.[22] From what has been said, 'tis easy to discover, what is so much inquired after, the *principium individuationis,* and that 'tis plain is existence itself, which determines a being of any sort to a particular time and place incommunicable to two beings of the same kind. This though it seems easier to conceive in simple substances or modes; yet when reflected on, is not more difficult in compounded ones, if care be taken to what it is applied; *v.g.* let us suppose an atom, *i.e.* a continued body under one immutable superficies, existing in a determined time and place; 'tis evident, that, considered in any instant of its existence, it is, in that instant, the same with itself. For being, at that instant what it is, and nothing else, it is the same, and so must continue, as long as its existence is continued: for so long it will be the same, and no other. In like manner, if two or more atoms be joined together into the same mass, every one of those atoms will be the same, by the foregoing rule: and whilst they exist united together, the mass, consisting of the same atoms, must be the same mass, or the same body, let the parts be never so differently jumbled: but if one of these atoms be taken away, or one new one added, it is no longer the same mass, or the same body. In the state of living creatures, their identity depends not on a mass of the same particles; but on something else. For in them the variation of great parcels of matter alters not the identity: an oak, growing from a plant to a great tree, and then lopped, is still the same oak:

22. *principium individuationis,* "principle of individuation," the factor responsible for a thing's distinctness from other things.

and a colt grown up to a horse, sometimes fat, sometimes lean, is all the while the same horse: though, in both these cases, there may be a manifest change of the parts: so that truly they are not either of them the same masses of matter, though they be truly one of them the same oak, and the other the same horse. The reason whereof is, that in these two cases of a mass of matter, and a living body, *identity* is not applied to the same thing.

4. *Identity of vegetables.* We must therefore consider wherein an oak differs from a mass of matter, and that seems to me to be in this; that the one is only the cohesion of particles anyhow united, the other such a disposition of them as constitutes the parts of an oak; and such an organization of those parts, as is fit to receive, and distribute nourishment, so as to continue, and frame the wood, bark, and leaves, *&c.* of an oak, in which consists the vegetable life. That being then one plant, which has such an organization of parts in one coherent body, partaking of one common life, it continues to be the same plant, as long as it partakes of the same life, though that life be communicated to new particles of matter vitally united to the living plant, in a like continued organization, conformable to that sort of plants. For this organization being at any one instant in any one collection of *matter,* is in that particular concrete distinguished from all other, and is that individual life, which existing constantly from that moment both forwards and backwards in the same continuity of insensibly succeeding parts united to the living body of the plant, it has that identity, which makes the same plant, and all the parts of it, parts of the same plant, during all the time that they exist united in that continued organization, which is fit to convey that common life to all the parts so united.

5. *Identity of animals.* The case is not so much different in *brutes,* but that anyone may hence see what makes an animal, and continues it the same. Something we have like this in machines, and may serve to illustrate it. For example, what is a watch? 'Tis plain 'tis nothing but a fit organization, or construction of parts, to a certain end, which, when a sufficient force is added to it, it is capable to attain. If we would suppose this machine one continued body, all whose organized parts were repaired, increased or diminished, by a constant addition or separation of insensible parts, with one common life, we should have something very much like the body of an animal, with this difference, that in an animal the fitness of the organization, and the motion wherein life consists, begin together, the motion coming from within; but in machines the force, coming sensibly from without, is often away, when the organ is in order, and well fitted to receive it.

6. *Identity of man.* This also shows wherein the identity of the same *man* consists; *viz.* in nothing but a participation of the same continued life, by constantly fleeting particles of matter, in succession vitally united to the same organized body. He that shall place the *identity* of man in anything else, but like that of other animals in one fitly organized body taken in any one instant, and from thence continued under one organization of life in several successively fleeting particles of matter, united to it, will find it hard, to make an *embryo,* one of years, mad, and sober, the same man, by any supposition, that will not make it possible for *Seth, Ismael, Socrates, Pilate,* St. *Austin,* and *Cæsar Borgia* to be the same man. For if the *identity* of soul alone makes the same man, and there be nothing in the nature of matter, why the same individual spirit may not be united to different bodies, it will be possible, that those men, living in distant ages, and of different tempers, may have been the same man: which way of speaking must be from a very strange use of the word *man,* applied to an *idea,* out of which body and shape is excluded: and that way of speaking would agree yet worse with the notions of those philosophers, who allow of transmigration, and are of opinion that the souls of men may, for their miscarriages, be detruded into the bodies of beasts, as fit habitations with organs suited to the satisfaction of their brutal inclinations. But yet I think nobody, could he be sure that the soul of *Heliogabalus* were in one of his hogs, would yet say that hog were a *man* or *Heliogabalus.*

7. *Identity suited to the* idea. 'Tis not therefore unity of substance that comprehends all sorts of *identity,* or will determine it in every case: but to conceive, and judge of it aright, we must consider what *idea* the word it is applied to stands for: it being one thing to be the same *substance,* another the same *man,* and a third the same *person,* if *person, man,* and *substance,* are three names standing for three different *ideas;* for such as is the *idea* belonging to that name, such must be the *identity;* which if it had been a little more carefully attended to, would possibly have prevented a great deal of that confusion, which often occurs about this matter, with no small seeming difficulties; especially concerning *personal identity,* which therefore we shall in the next place a little consider.

8. *Same man.* An animal is a living organized body; and consequently, the same animal, as we have observed, is the same continued life communicated to different particles of matter, as they happen successively to be united to that organized living body: and that our notion of a *man,* whatever is talked of other definitions, is but of a particular sort of animal, I doubt

not. Since I think I may be confident, that whoever should see a creature of his own shape and make, though it had no more reason all its life, than a *cat* or a *parrot,* would call him still a *man;* or whoever should hear a *cat* or a *parrot* discourse, reason and philosophize, would call or think it nothing but a *cat* or a *parrot;* and say, the one was a dull irrational *man,* and the other a very intelligent rational *parrot*. . . . For I presume 'tis not the *idea* of a thinking or rational being alone, that makes the *idea* of a *man* in most people's sense; but of a body so and so shaped joined to it; and if that be the *idea* of a *man,* the same successive body not shifted all at once, must as well as the same immaterial spirit go to the making of the same *man.*

9. *Personal identity.* This being premised to find wherein *personal identity* consists, we must consider what *person* stands for; which, I think, is a thinking intelligent being, that has reason and reflection, and can consider itself as itself, the same thinking thing in different times and places; which it does only by that consciousness, which is inseparable from thinking, and as it seems to me essential to it: it being impossible for anyone to perceive, without perceiving, that he does perceive. When we see, hear, smell, taste, feel, meditate, or will anything, we know that we do so. Thus it is always as to our present sensations and perceptions: and by this everyone is to himself, that which he calls *self:* it not being considered in this case, whether the same *self* be continued in the same, or divers substances. For since consciousness always accompanies thinking, and 'tis that, that makes everyone to be, what he calls *self;* and thereby distinguishes himself from all other thinking things, in this alone consists *personal identity, i.e.* the sameness of a rational being: and as far as this consciousness can be extended backwards to any past action or thought, so far reaches the identity of that *person;* it is the same *self* now it was then; and 'tis by the same *self* with this present one that now reflects on it, that that action was done.

10. *Consciousness makes personal identity.* But it is farther inquired whether it be the same identical substance. This few would think they had reason to doubt of, if these perceptions, with their consciousness, always remained present in the mind, whereby the same thinking thing would be always consciously present, and, as would be thought, evidently the same to itself. But that which seems to make the difficulty is this, that the consciousness, being interrupted always by forgetfulness, there being no moment of our lives wherein we have the whole train of all our past actions before our eyes in one view: but even the best memories losing the sight of one part whilst they are viewing another; and we sometimes, and that the greatest part of

our lives, not reflecting on our past selves, being intent on our present thoughts, and in sound sleep, having no thoughts at all, or at least none with that consciousness, which remarks our waking thoughts. I say, in all these cases, our consciousness being interrupted, and we losing the sight of our past *selves,* doubts are raised whether we are the same thinking thing; *i.e.* the same substance or no. Which however reasonable, or unreasonable concerns not *personal identity* at all. The question being what makes the same *person,* and not whether it be the same identical substance, which always thinks in the same *person,* which in this case matters not at all. Different substances, by the same consciousness (where they do partake in it) being united into one person; as well by different bodies, by the same life are united into one animal, whose *identity* is preserved, in that change of substances, by the unity of one continued life. For it being the same consciousness that makes a man be himself to himself, *personal identity* depends on that only, whether it be annexed only to one individual substance, or can be continued in a succession of several substances. For as far as any intelligent being can repeat the *idea* of any past action with the same consciousness it had of it at first, and with the same consciousness it has of any present action; so far it is the same *personal self.* For it is by the consciousness it has of its present thoughts and actions, that is is *self* to it*self* now, and so will be the same *self* as far as the same consciousness can extend to actions past or to come; and would be by distance of time, or change of substance, no more two *persons* than a man be two men, by wearing other clothes today than he did yesterday, with a long or short sleep in between: the same consciousness uniting those distant actions into the same *person,* whatever substances contributed to their production.

11. *Personal identity in change of substances.* That this is so, we have some kind of evidence in our very bodies, all whose particles, whilst vitally united to this same thinking conscious self, so that we feel when they are touched, and are affected by, and conscious of good or harm that happens to them, are a part of our *selves; i.e* of our thinking conscious *self.* Thus the limbs of his body is to everyone a part of *himself:* he sympathizes and is concerned for them. Cut off an hand, and thereby separate it from that consciousness, we had of its heat, cold, and other affections; and it is then no longer a part of that which is *himself,* any more than the remotest part of matter. Thus we see the *substance,* whereof *personal self* consisted at one time, may be varied at another, without the change of personal *identity:* there being no question about the same person, though the limbs, which but now were a part of it, be cut off.

12. *Whether in the change of thinking substances.* But the question is, whether if the same substance, which thinks, be changed, it can be the same person, or remaining the same, it can be different persons.

And to this I answer first, this can be no question at all to those, who place thought in a purely material, animal, constitution, void of an immaterial substance. For, whether their supposition be true or no, 'tis plain they conceive personal identity preserved in something else than identity of substance; as animal identity is preserved in identity of life, not of substance. And therefore those, who place thinking in an immaterial substance only, before they can come to deal with these men, must show why personal identity cannot be preserved in the change of immaterial substances, or variety of particular immaterial substances, as well as animal identity is preserved in the change of material substances, or variety of particular bodies; unless they will say, 'tis one immaterial spirit, that makes the same life in brutes; as it is one immaterial spirit that makes the same person in men, which the *Cartesians* at least will not admit, for fear of making brutes thinking things too.[23]

13. But next, as to the first part of the question, whether if the same thinking substance (supposing immaterial substances only to think) be changed, it can be the same person. I answer, that cannot be resolved, but by those, who know what kind of substances they are, that do think; and whether the consciousness of past actions can be transferred from one thinking substance to another. I grant, were the same consciousness the same individual action, it could not: but it being but a present representation of a past action, why it may not be possible, that that may be represented to the mind to have been, which really never was, will remain to be shown. And therefore how far the consciousness of past actions is annexed to any individual agent, so that another cannot possibly have it, will be hard for us to determine, till we know what kind of action it is, that cannot be done with a reflex act of perception accompanying it, and how performed by thinking substances, who cannot think without being conscious of it. But that which we call the *same consciousness,* not being the same individual act, why one intellectual substance may not have represented to it, as done by itself, what it never did, and was perhaps done by some other agent, why I say such a representation may not possibly be without reality of matter of fact, as well as several representations in dreams are, which yet, whilst dreaming, we take for true,

23. The Cartesians are the followers of René Descartes (1596–1650). They believed that animals are mere mechanisms or machines, incapable of thought and feeling.

will be difficult to conclude from the nature of things. And that it never is so, will by us, till we have clearer views of the nature of thinking substances, be best resolved into the goodness of God, who as far as the happiness or misery of any of his sensible creatures is concerned in it, will not by a fatal error of theirs transfer from one to another, that consciousness, which draws reward or punishment with it. How far this may be an argument against those who would place thinking in a system of fleeting animal spirits, I leave to be considered. But yet to return to the question before us, it must be allowed, that if the same consciousness (which, as has been shown, is quite a different thing from the same numerical figure or motion in body) can be transferred from one thinking substance to another, it will be possible, that two thinking substances may make but one person. For the same consciousness being preserved, whether in the same or different substances, the personal identity is preserved.

14. As to the second part of the question, whether the same immaterial substance remaining, there may be two distinct persons; which question seems to me to be built on this, whether the same immaterial being, being conscious of the actions of its past duration, may be wholly stripped of all the consciousness of its past existence, and lose it beyond the power of ever retrieving it again: and so as it were beginning a new account from a new period, have a consciousness that cannot reach beyond this new state. All those who hold pre-existence, are evidently of this mind, since they allow the soul to have no remaining consciousness of what it did in that pre-existent state, either wholly separate from body, or informing any other body; and if they should not, 'tis plain experience would be against them. So that personal identity reaching no farther than consciousness reaches, a pre-existent spirit not having continued so many ages in a state of silence, must needs make different persons. Suppose a Christian *Platonist* or *Pythagorean,* should upon God's having ended all his works of creation the seventh day, think his soul has existed ever since; and should imagine it has revolved in several human bodies, as I once met with one, who was persuaded his had been the soul of *Socrates* (how reasonably I will not dispute. This I know, that in the post he filled, which was no inconsiderable one, he passed for a very rational man, and the press has shown, that he wanted not parts or learning) would anyone say, that he, being not conscious of any of *Socrates's* actions or thoughts, could be the same person with *Socrates?*[24] Let anyone reflect upon himself, and conclude, that he has

24. Christian Platonists sought to combine the philosophy of Plato (428–347 B.C.) with Christian doctrine; Pythagoreans were followers of Pythagoras (c. 570–c. 495 B.C.). Both

in himself an immaterial spirit, which is that which thinks in him, and in the constant change of his body keeps him the same; and is that which he calls himself: let him also suppose it to be the same soul, that was in *Nestor* or *Thersites,* at the siege of *Troy,* (for souls being, as far as we know anything of them in their nature, indifferent to any parcel of matter, the supposition has no apparent absurdity in it) which it may have been, as well as it is now, the soul of any other man: but he, now having no consciousness of any of the actions either of *Nestor* or *Thersites,* does, or can he, conceive himself the same person with either of them? Can he be concerned in either of their actions? Attribute them to himself, or think them his own more than the actions of any other man, that ever existed? So that this consciousness not reaching to any of the actions of either of those men, he is no more one *self* with either of them, than if the soul or immaterial spirit, that now informs him, had been created, and began to exist, when it began to inform his present body, though it were never so true, that the same spirit that informed *Nestor*'s or *Thersites*'s body, were numerically the same that now informs his. For this would no more make him the same person with *Nestor,* than if some of the particles of matter, that were once a part of *Nestor,* were now a part of this man, the same immaterial substance without the same consciousness, no more making the same person by being united to any body, than the same particle of matter without consciousness united to any body, makes the same person. But let him once find himself conscious of any of the actions of *Nestor,* he then finds himself the same person with *Nestor.*

15. And thus we may be able without any difficulty to conceive, the same person at the Resurrection, though in a body not exactly in make or parts the same which he had here, the same consciousness going along with the soul that inhabits it.[25] But yet the soul alone in the change of bodies, would scarce to anyone, but to him that makes the soul the *man,* be enough to make the same *man.* For should the soul of a prince, carrying with it the consciousness of the prince's past life, enter and inform the body of a cobbler as soon as deserted by his own soul, everyone sees, he would be the same person with the prince, accountable only for the prince's actions: but who would say it was the same man? The body too goes to the making the man, and would, I guess, to everybody determine the man in this case,

---

Christian Platonists and Pythagoreans were reputed to believe in the reincarnation or transmigration of souls.

25. The Resurrection is the raising of the dead; see footnote 6.

wherein the soul, with all its princely thoughts about it, would not make another man: but he would be the same cobbler to everyone besides himself. I know that in the ordinary way of speaking, the same person, and the same man, stand for one and the same thing. And indeed everyone will always have a liberty to speak, as he pleases, and to apply what articulate sounds to what *ideas* he thinks fit, and change them as often as he pleases. But yet when we will inquire, what makes the same *spirit, man,* or *person,* we must fix the *ideas* of *spirit, man,* or *person,* in our minds; and having resolved with ourselves what we mean by them, it will not be hard to determine, in either of them, or the like, when it is the *same,* and when not.

16. *Consciousness makes the same person.* But though the same immaterial substance, or soul does not alone, wherever it be, and in whatsoever state, make the same man; yet 'tis plain consciousness, as far as ever it can be extended, should it be to ages past, unites existences, and actions, very remote in time, into the same person, as well as it does the existence and actions of the immediately preceding moment: so that whatever has the consciousness of present and past actions, is the same person to whom they both belong. Had I the same consciousness, that I saw the Ark and *Noah*'s flood, as that I saw an overflowing of the *Thames* last winter, or as that I write now, I could no more doubt that I, that write this now, that saw the *Thames* overflowed last winter, and that viewed the flood at the general deluge, was the same *self,* place that *self* in whatever substance you please, than that I that write this am the same *myself* now whilst I write (whether I consist of all the same substance, material or immaterial, or no) that I was yesterday. For as to this point of being the same *self,* it matters not whether this present *self* be made up of the same or other substances, I being as much concerned, and as justly accountable for any action was done a thousand years since, appropriated to me now by this self-consciousness, as I am, for what I did the last moment.

17. *Self depends on consciousness. Self* is that conscious thinking thing, (whatever substance made up of whether spiritual, or material, simple, or compounded, it matters not) which is sensible, or conscious of pleasure and pain, capable of happiness or misery, and so is concerned for it*self,* as far as that consciousness extends. Thus everyone finds, that whilst comprehended under that consciousness, the little finger is as much a part of it*self,* as what is most so. Upon separation of this little finger, should this consciousness go along with the little finger, and leave the rest of the body, 'tis evident the little finger would be the *person,* the *same person;* and self

then would have nothing to do with the rest of the body. As in this case it is the consciousness that goes along with the substance, when one part is separate from another, which makes the same *person,* and constitutes this inseparable *self:* so it is in reference to substances remote in time. That with which the *consciousness* of this present thinking thing can join itself, makes the same *person,* and is one *self* with it, and with nothing else; and so attributes to it*self,* and owns all the actions of that thing, as its own, as far as that consciousness reaches, and no farther; as everyone who reflects will perceive.

18. *Object of reward and punishment.* In this *personal identity* is founded all the right and justice of reward and punishment; happiness and misery, being that, for which everyone is concerned for *himself,* not mattering what becomes of any substance, not joined to, or affected with that consciousness. For as it is evident in the instance I gave but now, if the consciousness went along with the little finger, when it was cut off, that would be the same *self* which was concerned for the whole body yesterday, as making a part of it*self,* whose actions then it cannot but admit as its own now. Though if the same body should still live, and immediately from the separation of the little finger have its own peculiar consciousness, whereof the little finger knew nothing, it would not at all be concerned for it, as a part of it*self,* or could own any of its actions, or have any of them imputed to him.

19. This may show us wherein *personal identity* consists, not in the identity of substance, but, as I have said, in the identity of *consciousness,* wherein, if *Socrates* and the present Mayor of *Quinborough* agree, they are the same person: if the same *Socrates* waking and sleeping do not partake of the same *consciousness, Socrates* waking and sleeping is not the same person. And to punish *Socrates* waking, for what sleeping *Socrates* thought, and waking *Socrates* was never conscious of, would be no more of right, than to punish one twin for what his brother-twin did, whereof he knew nothing, because their outsides were so alike, that they could not be distinguished; for such twins have been seen.

20. But yet possibly it will still be objected, suppose I wholly lose the memory of some parts of my life, beyond a possibility of retrieving them, so that perhaps I shall never be conscious of them again; yet am I not the same person, that did those actions, had those thoughts, that I was once conscious of, though I have now forgot them? To which I answer, that we must here take notice what the word *I* is applied to, which in this case is the man

only. And the same man being presumed to be the same person, *I* is easily here supposed to stand also for the same person. But if it be possible for the same man to have distinct incommunicable consciousnesses at different times, it is past doubt the same man would at different times make different persons; which, we see, is the sense of mankind in the solemnest declaration of their opinions, human laws not punishing the *madman* for the *sober man's* actions, nor the *sober man* for what the *madman* did, thereby making them two persons; which is somewhat explained by our way of speaking in *English,* when we say such an one *is not himself,* or is *besides himself;* in which phrases it is insinuated, as if those who now, or, at least, first used them, thought, that *self* was changed, the *self*same person was no longer in that man.

21. *Difference between identity of man and person.* But yet 'tis hard to conceive, that *Socrates* the same individual man should be two persons. To help us a little in this, we must consider what is meant by *Socrates,* or the same individual *man.*

First, it must be either the same individual, immaterial, thinking substance; in short, the same numerical soul, and nothing else.

Secondly, or the same animal, without regard to an immaterial soul.

Thirdly, or the same immaterial spirit united to the same animal.

Now take which of these suppositions you please, it is impossible to make personal identity to consist in anything but consciousness; or reach any farther than that does.

For by the first of them, it must be allowed possible that a man born of different women, and in distant times, may be the same man. A way of speaking, which whoever admits, must allow it possible, for the same man to be two distinct persons, as any two that have lived in different ages without the knowledge of one another's thoughts.

By the second and third, *Socrates* in this life, and after it, cannot be the same man any way, but by the same consciousness; and so making *human identity* to consist in the same thing wherein we place *personal identity,* there will be no difficulty to allow the same man to be the same person. But then they who place *human identity* in consciousness only, and not in something else, must consider how they will make the infant *Socrates* the same man with *Socrates* after the Resurrection. But whatsoever to some men makes a *man,* and consequently the same individual man, wherein perhaps few are agreed, personal identity can by us be placed in nothing but consciousness (which is that alone which makes what we call *self*) without involving us in great absurdities.

22. But is not a man drunk and sober the same person, why else is he punished for the fact he commits when drunk, though he be never afterwards conscious of it? Just as much the same person, as a man that walks, and does other things in his sleep, is the same person, and is answerable for any mischief he shall do in it. Human laws punish both with a justice suitable to their way of knowledge: because in these cases, they cannot distinguish certainly what is real, what counterfeit; and so the ignorance in drunkenness or sleep is not admitted as a plea. For though punishment be annexed to personality, and personality to consciousness, and the drunkard perhaps be not conscious of what he did; yet human judicatures justly punish him; because the fact is proved against him, but want of consciousness cannot be proved for him. But in the great day,wherein the secrets of all hearts shall be laid open, it may be reasonable to think, no one shall be made to answer for what he knows nothing of; but shall receive his doom, his conscience accusing or excusing him.

23. *Consciousness alone makes self.* Nothing but consciousness can unite remote existences into the same person, the identity of substance will not do it. For whatever substance there is, however framed, without consciousness, there is no person: and a carcass may be a person, as well as any sort of substance be so without consciousness.

Could we suppose two distinct incommunicable consciousnesses acting the same body, the one constantly by day, the other by night; and on the other side the same consciousness acting by intervals two distinct bodies: I ask in the first case, whether the *day* and the *night-man* would not be two as distinct persons, as *Socrates* and *Plato;* and whether in the second case, there would not be one person in two distinct bodies, as much as one man is the same in two distinct clothings. Nor is it at all material to say, that this same, and this distinct *consciousness* in the cases above-mentioned, is owing to the same and distinct immaterial substances, bringing it with them to those bodies, which whether true or no, alters not the case: since 'tis evident the *personal identity* would equally be determined by consciousness, whether that consciousness were annexed to some individual immaterial substance or no. For granting that the thinking substance in man must be necessarily supposed immaterial, 'tis evident, that immaterial thinking thing may sometimes part with its past consciousness, and be restored to it again, as appears in the forgetfulness men often have of their past actions, and the mind many times recovers the memory of a past consciousness, which it had lost for twenty years together. Make these intervals of memory and forgetfulness to take their turns regularly by day and night, and you have two persons with the same immaterial spirit, as much as in the former instance two persons with the same body. So that *self* is not determined by identity or diversity of substance, which it cannot be sure of, but only by identity of consciousness.

24. Indeed it may conceive the substance whereof it is now made up, to have existed formerly, united in the same conscious being: but consciousness removed, that substance is no more it*self,* or makes no more a part of it, than any other substance, as is evident in the instance, we have already given, of a limb cut off, of whose heat, or cold, or other affections, having no longer any consciousness, it is no more of a man's self than any other matter of the universe. In like manner it will be in reference to any immaterial substance, which is void of that consciousness whereby I am my*self* to my*self:* if there be any part of its existence, which I cannot upon recollection join with that present consciousness, whereby I am now my*self,* it is in that part of its existence no more my*self,* than any other immaterial being. For whatsoever any substance has thought or done, which I cannot recollect, and by my consciousness make my own thought and action, it will no more belong to me, whether a part of me thought or did it, than if it had been thought or done by any other immaterial being anywhere existing.

25. I agree the more probable opinion is, that this consciousness is annexed to, and the affection of one individual immaterial substance.

But let men according to their divers hypotheses resolve of that as they please. This every intelligent being, sensible of happiness or misery, must grant, that there is something that is *himself,* that he concerned for, and would have happy; that this *self* has existed in a continued duration more than one instant, and therefore 'tis possible may exist, as it has done, months and years to come, without any certain bounds to be set to its duration; and may be the same *self,* by the same consciousness, continued on for the future. And thus, by this consciousness, he finds himself to be the *same self* which did such or such an action some years since, by which he comes to be happy or miserable now. In all which account of *self,* the same numerical substance is not considered, as making the same *self:* but the same continued consciousness, in which several substances may have been united, and again separated from it, which, whilst they continued in a vital union with that, wherein this consciousness then resided, made a part of that same *self.* Thus any part of our bodies vitally united to that, which is conscious in us, makes a part of our *selves:* but upon separation from the vital union, by which that consciousness is communicated, that, which a moment since was part of our *selves,* is now no more so, than a part of another man's *self* is part of me; and 'tis not impossible, but in a little time may become a real part of another person. And so we have the same numerical substance become a part of two different persons; and the same person preserved under the change of various substances. Could we suppose any spirit wholly stripped of all its memory or consciousness of past actions, as we find our minds always are of a great part of ours, and sometimes of them all, the union or separation of such a spiritual substance would make no variation of personal identity, any more than that of any particle of matter does. Any substance vitally united to the present thinking being, is part of that very *same self* which now is: anything united to it by a consciousness of former actions makes also a part of the *same self,* which is the same both then and now.

26. *Person a forensic term. Person,* as I take it, is the name for this *self.* Wherever a man finds, what he calls *himself,* there I think another may say is the same *person.* It is a forensic term appropriating actions and their merit; and so belongs only to intelligent agents capable of a law, and happiness and misery. This personality extends it*self* beyond present existence to what is past, only by consciousness, whereby it becomes concerned and accountable, owns and imputes to it*self* past actions, just upon the same ground, and for the same reason, that it does the present. All which is founded in a concern for happiness the unavoidable concomitant of consciousness, that which is conscious of pleasure and pain, desiring, that that *self,* that is conscious, should be happy. And therefore whatever past actions it cannot reconcile or appropriate to that present *self* by consciousness, it can be no more concerned in, than if they had never been done: and to receive pleasure or pain; *i.e.* reward or punishment, on the account of any such action, is all one, as to be made happy or miserable in its first being, without any demerit at all. For supposing a man punished now, for what he had done in another life, whereof he could be made to have no consciousness at all, what difference is there between that punishment, and being created miserable? And therefore conformable to this, the apostle tells us, that at the great day, when everyone shall *receive according to his doings, the secrets of all hearts shall be laid open.*[26] The sentence shall be justified by the consciousness all persons shall have, that they *themselves* in what bodies soever they appear, or what substances soever that consciousness adheres

26. *receive according to . . . doings,* 2 Corinthians 5:10; *the secrets . . . shall be . . . open,* 1 Corinthians 14:25.

to, are the *same,* that committed those actions, and deserve that punishment for them.

27. I am apt enough to think I have in treating of this subject made some suppositions that will look strange to some readers, and possibly they are so in themselves. But yet I think, they are such, as are pardonable in this ignorance we are in of the nature of that thinking thing, that is in us, and which we look on as our*selves*. Did we know what it was, or how it was tied to a certain system of fleeting animal spirits; or whether it could, or could not perform its operations of thinking and memory out of a body organized as ours is; and whether it has pleased God, that no one such spirit shall ever be united to any but one such body, upon the right constitution of whose organs its memory should depend, we might see the absurdity of some of those suppositions I have made. But taking, as we ordinarily now do, (in the dark concerning these matters) the soul of a man, for an immaterial substance, independent from matter, and indifferent alike to it all, there can from the nature of things, be no absurdity at all, to suppose, that the same soul may, at different times be united to different bodies, and with them make up, for that time, one man; as well as we suppose part of a sheep's body yesterday should be a part of a man's body tomorrow, and in that union make a vital part of *Melibœus* as well as it did of his ram.

28. *The difficulty from ill use of names.* To conclude, whatever substance begins to exist, it must, during its existence, necessarily be the same: whatever compositions of substances begin to exist, during the union of those substances, the concrete must be the same: whatsoever mode begins to exist, during its existence, it is the same: and so if the composition be of distinct substances, and different modes, the same rule holds. Whereby it will appear, that the difficulty or obscurity, that has been about this matter, rather rises from the names ill used, than from any obscurity in things themselves. For whatever makes the specific *idea,* to which the name is applied, if that *idea* be steadily kept to, the distinction of anything into the same, and divers will easily be conceived, and there can arise no doubt about it.

29. *Continued existence makes identity.* For supposing a rational spirit be the *idea* of a *man,* 'tis easy to know, what is the *same man, viz.* the *same spirit,* whether separate or in a body will be the *same man.* Supposing a rational spirit vitally united to a body of a certain conformation of parts to make a *man,* whilst that rational spirit, with that vital conformation of parts,

though continued in a fleeting successive body, remains, it will be the *same man*. But if to anyone the *idea* of a *man* be, but the vital union of parts in a certain shape; as long as that vital union and shape remains, in a concrete no otherwise the same, but by a continued succession of fleeting particles, it will be the same *man*. For whatever be the composition whereof the complex *idea* is made, whenever existence makes it one particular thing under any denomination, the same existence continued, preserves it the same individual under the same denomination.

CHAP. XXVIII.
Of other relations.

1. Besides the before-mentioned occasions of time, place, and causality of comparing, or referring things one to another, there are, as I have said, infinite others. . . .

2. *Natural*. . . . Another occasion of comparing things together, or considering one thing, so as to include in that consideration some other thing, is the circumstances of their origin or beginning; which being not afterwards to be altered, make the relations, depending thereon, as lasting as the subjects to which they belong; *v.g. father* and *son, brothers, cousin-germains,* &c. . .; and these I call *natural relations:* wherein we may observe, that mankind have fitted their notions and words to the use of common life, and not to the truth and extent of things. For 'tis certain, that in reality, the relation is the same, betwixt the begetter, and the begotten, in the several races of other animals, as well as men: but yet 'tis seldom said, this bull is the grandfather of such a calf; or that two pigeons are cousin-germains. . . .

3. *Instituted*. . . . Sometimes the foundation of considering things, with reference to one another, is some act, whereby anyone comes by a moral right, power, or obligation to do something. Thus a *general* is one, that has power to command an army; and an army under a general, is a collection of armed men, obliged to obey one man. A *citizen,* or a *burgher,* is one who has a right to certain privileges in this or that place. All this sort depending upon men's wills, or agreement in society, I call *instituted,* or *voluntary;* and may be distinguished from the natural, in that they are most, if not all of them, some way or other alterable, and separable from the persons, to

whom they have sometimes belonged, though neither of the substances, so related, be destroyed. . . .

4. *Moral*. . . . There is another sort of relation, which is the conformity, or disagreement, men's voluntary actions have to a rule, to which they are referred, and by which they are judged of: which, I think, may be called *moral relations;* as being that, which denominates our moral actions, and deserves well to be examined, there being no part of knowledge wherein we should be more careful to get determined *ideas,* and avoid, as much as may be, obscurity and confusion. Human actions, when with their various ends, objects, manners, and circumstances, they are framed into distinct complex *ideas,* are, as has been shown, so many *mixed modes,* a great part whereof have names annexed to them. Thus supposing gratitude to be a readiness to acknowledge and return kindness received; polygamy to be the having more wives than one at once: when we frame these notions thus in our minds, we have there so many determined *ideas* of mixed modes. But this is not all that concerns our actions; it is not enough to have determined *ideas* of them, and to know what names belong to such and such combinations of *ideas*. We have a farther and greater concernment, and that is, to know whether such actions so made up, are morally good, or bad.

5. *Moral good and evil*. Good and evil, as has been shown, B. II. Ch. xx. §.2. and Ch. xxi §.42. are nothing but pleasure or pain, or that which occasions, or procures pleasure or pain to us. *Morally good and evil* then, is only the conformity or disagreement of our voluntary actions to some law, whereby good or evil is drawn on us, from the will and power of the lawmaker; which good and evil, pleasure or pain, attending our observance, or breach of the law, by the decree of the lawmaker, is that we call *reward* and *punishment*.

6. *Moral rules*. Of these *moral rules,* or laws, to which men generally refer, and by which they judge of the rectitude or pravity of their actions, there seem to me to be *three sorts,* with their three different enforcements, or reward and punishments. For since it would be utterly in vain, to suppose a rule set to the free actions of man, without annexing to it some enforcement of good and evil, to determine his will, we must, wherever we suppose a law, suppose also some reward or punishment annexed to that law. . . . This, if I mistake not, is the true nature of all *law,* properly so called.

7. *Laws*. The *laws* that men generally refer their actions to, to judge of their rectitude, or obliquity, seem to me to be these three. 1. The *divine* law.

2. The *civil* law. 3. The law of *opinion* or *reputation,* if I may so call it. By the relation they bear to the first of these, men judge whether their actions are sins, or duties; by the second, whether they be criminal, or innocent; and by the third, whether they be virtues or vices.

8. *Divine law, the measure of sin and duty. First,* the *divine* law, whereby I mean, that law which God has set to the actions of men, whether promulgated to them by the light of nature, or the voice of revelation. That God has given a rule whereby men should govern themselves, I think there is nobody so brutish as to deny. He has a right to do it, we are his creatures: he has goodness and wisdom to direct our actions to that which is best: and he has power to enforce it by rewards and punishments, of infinite weight and duration, in another life: for nobody can take us out of his hands. This is the only true touchstone of *moral rectitude;* and by comparing them to this law, it is, that men judge of the most considerable *moral good* or *evil* of their actions; that is, whether as *duties, or sins,* they are like to procure them happiness, or misery, from the hands of the ALMIGHTY.

9. *Civil law, the measure of crimes and innocence. Secondly,* the *civil* law, the rule set by the commonwealth, to the actions of those, who belong to it, is another rule, to which men refer their actions, to judge whether they be *criminal,* or no. . . .

10. *Philosophical law, the measure of virtue and vice. Thirdly,* the *law of opinion or reputation.* Virtue and vice are names pretended, and supposed everywhere to stand for actions in their own nature right and wrong: and as far as they really are so applied, they so far are coincident with the *divine law* above-mentioned. But yet, whatever is pretended, this is visible, that these names, *virtue* and *vice,* in the particular instances of their application, through the several nations and societies of men in the world, are constantly attributed only to such actions, as in each country and society are in reputation or discredit. . . . For though men uniting into politic societies, have resigned up to the public the disposing of all their force, so that they cannot employ it against any fellow-citizen, any farther than the law of the country directs: yet they retain still the power of thinking well or ill; approving or disapproving of the actions of those whom they live amongst, and converse with: and by this approbation and dislike they establish amongst themselves, what they will call *virtue* and *vice*.

. . . .

14. *Morality is the relation of actions to these rules.* Whether the rule, to which, as to a touchstone, we bring our voluntary actions, to examine them by, and try their goodness, and accordingly to name them; which is, as it were, the mark of the value we set upon them: whether, I say, we take that rule from the fashion of the country, or the will of a lawmaker, the mind is easily able to observe the relation any action has to it; and to judge, whether the action agrees, or disagrees with the rule: and so has a notion of *moral goodness or evil,* which is either conformity, or not conformity of any action to that rule: and therefore, is often called moral rectitude. This rule being nothing but a collection of several simple *ideas,* the conformity thereto is but so ordering the action, that the simple *ideas,* belonging to it, may correspond to those, which the law requires. And thus we see, how moral beings and notions, are founded on, and terminated in these simple *ideas,* we have received from sensation or reflection. For example, let us consider the complex *idea,* we signify by the word murder: and when we have taken it asunder, and examined all the particulars, we shall find them to amount to a collection of simple *ideas,* derived from reflection or sensation, *viz. first,* from reflection on the operations of our own minds, we have the *ideas* of willing, considering, purposing beforehand, malice, or wishing ill to another; and also of life, or perception, and self-motion. *Secondly,* from sensation, we have the collection of those simple sensible *ideas* which are to be found in a man, and of some action, whereby we put an end to perception, and motion in the man; all which simple *ideas,* are comprehended in the word murder. This collection of simple *ideas,* being found by me to agree or disagree, with the esteem of the country I have been bred in; and to be held by most men there, worthy praise, or blame, I call the action virtuous or vicious: if I have the will of a supreme, invisible lawmaker for my rule: then, as I supposed the action commanded, or forbidden by God, I call it good or evil, sin or duty: and if I compare it to the civil law, the rule made by the legislative of the country, I call it lawful, or unlawful, a crime, or no crime. . . .

15. To conceive rightly of *moral actions,* we must take notice of them, under this twofold consideration. *First,* as they are in themselves each made up of such a collection of simple *ideas.* . . . *Secondly,* our actions are considered, as good, bad, *or* indifferent; and in this respect, they are *relative,* it being their conformity to, or disagreement with some rule, that makes them to be regular or irregular, good or bad: and so, as far as they are compared with a rule, and thereupon denominated, they come under relation. . . .

. . . .

17. *Relations innumerable*. . . . 'Twould make a volume, to go over all sorts of *relations:* 'tis not therefore to be expected, that I should here mention them all. It suffices to our present purpose, to show by these, what the *ideas* are, we have *of* this comprehensive consideration, called *relation*. Which is so *various,* and the occasions of it so *many,* (as many as there can be of comparing things one to another,) that it is not very easy to reduce it to rules, or under just heads. . . .

. . . .

CHAP. XXIX.

Of clear and obscure, distinct and confused ideas.

1. Ideas *some clear and distinct, others obscure and confused*. Having shown the original of our *ideas,* and taken a view of their several sorts; considered the difference between the simple and the complex; and observed how the complex ones are divided into those of modes, substances and relations, all which, I think, is necessary to be done by anyone, who would acquaint himself thoroughly with the progress of the mind, in its apprehension and knowledge of things, it will, perhaps, be thought I have dwelt long enough upon the examination of *ideas*. I must, nevertheless, crave leave to offer some few other considerations concerning them. The first is, that some are *clear,* and others *obscure;* some *distinct,* and others *confused*.

2. *Clear and obscure, explained by sight*. The perception of the mind being most aptly explained by words relating to the sight, we shall best understand what is meant by *clear* and *obscure* in our *ideas,* by reflecting on what we call *clear* and *obscure* in the objects of sight. Light being that which discovers to us visible objects, we give the name of *obscure,* to that, which is not placed in a light sufficient to discover minutely to us the figure and colors, which are observable in it, and which, in a better light, would be discernible. In like manner, our *simple ideas* are *clear,* when they are such as the objects themselves, from whence they were taken, did or might, in a well-ordered sensation or perception, present them. Whilst the memory retains them thus, and can produce them to the mind, whenever it has occasion to consider them, they are *clear ideas*. So far as they either want

anything of the original exactness, or have lost any of their first freshness, and are, as it were, faded or tarnished by time, so far are they *obscure. Complex ideas,* as they are made up of simple ones; so they are *clear,* when the *ideas* that go to their composition are clear; and the number and order of those simple *ideas,* that are the ingredients of any complex one, is determinate and certain.

. . . .

4. *Distinct and confused, what.* As a *clear idea* is that whereof the mind has such a full and evident perception, as it does receive from an outward object operating duly on a well-disposed organ, so a *distinct idea* is that wherein the mind perceives a difference from all other; and a *confused idea* is such an one, as is not sufficiently distinguishable from another, from which it ought to be different.

. . . .

10. *Confusion without reference to names, hardly conceivable. . . .* We may observe how much *names,* as supposed steady signs of things, and by their difference to stand for, and keep things distinct, that in themselves are different, are the *occasion of denominating* ideas *distinct or confused,* by a secret and unobserved reference, the mind makes of its *ideas* to such names. This, perhaps, will be fuller understood, after what I say of words, in the third book, has been read and considered. But without taking notice of such a reference of *ideas* to distinct names, as the signs of distinct things, it will be hard to say what a *confused idea* is. And therefore when a man designs, by any name, a sort of things, or any one particular thing, distinct from all others, the complex *idea* he annexes to that name is the more distinct, the more particular the *ideas* are, and the greater and more determinate the number and order of them is, whereof it is made up. For the more it has of these, the more it has still of the perceivable differences, whereby it is kept separate and distinct from all *ideas* belonging to other names, even those that approach nearest to it, and thereby all confusion with them is avoided.

11. *Confusion concerns always two* ideas. *Confusion,* making it a difficulty to separate two things that should be separated, *concerns always two ideas;* and those most, which most approach one another. Whenever therefore we suspect any *idea* to be *confused,* we must examine what other it is in danger to be confounded with, or which it cannot easily be separated from, and that will always be found an *idea* belonging to another name, and so should

be a different thing, from which yet it is not sufficiently distinct: being either the same with it, or making a part of it, or, at least, as properly called by that name, as the other it is ranked under; and so keeps not that difference from that other *idea,* which the different names import.

. . . .

13. *Complex* ideas *may be distinct in one part, and confused in another.* Our *complex ideas* being made up of collections, and so variety of simple ones, *may* accordingly *be very clear and distinct in one part, and very obscure and confused in another.* In a man who speaks of a *chiliaëdron,* or a body of a thousand sides, the *idea* of the figure may be very confused, though that of the number be very distinct; so that he being able to discourse and demonstrate concerning that part of his complex *idea,* which depends upon the number of a thousand, he is apt to think, he has a distinct *idea* of a *chiliaëdron;* though it be plain, he has no precise *idea* of its figure, so as to distinguish it, by that, from one that has but 999 sides: the not observing whereof, causes no small error in men's thoughts, and confusion in their discourses.

. . . .

15. *Instance in eternity.* Having frequently in our mouths the name *eternity,* we are apt to think, we have a positive comprehensive *idea* of it, which is as much as to say, that there is no part of that duration, which is not clearly contained in our *idea.* 'Tis true, that he that thinks so, may have a very clear *idea* of duration; he may also have a clear *idea* of a very great length of duration; he may also have a clear *idea* of the comparison of that great one, with still a greater: but it not being possible for him to include in his *idea* of any duration, let it be as great as it will, the whole extent together of a duration, where he supposes no end, that part of his *idea,* which is still beyond the bounds of that large duration, he represents to his own thoughts, is very obscure and undetermined. And hence it is, that in disputes and reasonings concerning eternity, or any other *infinite,* we are very apt to blunder, and involve ourselves in manifest absurdities.

16. *Divisibility of matter.* In matter, we have no clear *ideas* of the smallness of parts, much beyond the smallest, that occur to any of our senses: and therefore when we talk of the divisibility of matter *in infinitum,* though we have clear *ideas* of division and divisibility, and have also clear *ideas* of parts,

made out of a whole, by division; yet we have but very obscure, and confused *ideas* of corpuscles, or minute bodies, so to be divided, when by former divisions, they are reduced to a smallness, much exceeding the perception of any of our senses; and so all that we have clear, and distinct *ideas* of, is of what division in general, or abstractly is, and the relation of *totum* and *pars:* but of the bulk of the body, to be thus infinitely divided after certain progressions, I think, we have no clear, nor distinct *idea* at all.[27] . . . And so likewise in eternity, he that has an *idea* of but four years, has as much a positive complete *idea* of eternity, as he that has one of 400,000,000 of years: for what remains of eternity beyond either of these two numbers of years, is as clear to the one as the other; *i.e.* neither of them has any clear positive *idea* of it at all. For he that adds only 4 years to 4, and so on, shall as soon reach eternity, as he that adds 400,000,000 of years, and so on; or if he please, doubles the increase as often as he will: the remaining abyss being still as far beyond the end of all these progressions, as it is from the length of a day, or an hour. For nothing finite bears any proportion to infinite; and therefore our *idea*s, which are all finite, cannot bear any. Thus it is also in our *idea* of *extension,* when we increase it by addition, as well as when we diminish it by division, and would enlarge our thoughts to infinite space. After a few doublings of those *ideas* of extension, which are the largest we are accustomed to have, we lose the clear distinct *idea* of that space: it becomes a confusedly great one, with a surplus of still greater; about which, when we would argue, or reason, we shall always find ourselves at a loss; confused *ideas,* in our arguings and deductions from that part of them which is confused, always leading us into confusion.

CHAP. XXX.
Of real and fantastical ideas.

1. *Real* ideas *are conformable to their archetypes.* Besides what we have already mentioned, concerning *idea*s, other considerations belong to them, in reference to things from whence they are taken, or which they may be supposed to represent; and thus, I think, they may come under a threefold distinction; and are,

27. *totum*, whole; *pars*, part.

First, either real, or fantastical.

Secondly, adequate, or inadequate.

Thirdly, true, or false.

First, by *real ideas*, I mean such as have a foundation in nature; such as have a conformity with the real being, and existence of things, or with their archetypes. *Fantastical* or *chimerical,* I call such as have no foundation in nature, nor have any conformity with that reality of being, to which they are tacitly referred, as to their archetypes. If we examine the several sorts of *ideas* before-mentioned, we shall find, that,

2. *Simple* ideas *all real.* First, our *simple* ideas *are all real,* all agree to the reality of things. Not that they are all of them the images, or representations of what does exist, the contrary whereof, in all but the primary qualities of bodies, has been already showed. But though whiteness and coldness are no more in snow, than pain is; yet those *ideas* of whiteness, and coldness, pain, *&c.* being in us the effects of powers in things without us, ordained by our maker, to produce in us such sensations; they are real *ideas* in us, whereby we distinguish the qualities, that are really in things themselves. For these several appearances, being designed to be the marks, whereby we are to know, and distinguish things, which we have to do with; our *ideas* do as well serve us to that purpose, and are as real distinguishing characters, whether they be only constant effects, or else exact resemblances of something in the things themselves: the reality lying in that steady correspondence, they have with the distinct constitutions of real beings. But whether they answer to those constitutions, as to causes, or patterns, it matters not; it suffices, that they are constantly produced by them. And thus our simple *ideas* are all real and true, because they answer and agree to those powers of things, which produce them in our minds, that being all that is requisite to make them real, and not fictions at pleasure. For in simple *ideas,* (as has been shown,) the mind is wholly confined to the operation of things upon it; and can make to itself no simple *idea,* more than what it has received.

3. *Complex* ideas *are voluntary combinations.* Though the mind be wholly passive, in respect of its simple *ideas:* yet, I think, we may say, it is not so, in respect of its complex *ideas:* for those being combinations of simple *ideas,* put together, and united under one general name; 'tis plain, that the mind of man uses some kind of liberty, in forming those complex *ideas:* how else comes it to pass, that one man's *idea* of gold, or justice, is different from another's, but because he has put in, or left out of his, some simple *idea*

which the other has not? The question then is, which of these are real, and which barely imaginary combinations? What collections agree to the reality of things, and what not? And to this I say, that

4. *Mixed modes made of consistent* ideas *are real. Secondly, mixed modes and relations,* having no other *reality,* but what they have in the minds of men, there is nothing more required to those kind of *ideas,* to make them *real,* but that they be so framed, that there be a possibility of existing conformable to them. These *ideas,* being themselves archetypes, cannot differ from their archetypes, and so *cannot be chimerical,* unless anyone will jumble together in them inconsistent *ideas.* Indeed, as any of them have the names of a known language assigned to them, by which, he that has them in his mind, would signify them to others, so bare possibility of existing is not enough; they must have a conformity to the ordinary signification of the name, that is given them, that they may not be thought fantastical: as if a man would give the name of justice to that *idea,* which common use calls liberality. But this fantasticalness relates more to propriety of speech, than reality of *ideas.* For a man to be undisturbed in danger, sedately to consider what is fittest to be done, and to execute it steadily, is a mixed mode, or a complex *idea* of an action which may exist. But to be undisturbed in danger, without using one's reason or industry, is what is also possible to be; and so is as real an *idea* as the other. Though the first of these having the name courage given to it, may, in respect of that name, be a right or wrong *idea:* but the other, whilst it has not a common received name of any known language assigned to it, is not capable of any deformity, being made with no reference to anything but itself.

5. Ideas *of substances are real, when they agree with the existence of things. Thirdly,* our *complex* ideas *of substances,* being made all of them in reference to things existing without us, and intended to be representations of substances, as they really are, are no farther *real,* than as they are such combinations of simple *ideas,* as are really united, and coexist in things without us. On the contrary, those are *fantastical,* which are made up of such collections of simple *ideas,* as were really never united, never were found together in any substance; *v.g.* a rational creature, consisting of a horse's head, joined to a body of human shape, or such as the *centaurs* are described: or, a body, yellow, very malleable, fusible, and fixed; but lighter than common water: or, an uniform, unorganized body, consisting as to sense, all of similar parts, with perception and voluntary motion joined to it. Whether such substances, as these, can possibly exist, or no, 'tis

probable we do not know: but be that as it will, these *ideas* of substances, being made conformable to no pattern existing that we know; and consisting of such collections of *ideas,* as no substance ever showed us united together, they ought to pass with us for barely imaginary: but much more are those complex *ideas* so, which contain in them any inconsistency or contradiction of their parts.

CHAP. XXXI.

Of adequate and inadequate ideas.

1. *Adequate* ideas, *are such as perfectly represent their archetypes.* Of our real *ideas,* some are adequate, and some are inadequate. Those I call *adequate,* which perfectly represent those archetypes, which the mind supposes them taken from; which it intends them to stand for, and to which it refers them. *Inadequate ideas* are such, which are but a partial, or incomplete representation of those archetypes to which they are referred. Upon which account it is plain,

2. *Simple ideas* all *adequate. First,* that *all our simple* ideas *are adequate.* Because being nothing but the effects of certain powers in things, fitted and ordained by GOD to produce such sensations in us, they cannot but be correspondent, and adequate to those powers: and we are sure they agree to the reality of things. For if sugar produce in us the *ideas,* which we call whiteness, and sweetness, we are sure there is a power in sugar to produce those *ideas* in our minds, or else they could not have been produced by it. And so each sensation answering the power, that operates on any of our senses, the *idea* so produced, is a real *idea,* and not a fiction of the mind, which has no power to produce any simple *idea*; and cannot but be adequate, since it ought only to answer that power: and so all simple *ideas* are adequate. 'Tis true, the things producing in us these simple *ideas,* are but few of them denominated by us, as if they were only the causes of them; but as if those *ideas* were real beings in them. For though fire be called painful to the touch, whereby is signified the power of producing in us the *idea* of pain; yet it is denominated also light, and hot; as if light and heat, were really something in the fire, more than a power to excite these *ideas* in us; and therefore are called *qualities* in, or of the fire. But these being nothing, in truth, but powers to excite such *ideas* in us, I must, in that sense,

be understood, when I speak of secondary *qualities,* as being in things; or of their *idea*s, as being in the objects that excite them in us. Such ways of speaking, though accommodated to the vulgar notions, without which, one cannot be well understood; yet truly signify nothing, but those powers, which are in things, to excite certain sensations or *ideas* in us. Since were there no fit organs to receive the impressions fire makes on the sight and touch; nor a mind joined to those organs to receive the *ideas* of light and heat, by those impressions from the fire, or the sun, there would yet be no more light, or heat in the world, than there would be pain if there were no sensible creature to feel it, though the sun should continue just as it is now, and Mount Aetna flame higher than ever it did. Solidity, and extension, and the termination of it, figure, with motion and rest, whereof we have the *ideas,* would be really in the world as they are, whether there were any sensible being to perceive them or no: and therefore those we have reason to look on, as the real modifications of matter; and such as are the exciting causes of all our various sensations from bodies. But this being an inquiry not belonging to this place, I shall enter no farther into it, but proceed to show, what complex *ideas* are *adequate,* and what not.

3. *Modes are all adequate. Secondly,* our *complex* ideas *of modes,* being voluntary collections of simple *ideas,* which the mind puts together, without reference to any real archetypes, or standing patterns, existing anywhere, *are,* and cannot but be *adequate ideas*. Because they not being intended for copies of things really existing, but for archetypes made by the mind, to rank and denominate things by, cannot want anything: they having each of them that combination of *ideas,* and thereby that perfection which the mind intended they should: so that the mind acquiesces in them, and can find nothing wanting. . . . But in our *ideas* of *substances,* it is otherwise. For there desiring to copy things, as they really do exist; and to represent to ourselves that constitution, on which all their properties depend, we perceive our *ideas* attain not that perfection we intend: we find they still want something, we should be glad were in them; and so are all *inadequate*. But *mixed modes* and *relations,* being archetypes without patterns, and so having nothing to represent but themselves, cannot but be adequate, everything being so to itself. . . .

. . . .

5. *Modes in reference to settled names, may be inadequate*. . . . These *complex* ideas *of modes,* when they are referred by the mind, and intended to

correspond to the *ideas* in the mind of some other intelligent being, expressed by the names we apply to them, they *may be* very deficient, wrong, and *inadequate*. Because they agree not to that, which the mind designs to be their archetype, and pattern: in which respect only, any *idea* of *modes* can be wrong, imperfect, or *inadequate*. And on this account, our *ideas* of *mixed modes* are the most liable to be faulty of any other; but this refers more to proper speaking, than knowing right.

6. Ideas *of substances, as referred to real essences not adequate. Thirdly,* what *ideas we have of substances,* I have above showed: now those *ideas* have in the mind a double reference: 1. Sometimes they are referred to a supposed real essence of each species of things. 2. Sometimes they are only designed to be pictures and representations in the mind, of things that do exist, by *ideas* of those qualities that are discoverable in them. In both which ways, these copies of those originals, and archetypes, *are* imperfect and *inadequate*.

First, it is usual for men to make the names of substances, stand for things, as supposed to have certain real essences, whereby they are of this or that species: and names standing for nothing but the *ideas,* that are in men's minds, they must consequently refer their *ideas* to such real essences, as to their archetypes. That men (especially such as have been bred up in the learning taught in this part of the world) do suppose certain specific essences of substances, which each individual in its several kinds is made conformable to, and partakes of, is so far from needing proof, that it will be thought strange, if anyone should do otherwise. And thus they ordinarily apply the specific names, they rank particular substances under, to things, as distinguished by such specific real essences. Who is there almost, who would not take it amiss, if it should be doubted, whether he called himself man, with any other meaning, than as having the real essence of a man? And yet if you demand, what those real essences are, 'tis plain men are ignorant, and know them not. From whence it follows, that the *ideas* they have in their minds, being referred to real essences as to archetypes which are unknown, must be so far from being *adequate,* that they cannot be supposed to be any representation of them at all. The complex *ideas* we have of substances, are, as it has been shown, certain collections of simple *ideas,* that have been observed or supposed constantly to exist together. But such a complex *idea* cannot be the real essence of any substance; for then the properties we discover in that body, would depend on that complex *idea,* and be deducible from it, and their necessary connection with it be known; as all properties of a triangle depend on, and as far as they are discoverable, are deducible from the complex *idea* of three lines, including a space. But it is plain, that in our complex *ideas* of substances, are not contained such *idea*s, on which all the other qualities, that are to be found in them, do depend. The common *idea* men have of *iron,* is a body of a certain color, weight and hardness; and a property that they look on as belonging to it, is malleableness. But yet this property has no necessary connection with that complex *idea,* or any part of it: and there is no more reason to think, that malleableness depends on that color, weight, and hardness, than that color, or that weight depends on its malleableness. And yet, though we know nothing of these real essences, there is nothing more ordinary, than that men should attribute the sorts of things to such essences. The particular parcel of matter, which makes the ring I have on my finger, is forwardly, by most men, supposed to have a real essence, whereby it is *gold;* and from whence those qualities flow, which I find in it, *viz.* its peculiar color, weight, hardness, fusibility, fixedness, and change of color upon a slight touch of mercury, *&c.* This essence, from which all these properties flow, when I inquire into it, and search after it, I plainly perceive I cannot discover: the farthest I can go is only to presume, that it being nothing but body, its real essence, or internal constitution, on which these qualities depend, can be nothing but the figure, size, and connection of its solid parts; of neither of which, I having any distinct perception at all, I can have no *idea* of its essence, which is the cause that it has that particular shining yellowness; a greater weight than anything I know of the same bulk; and a fitness to have its color changed by the touch of quicksilver. If anyone will say, that the real essence, and internal constitution, on which these properties depend, is not the figure, size, and arrangement or connection of its solid parts, but something else, called its particular *form;* I am farther from having any *idea* of its real essence, than I was before, for I have an *idea* of figure, size, and situation of solid parts in general, though I have none of the particular figure, size, or putting together of parts, whereby the qualities above-mentioned are produced; which qualities I find in that particular parcel of matter, that is on my finger, and not in another parcel of matter, with which I cut the pen I write with. But when I am told, that something besides the figure, size, and posture of the solid parts of that body, is its essence, something called *substantial form,* of that, I confess, I have no *idea* at all, but only of the sound *form;* which is far enough from an *idea* of its real essence, or constitution. The like ignorance as I have of the real essence of this particular substance, I have also of the real essence of all other natural ones: of which essences, I confess, I have no distinct *ideas* at all; and I am apt to suppose others, when they examine their own knowledge, will find in themselves, in this one point, the same sort of ignorance.

7. Now then, when men apply to this particular parcel of matter on my finger, a general name already in use, and denominate it *gold,* do they not ordinarily, or are they not understood to give it that name as belonging to a particular species of bodies, having a real internal essence; by having of which essence, this particular substance comes to be of that species, and to be called by that name? If it be so, as it is plain it is, the name, by which things are marked, as having that essence, must be referred primarily to that essence; and consequently the *idea* to which that name is given, must be referred also to that essence, and be intended to represent it. Which essence, since they, who so use the names, know not, their ideas *of substances* must be *all inadequate* in that respect, as not containing in them that real essence, which the mind intends they should.

8. Ideas *of substances, as collections of their qualities, are all inadequate. Secondly,* those who, neglecting that useless supposition of unknown real essences, whereby they are distinguished, endeavor to copy the substances, that exist in the world, by putting together the *ideas* of those sensible qualities, which are found coexisting in them, though they come much nearer a likeness of them, than those who imagine, they know not what real specific essences: yet they arrive not at perfectly adequate *ideas* of those substances, they would thus copy into their minds: nor do those copies, exactly, and fully, contain all that is to be found in their archetypes. Because those qualities, and powers of substances, whereof we make their complex *ideas,* are so many and various, that no man's complex *idea* contains them all. That our abstract *ideas* of substances, do not contain in them all the simple *ideas,* that are united in the things themselves, is evident, in that men do rarely put into their complex *idea* of any substance, all the simple *ideas* they do know to exist in it. Because endeavoring to make the signification of their specific names as clear, and as little cumbersome as they can, they make their specific *ideas* of the sorts of substances, for the most part, of a few of those simple *ideas* which are to be found in them: but these having no original precedency, or right to be put in, and make the specific *idea,* more than others that are left out, 'tis plain, that both these ways, *our* ideas *of substances* are deficient, and *inadequate*. The simple *ideas* whereof we make our complex ones of substances, are all of them (bating only the figure and bulk of some sorts) powers which being relations to other substances, we can never be sure that we know all the powers, that are in any one body, till we have tried what changes it is fitted to give to, or receive from other substances, in their several ways of application: which being impossible to be tried upon any one body, much less upon all, it is impossible we should

have adequate *ideas* of any substance, made up of a collection of all its properties.

9. Whosoever first light on a parcel of that sort of substance, we denote by the word *gold,* could not rationally take the bulk and figure he observed in that lump, to depend on its real essence, or internal constitution. Therefore those never went into his *idea* of that species of body; but its peculiar color, perhaps, and weight, were the first he abstracted from it, to make the complex *idea* of that species. Which both are but powers; the one to affect our eyes, after such a manner, and to produce in us that *idea,* we call yellow; and the other to force upwards any other body of equal bulk, they being put into a pair of equal scales, one against another. Another, perhaps, added to these, the *ideas* of fusibility, and fixedness, two other passive powers, in relation to the operation of fire upon it; another, its ductility, and solubility in *aqua regia,* two other powers, relating to the operation of other bodies, in changing its outward figure or separation of it, into insensible parts. These, or part of these, put together, usually make the complex *idea* in men's minds, of that sort of body we call *gold.*

10. But no one, who has considered the properties of bodies in general, or this sort in particular, can doubt that this, called *gold,* has infinite other properties, not contained in that complex *idea*. . . .

11. So that *all our complex* ideas *of substances are* imperfect and *inadequate.* Which would be so also in mathematical figures, if we were to have our complex *ideas* of them, only by collecting their properties, in reference to other figures. How uncertain, and imperfect would our *ideas* be of an *ellipsis,* if we had no other *idea* of it, but some few of its properties? Whereas having in our plain *idea,* the whole essence of that figure, we from thence discover those properties, and demonstratively see how they flow, and are inseparable from it.

12. *Simple ideas* ἔκτυπα, *and adequate.*[28] Thus the mind has three sorts of abstract *ideas,* or nominal essences:

First, simple *idea*s, which are ἔκτυπα, or *copies;* but yet certainly *adequate.* Because being intended to express nothing but the power in things to produce in the mind such a sensation, that sensation, when it is produced, cannot but be the effect of that power. . . .

28. ἔκτυπα, ectypes or copies (of an original or archetype).

13. Ideas *of substances are* ἔκτυπα, inadequate. Secondly, the *complex* ideas *of substances are ectypes, copies* too; but not perfect ones, not *adequate* . . . .

14. Ideas *of modes and relations are archetypes, and cannot but be adequate. Thirdly, complex* ideas *of modes and relations are* originals, and *archetypes;* are not copies, nor made after the pattern of any real existence, to which the mind intends them to be conformable, and exactly to answer. . . .

CHAP. XXXII.

Of true and false ideas.

1. *Truth and falsehood properly belong to propositions.* Though truth and falsehood belong, in propriety of speech, only to propositions; yet *ideas* are oftentimes termed *true or false* (as what words are there, that are not used with great latitude, and with some deviation from their strict and proper significations?) Though, I think, that when *ideas* themselves are termed true or false, there is still some secret or tacit proposition, which is the foundation of that denomination: as we shall see, if we examine the particular occasions, wherein they come to be called true or false. In all which, we shall find some kind of affirmation or negation, which is the reason of that denomination. For our *ideas,* being nothing but bare appearances or perceptions in our minds, cannot properly and simply in themselves be said to be *true* or *false,* no more than a single name of anything can be said to be *true* or *false.*

2. *Metaphysical truth contains a tacit proposition.* Indeed, both *ideas* and words, *may* be said to be *true in a metaphysical sense* of the word truth; as all other things, that any way exist, are said to be true, *i.e.* really to be such as they exist. Though in things called *true,* even in that sense, there is, perhaps, a secret reference to our *idea*s, looked upon as the standards of that truth, which amounts to a mental proposition, though it be usually not taken notice of.

3. *No* idea *as an appearance in the mind true or false.* But 'tis not in that metaphysical sense of truth, which we inquire here, when we examine, whether our *ideas* are capable of being *true* or *false;* but in the more ordinary acceptation of those words: and so I say, that the *ideas* in our minds, being

only so many perceptions, or appearances there, none of them are *false.* The *idea* of a centaur, having no more falsehood in it, when it appears in our minds; than the name centaur has falsehood in it, when it is pronounced by our mouths, or written on paper. For truth or falsehood, lying always in some affirmation, or negation, mental or verbal, our *ideas* are *not capable* any of them *of being false,* till the mind passes some judgment on them; that is, affirms or denies something of them.

4. Ideas *referred to anything may be true or false*. Whenever the mind refers any of its *ideas* to anything extraneous to them, they are then *capable to be called true or false*. Because the mind in such a reference, makes a tacit supposition of their conformity to that thing: which supposition, as it happens to be *true* or *false;* so the *ideas* themselves come to be denominated. The most usual cases wherein this happens, are these following:

5. *Other men's* ideas, *real existence, and supposed real essences, are what men usually refer their* ideas *to. First,* when the mind supposes any *idea* it has, *conformable* to that in *other men's* minds called by the same common name; *v.g.* when the mind intends, or judges its *ideas* of *justice, temperance, religion,* to be the same, with what other men give those names to.

Secondly, when the mind supposes any *idea* it has in itself, to be *conformable to some real existence*. . . .

Thirdly, when the mind *refers* any of its *ideas to* that *real* constitution, and *essence* of anything, whereon all its properties depend: and thus the greatest part, if not all our *ideas* of substances, are *false*.

. . . .

9. *Simple* ideas *may be false in reference to others of the same name, but are least liable to be so. First* then, I say, that *when the truth of our* ideas *is judged of, by the conformity they have to the* ideas *which other men have, and commonly signify by the same name, they may be any of them false*. But yet *simple* ideas are *least* of all *liable to be so mistaken*. Because a man by his senses and every day's observation, may easily satisfy himself, what the simple *ideas* are, which their several names, that are in common use stand for, they being but few in number, and such, as if he doubts or mistakes in, he may easily rectify by the objects they are to be found in. Therefore it is seldom, that anyone mistakes in his names of simple *idea*s; or applies the name *red,* to the *idea* of green; or the name sweet, to the *idea* bitter: much less are men apt to confound the names of *ideas,* belonging to different senses; and call a color,

by the name of a taste, *&c.* whereby it is evident, that the simple *ideas,* they call by any name, are commonly the same, that others have and mean, when they use the same names.

10. Ideas *of mixed modes most liable to be false in this sense. Complex* ideas *are much more liable to be false in this respect; and the complex* ideas *of mixed modes, much more than those of substances:* because in substances, (especially those, which the common and unborrowed names of any language are applied to,) some remarkable sensible qualities, serving ordinarily to distinguish one sort from another, easily preserve those, who take any care in the use of their words, from applying them to sorts of substances, to which they do not at all belong. But in mixed modes, we are much more uncertain, it being not so easy to determine of several actions; whether they are to be called *justice,* or *cruelty; liberality,* or *prodigality*. And so in referring our *ideas* to those of other men, called by the same names, ours may be *false;* and the *idea* in our minds, which we express by the word *justice,* may, perhaps, be that, which ought to have another name.

11. *Or at least to be thought false*. But whether or no our *ideas* of mixed modes are more liable than any sort, to be different from those of other men, which are marked by the same names: this at least is certain, that *this sort of falsehood is much more familiarly attributed to* our *ideas* of *mixed modes, than to any other*. When a man is thought to have a false *idea* of *justice,* or *gratitude,* or *glory,* it is for no other reason, but that his agrees not with the *ideas,* which each of those names are the signs of in other men.

12. *And why*. The *reason whereof* seems to me to be this, that the abstract *ideas* of mixed modes, being men's voluntary combinations of such a precise collection of simple *ideas;* and so the essence of each species, being made by men alone, whereof we have no other sensible standard, existing anywhere, but the name itself, or the definition of that name: we have nothing else to refer these our *ideas* of mixed modes to as a standard, to which we would conform them, but the *ideas* of those, who are thought to use those names in their most proper significations; and so as our *ideas* conform, or differ from them, they pass for true or false. And thus much concerning the *truth* and *falsehood* of our *idea*s, in reference to their names.

13. *As referred to real existences, none of our* ideas *can be false, but those of substances. Secondly,* as to the *truth and falsehood of our* ideas, *in reference* to the *real existence* of things, when that is made the standard of their truth,

none of them can be termed false, but only our complex *ideas* of substances.

14. *First, simple* ideas *in this sense not false, and why. First,* our simple *ideas,* being barely such perceptions, as God has fitted us to receive, and given power to external objects to produce in us by established laws, and ways, suitable to his wisdom and goodness, though incomprehensible to us, their truth consists in nothing else, but in such appearances, as are produced in us, and must be suitable to those powers, he has placed in external objects, or else they could not be produced in us: and thus answering those powers, they are what they should be, *true ideas*. Nor do they become liable to any imputation of *falsehood,* if the mind (as in most men I believe it does) judges these *ideas* to be in the things themselves. For God in his wisdom, having set them as marks of distinction in things, whereby we may be able to discern one thing from another; and so choose any of them for our uses, as we have occasion, it alters not the nature of our simple *idea,* whether we think, that the *idea* of blue, be in the violet itself, or in our mind only; and only the power of producing it by the texture of its parts, reflecting the particles of light, after a certain manner, to be in the violet itself. For that texture in the object, by a regular and constant operation, producing the same *idea* of blue in us, it serves us to distinguish, by our eyes, that from any other thing, whether that distinguishing mark, as it is really in the *violet,* be only a peculiar texture of parts, or else that very color, the *idea* whereof (which is in us) is the exact resemblance. And it is equally from that appearance, to be denominated *blue,* whether it be that real color, or only a peculiar texture in it, that causes in us that *idea:* since the name *blue* notes properly nothing, but that mark of distinction, that is in a *violet,* discernible only by our eyes, whatever it consists in, that being beyond our capacities distinctly to know, and, perhaps, would be of less use to us, if we had faculties to discern.

15. *Though one man's* idea *of blue, should be different from another's*. Neither would it carry any imputation of *falsehood* to our simple *ideas*, *if* by the different structure of our organs, it were so ordered, that *the same object should produce in several men's minds different* ideas at the same time: *v.g.* if the *idea,* that a violet produced in one man's mind by his eyes, were the same that a *marigold* produced in another man's, and *vice versa*. For since this could never be known: because one man's mind could not pass into another man's body, to perceive, what appearances were produced by those organs; neither the *ideas* hereby, nor the names, would be at all confounded, or any *falsehood* be in either. For all things, that had the texture of a *violet,*

producing constantly the *idea,* which he called *blue;* and those which had the texture of a *marigold,* producing constantly the *idea,* which he as constantly called *yellow,* whatever those appearances were in his mind; he would be able as regularly to distinguish things for his use by those appearances, and understand, and signify those distinctions, marked by the names *blue* and *yellow,* as if the appearances, or *ideas* in his mind, received from those two flowers, were exactly the same, with the *ideas* in other men's minds. I am nevertheless very apt to think, that the sensible *ideas,* produced by any object in different men's minds, are most commonly very near and undiscernibly alike. For which opinion, I think, there might be many reasons offered: but that being besides my present business, I shall not trouble my reader with them; but only mind him, that the contrary supposition, if it could be proved, is of little use, either for the improvement of our knowledge, or conveniency of life; and so we need not trouble ourselves to examine it.

16. From what has been said concerning our simple *idea*s, I think it evident, that our *simple* ideas can *none of them* be *false, in respect of things* existing without us. . . .

17. *Secondly, modes not false. Secondly, neither can* our *complex* ideas *of modes, in reference to the essence of anything really existing, be false.* Because whatever complex *idea* I have of any mode, it has no reference to any pattern existing, and made by nature: it is not supposed to contain in it any other *ideas,* than what it has; nor to represent anything, but such a complication of *ideas,* as it does. . . .

18. *Thirdly,* ideas *of substances when false. Thirdly,* our complex *ideas of substances, being all referred to patterns in things themselves, may be false.* That they are all *false,* when looked upon as the representations of the unknown essences of things, is so evident, that there needs nothing to be said of it. I shall therefore pass over that chimerical supposition, and consider them as collections of simple *ideas* in the mind, taken from combinations of simple *ideas* existing together constantly in things, of which patterns, they are the supposed copies: and in this reference of them, to the existence of things, they *are false* ideas. 1. *When* they put together simple *ideas,* which in the real existence of things, have no union: as when to the shape, and size, that exist together in a horse, is joined, in the same complex *idea,* the power of barking like a dog: which three *ideas,* however put together into one in the mind, were never united in nature: and this therefore may be called a *false*

idea of a horse. 2. *Ideas* of substances are, in this respect, also *false,* when from any collection of simple *ideas,* that do always exist together, there is separated, by a direct negation, any other simple *idea,* which is constantly joined with them. Thus if to extension, solidity, fusibility, the peculiar weightiness, and yellow color of gold, anyone join in his thoughts the negation of a greater degree of fixedness, than is in lead or copper, he may be said to have a false complex *idea,* as well as when he joins to those other simple ones, the *idea* of perfect absolute fixedness. For either way, the complex *idea* of gold being made up of such simple ones, as have no union in nature, may be termed false. But if he leave out of this his complex *idea,* that of fixedness quite, without either actually joining to, or separating of it from the rest in his mind, it is, I think, to be looked on, as an inadequate and imperfect *idea,* rather than a *false* one: since though it contains not all the simple *ideas,* that are united in nature, yet it puts none together, but what do really exist together.

19. *Truth or falsehood always supposes affirmation or negation.* Though in compliance with the ordinary way of speaking, I have showed in what sense, and upon what ground our *ideas* may be sometimes called *true,* or *false;* yet if we will look a little nearer into the matter in all cases, where any *idea* is called *true,* or *false,* it is from some judgment that the mind makes, or is supposed to make, that is *true,* or *false.* For *truth,* or *falsehood,* being *never without some affirmation, or negation,* express, or tacit, it is not to be found, but where signs are joined or separated, according to the agreement, or disagreement, of the things they stand for. The signs we chiefly use, are either *ideas,* or words, wherewith we make either mental, or verbal propositions. *Truth* lies in so joining or separating these representatives, as the things they stand for, do, in themselves, agree, or disagree: and *falsehood* in the contrary, as shall be more fully showed hereafter.

20. Ideas *in themselves neither true nor false.* Any *idea* then which we have in our minds, whether conformable, or not, to the existence of things, or to any *ideas* in the minds of other men, cannot properly for this alone be called *false*. . . .

. . . .

26. *More properly to be called right or wrong.* Upon the whole matter, I think, that our *idea*s, as they are considered by the mind, either in reference to the proper signification of their names; or in reference to the reality of things,

may very fitly *be called right, or wrong* ideas, according as they agree, or disagree to those patterns to which they are referred. But if anyone had rather call them *true,* or *false,* 'tis fit he use a liberty which everyone has, to call things by those names he thinks best; though, in propriety of speech, *truth,* or *falsehood* will, I think, scarce agree to them, but as they, some way or other, virtually contain in them some mental proposition. The *ideas* that are in a man's mind, simply considered, cannot be wrong, unless complex ones, wherein inconsistent parts are jumbled together. All other *ideas* are in themselves right; and the knowledge about them right and true knowledge: but when we come to refer them to anything, as to their patterns and archetypes, then they are capable of being wrong, as far as they disagree with such archetypes.

CHAP. XXXIII.
Of the association of ideas.

1. *Something unreasonable in most men.* There is scarce anyone that does not observe something that seems odd to him, and is in itself really extravagant in the opinions, reasonings, and actions of other men. The least flaw of this kind, if at all different from his own, everyone is quick-sighted enough to espy in another, and will by the authority of reason forwardly condemn, though he be guilty of much greater unreasonableness in his own tenets and conduct, which he never perceives; and will very hardly, if at all, be convinced of.

. . . .

3. *Not wholly from education.* This sort of unreasonableness is usually imputed to education and prejudice, and for the most part truly enough, though that reaches not the bottom of the disease, nor shows distinctly enough whence it rises, or wherein it lies. Education is often rightly assigned for the cause, and prejudice is a good general name for the thing itself: but yet, I think, he ought to look a little farther, who would trace this sort of madness to the root it springs from, and so explain it, as to show whence this flaw has its original in very sober and rational minds, and wherein it consists.

4. *A degree of madness.* I shall be pardoned for calling it by so harsh a name as madness, when it is considered, that opposition to reason deserves that name, and is really madness; and there is scarce a man so free from it, but that if he should always on all occasions argue or do as in some cases he constantly does, would not be thought fitter for *Bedlam,* than civil conversation. I do not here mean when he is under the power of an unruly passion, but in the steady calm course of his life. That which will yet more apologize for this harsh name, and ungrateful imputation on the greatest part of mankind, is, that inquiring a little by the by into the nature of madness, . . . I found it to spring from the very same root, and to depend on the very same cause we are here speaking of. This consideration of the thing itself, at a time when I thought not the least on the subject which I am now treating of, suggested it to me. And if this be a weakness to which all men are so liable; if this be a taint which so universally infects mankind, the greater care should be taken to lay it open under its due name, thereby to excite the greater care in its prevention and cure.

5. *From a wrong connection of* ideas. Some of our *ideas* have a natural correspondence and connection one with another: it is the office and excellency of our reason to trace these, and hold them together in that union and correspondence which is founded in their peculiar beings. Besides this there is another connection of *ideas* wholly owing to chance or custom, *ideas* that in themselves are not at all of kin, come to be so united in some men's minds, that 'tis very hard to separate them, they always keep in company, and the one no sooner at any time comes into the understanding but its associate appears with it; and if they are more than two which are thus united, the whole gang always inseparable show themselves together.

6. *This connection how made.* This strong combination of *ideas,* not allied by nature, the mind makes in itself either voluntarily, or by chance, and hence it comes in different men to be very different, according to their different inclinations, educations, interests, *&c.* Custom settles habits of thinking in the understanding, as well as of determining in the will, and of motions in the body; all which seems to be but trains of motion in the animal spirits, which once set agoing continue on in the same steps they have been used to, which by often treading are worn into a smooth path, and the motion in it becomes easy and as it were natural. As far as we can comprehend thinking, thus *ideas* seem to be produced in our minds, or if they are not, this may serve to explain their following one another in an habitual train,

when once they are put into that tract, as well as it does to explain such motions of the body. . . .

7. *Some antipathies an effect of it.* That there are such associations of them made by custom in the minds of most men, I think nobody will question who has well considered himself or others; and to this, perhaps, might be justly attributed most of the sympathies and antipathies observable in men, which work as strongly, and produce as regular effects as if they were natural, and are therefore called so, though they at first had no other original but the accidental connection of two *ideas,* which either the strength of the first impression, or future indulgence so united, that they always afterwards kept company together in that man's mind, as if they were but one *idea.* I say most of the antipathies, I do not say all, for some of them are truly natural, depend upon our original constitution, and are born with us; but a great part of those which are counted natural, would have been known to be from unheeded, though, perhaps, early impressions, or wanton fancies at first, which would have been acknowledged the original of them, if they had been warily observed. . . .

. . . .

9. *A great cause of errors.* This wrong connection in our minds of *ideas* in themselves, loose and independent one of another has such an influence, and is of so great force to set us awry in our actions, as well moral as natural, passions, reasonings, and notions themselves, that, perhaps, there is not any one thing that deserves more to be looked after.

. . . .

13. *Why time cures some disorders in the mind which reason cannot.* When this combination is settled and whilst it lasts, it is not in the power of reason to help us, and relieve us from the effects of it. *Ideas* in our minds, when they are there, will operate according to their natures and circumstances; and here we see the cause why time cures certain affections, which reason, though in the right, and allowed to be so, has not power over, nor is able against them to prevail with those who are apt to hearken to it in other cases. The death of a child, that was the daily delight of his mother's eyes, and joy of her soul, rends from her heart the whole comfort of her life, and gives her all the torment imaginable; use the consolations of reason in this case, and you were as good preach ease to one on the rack, and hope to allay,

by rational discourses, the pain of his joints tearing asunder. Till time has by disuse separated the sense of that enjoyment and its loss from the *idea* of the child returning to her memory, all representations, though never so reasonable, are in vain; and therefore some in whom the union between these *ideas* is never dissolved, spend their lives in mourning, and carry an incurable sorrow to their graves.

. . . .

17. *Its influence on intellectual habits.* Intellectual habits and defects this way contracted are not less frequent and powerful, though less observed. Let the *ideas* of being and matter be strongly joined either by education or much thought, whilst these are still combined in the mind, what notions, what reasonings, will there be about separate spirits? Let custom from the very childhood have joined figure and shape to the *idea* of God, and what absurdities will that mind be liable to about the deity?

Let the *idea* of infallibility be inseparably joined to any person, and these two constantly together possess the mind, and then one body in two places at once, shall unexamined be swallowed for a certain truth, by an implicit faith, whenever that imagined infallible person dictates and demands assent without inquiry.

. . . .

19. *Conclusion.* Having thus given an account of the original, sorts, and extent of our *ideas,* with several other considerations, about these (I know not whether I may say) instruments, or materials, of our knowledge, the method I at first proposed to myself, would now require, that I should immediately proceed to show, what use the understanding makes of them, and what knowledge we have by them. This was that, which, in the first general view I had of this subject, was all that I thought I should have to do: but upon a nearer approach, I find, that there is so close a connection between *ideas* and words; and our abstract *ideas,* and general words, have so constant a relation one to another, that it is impossible to speak clearly and distinctly of our knowledge, which all consists in propositions, without considering, first, the nature, use, and signification of language; which therefore must be the business of the next book.

BOOK III.

CHAP. I.

Of words or language in general.

1. *Man fitted to form articulate sounds.* GOD having designed man for a sociable creature, made him not only with an inclination, and under a necessity to have fellowship with those of his own kind; but furnished him also with language, which was to be the great instrument, and common tie of society. *Man* therefore had by nature his organs so fashioned, as to be *fit to frame articulate sounds,* which we call words. But this was not enough to produce language; for parrots, and several other birds, will be taught to make articulate sounds distinct enough, which yet, by no means, are capable of language.

2. *To make them signs of* ideas. Besides articulate sounds therefore, it was farther necessary, that he should be *able to use these sounds, as signs of internal conceptions;* and to make them stand as marks for the *ideas* within his own mind, whereby they might be made known to others, and the thoughts of men's minds be conveyed from one to another.

3. *To make general signs.* But neither was this sufficient to make words so useful as they ought to be. It is not enough for the perfection of language, that sounds can be made signs of *ideas,* unless those *signs* can be so made use of, as *to comprehend several particular things:* for the multiplication of words would have perplexed their use, had every particular thing need of a distinct name to be signified by. To remedy this inconvenience, language had yet a farther improvement in the use of general terms, whereby one word was made to mark a multitude of particular existences: which advantageous use of sounds was obtained only by the difference of the *ideas* they were made signs of. Those names becoming general, which are made to stand for general *ideas,* and those remaining particular, where the *ideas* they are used for are particular.

4. Besides these names which stand for *ideas,* there be other words which men make use of, not to signify any *idea,* but the want or absence of some

ideas simple or complex, or all *ideas* together; such as are *nihil* in Latin, and in English, *ignorance* and *barrenness.* All which negative or privative words, cannot be said properly to belong to, or signify no *ideas:* for then they would be perfectly insignificant sounds; but they relate to positive *ideas,* and signify their absence.

5. *Words ultimately derived from such as signify sensible* ideas. It may also lead us a little towards the original of all our notions and knowledge, if we remark, how great a dependence our *words* have on common sensible *ideas;* and how those, which are made use of to stand for actions and notions quite removed from sense, *have their rise from thence, and from obvious sensible* ideas *are transferred to more abstruse significations,* and made to stand for *ideas* that come not under the cognizance of our senses; *v.g.* to *imagine, apprehend, comprehend, adhere, conceive, instill, disgust, disturbance, tranquility, &c.* are all words taken from the operations of sensible things, and applied to certain modes of thinking. *Spirit,* in its primary signification, is breath: *angel,* a messenger: and I doubt not, but if we could trace them to their sources, we should find, in all languages, the names, which stand for things that fall not under our senses, to have had their first rise from sensible *ideas.* . . .

6. *Distribution.* But to understand better the use and force of language, as subservient to instruction and knowledge, it will be convenient to consider,

First, to what it is that names, in the use of language, are immediately applied.

Secondly, since all (except proper) names are general, and so stand not particularly for this or that single thing; but for sorts and ranks of things, it will be necessary to consider, in the next place, what the sorts and kinds, or, if you rather like the Latin names, *what the species and genera of things* are; wherein they consist; and how they come to be made. These being (as they ought) well looked into, we shall the better come to find the right use of words; the natural advantages and defects of language; and the remedies that ought to be used, to avoid the inconveniences of obscurity or uncertainty in the signification of words, without which, it is impossible to discourse with any clearness, or order, concerning knowledge: which being conversant about propositions, and those most commonly universal ones, has greater connection with words, than perhaps is suspected.

These considerations therefore, shall be the matter of the following chapters.

CHAP. II.
Of the signification of words.

1. *Words are sensible signs necessary for communication.* Man, though he have great variety of thoughts, and such, from which others, as well as himself, might receive profit and delight; yet they are all within his own breast, invisible, and hidden from others, nor can of themselves be made appear. The comfort, and advantage of society, not being to be had without communication of thoughts, it was necessary, that man should find out some external sensible signs, whereof those invisible *ideas,* which his thoughts are made up of, might be made known to others. For this purpose, nothing was so fit, either for plenty or quickness, as those articulate sounds, which with so much ease and variety, he found himself able to make. Thus we may conceive how *words,* which were by nature so well adapted to that purpose, come to be made use of by men, as *the signs of* their *ideas;* not by any natural connection, that there is between particular articulate sounds and certain *ideas,* for then there would be but one language amongst all men; but by a voluntary imposition, whereby such a word is made arbitrarily the mark of such an *idea.* The use then of words, is to be sensible marks of *ideas;* and the *ideas* they stand for, are their proper and immediate signification.

2. *Words are the sensible signs of his* ideas *who uses them.* The use men have of these marks, being either to record their own thoughts for the assistance of their own memory; or as it were, to bring out their *ideas,* and lay them before the view of others: *words in their primary and immediate signification, stand for nothing, but the* ideas *in the mind of him that uses them,* how imperfectly soever, or carelessly those *ideas* are collected from the things, which they are supposed to represent. When a man speaks to another, it is that he may be understood; and the end of speech is, that those sounds, as marks, may make known his *ideas* to the hearer. . . .

. . . .

4. *Words often secretly referred, first, to the* ideas *in other men's minds.* But though words, as they are used by men, can properly and immediately signify nothing but the *ideas,* that are in the mind of the speaker; yet they in their thoughts give them a secret reference to two other things.

First, they suppose their words to be marks of the ideas *in the minds also of other men, with whom they communicate:* for else they should talk in vain, and could not be understood, if the sounds they applied to one *idea,* were such, as by the hearer, were applied to another, which is to speak two languages. But in this, men stand not usually to examine, whether the *idea* they, and those they discourse with have in their minds, be the same: but think it enough, that they use the word, as they imagine, in the common acceptation of that language; in which case they suppose, that the *idea,* they make it a sign of, is precisely the same, to which the understanding men of that country apply that name.

5. *Secondly, to the reality of things. Secondly,* because *men* would not be thought to talk *barely* of their own imaginations, but of things as really they are; therefore they *often suppose their words to stand also for the reality of things.* But this relating more particularly to substances, and their names, as perhaps the former does to simple *ideas* and modes, we shall speak of these two different ways of applying words more at large, when we come to treat of the names of mixed modes, and substances, in particular: though give me leave here to say, that it is a perverting the use of words, and brings unavoidable obscurity and confusion into their signification, whenever we make them stand for anything, but those *ideas* we have in our own minds.

. . . .

7. *Words often used without signification.* . . . Though the proper and immediate signification of words, are *ideas* in the mind of the speaker; yet because by familiar use from our cradles, we come to learn certain articulate sounds very perfectly, and have them readily on our tongues, and always at hand in our memories; but yet are not always careful to examine, or settle their significations perfectly; it *often* happens that *men,* even when they would apply themselves to an attentive consideration, do *set their thoughts more on words than things.* Nay, because words are many of them learned, before the *ideas* are known for which they stand: therefore some, not only children, but men, speak several words, no otherwise than parrots do, only because they have learned them, and have been accustomed to those sounds. But so far as words are of use and signification, so far is there a constant connection between the sound and the *idea;* and a designation, that the one stand for the other: without which application of them, they are nothing but so much insignificant noise.

8. *Their signification perfectly arbitrary. Words* by long and familiar use, as has been said, come to excite in men certain *ideas* so constantly and readily, that they are apt to suppose a natural connection between them. But that they *signify* only men's peculiar *ideas,* and that *by a perfect arbitrary imposition,* is evident, in that they often fail to excite in others (even that use the same language) the same *ideas,* we take them to be the signs of. . . .

CHAP. III.

Of general terms.

1. *The greatest part of words general.* All things, that exist, being particulars, it may perhaps be thought reasonable, that words, which ought to be conformed to things, should be so too, I mean in their signification: but yet we find the quite contrary. The far *greatest part of words,* that make all languages, *are general terms:* which has not been the effect of neglect, or chance, but of reason, and necessity.

2. *For every particular thing to have a name is impossible. First, it is impossible, that every particular thing should have a distinct peculiar name.* . . . It is beyond the power of human capacity to frame and retain distinct *ideas* of all the particular things we meet with: every bird, and beast men saw; every tree, and plant, that affected the senses, could not find a place in the most capacious understanding. . . .

3. *And useless. Secondly,* if it were possible, *it would yet be useless;* because it would not serve to the chief end of language. Men would in vain heap up names of particular things, that would not serve them to communicate their thoughts. Men learn names, and use them in talk with others, only that they may be understood: which is then only done, when by use or consent, the sound I make by the organs of speech, excites in another man's mind, who hears it, the *idea* I apply it to in mine, when I speak it. This cannot be done by names, applied to particular things, whereof I alone having the *ideas* in my mind, the names of them could not be significant, or intelligible to another, who was not acquainted with all those very particular things, which had fallen under my notice.

4. *Thirdly,* but yet granting this also feasible; (which I think is not,) yet *a distinct name for every particular thing, would not be of any great use for the improvement of knowledge:* which, though founded in particular things, enlarges itself by general views; to which, things reduced into sorts under general names, are properly subservient. . . .

. . . .

6. *How general words are made.* The next thing to be considered is, *how general words come to be made.* For since all things that exist are only particulars, how come we by general terms, or where find we those general natures they are supposed to stand for? Words become general, by being made the signs of general *ideas:* and *ideas* become general, by separating from them the circumstances of time, and place, and any other *ideas,* that may determine them to this or that particular existence. By this way of abstraction they are made capable of representing more individuals than one; each of which, having in it a conformity to that abstract *idea,* is (as we call it) of that sort.

7. But to deduce this a little more distinctly, it will not perhaps be amiss, to trace our notions, and names from their beginning, and observe by what degrees we proceed, and by what steps we enlarge our *ideas* from our first infancy. There is nothing more evident, than that the *ideas* of the persons children converse with, (to instance in them alone) are like the persons themselves, only particular. The *ideas* of the nurse, and the mother, are well framed in their minds; and, like pictures of them there, represent only those individuals. The names they first gave to them, are confined to these individuals; and the names of *nurse* and *mamma,* the child uses, determine themselves to those persons. Afterwards, when time and a larger acquaintance has made them observe, that there are a great many other things in the world, that in some common agreements of shape, and several other qualities, resemble their father and mother, and those persons they have been used to, they frame an *idea,* which they find those many particulars do partake in; and to that they give, with others, the name *man,* for example. And *thus they come to have a general name,* and a general *idea.* Wherein they make nothing new, but only leave out of the complex *idea* they had of *Peter* and *James, Mary* and *Jane,* that which is peculiar to each, and retain only what is common to them all.

8. By the same way, that they come by the general name and *idea* of *man,* they easily *advance to more general names* and notions. For observing, that

several things that differ from their *idea* of *man,* and cannot therefore be comprehended under that name, have yet certain qualities, wherein they agree with *man,* by retaining only those qualities, and uniting them into one *idea,* they have again another and more general *idea;* to which having given a name, they make a term of a more comprehensive extension: which new *idea* is made, not by any new addition, but only, as before, by leaving out the shape, and some other properties signified by the name *man,* and retaining only a body, with life, sense, and spontaneous motion, comprehended under the name *animal.*

9. *General natures are nothing but abstract* ideas. That this is the *way, whereby men first formed general* ideas, *and general names to them,* I think, is so evident, that there needs no other proof of it, but the considering of a man's self, or others, and the ordinary proceedings of their minds in knowledge: and he that thinks general natures or notions, are anything else but such abstract and partial *ideas* of more complex ones, taken at first from particular existences, will, I fear, be at a loss where to find them. For let anyone reflect, and then tell me, wherein does his *idea* of *man* differ from that of *Peter,* and *Paul,* or his *idea* of *horse,* from that of *Bucephalus,* but in the leaving out something, that is peculiar to each individual; and retaining so much of those particular complex *ideas,* of several particular existences, as they are found to agree in? Of the complex *ideas,* signified by the names *man,* and *horse,* leaving out but those particulars wherein they differ, and retaining only those wherein they agree, and of those, making a new distinct complex *idea,* and giving the name *animal* to it, one has a more general term, that comprehends, with man, several other creatures. Leave out of the *idea* of *animal,* sense and spontaneous motion, and the remaining complex *idea,* made up of the remaining simple ones of body, life, and nourishment, becomes a more general one, under the more comprehensive term, *vivens.*[29] And not to dwell longer upon this particular, so evident in itself, by the same way the mind proceeds to *body, substance,* and at last to *being, thing,* and such universal terms, which stand for any of our *ideas* whatsoever. To conclude, this whole *mystery* of *genera* and *species,* which make such a noise in the schools, and are, with justice, so little regarded out of them, is nothing else but abstract *ideas,* more or less comprehensive, with names annexed to them. In all which, this is constant and unvariable, that every more general term, stands for such an *idea,* and is but a part of any of those contained under it.

29. *vivens,* living.

10. *Why the* genus *is ordinarily made use of in definitions.* This may show us the reason, *why, in the defining of words,* which is nothing but declaring their signification, *we make use of the genus,* or next general word that comprehends it. Which is not out of necessity, but only to save the labor of enumerating the several simple *ideas,* which the next general word, or *genus,* stands for; or, perhaps, sometimes the shame of not being able to do it. But though defining by *genus* and *differentia,* (I crave leave to use these terms of art, though originally Latin, since they most properly suit those notions they are applied to;) I say, though defining by the *genus* be the shortest way; yet, I think, it may be doubted whether it be the best.[30] This I am sure, it is not the only, and so not absolutely necessary. For definition being nothing but making another understand by words, what *idea,* the term defined stands for, a definition is best made by enumerating those simple *ideas* that are combined in the signification of the term defined: and if instead of such an enumeration, men have accustomed themselves to use the next general term, it has not been out of necessity, or for greater clearness; but for quickness and dispatch sake. . . .

11. *General and universal are creatures of the understanding.* To return to general words, it is plain, by what has been said, that *general and universal,* belong not to the real existence of things; but *are the inventions and creatures of the understanding,* made by it for its own use, *and concern only signs,* whether words, or *ideas.* Words are general, as has been said, when used, for signs of general *ideas;* and so are applicable indifferently to many particular things; and *ideas* are general, when they are set up, as the representatives of many particular things: but universality belongs not to things themselves, which are all of them particular in their existence, even those words, and *ideas,* which in their signification, are general. When therefore we quit particulars, the generals that rest, are only creatures of our own making, their general nature being nothing but the capacity they are put into by the understanding, of signifying or representing many particulars. For the signification they have, is nothing but a relation, that by the mind of man is added to them.

30. A *genus* is a kind that includes several smaller kinds or *species.* Each species in the kind is differentiated from the others by a *differentia* or "difference." A standard illustration of definition by genus and differentia is the definition of "human being" as rational animal. Human beings form a species in the genus animal; rationality is what distinguishes human beings from other species in the genus.

12. *Abstract* ideas *are the essences of the* genera *and* species. The next thing therefore to be considered, is, *what kind of signification it is, that general words have.* For as it is evident, that they do not signify barely one particular thing; for then they would not be general terms, but proper names, so on the other side, 'tis as evident, they do not signify a plurality; for man and men would then signify the same; and the distinction of numbers (as grammarians call them) would be superfluous and useless. That then which general words signify, is a sort of things; and each of them does that, by being a sign of an abstract *idea* in the mind, to which *idea,* as things existing are found to agree, so they come to be ranked under that name; or, which is all one, be of that sort. Whereby it is evident, that the *essences of* the *sorts, or* (if the Latin word pleases better) *species* of things, are nothing else but these abstract *ideas.* For the having the essence of any species, being that which makes anything to be of that species, and the conformity to the *idea,* to which the name is annexed, being that which gives a right to that name; the having the essence, and the having that conformity, must needs be the same thing: since to be of any species, and to have a right to the name of that species, is all one. . . . From whence it is easy to observe, that the essences of the sorts of things, and consequently the sorting of things, is the workmanship of the understanding, since it is the understanding that abstracts and makes those general *ideas.*

13. *They are the workmanship of the understanding, but have their foundation in the similitude of things.* I would not here be thought to forget, much less to deny, that nature in the production of things, makes several of them alike: there is nothing more obvious, especially in the races of animals, and all things propagated by seed. But yet, I think, we may say, the *sorting* of them under names, *is the workmanship of the understanding, taking occasion from the similitude* it observes amongst them, to make abstract general *ideas,* and set them up in the mind, with names annexed to them, as patterns, or forms, (for in that sense the word form has a very proper signification,) to which, as particular things existing are found to agree, so they come to be of that species, have that denomination, or are put into that *classis.*[31] . . . And therefore the supposed real essences of substances, if different from our abstract *ideas,* cannot be the essences of the species we rank things into. For two species may be one, as rationally, as two different essences be the essence of one species: and I demand, what are the alterations may, or may not be made in a *horse,* or *lead,* without making either of them to be of

31. *classis,* class.

another species? In determining the species of things by our abstract *ideas,* this is easy to resolve: but if anyone will regulate himself herein, by supposed real essences, he will, I suppose, be at a loss: and he will never be able to know when anything precisely ceases to be of the species of an *horse,* or *lead.*

. . . .

15. *Real and nominal essence.* But since the *essences* of things are thought, by some, (and not without reason,) to be wholly unknown; it may not be amiss to consider the *several significations of the word essence.*

First, essence may be taken for the very being of anything, whereby it is, what it is. And thus the real internal, but generally in substances, unknown constitution of things, whereon their discoverable qualities depend, may be called their *essence.* This is the proper original signification of the word, as is evident from the formation of it; *essentia,* in its primary notation signifying properly *being.* And in this sense it is still used, when we speak of the essence of particular things, without giving them any name.

Secondly, the learning and disputes of the schools, having been much busied about *genus* and *species,* the word *essence* has almost lost its primary signification; and instead of the real constitution of things, has been almost wholly applied to the artificial constitution of *genus* and *species.* 'Tis true, there is ordinarily supposed a real constitution of the sorts of things; and 'tis past doubt, there must be some real constitution, on which any collection of simple *ideas* coexisting, must depend. But it being evident, that things are ranked under names into sorts or *species,* only as they agree to certain abstract *ideas,* to which we have annexed those names, the *essence* of each *genus,* or sort, comes to be nothing but that abstract *idea,* which the general, or *sortal* (if I may have leave so to call it from *sort,* as I do *general* from *genus,*) name stands for. And this we shall find to be that, which the word *essence* imports, in its most familiar use. These two sorts of *essences,* I suppose, may not unfitly be termed, the one the *real,* the other the *nominal essence.*

16. *Constant connection between the name and nominal essence. Between the nominal essence, and the name,* there is so *near* a *connection,* that the name of any sort of things cannot be attributed to any particular being, but what has this *essence,* whereby it answers that abstract *idea,* whereof that name is the sign.

17. *Supposition that species are distinguished by their real essences useless.* Concerning the real essences of corporeal substances, (to mention these only,) there are, if I mistake not, two opinions. The one is of those, who using the word *essence,* for they know not what, suppose a certain number of those essences, according to which, all natural things are made, and wherein they do exactly every one of them partake, and so become of this or that *species.* The other, and more rational opinion, is of those, who look on all natural things to have a real, but unknown constitution of their insensible parts, from which flow those sensible qualities, which serve us to distinguish them one from another, according as we have occasion to rank them into sorts, under common denominations. The former of these opinions, which supposes these *essences,* as a certain number of forms or molds, wherein all natural things, that exist, are cast, and do equally partake, has, I imagine, very much perplexed the knowledge of natural things. The frequent productions of monsters, in all the species of animals, and of changelings, and other strange issues of human birth, carry with them difficulties, not possible to consist with this *hypothesis:* since it is as impossible, that two things, partaking exactly of the same real *essence,* should have different properties, as that two figures partaking of the same real *essence* of a circle, should have different properties. But were there no other reason against it, yet the *supposition of essences, that cannot be known;* and the making of them nevertheless to be that, which distinguishes the species of things, *is* so *wholly useless,* and unserviceable to any part of our knowledge, that that alone were sufficient, to make us lay it by; and content ourselves with such *essences* of the sorts or species of things, as come within the reach of our knowledge: which, when seriously considered, will be found, as I have said, to be nothing else, but those abstract complex *ideas,* to which we have annexed distinct general names.

18. *Real and nominal essence the same in simple* ideas *and modes, different in substances. Essences* being thus distinguished into *nominal and real,* we may farther observe, that *in* the species of *simple* ideas *and modes,* they *are always the same:* but *in substances, always quite different.* Thus a figure including a space between three lines, is the real, as well as nominal *essence* of a triangle; it being not only the abstract *idea* to which the general name is annexed, but the very *essentia,* or being, of the thing itself, that foundation from which all its properties flow, and to which they are all inseparably annexed.[32] But it is far otherwise concerning that parcel of matter, which makes the ring on my

32. *essentia,* essence.

finger, wherein these two *essences* are apparently different. For it is the real constitution of its insensible parts, on which depend all those properties of color, weight, fusibility, fixedness, *&c.* which are to be found in it. Which constitution we know not; and so having no particular *idea* of, have no name that is the sign of it. But yet it is its color, weight, fusibility, fixedness, *&c.* which makes it to be *gold*, or gives it a right to that name, which is therefore its nominal *essence*. Since nothing can be called *gold*, but what has a conformity of qualities to that abstract complex *idea*, to which that name is annexed. But this distinction of *essences*, belonging particularly to substances, we shall, when we come to consider their names, have an occasion to treat of more fully.

. . . .

20. *Recapitulation.* To conclude, this is that, which in short I would say, (*viz.*) that all the great business of *genera* and *species*, and their *essences*, amounts to no more but this, that men making abstract *ideas*, and settling them in their minds, with names annexed to them, do thereby enable themselves to consider things, and discourse of them, as it were in bundles, for the easier and readier improvement, and communication of their knowledge, which would advance but slowly, were their words and thoughts confined only to particulars.

CHAP. IV.

Of the names of simple ideas.

1. *Names of simple* ideas, *modes, and substances, have each something peculiar.* Though all words, as I have shown, signify nothing immediately, but the *ideas* in the mind of the speaker; yet upon a nearer survey, we shall find that the *names of simple* ideas, *mixed modes*, (under which I comprise relations too,) *and natural substances, have each of them something peculiar*, and different from the other. For example:

2. *First, names of simple* ideas *and substances, intimate real existence. First*, the *names of simple* ideas *and substances*, with the abstract *ideas* in the mind, which they immediately signify, *intimate* also *some real existence*, from which was derived their original pattern. But the *names of mixed modes, terminate in*

the idea that is in the mind, and lead not the thoughts any farther, as we shall see more at large in the following chapter.

3. *Secondly, names of simple* ideas *and modes signify always both real and nominal essence. Secondly,* the *names of simple* ideas *and modes, signify always the real, as well as nominal essence of their species.* But *the names of natural substances, signify* rarely, if ever, anything but *barely the nominal essences* of those species, as we shall show in the chapter, that treats of the names of substances in particular.

4. *Thirdly, names of simple* ideas *undefinable. Thirdly,* the *names of simple* ideas *are not capable of any definitions;* the names of all complex *ideas* are. . . .

5. *If all were definable, 'twould be a process* in infinitum. I will not here trouble myself, to prove that all terms are not definable from that progress, *in infinitum,* which it will visibly lead us into, if we should allow, that all names could be defined. For if the terms of one definition, were still to be defined by another, where at last should we stop? But I shall from the nature of our *ideas,* and the signification of our words show, *why some names can, and others cannot be defined,* and which they are.

6. *What a definition is.* I think, it is agreed, that *a definition is* nothing else, but *the showing the meaning of one word by several other not synonymous terms.* The meaning of words, being only the *ideas* they are made to stand for by him that uses them; the meaning of any term is then showed, or the word is defined when by other words, the *idea* it is made the sign of, and annexed to in the mind of the speaker, is as it were represented, or set before the view of another; and thus its signification ascertained: this is the only use and end of definitions; and therefore the only measure of what is, or is not a good definition.

7. *Simple* ideas *why undefinable.* This being premised, I say, that *the names of simple* ideas, and those only, *are incapable of being defined.* The reason whereof is this, that the several terms of a definition, signifying several *ideas,* they can all together by no means represent an *idea,* which has no composition at all: and therefore a definition, which is properly nothing but the showing the meaning of one word by several others not signifying each the same thing, can in the names of simple *ideas* have no place.

. . . .

12. *The contrary showed in complex* ideas. The case is quite otherwise *in complex ideas;* which consisting of several simple ones, it is in the power of words, standing for the several *ideas,* that make that composition, to imprint complex *ideas* in the mind, which were never there before, and so make their names be understood. In such collections of *ideas,* passing under one name, *definition,* or the teaching the signification of one word, by several others, has place, and *may make us understand the names* of things, which never came within the reach of our senses; and frame *ideas* suitable to those in other men's minds, when they use those names: provided that none of the terms of the definition stand for any such simple *ideas,* which he to whom the explication is made, has never yet had in his thoughts. . . .

. . . .

17. *Names of simple* ideas *stand for* ideas *not at all arbitrary.* . . . The names of simple *ideas,* substances, and mixed modes, have also this difference; that those *of mixed modes* stand for *ideas* perfectly *arbitrary:* those *of substances,* are not perfectly so; but *refer to a pattern, though with some latitude: and those of simple* ideas *are* perfectly taken from the existence of things, and *are not arbitrary at all.* Which what difference it makes in the significations of their names, we shall see in the following chapters.

The names of simple modes, differ little from those of simple *ideas.*

CHAP. V.

Of the names of mixed modes and relations.

1. *They stand for abstract* ideas, *as other general names.* The names of mixed modes being general, they stand, as has been shown, for sorts or species of things, each of which has its peculiar essence. The essences of these species also, as has been showed, are nothing but the abstract *ideas* in the mind, to which the name is annexed. Thus far the names and essences of mixed modes, have nothing but what is common to them, with other *ideas:* but if we take a little nearer survey of them, we shall find, that they have something peculiar, which, perhaps, may deserve our attention.

2. *First, the* ideas *they stand for, are made by the understanding.* The first particularity I shall observe in them is, that the abstract *ideas,* or, if you please, the essences of the several species *of mixed modes are made by the understanding,* wherein they differ from those of *simple ideas.* . . .

3. *Secondly, made arbitrarily, and without patterns.* In the next place, these *essences of the species of mixed modes, are* not only *made* by the mind, but made *very arbitrarily,* made without patterns, or reference to any real existence. Wherein they differ from those of substances, which carry with them the supposition of some real being, from which they are taken, and to which they are conformable. . . .

. . . .

7. *But still subservient to the end of language.* But though these complex *ideas,* or *essences of mixed modes,* depend on the mind, and are made by it with great liberty; yet they *are not made at random,* and jumbled together without any reason at all. Though these complex *ideas* be not always copied from nature, yet they are always suited to the end for which abstract *ideas* are made: and though they be combinations made of *ideas,* that are loose enough, and have as little union in themselves, as several other, to which the mind never gives a connection that combines them into one *idea;* yet they are always made for the convenience of communication, which is the chief end of language. The use of language is, by short sounds to signify with ease and dispatch general conceptions: wherein not only abundance of particulars may be contained, but also a great variety of independent *ideas,* collected into one complex one. . . .

8. *Whereof the intranslatable words of divers languages are a proof.* A moderate skill *in different languages,* will easily satisfy one of the truth of this, it being so obvious to observe great store of *words in one* language, *which have not any that answer them in another.* Which plainly shows, that those of one country, by their customs and manner of life, have found occasion to make several complex *ideas,* and given names to them, which others never collected into specific *ideas.* This could not have happened, if these species were the steady workmanship of nature; and not collections made and abstracted by the mind, in order to naming, and for the convenience of communication. . . .

. . . .

12. *For the originals of mixed modes, we look no farther than the mind, which also shows them to be the workmanship of the understanding.* Conformable also to what has been said, concerning the *essences* of the *species* of *mixed modes,* that they are the creatures of the understanding, rather than the works of nature; conformable, I say, to this, we find, that *their names lead our thoughts to the mind, and no farther.* When we speak of *justice,* or *gratitude,* we frame to ourselves no imagination of any thing existing, which we would conceive; but our thoughts terminate in the abstract *ideas* of those virtues, and look not farther; as they do, when we speak of a *horse,* or *iron,* whose specific *ideas* we consider not, as barely in the mind, but as in things themselves, which afford the original patterns of those *ideas.* But in mixed modes, at least the most considerable parts of them, which are moral beings, we consider the original patterns, as being in the mind; and to those we refer for the distinguishing of particular beings under names. And hence I think it is, that these *essences* of the *species* of mixed modes, are by a more particular name called *notions;* as by a peculiar right, appertaining to the understanding.

. . . .

16. *Reason of my being so large on this subject.* What has been said here of mixed modes, is with very little difference applicable also to relations; which since every man himself may observe, I may spare myself the pains to enlarge on: especially, since what I have here said concerning words in this third book, will possibly be thought by some to be much more than what so slight a subject required. I allow, it might be brought into a narrower compass: but I was willing to stay my reader on an argument, that appears to me new, and a little out of the way, (I am sure 'tis one, I thought not of, when I began to write,) that by searching it to the bottom, and turning it on every side, some part or other might meet with everyone's thoughts, and give occasion to the most averse, or negligent, to reflect on a general miscarriage; which, though of great consequence, is little taken notice of. When it is considered, what a pudder is made about *essences,* and how much all sorts of knowledge, discourse and conversation, are pestered and disordered by the careless, and confused use and application of words, it will, perhaps, be thought worthwhile thoroughly to lay it open. . . . I shall imagine I have done some service to truth, peace, and learning, if, by any enlargement on this subject, I can make men reflect on their own use of language; and give them reason to suspect, that since it is frequent for others, it may also be possible for them, to have sometimes very good and approved words in their mouths, and writings, with very uncertain, little, or no signification. . . .

CHAP. VI.
Of the names of substances.

1. *The common names of substances stand for sorts. The common names of substances,* as well as other general terms, *stand for sorts;* which is nothing else but the being made signs of such complex *ideas,* wherein several particular substances do, or might agree, by virtue of which, they are capable to be comprehended in one common conception, and be signified by one name. I say, do or might agree: for though there be but one sun existing in the world, yet the *idea* of it being abstracted, so that more substances (if there were several) might each agree in it; it is as much a sort, as if there were as many suns, as there are stars. They want not their reasons, who think there are, and that each fixed star, would answer the *idea* the name *sun* stands for, to one who was placed in a due distance; which, by the way, may show us how much the sorts, or, if you please, *genera* and *species* of things (for those Latin terms signify to me, no more than the English word *sort*) depend on such collections of *ideas,* as men have made; and not on the real nature of things: since 'tis not impossible, but that in propriety of speech, that might be a sun to one, which is a star to another.

2. *The essence of each sort is the abstract* idea. The measure and boundary of each sort, or *species,* whereby it is constituted that particular sort, and distinguished from others, is that we call its *essence,* which *is* nothing but that *abstract* idea *to which the name is annexed:* so that everything contained in that *idea,* is essential to that sort. This, though it be all the *essence* of natural substances, that we know, or by which we distinguish them into sorts; yet I call it by a peculiar name, the *nominal essence,* to distinguish it from that real constitution of substances, upon which depends this *nominal essence,* and all the properties of that sort; which therefore, as has been said, may be called the *real essence: v.g.* the *nominal essence* of *gold,* is that complex *idea* the word *gold* stands for, let it be, for instance, a body yellow, of a certain weight, malleable, fusible, and fixed. But the *real essence* is the constitution of the insensible parts of that body, on which those qualities, and all the other properties of *gold* depend. How far these two are different, though they are both called *essence,* is obvious, at first sight, to discover.

3. *The nominal and real essence different.* For though, perhaps, voluntary motion, with sense and reason, joined to a body of a certain shape, be the

complex *idea,* to which I, and others, annex the name *man;* and so be the *nominal essence* of the *species* so called: yet nobody will say, that complex *idea* is the *real essence* and source of all those operations, which are to be found in any individual of that sort. The foundation of all those qualities, which are the ingredients of our complex *idea,* is something quite different: and had we such a knowledge of that constitution of *man,* from which his faculties of moving, sensation, and reasoning, and other powers flow; and on which his so regular shape depends, as 'tis possible angels have, and 'tis certain his maker has, we should have a quite other *idea* of his *essence,* than what now is contained in our definition of that *species,* be it what it will: and our *idea* of any individual *man* would be as far different from what it now is, as is his, who knows all the springs and wheels, and other contrivances within, of the famous clock at *Strasburg,* from that which a gazing country-man has of it, who barely sees the motion of the hand, and hears the clock strike, and observes only some of the outward appearances.

4. *Nothing essential to individuals.* That *essence,* in the ordinary use of the word, relates to *sorts,* and that it is considered in particular beings, no farther than as they are ranked into *sorts,* appears from hence: that take but away the abstract *ideas,* by which we sort individuals, and rank them under common names, and then the thought of anything *essential* to any of them, instantly vanishes; we have no notion of the one, without the other: which plainly shows their relation. 'Tis necessary for me to be as I am; GOD and nature has made me so: but there is nothing I have, is essential to me. An accident, or disease, may very much alter my color, or shape; a fever, or fall, may take away my reason, or memory, or both; and an apoplexy leave neither sense, nor understanding, no nor life. Other creatures of my shape, may be made with more, and better, or fewer, and worse faculties than I have: and others may have reason, and sense, in a shape and body very different from mine. None of these are essential to the one, or the other, or to any individual whatsoever, till the mind refers it to some sort or *species* of things; and then presently, according to the abstract *idea* of that sort, something is found *essential.* Let anyone examine his own thoughts, and he will find, that as soon as he supposes or speaks of *essential,* the consideration of some *species,* or the complex *idea,* signified by some general name, comes into his mind: and 'tis in reference to that, that this or that quality is said to be *essential.* So that if it be asked, whether it be *essential* to me, or any other particular corporeal being to have reason? I say no; no more than it is *essential* to this white thing I write on, to have words in it. But if that particular being be to be counted of the sort *man,* and to have the name *man*

given it, then reason is *essential* to it, supposing reason to be a part of the complex *idea* the name *man* stands for: as it is *essential* to this thing I write on, to contain words, if I will give it the name *treatise,* and rank it under that *species.* So that *essential, and not essential, relate only to our abstract ideas, and the names annexed to them;* which amounts to no more than this, that whatever particular thing, has not in it those qualities, which are contained in the abstract *idea,* which any general term stands for, cannot be ranked under that *species,* nor be called by that name, since that abstract *idea* is the very *essence* of that *species.*

5. Thus if the *idea* of *body,* with some people, be bare extension, or space, then solidity is not *essential* to body: if others make the *idea,* to which they give the name *body,* to be solidity and extension, then solidity is essential also to *body.* That therefore, and *that alone is* considered as *essential, which makes a part of the complex* idea *the name of a sort stands for,* without which, no particular thing can be reckoned of that sort, nor be entitled to that name. Should there be found a parcel of matter, that had all the other qualities that are in *iron,* but wanted obedience to the lodestone; and would neither be drawn by it, nor receive direction from it, would anyone question, whether it wanted anything *essential*? It would be absurd to ask, whether a thing really existing, wanted anything *essential* to it. Or could it be demanded, whether this made an *essential* or *specific* difference, or no; since we have no other measure of *essential* or *specific,* but our abstract ideas? And to talk of specific differences in nature, without reference to general *ideas* and names, is to talk unintelligibly. For I would ask anyone, what is sufficient to make an *essential* difference in nature, between any two particular beings, without any regard had to some abstract *idea,* which is looked upon as the essence and standard of a *species*? All such patterns and standards, being quite laid aside, particular beings, considered barely in themselves, will be found to have all their qualities equally *essential;* and everything, in each individual, will be *essential* to it, or, which is more true, nothing at all. For though it may reasonably be asked, whether obeying the magnet be *essential* to *iron*? yet, I think, it is very improper and insignificant to ask, whether it be *essential* to the particular parcel of matter I cut my pen with, without considering it under the name *iron,* or as being of a certain *species*? And if, as has been said, our abstract *ideas,* which have names annexed to them, are the boundaries of *species,* nothing can be *essential* but what is contained in those *ideas.*

6. 'Tis true, I have often mentioned a *real essence,* distinct in substances, from those abstract *ideas* of them, which I call their *nominal essences.* By this

real essence, I mean, that real constitution of anything, which is the foundation of all those properties, that are combined in, and are constantly found to coexist with the *nominal essence;* that particular constitution, which everything has within itself, without any relation to anything without it. But *essence,* even in this sense, *relates to a sort,* and supposes a *species:* for being that real constitution, on which the properties depend, it necessarily supposes a sort of things, properties belonging only to *species,* and not to individuals; *v.g.* supposing the nominal essence of *gold,* to be a body of such a peculiar color and weight, with malleability and fusibility, the real essence is that constitution of the parts of matter, on which these qualities, and their union, depend; and is also the foundation of its solubility in *aqua regia,* and other properties accompanying that complex *idea.* Here are *essences* and *properties,* but all upon supposition of a sort, or general abstract *idea,* which is considered as immutable: but there is no individual parcel of matter, to which any of these qualities are so annexed, as to be *essential* to it, or inseparable from it. That which is *essential,* belongs to it as a condition, whereby it is of this or that sort: but take away the consideration of its being ranked under the name of some abstract *idea,* and then there is nothing necessary to it, nothing inseparable from it. Indeed, as to the *real essences* of substances, we only suppose their being, without precisely knowing what they are: but that which annexes them still to the *species,* is the nominal essence, of which they are the supposed foundation and cause.

7. *The nominal essence bounds the species.* The next thing to be considered is, by which of those essences it is, that *substances are determined into* sorts, or *species;* and that 'tis evident, is *by the nominal essence.* For 'tis that alone, that the name, which is the mark of the sort, signifies. 'Tis impossible therefore, that anything should determine the sorts of things, which we rank under general names, but that *idea,* which that name is designed as a mark for; which is that, as has been shown, which we call the *nominal essence.* Why do we say, this is a *horse,* that a *mule;* this is an *animal,* that an *herb*? How comes any particular thing to be of this or that sort, but because it has that nominal essence, or, which is all one, agrees to that abstract *idea,* that name is annexed to? And I desire anyone but to reflect on his own thoughts, when he hears or speaks any of those, or other names of substances, to know what sort of *essences* they stand for.

8. And that the *species of things to us, are nothing but the ranking them under distinct names, according to the complex* ideas *in us;* and not according to precise, distinct, real *essences* in them, is plain from hence, that we find

many of the individuals that are ranked into one sort, called by one common name, and so received as being of one *species,* have yet qualities depending on their real constitutions, as far different one from another, as from others, from which they are accounted to differ *specifically.* This, as it is easy to be observed by all, who have to do with natural bodies; so chemists especially are often, by sad experience, convinced of it, when they, sometimes in vain, seek for the same qualities in one parcel of sulphur, antimony, or vitriol, which they have found in others. For though they are bodies of the same *species,* having the same nominal *essence,* under the same name; yet do they often, upon severe ways of examination, betray qualities so different one from another, as to frustrate the expectation and labor of very wary chemists. . . .

9. *Not the real essence which we know not.* Nor indeed *can we* rank, and *sort things,* and consequently (which is the end of sorting) denominate them *by their real essences,* because we know them not. Our faculties carry us no farther towards the knowledge and distinction of substances, than a collection of those sensible *ideas,* which we observe in them; which however made with the greatest diligence and exactness, we are capable of, yet is more remote from the true internal constitution, from which those qualities flow, than, as I said, a country-man's *idea* is from the inward contrivance of that famous clock at *Strasburg,* whereof he only sees the outward figure and motions. There is not so contemptible a plant or animal, that does not confound the most enlarged understanding. . . . The workmanship of the all-wise, and powerful God, in the great fabric of the universe, and every part thereof, farther exceeds the capacity and comprehension of the most inquisitive and intelligent man, than the best contrivance of the most ingenious man, does the conceptions of the most ignorant of rational creatures. Therefore we in vain pretend to range things into sorts, and dispose them into certain classes, under names, by their *real essences,* that are so far from our discovery or comprehension. A blind man may as soon sort things by their colors, and he that has lost his smell, as well distinguish a lily and a rose by their odors, as by those internal constitutions which he knows not. . . .

. . . .

12. *There are probably numberless species of spirits.* It is not impossible to conceive, nor repugnant to reason, that there may be many *species of spirits,* as much separated and diversified one from another by distinct properties,

whereof we have no *ideas,* as the *species* of sensible things are distinguished one from another, by qualities, which we know, and observe in them. That there should be more *species* of intelligent creatures above us, than there are of sensible and material below us, is probable to me from hence; that in all the visible corporeal world, we see no chasms, or gaps. All quite down from us, the descent is by easy steps, and a continued series of things, that in each remove, differ very little one from the other. There are fishes that have wings, and are not strangers to the airy region: and there are some birds, that are inhabitants of the water; whose blood is cold as fishes, and their flesh so like in taste, that the scrupulous are allowed them on fish-days. There are animals so near of kin both to birds and beasts, that they are in the middle between both: amphibious animals link the terrestrial and aquatic together; seals live at land and at sea, and porpoises have the warm blood and entrails of a hog, not to mention what is confidently reported of mermaids, or sea-men. There are some brutes, that seem to have as much knowledge and reason, as some that are called men; and the animal and vegetable kingdoms, are so nearly joined, that if you will take the lowest of one, and the highest of the other, there will scarce be perceived any great difference between them; and so on till we come to the lowest and the most inorganical parts of matter, we shall find everywhere, that the several *species* are linked together, and differ but in almost insensible degrees. And when we consider the infinite power and wisdom of the maker, we have reason to think, that it is suitable to the magnificent harmony of the universe, and the great design and infinite goodness of the architect, that the *species* of creatures should also, by gentle degrees, ascend upward from us toward his infinite perfection, as we see they gradually descend from us downwards: which if it be probable, we have reason then to be persuaded, that there are far more *species* of creatures above us, than there are beneath; we being in degrees of perfection much more remote from the infinite being of GOD, than we are from the lowest state of being, and that which approaches nearest to nothing. And yet of all those distinct *species* . . . we have no clear distinct *ideas.*

. . . .

14. *Difficulties against a certain number of real essences.* To distinguish substantial beings into *species,* according to the usual supposition, that there are certain precise *essences* or *forms* of things, whereby all the individuals existing, are, by nature, distinguished into *species,* these things are necessary:

15. *First,* to be assured, that nature, in the production of things, always designs them to partake of certain regulated established *essences,* which are

to be the models of all things to be produced. This, in that crude sense, it is usually proposed, would need some better explication, before it can fully be assented to.

16. *Secondly,* it would be necessary to know, whether nature always attains that *essence,* it designs in the production of things. The irregular and monstrous births, that in divers sorts of animals have been observed, will always give us reason to doubt of one, or both of these.

17. *Thirdly,* it ought to be determined, whether those we call *monsters,* be really a distinct *species,* according to the scholastic notion of the word *species;* since it is certain, that everything that exists, has its particular constitution: and yet we find, that some of these monstrous productions, have few or none of those qualities, which are supposed to result from, and accompany the *essence* of that *species,* from whence they derive their originals, and to which, by their descent, they seem to belong.

18. *Fourthly,* the *real essences* of those things, which we distinguish into *species,* and as so distinguished we name, ought to be known; *i.e.* we ought to have *ideas* of them. But since we are ignorant in these four points, *the supposed real essences of things, stand us not in stead for the distinguishing substances into species.*

19. *Our nominal essences of substances, not perfect collections of properties. Fifthly,* the only imaginable help in this case would be, that having framed perfect complex *ideas* of the *properties* of things, flowing from their different real essences, we should thereby distinguish them into *species.* But neither can this be done: for being ignorant of the real essence itself, it is impossible to know all those properties, that flow from it, and are so annexed to it, that any one of them being away, we may certainly conclude, that that essence is not there, and so the thing is not of that *species.* We can never know what is the precise number of properties depending on the real essence of *gold,* any one of which failing, the real essence of gold, and consequently gold, would not be there, unless we knew the real essence of gold itself, and by that determined that *species.* By the word *gold* here, I must be understood to design a particular piece of matter; *v.g.* the last guinea that was coined. For if it should stand here in its ordinary signification for that complex *idea,* which I, or anyone else calls gold; *i.e.* for the nominal essence of gold, it would be *jargon:* so hard is it, to show the various meaning and imperfection of words, when we have nothing else but words to do it by.

20. By all which it is clear, that our *distinguishing substances into species* by names, *is not* at all *founded on their real essences;* nor can we pretend to range, and determine them exactly into species, according to internal essential differences.

. . . .

22. *Our abstract* ideas *are to us the measures of species, instance in that of man.* There are creatures in the world, that have shapes like ours, but are hairy, and want language, and reason. There are naturals amongst us, that have perfectly our shape, but want reason, and some of them language too. There are creatures, as 'tis said (*sit fides penes authorem,* but there appears no contradiction, that there should be such) that with language, and reason, and a shape in other things agreeing with ours, have hairy tails; others where the males have no beards, and others where the females have.[33] If it be asked, whether these be all *men,* or no, all of human *species;* 'tis plain, the question refers only to the nominal essence: for those of them to whom the definition of the word *man,* or the complex *idea* signified by that name, agrees are *men,* and the other not. But if the inquiry be made concerning the supposed real essence; and whether the internal constitution and frame of these several creatures be specifically different, it is wholly impossible for us to answer, no part of that going into our specific *idea:* only we have reason to think, that where the faculties, or outward frame so much differs, the internal constitution is not exactly the same: but, what difference in the internal real constitution makes a specific difference, it is in vain to inquire; whilst our *measures of species* be, as they *are, only our abstract* ideas, which we know; and not that internal constitution, which makes no part of them. . . .

23. *Species not distinguished by generation.* Nor let anyone say, that the power of propagation in animals by the mixture of male and female, and in plants by seeds, keeps the supposed real *species* distinct and entire. For granting this to be true, it would help us in the distinction of the *species* of things no farther than the tribes of animals and vegetables. What must we do for the rest? But in those too it is not sufficient: for if history lie not, women have conceived by drills; and what real *species,* by that measure, such a production will be in nature, will be a new question; and we have reason to think this is not impossible, since mules and gimars, the one from the mixture of

33. *sit fides penes authorem,* may the author be trusted.

an ass and a mare, the other from the mixture of a bull and a mare, are so frequent in the world. . . .

. . . .

25. *The specific essences are made by the mind.* But supposing that the *real essences* of substances were discoverable, by those, that would severely apply themselves to that inquiry; yet we could not reasonably think, that the *ranking of things under general names, was regulated by* those internal real constitutions, or anything else but *their obvious appearances.* Since languages, in all countries, have been established long before sciences. So that they have not been philosophers, or logicians, or such who have troubled themselves about *forms* and *essences,* that have made the general names, that are in use amongst the several nations of men; but those, more or less comprehensive terms, have, for the most part, in all languages, received their birth and signification, from ignorant and illiterate people, who sorted and denominated things, by those sensible qualities they found in them, thereby to signify them, when absent, to others, whether they had an occasion to mention a sort, or a particular thing.

26. *Therefore very various and uncertain.* Since then it is evident, that we sort and name substances by their *nominal,* and not by their real *essences,* the next thing to be considered is, how, and by whom these *essences* come to be made. As to the latter, 'tis evident they *are made by the mind,* and not by nature: for were they nature's workmanship, they could not be so various and different in several men, as 'tis evident they are. For if we will examine it, we shall not find the nominal essence of any one *species* of substances, in all men the same; no not of that, which of all others we are the most intimately acquainted with. It could not possibly be, that the abstract *idea,* to which the name *man* is given, should be different in several men, if it were of nature's making. . . .

27. Wherein then, would I gladly know, consist the precise and *unmovable boundaries of* that *species*? 'Tis plain, if we examine, there is *no* such thing *made by nature,* and established by her amongst men. The real essence of that, or any other sort of substances, 'tis evident we know not; and therefore are so undetermined in our nominal essences, which we make ourselves, that if several men were to be asked concerning some oddly shaped *fetus,* as soon as born, whether it were a *man,* or no, 'tis past doubt, one should meet with different answers . . . I think, I may say, that the certain boundaries of

that *species,* are so far from being determined, and the precise number of simple *ideas,* which make the nominal essence, so far from being settled, and perfectly known, that very material doubts may still arise about it: and I imagine, none of the definitions of the word *man,* which we yet have, nor descriptions of that sort of animal, are so perfect and exact, as to satisfy a considerate inquisitive person; much less to obtain a general consent, and to be that which men would everywhere stick by, in the decision of cases, and determining of life and death, baptism or no baptism, in productions that might happen.

28. *But not so arbitrary as mixed modes.* But though these *nominal essences of substances* are made by the mind, they are *not* yet *made so arbitrarily, as those of mixed modes.* To the making of any nominal essence, it is necessary, *first,* that the *ideas* whereof it consists, have such an union as to make but one *idea,* how compounded soever. *Secondly,* that the particular *ideas* so united, be exactly the same, neither more nor less. For if two abstract complex *ideas,* differ either in number, or sorts, of their component parts, they make two different, and not one and the same essence. In the first of these, the mind, in making its complex *ideas* of substances, only follows nature; and puts none together, which are not supposed to have an union in nature. . . . For though men may make what complex *ideas* they please, and give what names to them they will: yet if they will be understood, when they speak of things really existing, they must, in some degree, conform their *ideas* to the things they would speak of: or else men's language will be like that of *Babel;* and every man's words, being intelligible only to himself, would no longer serve to conversation, and the ordinary affairs of life, if the *ideas* they stand for, be not some way answering the common appearances and agreement of substances, as they really exist.

29. *Though very imperfect. Secondly,* though the mind of man, *in making* its *complex ideas of substances,* never puts any together that do not really, or are not supposed to coexist; and so it truly borrows that union from nature: yet *the number* it combines, *depends upon the various care, industry, or fancy of him that makes it.* Men generally content themselves with some few sensible obvious qualities; and often, if not always, leave out others as material, and as firmly united, as those that they take. . . .

. . . .

32. *The more general our* ideas *are, the more incomplete and partial they are.* If the *number of simple* ideas, *that make the nominal essence* of the lowest *species,*

or first sorting of individuals, *depends on the mind* of man, variously collecting them, it is much more evident, that they do so, in the more comprehensive *classes,* which, by the masters of logic are called *genera.* These are complex *ideas* designedly imperfect: and 'tis visible at first sight, that several of those qualities, that are to be found in the things themselves, are purposely left out of *generical ideas.* For as the mind, to make general *ideas,* comprehending several particulars, leaves out those of time, and place, and such other, that make them incommunicable to more than one individual, so to make other yet more general *ideas,* that may comprehend different sorts, it leaves out those qualities that distinguish them, and puts into its new collection, only such *ideas,* as are common to several sorts. . . .

. . . .

36. *Nature makes the similitude.* This then, in short, is the case: *nature makes many particular things, which do agree* one with another, in many sensible qualities, and probably too, in their internal frame and constitution: but 'tis not this real essence that distinguishes them into *species;* 'tis *men,* who, taking occasion from the qualities they find united in them, and wherein they observe often several individuals to agree, *range them into sorts, in order to their naming,* for the convenience of comprehensive signs; under which individuals, according to their conformity to this or that abstract *idea,* come to be ranked as under ensigns; so that this is of the blue, that the red regiment; this is a man, that a drill: and in this, I think, consists the whole business of *genus* and *species.*

. . . .

51. *Conclusion.* To conclude; what liberty *Adam* had at first to make any complex *ideas* of mixed modes, by no other pattern, but by his own thoughts, the same have all men ever since had. And the same necessity of conforming his *ideas* of substances to things without him, as to *archetypes* made by nature, that *Adam* was under, if he would not wilfully impose upon himself, the same are all men ever since under too. The same liberty also, that *Adam* had of affixing any new name to any *idea;* the same has anyone still, (especially the beginners of languages, if we can imagine any such,) but only with this difference, that in places, where men in society have already established a language amongst them, the significations of words are very warily and sparingly to be altered. Because men being furnished already with names for their *ideas,* and common use having appropriated

known names to certain *ideas,* an affected misapplication of them cannot but be very ridiculous. He that has new notions, will, perhaps, venture sometimes on the coining new terms to express them: but men think it a boldness, and 'tis uncertain, whether common use will ever make them pass for current. But in communication with others, it is necessary, that we conform the *ideas* we make the vulgar words of any language stand for, to their known proper significations, (which I have explained at large already,) or else to make known that new signification, we apply them to.

CHAP. VII.
Of particles.

1. *Particles connect parts, or whole sentences together.* Besides words, which are names of *ideas* in the mind, there are a great many others that are made use of, to signify the *connection* that the mind gives to *ideas, or propositions, one with another.* The mind, in communicating its thoughts to others, does not only need signs of the *ideas* it has then before it, but others also, to show or intimate some particular action of its own, at that time, relating to those *ideas.* This it does several ways; as *is,* and *is not,* are the general marks of the mind, affirming or denying. But besides affirmation, or negation, without which, there is in words no truth or falsehood, the mind does, in declaring its sentiments to others, connect, not only the parts of propositions, but whole sentences one to another, with their several relations and dependencies, to make a coherent discourse.

2. *In them consists the art of well speaking.* The words, whereby it signifies what connection it gives to the several affirmations and negations, that it unites in one continued reasoning or narration, are generally called *particles:* and 'tis in the right use of these, that more particularly consists the clearness and beauty of a good style. . . .

. . . .

4. *They show what relation the mind gives to its own thoughts.* Neither is it enough, for the explaining of these words, to render them, as is usually in dictionaries, by words of another tongue which came nearest to their signification: for what is meant by them, is commonly as hard to be

understood in one, as another language. They are all *marks of some action, or intimation of the mind;* and therefore to understand them rightly, the several views, postures, stands, turns, limitations, and exceptions, and several other thoughts of the mind, for which we have either none, or very deficient names, are diligently to be studied. . . .

. . . .

CHAP. IX.
Of the imperfection of words.

1. *Words are used for recording and communicating our thoughts.* From what has been said in the foregoing chapters, it is easy to perceive, what imperfection there is in language, and how the very nature of words, makes it almost unavoidable, for many of them to be doubtful and uncertain in their significations. To examine the perfection, or imperfection of words, it is necessary first to consider their use and end: for as they are more or less fitted to attain that, so they are more or less perfect. We have, in the former part of this discourse, often, upon occasion, mentioned *a double use of words.*

First, one for the recording of our own thoughts.

Secondly, the other for the communicating of our thoughts to others.

2. *Any words will serve for recording.* As to the first of these, *for the recording our own thoughts* for the help of our own memories, whereby, as it were, we talk to ourselves, any words will serve the turn. For since sounds are voluntary and indifferent signs of any *ideas,* a man may use what words he pleases, to signify his own *ideas* to himself: and there will be no imperfection in them, if he constantly use the same sign for the same *idea:* for then he cannot fail of having his meaning understood, wherein consists the right use and perfection of language.

3. *Communication by words, civil or philosophical. Secondly,* as to *communication by words,* that too *has a double use.*

I. *Civil.*
II. *Philosophical.*

First, by their *civil use,* I mean such a communication of thoughts and *ideas* by words, as may serve for the upholding common conversation and commerce, about the ordinary affairs and conveniencies of civil life, in the societies of men, one amongst another.

Secondly, by the *philosophical use* of words, I mean such an use of them, as may serve to convey the precise notions of things, and to express, in general propositions, certain and undoubted truths, which the mind may rest upon, and be satisfied with, in its search after true knowledge. These two uses are very distinct; and a great deal less exactness will serve in the one, than in the other, as we shall see in what follows.

4. *The imperfection of words is the doubtfulness of their signification.* The chief end of language in communication being to be understood, words serve not well for that end, neither in civil, nor philosophical discourse, when any word does not excite in the hearer, the same *idea* which it stands for in the mind of the speaker. Now since sounds have no natural connection with our *ideas,* but have all their signification from the arbitrary imposition of men, the *doubtfulness* and uncertainty *of their signification,* which *is the imperfection* we here are speaking of, has its cause more in the *ideas* they stand for, than in any incapacity there is in one sound, more than in another, to signify any *idea:* for in that regard, they are all equally perfect.

That then which makes doubtfulness and uncertainty in the signification of some more than other words, is the difference of *ideas* they stand for.

5. *Causes of their imperfection.* Words having naturally no signification, the *idea* which each stands for, must be learned and retained by those, who would exchange thoughts, and hold intelligible discourse with others, in any language. But this is hardest to be done, where,

First, the *ideas* they stand for, are very complex, and made up of a great number of *ideas* put together.

Secondly, where the *ideas* they stand for, have no certain connection in nature; and so no settled standard, anywhere in nature existing, to rectify and adjust them by.

Thirdly, when the signification of the word is referred to a standard, which standard is not easy to be known.

Fourthly, where the signification of the word, and the real essence of the thing, are not exactly the same.

These are difficulties that attend the signification of several words that are intelligible. Those which are not intelligible at all, such as names standing for any simple ideas, which another has not organs or faculties to attain; as the names of colors to a blind man, or sounds to a deaf man, need not here be mentioned.

In all these cases, we shall find an imperfection in words; which I shall . . . explain, in their particular application to our several sorts of *ideas:* for if we examine them, we shall find, that the *names of mixed modes are most liable to doubtfulness and imperfection, for the two first of these reasons; and the names of substances chiefly for the two latter.*

. . . .

11. If the signification of the names of mixed modes are uncertain, because there be no real standards existing in nature, to which those *ideas* are referred, and by which they may be adjusted, *the names of substances are of a doubtful signification,* for a contrary reason, *viz. because* the *ideas,* they stand for, are supposed conformable to the reality of things, and are *referred to standards* made by nature. In our *ideas* of substances we have not the liberty as in mixed modes, to frame what combinations we think fit, to be the characteristical notes, to rank and denominate things by. In these we must follow nature, suit our complex *ideas* to real existences, and regulate the signification of their names by the things themselves, if we will have our names to be signs of them, and stand for them. Here, 'tis true, we have patterns to follow; but patterns, that will make the signification of their names very uncertain: for names must be of a very unsteady and various meaning, if the *ideas* they stand for, be referred to standards without us, *that either cannot be known at all, or can be known but imperfectly and uncertainly.*

12. *Names of substances referred, first, to real essences that cannot be known.* The *names of substances have,* as has been showed, a double reference in their ordinary use.

First, sometimes they are made to stand for, and so their signification is supposed to agree to, *the real constitution of things,* from which all their properties flow, and in which they all center. But this real constitution, or (as it is apt to be called) essence, being utterly unknown to us, any sound that is put to stand for it, must be very uncertain in its application; and it will be impossible to know, what things are, or ought to be called an *horse,* or *antimony,* when those words are put for real essences, that we have no *ideas* of at all. And therefore in this supposition, the names of substances being referred to standards that cannot be known, their significations can never be adjusted and established by those standards.

13. *Secondly, to coexisting qualities, which are known but imperfectly. Secondly,* the *simple ideas* that are found to *coexist in substances,* being that which their names immediately signify, these, as united in the several sorts of things, *are* the proper *standards* to which their names are referred, and by which their significations may best be rectified. But neither will these *archetypes* so well serve to this purpose, as to leave these names without very various and uncertain significations. Because these simple *ideas* that coexist, and are united in the same subject, being very numerous, and having all an equal right to go into the complex specific *idea,* which the specific name is to stand for, men, though they propose to themselves the very same subject to consider, yet frame very different *ideas* about it; and so the name they use for it, unavoidably comes to have, in several men, very different significations. . . .

. . . .

18. *The names of simple* ideas *the least doubtful.* From what has been said, it is easy to observe, what has been before remarked. *viz.* that the *names of simple* ideas *are,* of all others the *least liable to mistakes,* and that for these reasons. *First,* because the *ideas* they stand for, being each but one single perception, are much easier got, and more clearly retained, than the more complex ones, and therefore are not liable to the uncertainty, which usually attends those compounded ones of *substances and mixed modes,* in which the precise number of simple *ideas,* that make them up, are not easily agreed, nor so readily kept in mind. And *secondly,* because they are never referred to any other essence, but barely that perception they immediately signify: which reference is that, which renders the signification of the names of substances naturally so perplexed, and gives occasion to so many disputes. . . .

. . . .

CHAP. X.
Of the abuse of words.

1. *Abuse of words.* Besides the imperfection that is naturally in language, and the obscurity and confusion that is so hard to be avoided in the use of words, there are *several wilful faults and neglects,* which men are guilty of, in this way of communication, whereby they render these signs less clear and distinct in their signification, than naturally they need to be.

2. *First, words without any, or without clear* ideas. *First,* in this kind, the first and most palpable abuse is, the using of words, without clear and distinct *ideas;* or, which is worse, signs without anything signified. Of these there are two sorts:

I. One may observe, in all languages, certain words, that if they be examined, will be found, in their first original, and their appropriated use, not to stand for any clear and distinct *ideas.* These, for the most part, the several *sects* of philosophy and religion have introduced. For their authors, or promoters, either affecting something singular, and out of the way of common apprehensions, or to support some strange opinions, or cover some weakness of their hypothesis, seldom fail to *coin* new words, and such as, when they come to be examined, may justly be called *insignificant terms.* For having either had no determinate collection of *ideas* annexed to them, when they were first invented; or at least such as, if well examined, will be found inconsistent, 'tis no wonder if afterwards, in the vulgar use of the same party, they remain empty sounds, with little or no signification, amongst those who think it enough to have them often in their mouths, as the distinguishing characters of their church, or school, without much troubling their heads to examine, what are the precise *ideas* they stand for. I shall not need here to heap up instances; everyone's reading and conversation will sufficiently furnish him: or if he wants to be better stored, the great mint-masters of these kind of terms, I mean the schoolmen and metaphysicians, (under which, I think the disputing natural and moral philosophers of these latter ages, may be comprehended,) have wherewithal abundantly to content him.

3. II. Others there be, who extend this abuse yet farther, who take so little care to lay by words, which in their primary notation have scarce any clear

and distinct *ideas* which they are annexed to, that by an unpardonable negligence, they familiarly *use words,* which the propriety of language has affixed to very important *ideas, without any distinct meaning* at all. *Wisdom, glory, grace,* &c. are words frequent enough in every man's mouth; but if a great many of those who use them, should be asked, what they mean by them? they would be at a stand, and not know what to answer: a plain proof, that though they have learned those sounds, and have them ready at their tongues' ends, yet there are no determined *ideas* laid up in their minds, which are to be expressed to others by them.

. . . .

5. *Secondly, unsteady application of them. Secondly,* another great abuse of words is, *inconstancy* in the use of them. It is hard to find a discourse written of any subject, especially of controversy, wherein one shall not observe, if he read with attention, the same words (and those commonly the most material in the discourse, and upon which the argument turns) used sometimes for one collection of simple *ideas,* and sometimes for another, which is a perfect abuse of language, words being intended for signs of my *ideas,* to make them known to others, not by any natural signification, but by a voluntary imposition, 'tis plain cheat and abuse, when I make them stand sometimes for one thing, and sometimes for another; the wilful doing whereof, can be imputed to nothing but great folly, or greater dishonesty. . . .

6. *Thirdly, affected obscurity by wrong application. Thirdly,* another abuse of language is, an *affected obscurity,* by either applying old words, to new and unusual significations; or introducing new and ambiguous terms, without defining either; or else putting them so together, as may confound their ordinary meaning. Though the Peripatetic philosophy has been most eminent in this way, yet other sects have not been wholly clear of it.[34] There is scarce any of them that are not cumbered with some difficulties, (such is the imperfection of human knowledge,) which they have been fain to cover with obscurity of terms, and to confound the signification of words, which, like a mist before people's eyes, might hinder their weak parts from being discovered. That *body* and *extension,* in common use, stand for two distinct ideas, is plain to anyone that will but reflect a little. For were their signification precisely the same, it would be as proper, and as intelligible to say, the *body of an extension,* as *the extension of a body;* and yet there are those

34. Peripatetic philosophy is the philosophy of Aristotle (384–322 B.C.) and his followers.

who find it necessary to confound their signification. To this abuse, and the mischiefs of confounding the signification of words, logic, and the liberal sciences, as they have been handled in the schools, have given reputation; and the admired art of disputing, has added much to the natural imperfection of languages, whilst it has been made use of, and fitted, to perplex the signification of words, more than to discover the knowledge and truth of things: and he that will look into that sort of learned writings, will find the words there much more obscure, uncertain, and undetermined in their meaning, than they are in ordinary conversation.

. . . .

12. *This art has perplexed religion and justice.* Nor has this mischief stopped in logical niceties, or curious empty speculations; it has invaded the great concernments of human life and society; obscured and perplexed the material truths of law and divinity; brought confusion, disorder and uncertainty into the affairs of mankind; and if not destroyed, yet in a great measure rendered useless, these two great rules, religion and justice. What have the greatest part of the comments and disputes upon the laws of GOD and man served for, but to make the meaning more doubtful, and perplex the sense? What have been the effect of those multiplied curious distinctions, and acute niceties, but obscurity and uncertainty, leaving the words more unintelligible, and the reader more at a loss? How else comes it to pass that princes, speaking or writing to their servants, in their ordinary commands, are easily understood; speaking to their people, in their laws, are not so? And . . . does it not often happen, that a man of an ordinary capacity, very well understands a text, or a law, that he reads, till he consults an expositor, or goes to counsel; who, by that time he has done explaining them, makes the words signify either nothing at all, or what he pleases.

. . . .

14. *Fourthly, taking them for things. Fourthly,* another great *abuse of words is, the taking them for things.* This, though it, in some degree, concerns all names in general; yet more particularly affects those of substances. To this abuse, those men are most subject, who most confine their thoughts to any one system, and give themselves up into a firm belief of the perfection of any received hypothesis: whereby they come to be persuaded, that the terms of that sect, are so suited to the nature of things, that they perfectly correspond with their real existence. Who is there, that has been bred up in

the Peripatetic philosophy, who does not think the ten names, under which are ranked the ten predicaments, to be exactly conformable to the nature of things?[35] Who is there, of that school, that is not persuaded, that *substantial forms, vegetative souls, abhorrence of a vacuum, intentional species,* &c. are something real?[36] These words men have learned from their very entrance upon knowledge, and have found their masters and systems lay great stress upon them: and therefore they cannot quit the opinion, that they are conformable to nature, and are the representations of something that really exists. The *Platonists* have their *soul of the world,* and the *Epicureans* their *endeavor towards motion* in their atoms, when at rest.[37] There is scarce any sect in philosophy has not a distinct set of terms, that others understand not. But yet this gibberish, which, in the weakness of human understanding, serves so well to palliate men's ignorance, and cover their errors, comes by familiar use amongst those of the same tribe, to seem the most important part of language, and of all other the terms the most significant. . . .

15. *Instance in matter.* How much *names taken for things,* are apt to *mislead the understanding,* the attentive reading of philosophical writers would abundantly discover; and that, perhaps, in words little suspected of any such misuse. I shall instance in one only, and that a very familiar one. How many intricate disputes have there been about *matter,* as if there were some such thing really in nature, distinct from *body;* as 'tis evident, the word *matter* stands for an *idea* distinct from the *idea* of body? For if the *ideas* these two terms stood for, were precisely the same, they might indifferently in all places be put for the other. But we see, that though it be proper to say, there is *one matter of all bodies,* one cannot say, there is *one body of all matters:* we familiarly say, one *body* is bigger than another, but it sounds harsh (and I

35. The predicaments are the ten categories of the Aristotelians, the basic kinds into which all things can be divided.

36. The notions Locke lists here were standard targets for seventeenth-century philosophers hostile (as Locke was) to Aristotle and scholasticism. A *substantial form* is a form which, when joined to matter, gives rise to a substance of a particular kind. A *vegetative soul* is an animating principle responsible for the characteristics of vegetative life, such as growth. *Abhorrence of a vacuum* is a principle or tendency meant to explain why air rushes in to fill space as it empties. *Intentional species* are internal representations used to explain how the mind thinks of things outside it.

37. Some Platonists (followers of Plato, 428–347 B.C.) believed in a soul of the world analogous to the souls of animals. The Epicureans (followers of Epicurus, 341–270 B.C.) were atomists; they traced the beginning of motion not to God, but to a tendency or "endeavor" toward motion contained in the atoms themselves.

think is never used) to say, one *matter* is bigger than another. Whence comes this then? *Viz.* from hence, that though *matter* and *body,* be not really distinct, but wherever there is one, there is the other; yet *matter* and *body,* stand for two different conceptions, whereof the one is incomplete, and but a part of the other. For *body* stands for a solid extended figured substance, whereof *matter* is but a partial and more confused conception, it seeming to me to be used for the substance and solidity of body, without taking in its extension and figure: and therefore it is that speaking of *matter,* we speak of it always as one, because in truth, it expressly contains nothing but the *idea* of a solid substance, which is everywhere the same, everywhere uniform. This being our *idea* of *matter,* we no more conceive, or speak of different *matters* in the world, than we do of different solidities; though we both conceive, and speak of different bodies, because extension and figure are capable of variation. But since solidity cannot exist without extension, and figure, the taking *matter* to be the name of something really existing under that precision, has no doubt produced those obscure and unintelligible discourses and disputes, which have filled the heads and books of philosophers concerning *materia prima;* which imperfection or abuse, how far it may concern a great many other general terms, I leave to be considered.[38] This, I think, I may at least say, that we should have a great many fewer disputes in the world, if words were taken for what they are, the signs of our *ideas* only, and not for things themselves. For when we argue about *matter,* or any the like term, we truly argue only about the *idea* we express by that sound, whether that precise *idea* agree to anything really existing in nature, or no. And if men would tell, what *ideas* they make their words stand for, there could not be half that obscurity or wrangling, in the search or support of truth, that there is.

. . . .

17. *Fifthly, setting them for what they cannot signify. Fifthly,* another *abuse of words, is the setting them in the place of things, which they do or can by no means signify.* We may observe, that in the general names of substances, whereof the nominal essences are only known to us, when we put them into propositions, and affirm or deny anything about them, we do most commonly tacitly suppose, or intend, they should stand for the real essence of a certain sort of substances. For when a man says *gold is malleable,* he means

38. *materia prima,* prime matter, an indeterminate substratum alleged (by some of the Aristotelians) to underlie all the forms that make something a thing of one kind rather than another.

and would insinuate something more than this, that *what I call gold is malleable,* (though truly it amounts to no more) but would have this understood, *viz.* that *gold;* i.e. *what has the real essence of gold is malleable,* which amounts to thus much, that *malleableness depends on, and is inseparable from the real essence of gold.* But a man, not knowing wherein that real essence consists, the connection in his mind of malleableness, is not truly with an essence he knows not, but only with the sound gold he puts for it. Thus when we say, that *animal rationale* is, and *animal implume bipes latis unguibus,* is not a good definition of a man; 'tis plain, we suppose the name man in this case to stand for the real essence of a species, and would signify, that a *rational animal* better described that real essence, than *a two-legged animal with broad nails, and without feathers.*[39] For else, why might not *Plato* as properly make the word ἄνθρωπος or *man* stand for his complex *idea,* made up of the *ideas* of a body, distinguished from others by a certain shape and other outward appearances, as *Aristotle,* make the complex *idea,* to which he gave the name ἄνθρωπος or *man,* of body, and the faculty of reasoning joined together; unless the name ἄνθρωπος or *man,* were supposed to stand for something else, than what it signifies; and to be put in the place of some other thing, than the *idea* a man professes he would express by it?[40]

. . . .

20. *The cause of this abuse, a supposition of nature's always working regularly.* That which, I think very much disposes men to substitute their names for the real essences of *species,* is the supposition before-mentioned, that nature works regularly in the production of things, and sets the boundaries to each of those *species,* by giving exactly the same real internal constitution to each individual, which we rank under one general name. Whereas anyone who observes their different qualities can hardly doubt, that many of the individuals, called by the same name, are, in their internal constitution, as different one from another, as several of those which are ranked under different specific names. *This supposition,* however *that the same precise internal constitution goes always with the same specific name, makes men forward to take* those *names for the representatives* of those real *essences,* though indeed they signify nothing but the complex *ideas* they have in their minds when they use them. So that, if I may so say, signifying one thing,

39. *animal rationale,* rational animal; *animal implume bipes latis unguibus,* two-legged featherless animal, with broad nails.

40. ἄνθρωπος, man or human being.

and being supposed for, or put in the place of another, they cannot but, in such a kind of use, cause a great deal of uncertainty in men's discourses; especially in those, who have thoroughly imbibed the doctrine of *substantial forms,* whereby they firmly imagine the several species of things to be determined and distinguished.

. . . .

22. *Sixthly, a supposition that words have a certain and evident signification. Sixthly,* there remains yet another more general, though, perhaps, less observed *abuse of words;* and that is, that men having by a long and familiar use annexed to them certain *ideas,* they are apt *to imagine so near and necessary a connection between the names and the signification* they use them in, that they forwardly suppose one cannot but understand what their meaning is; and therefore one ought to acquiesce in the words delivered, as if it were past doubt, that in the use of those common received sounds, the speaker and hearer had necessarily the same precise *ideas.* Whence presuming, that when they have in discourse used any term, they have thereby, as it were, set before others the very thing they talked of. And so likewise taking the words of others, as naturally standing for just what they themselves have been accustomed to apply them to, they never trouble themselves to explain their own, or understand clearly others' meaning. From whence commonly proceeds noise, and wrangling, without improvement or information; whilst men take words to be the constant regular marks of agreed notions, which in truth are no more but the voluntary and unsteady signs of their own *ideas.* . . .

. . . .

34. *Seventhly, figurative speech also an abuse of language.* Since wit and fancy find easier entertainment in the world, than dry truth and real knowledge, *figurative speeches,* and allusion in language, will hardly be admitted, as *an* imperfection or *abuse* of it. I confess, in discourses, where we seek rather pleasure and delight, than information and improvement, such ornaments as are borrowed from them, can scarce pass for faults. But yet, if we would speak of things as they are, we must allow, that all the art of rhetoric, besides order and clearness, all the artificial and figurative application of words eloquence has invented, are for nothing else but to insinuate wrong *ideas,* move the passions, and thereby mislead the judgment; and so indeed are perfect cheat: and therefore however laudable or allowable oratory may

render them in harangues and popular addresses, they are certainly, in all discourses that pretend to inform or instruct, wholly to be avoided; and where truth and knowledge are concerned, cannot but be thought a great fault, either of the language or person that makes use of them. What, and how various they are, will be superfluous here to take notice; the books of rhetoric which abound in the world, will instruct those, who want to be informed: only I cannot but observe, how little the preservation and improvement of truth and knowledge, is the care and concern of mankind; since the arts of fallacy are endowed and preferred. 'Tis evident how much men love to deceive, and be deceived, since rhetoric, that powerful instrument of error and deceit, has its established professors, is publicly taught, and has always been had in great reputation: and, I doubt not, but it will be thought great boldness, if not brutality in me, to have said thus much against it. . . .

CHAP. XI.

Of the remedies of the foregoing imperfections and abuses.

1. *They are worth seeking.* The natural and improved imperfections of languages, we have seen above at large: and speech being the great bond that holds society together, and the common conduit, whereby the improvements of knowledge are conveyed from one man, and one generation to another; it would well deserve our most serious thoughts, to consider what *remedies* are to be found *for these inconveniences* above-mentioned.

. . . .

8. *First, remedy to use no word without an* idea. *To remedy the defects of speech* before-mentioned, to some degree, and to prevent the inconveniences that follow from them, I imagine, the observation of these following rules may be of use, till somebody better able shall judge it worth his while, to think more maturely on this matter, and oblige the world with his thoughts on it.

First, a man shall take care *to use no word without a signification,* no name without an *idea* for which he makes it stand. . . .

9. *Secondly, to have distinct* ideas *annexed to them in modes. Secondly,* 'tis not enough a man *uses* his *words as signs of* some *ideas;* those *ideas* he annexes them to, if they be *simple* must be clear and distinct; if *complex* must be *determinate, i.e.* the precise collection of simple *ideas* settled in the mind, with that sound annexed to it, as the sign of that precise determined collection, and no other. This is very necessary in names of modes, and especially moral words; which having no settled objects in nature, from whence their *ideas* are taken, as from their originals, are apt to be very confused. *Justice* is a word in every man's mouth, but most commonly with a very undetermined loose signification: which will always be so, unless a man has in his mind a distinct comprehension of the component parts, that complex *idea* consists of; and if it be decompounded, must be able to resolve it still on, till he at last comes to the simple *ideas,* that make it up: and unless this be done, a man makes an ill use of the word, let it be *justice,* for example, or any other. I do not say, a man needs stand to recollect, and make this analysis at large, every time the word *justice* comes in his way: but this, at least, is necessary, that he have so examined the signification of that name, and settled the *idea* of all its parts in his mind, that he can do it when he pleases. . . .

10. *And conformable in substances.* In the names of *substances,* for a right use of them, something more is required than barely *determined ideas:* in these *the names must also be conformable to things,* as they exist: but of this, I shall have occasion to speak more at large by and by. This exactness is absolutely necessary in inquiries after philosophical knowledge, and in controversies about truth. And though it would be well too, if it extended itself to common conversation, and the ordinary affairs of life; yet I think, that is scarce to be expected. Vulgar notions suit vulgar discourses: and both, though confused enough, yet serve pretty well the market, and the wake. Merchants and lovers, cooks and tailors, have words wherewithal to dispatch their ordinary affairs; and so, I think, might philosophers and disputants too, if they had a mind to understand, and to be clearly understood.

11. *Thirdly, propriety. Thirdly,* 'tis not enough that men have *ideas,* determined *ideas,* for which they make these signs stand; but they *must* also take care to *apply their words,* as near as may be, *to such* ideas *as common use has annexed them to.* For words, especially of languages already framed, being no man's private possession, but the common measure of commerce and communication, 'tis not for anyone, at pleasure, to change the stamp they

are current in; nor alter the *ideas* they are affixed to; or at least when there is a necessity to do so, he is bound to give notice of it. . . .

12. *Fourthly, to make known their meaning. Fourthly.* But because common use has not so visibly annexed any signification to words, as to make men know always certainly what they precisely stand for: and because men in the improvement of their knowledge, come to have *ideas* different from the vulgar and ordinary received ones, for which they must either make new words, (which men seldom venture to do, for fear of being thought guilty of affectation, or novelty,) or else *must* use old ones, in a new signification. Therefore after the observation of the foregoing rules, it is sometimes necessary for the ascertaining the signification of words, to *declare their meaning;* where either common use has left it uncertain and loose; (as it has in most names of very complex *ideas*) or where a man uses them in a sense any way peculiar to himself; or where the term, being very material in the discourse, and that upon which it chiefly turns, is liable to any doubtfulness or mistake.

13. *And that three ways.* As the *ideas,* men's words stand for, are of different sorts: so the way of making known the *ideas,* they stand for, when there is occasion, is also different. For though defining be thought the proper *way, to make known the proper signification of words;* yet there be some words, that will not be defined, as there be others, whose precise meaning cannot be made known, but by definition: and, perhaps, a third, which partake somewhat of both the other, as we shall see in the names of simple *ideas,* modes, and substances.

14. *First, in simple* ideas *by synonymous terms or showing. First,* when a man makes use of the *name* of *any simple* idea, which he perceives is not understood, or is in danger to be mistaken, he is obliged by the laws of ingenuity, and the end of speech, to declare his meaning, and make known what *idea* he makes it stand for. This, as has been shown, cannot be done by definition: and therefore, when a synonymous word fails to do it, there is but one of these ways left. *First,* sometimes the *naming the subject, wherein that simple* idea *is* to be found, will make its name to be understood by those, who are acquainted with that subject, and know it by that name. So to make a country-man understand what *feuillemorte* color signifies, it may suffice to tell him, 'tis the color of withered leaves falling in *autumn. Secondly,* but the only sure way of making known the signification of the name of any

simple *idea,* is *by presenting to his senses that subject, which may produce it in his mind,* and make him actually have the *idea,* that word stands for.

15. *Secondly, in mixed modes by definition. Secondly, mixed modes,* especially those belonging to morality, being most of them such combinations of *ideas,* as the mind puts together of its own choice, and whereof there are not always standing patterns to be found existing, the signification of their names cannot be made known, as those of simple *ideas,* by any showing; but in recompense thereof, may be perfectly and exactly *defined.* For they being combinations of several *ideas,* that the mind of man has arbitrarily put together, without reference to any archetypes, men may, if they please, exactly know the *ideas,* that go to each composition, and so both use these words in a certain and undoubted signification, and perfectly declare, when there is occasion, what they stand for. This, if well considered, would lay great blame on those, who make not their discourses about moral things very clear and distinct. For since the precise signification of the names of mixed modes, or, which is all one, the real essence of each species, is to be known, they being not of nature's, but man's making, it is a great negligence and perverseness, to discourse of moral things with uncertainty and obscurity, which is more pardonable in treating of natural substances, where doubtful terms are hardly to be avoided, for a quite contrary reason, as we shall see by and by.

16. *Morality capable of demonstration.* Upon this ground it is, that I am bold to think, that *morality is capable of demonstration,* as well as mathematics: since the precise real essence of the things moral words stand for, may be perfectly known; and so the congruity or, incongruity of the things themselves, be certainly discovered, in which consists perfect knowledge. Nor let anyone object, that the names of substances are often to be made use of in morality, as well as those of modes, from which will arise obscurity. For as to substances, when concerned in moral discourses, their divers natures are not so much inquired into, as supposed; *v.g.* when we say that *man is subject to law:* we mean nothing by *man,* but a corporeal rational creature: what the real essence or other qualities of that creature are in this case, is no way considered. And therefore, whether a child or changeling be a *man* in a physical sense, may amongst the naturalists be as disputable as it will, it concerns not at all the *moral man,* as I may call him, which is this immovable unchangeable *idea, a corporeal rational being.* For were there a monkey, or any other creature to be found, that had the use of reason, to such a degree, as to be able to understand general signs, and to deduce

consequences about general *ideas,* he would no doubt be subject to law, and, in that sense, be a *man,* how much soever he differed in shape from others of that name. The names of substances, if they be used in them, as they should, can no more disturb moral, than they do mathematical discourses: where, if the mathematician speaks of a *cube* or *globe* of *gold,* or any other body, he has his clear settled *idea,* which varies not, though it may, by mistake be applied to a particular body, to which it belongs not.

17. *Definitions can make moral discourses clear.* This I have here mentioned by the by, to show of what consequence it is for men, in their names of mixed modes, and consequently, in all their moral discourses, to define their words when there is occasion: since thereby moral knowledge may be brought, to so great clearness and certainty. And it must be great want of ingenuity, (to say no worse of it) to refuse to do it: since a *definition is the only way, whereby the precise meaning of moral words can be known;* and yet a way, whereby their meaning may be known *certainly,* and without leaving any room for any contest about it. And therefore the negligence or perverseness of mankind, cannot be excused, if their discourses in morality be not much more clear, than those in natural philosophy: since they are about *ideas* in the mind, which are none of them false or disproportionate; they having no external beings for *archetypes* which they are referred to, and must correspond with. It is far easier for men to frame in their minds an *idea,* which shall be the standard to which they will give the name *justice,* with which pattern so made, all actions that agree shall pass under that denomination, than, having seen *Aristides,* to frame an *idea,* that shall in all things be exactly like him, who is as he is, let men make what *idea,* they please of him. For the one, they need but know the combination of *ideas* that are put together in their own minds; for the other, they must inquire into the whole nature, and abstruse hidden constitution, and various qualities of a thing existing without them.

. . . .

19. *Thirdly, in substances, by showing and defining. Thirdly, for the explaining* the signification of *the names of substances* as they stand for the *ideas* we have of their distinct species, both the forementioned ways, *viz.* of *showing and defining, are requisite,* in many cases, to be made use of. For there being ordinarily in each sort some leading qualities, to which we suppose the other *ideas,* which make up our complex *idea* of that species, annexed, we forwardly give the specific name to that thing, wherein that characteristical

mark is found, which we take to be the most distinguishing *idea* of that species. These leading or characteristical (as I may call them) *ideas,* in the sorts of animals and vegetables, is . . . mostly figure, and in inanimate bodies color, and in some both together.

. . . .

21. Ideas *of the leading qualities of substances, are best got by showing.* Now *these leading qualities, are best made known by showing,* and can hardly be made known otherwise. . . .

22. *The* ideas *of their powers best by definition.* But because many of the simple *ideas* that make up our specific *ideas* of substances, are powers, which lie not obvious to our senses in the things as they ordinarily appear; therefore *in* the signification of our *names of substances, some part of the signification will be better made known, by enumerating those simple* ideas, *than in showing the substance itself.* For he that, to the yellow shining color of *gold* got by sight, shall, from my enumerating them, have the *ideas* of great ductility, fusibility, fixedness, and solubility, in *aqua regia,* will have a perfecter *idea of gold,* than he can have by seeing a piece of *gold,* and thereby imprinting in his mind only its obvious qualities. But if the formal constitution of this shining, heavy, ductile thing (from whence all these its properties flow) lay open to our senses, as the formal constitution, or essence of a triangle does, the signification of the word *gold,* might as easily be ascertained, as that of triangle.

23. *A reflection on the knowledge of spirits.* Hence we may take notice, how much the foundation of all *our knowledge of corporeal things, lies in our senses.* For how spirits, separate from bodies, (whose knowledge and *ideas* of these things are certainly much more perfect than ours) know them, we have no notion, no *idea* at all. The whole extent of our knowledge, or imagination, reaches not beyond our own *ideas,* limited to our ways of perception. Though yet it be not to be doubted, that spirits of a higher rank than those immersed in flesh, may have as clear *ideas* of the radical constitution of substances, as we have of a triangle, and so perceive how all their properties and operations flow from thence: but the manner how they come by that knowledge, exceeds our conceptions.

24. Ideas *also of substances must be conformable to things.* But though definitions will serve to explain the names of substances, as they stand for our

ideas; yet they leave them not without great imperfection, as they stand for things. For our names of substances being not put barely for our *ideas,* but being made use of ultimately to represent things, and so are put in their place, their signification must agree with the truth of things, as well as with men's *ideas.* And therefore in substances, we are not always to rest in the ordinary complex *idea,* commonly received as the signification of that word, but must go a little farther, and inquire into the nature and properties of the things themselves, and thereby perfect, as much as we can, our *ideas* of their distinct species; or else learn them from such as are used to that sort of things, and are experienced in them. For since 'tis intended their names should stand for such collections of simple *ideas,* as do really exist in things themselves, as well as for the complex *idea* in other men's minds, which in their ordinary acceptation they stand for: therefore *to define their names right, natural history is to be inquired into;* and their properties are, with care and examination, to be found out. For it is not enough, for the avoiding inconveniencies in discourse and arguings about natural bodies and substantial things, to have learned, from the propriety of the language, the common but confused, or very imperfect *idea,* to which each word is applied, and to keep them to that *idea* in our use of them: but we must, by acquainting ourselves with the history of that sort of things rectify and settle our complex *idea,* belonging to each specific name; and in discourse with others, (if we find them mistake us) we ought to tell, what the complex *idea* is, that we make such a name stand for. This is the more necessary to be done by all those, who search after knowledge, and philosophical verity, in that children being taught words whilst they have but imperfect notions of things, apply them at random, and without much thinking, and seldom frame determined *ideas* to be signified by them. Which custom, (it being easy, and serving well enough for the ordinary affairs of life and conversation) they are apt to continue, when they are men: and so begin at the wrong end, learning words first, and perfectly, but make the notions, to which they apply those words afterwards, very overtly. By this means it comes to pass, that men speaking the proper language of their country, *i.e.* according to grammar-rules of that language, do yet speak very improperly of things themselves; and by their arguing one with another, make but small progress in the discoveries of useful truths, and the knowledge of things, as they are to be found in themselves, and not in our imaginations; and it matters not much, for the improvement of our knowledge, how they are called.

25. *Not easy to be made so.* It were therefore to be wished, that men, versed in physical inquiries, and acquainted with the several sorts of natural bodies,

would set down those simple *ideas,* wherein they observe the individuals of each sort constantly to agree. This would remedy a great deal of that confusion,which comes from several persons, applying the same name to a collection of a smaller, or greater number of sensible qualities, proportionably as they have been more or less acquainted with, or accurate in examining the qualities of any sort of things, which come under one denomination. But a dictionary of this sort, containing, as it were, a natural history, requires too many hands, as well as too much time, cost, pains, and sagacity, ever to be hoped for; and till that be done, we must content ourselves with such definitions of the names of substances, as explain the sense men use them in. . . . But though such a dictionary . . . will require too much time, cost, and pains, to be hoped for in this age; yet, methinks, it is not unreasonable to propose, that words standing for things, which are known and distinguished by their outward shapes, should be expressed by little drafts and prints made of them. A vocabulary made after this fashion, would, perhaps with more ease, and in less time, teach the true signification of many terms, especially in languages of remote countries or ages, and settle truer *ideas* in men's minds of several things, whereof we read the names in ancient authors, than all the large and laborious comments of learned critics. Naturalists, that treat of plants and animals, have found the benefit of this way: and he that has had occasion to consult them, will have reason to confess, that he has a clearer idea of *apium,* or *ibex* from a little print of that herb, or beast, than he could have from a long definition of the names of either of them. And so, no doubt, he would have of *strigil* and *sistrum,* if instead of a *curry-comb,* and *cymbal,* which are the English names dictionaries render them by, he could see stamped in the margin, small pictures of these instruments, as they were in use amongst the ancients. *Toga, tunica, pallium,* are words easily translated by *gown, coat,* and *cloak:* but we have thereby no more true *ideas* of the fashion of those habits amongst the *Romans,* than we have of the faces of the tailors who made them. Such things as these, which the eye distinguishes by their shapes, would be best let into the mind by drafts made of them, and more determine the signification of such words, than any other words set for them, or made use of to define them. But this only by the by.

26. *Fifthly, by constancy in their signification. Fifthly,* if men will not be at the pains to declare the meaning of their words, and definitions of their terms are not to be had; yet this is the least that can be expected, that in all discourses, wherein one man pretends to instruct or convince another, he should *use the same word constantly in the same sense:* if this were done, (which

nobody can refuse, without great disingenuity) many of the books extant might be spared; many of the controversies in dispute would be at an end; several of those great volumes, swollen with ambiguous words, now used in one sense, and by and by in another, would shrink into a very narrow compass; and many of the philosophers' (to mention no other,) as well as poets' works, might be contained in a nutshell.

27. *When the variation is to be explained.* But after all, the provision of words is so scanty in respect to that infinite variety of thoughts, that men, wanting terms to suit their precise notions, will, notwithstanding their utmost caution, be forced often to use the same word, in somewhat different senses. And though in the continuation of a discourse, or the pursuit of an argument, there be hardly room to digress into a particular definition, as often as a man varies the signification of any term; yet the import of the discourse will, for the most part, if there be no designed fallacy, sufficiently lead candid and intelligent readers, into the true meaning of it: but where there is not sufficient to guide the reader, there it concerns the writer to explain his meaning, and show in what sense he there uses that term.

BOOK IV.

CHAP. I.

Of knowledge in general.

1. *Our knowledge conversant about our* ideas. Since *the mind,* in all its thoughts and reasonings, has no other immediate object but its own *ideas,* which it alone does or can contemplate, it is evident, that our knowledge is only conversant about them.

2. *Knowledge is the perception of the agreement or disagreement of two* ideas. *Knowledge* then seems to me to be nothing but *the perception of the connection and agreement, or disagreement and repugnancy of any of our ideas.* In this alone it consists. Where this perception is, there is knowledge, and where it is not, there, though we may fancy, guess, or believe, yet we always come short of knowledge. For when we know that *white is not black,* what do we else but perceive, that these two ideas do not agree? When we possess ourselves with the utmost security of the demonstration, that *the three angles of a triangle are equal to two right ones,* what do we more but perceive, that equality to two right ones does necessarily agree to, and is inseparable from the three angles of a triangle?

3. *This agreement fourfold.* But to understand a little more distinctly, wherein this agreement or disagreement consists, I think we may reduce it all to these four sorts:

1. *Identity,* or *diversity.*
2. *Relation.*
3. *Coexistence,* or *necessary connection.*
4. *Real existence.*

4. *First, of identity or diversity. First,* as to the first sort of agreement or disagreement, *viz. identity,* or *diversity.* 'Tis the first act of the mind, when it has any sentiments or *ideas* at all, to perceive its *ideas,* and so far as it perceives them, to know each what it is, and thereby also to perceive their

difference, and that one is not another. This is so absolutely necessary, that without it there could be no knowledge, no reasoning, no imagination, no distinct thoughts at all. By this the mind clearly and infallibly perceives each *idea* to agree with itself, and to be what it is; and all distinct *ideas* to disagree, *i.e.* the one not to be the other: and this it does without pains, labor, or deduction; but at first view, by its natural power of perception and distinction. And though men of art have reduced this into those general rules, *what is, is; and it is impossible for the same thing to be, and not to be;* for ready application in all cases, wherein there may be occasion to reflect on it; yet it is certain, that the first exercise of this faculty, is about particular *ideas.* A man infallibly knows, as soon as ever he has them in his mind that the *ideas* he calls *white* and *round,* are the very *ideas* they are, and that they are not other *ideas* which he calls *red* or *square.* Nor can any maxim or proposition in the world make him know it clearer or surer than he did before, and without any such general rule. This then is the first agreement, or disagreement, which the mind perceives in its *ideas;* which it always perceives at first sight: and if there ever happen any doubt about it, 'twill always be found to be about the names, and not the *ideas* themselves, whose identity and diversity will always be perceived, as soon and clearly as the *ideas* themselves are, nor can it possibly be otherwise.

5. *Secondly, relative. Secondly,* the next sort of agreement, or disagreement, the mind perceives in any of its *ideas,* may, I think, be called *relative,* and is nothing but *the perception of the relation between any two ideas,* of what kind soever, whether substances, modes, or any other. For since all distinct *ideas* must eternally be known not to be the same, and so be universally and constantly denied one of another, there could be no room for any positive knowledge at all, if we could not perceive any relation between our *ideas,* and find out the agreement or disagreement, they have one with another, in several ways the mind takes of comparing them.

6. *Thirdly, of coexistence. Thirdly,* the third sort of agreement, or disagreement, to be found in our *ideas,* which the perception of the mind is employed about, is *coexistence,* or *non-coexistence* in the same subject; and this belongs particularly to substances. Thus when we pronounce concerning *gold,* that it is fixed, our knowledge of this truth amounts to no more but this, that fixedness, or a power to remain in the fire unconsumed, is an *idea,* that always accompanies, and is joined with that particular sort of yellowness, weight, fusibility, malleableness, and solubility in *aqua regia,* which make our complex *idea,* signified by the word *gold.*

7. *Fourthly, of real existence. Fourthly,* the fourth and last sort is that of *actual real existence* agreeing to any *idea.* Within these four sorts of agreement or disagreement, is, I suppose, contained all the knowledge we have, or are capable of: for all the inquiries we can make, concerning any of our *ideas,* all that we know, or can affirm concerning any of them, is, that it is, or is not the same with some other; that it does, or does not always coexist with some other *idea* in the same subject; that it has this or that relation to some other *idea;* or that it has a real existence without the mind. Thus *blue is not yellow,* is of identity. *Two triangles upon equal basis, between two parallels are equal,* is of relation. *Iron is susceptible of magnetical impressions,* is of coexistence, *GOD is,* is of real existence. Though identity and co-existence are truly nothing but relations, yet they are so peculiar ways of agreement, or disagreement of our *ideas,* that they deserve well to be considered as distinct heads, and not under relation in general; since they are so different grounds of affirmation and negation, as will easily appear to anyone, who will but reflect on what is said in several places of this essay. I should now proceed to examine the several degrees of our knowledge, but that it is necessary first, to consider the different acceptations of the word *knowledge.*

8. *Knowledge actual or habitual.* There are several ways wherein the mind is possessed of truth; each of which is called *knowledge.*

1. There is *actual knowledge,* which is the present view the mind has of the agreement, or disagreement of any of its *ideas,* or of the relation they have one to another.

2. A man is said to know any proposition, which having been once laid before his thoughts, he evidently perceived the agreement, or disagreement of the *ideas* whereof it consists; and so lodged it in his memory, that whenever that proposition comes again to be reflected on, he, without doubt or hesitation, embraces the right side, assents to, and is certain of the truth of it. This, I think, one may call *habitual knowledge:* and thus a man may be said to know all those truths, which are lodged in his memory, by a foregoing clear and full perception, whereof the mind is assured past doubt, as often as it has occasion to reflect on them. For our finite understandings being able to think, clearly and distinctly, but on one thing at once, if men had no knowledge of any more than what they actually thought on, they would all be very ignorant: and he that knew most, would know but one truth, that being all he was able to think on at one time.

9. *Habitual knowledge twofold.* Of habitual knowledge, there are also, vulgarly speaking two degrees:

First, the one is of *such truths laid up in the memory, as whenever they occur to the mind, it actually perceives the relation is between those ideas.* And this is in all those truths, whereof we have an *intuitive knowledge,* where the *ideas* themselves, by an immediate view, discover their agreement or disagreement one with another.

Secondly, the other is of *such truths, whereof the mind having been convinced, it retains the memory of the conviction, without the proofs.* Thus a man that remembers certainly, that he once perceived the demonstration, that the three angles of a triangle are equal to two right ones, is certain that he knows it, because he cannot doubt the truth of it. In his adherence to a truth, where the demonstration, by which it was at first known, is forgot, though a man may be thought rather to believe his memory, than really to know, and this way of entertaining a truth seemed formerly to me like something between opinion and knowledge, a sort of assurance which exceeds bare belief, for that relies on the testimony of another; yet upon a due examination I find it comes not short of perfect certainty, and is in effect true knowledge. That which is apt to mislead our first thoughts into a mistake in this matter is, that the agreement or disagreement of the *ideas* in this case is not perceived, as it was at first, by an actual view of all the intermediate *ideas* whereby the agreement or disagreement of those in the proposition was at first perceived; but by other intermediate *ideas,* that show the agreement or disagreement of the *ideas* contained in the proposition whose certainty we remember. For example, in this proposition, that the three angles of a triangle are equal to two right ones, one, who has seen and clearly perceived the demonstration of this truth, knows it to be true, when that demonstration is gone out of his mind; so that at present it is not actually in view, and possibly cannot be recollected: but he knows it in a different way, from what he did before. The agreement of the two *ideas* joined in that proposition is perceived, but it is by the intervention of other *ideas* than those which at first produced that perception. He remembers, *i.e.* he knows (for remembrance is but the reviving of some past knowledge) that he was once certain of the truth of this proposition, that the three angles of a triangle are equal to two right ones. The immutability of the same relations between the same immutable things, is now the *idea* that shows him, that if the three angles of a triangle were once equal to two right ones, they will always be equal to two right ones. And hence he comes to be certain, that what was once true in the case, is always true; what *ideas* once agreed will always agree; and consequently what he once knew to be true he will always know to be true, as long as he can remember that he once knew it. Upon this ground it is, that particular demonstrations in mathematics afford general knowledge. If then the perception that the same ideas will eternally have the same habitudes and relations be not a sufficient ground of knowledge, there could be no knowledge of general propositions in mathematics, for no mathematical demonstration would be any other than particular: and when a man had demonstrated any proposition concerning one triangle or circle, his knowledge would not reach beyond that particular diagram. If he would extend it farther he must renew his demonstration in another instance, before he could know it to be true in another like triangle, and so on: by which means one could never come to the knowledge of any general propositions. Nobody, I think can deny that Mr. *Newton* certainly knows any proposition, that he now at any time reads in his book, to be true, though he has not in actual view that admirable chain of intermediate *ideas,* whereby he at first discovered it to be true.[41] Such a memory as that, able to retain such a train of particulars, may be well thought beyond the reach of human faculties. When the very discovery, perception, and laying together that wonderful connection of *ideas* is found to surpass most readers' *comprehension.* But yet 'tis evident, the author himself knows the proposition to be true, remembering he once saw the connection of those *ideas,* as certainly as he knows such a man wounded another, remembering that he saw him run him through. But because the memory is not always so clear as actual perception, and does in all men more or less decay in length of time, this amongst other differences is one, which shows, that *demonstrative knowledge,* is much more imperfect than *intuitive,* as we shall see in the following chapter.

CHAP. II.

Of the degrees of our knowledge.

1. *Intuitive.* All our knowledge consisting, as I have said, in the view the mind has of its own *ideas,* which is the utmost light and greatest certainty we, with our faculties, and in our way of knowledge are capable of, it may not be amiss, to consider a little the degrees of its evidence. The different clearness of our knowledge seems to me to lie in the different way of perception, the mind has of the agreement, or disagreement of any of its

41. Isaac Newton (1642–1727), British scientist; the book is *Mathematical Principles of Natural Philosophy,* published in 1687.

ideas. For if we will reflect on our own ways of thinking, we shall find, that sometimes the mind perceives the agreement or disagreement of two *ideas* immediately by themselves, without the intervention of any other: and this, I think, we may call *intuitive knowledge.* For in this the mind is at no pains of proving or examining, but perceives the truth, as the eye does light, only by being directed toward it. Thus the mind perceives, that *white* is not *black,* that a *circle* is not a *triangle,* that *three* are more than *two,* and equal to *one* and *two.* Such kind of truths, the mind perceives at the first sight of the *ideas* together, by bare *intuition,* without the intervention of any other *idea;* and this kind of knowledge is the clearest, and most certain, that human frailty is capable of. This part of knowledge is irresistible, and like the bright sunshine, forces itself immediately to be perceived, as soon as ever the mind turns its view that way; and leaves no room for hesitation, doubt, or examination, but the mind is presently filled with the clear light of it. 'Tis on this *intuition,* that depends all the certainty and evidence of all our knowledge, which certainty everyone finds to be so great, that he cannot imagine, and therefore not require a greater: for a man cannot conceive himself capable of a greater certainty, than to know that any *idea* in his mind is such, as he perceives it to be; and that two *ideas,* wherein he perceives a difference, are different, and not precisely the same. He that demands a greater certainty than this, demands he knows not what, and shows only that he has a mind to be a skeptic, without being able to be so. Certainty depends so wholly on this intuition, that in the next degree of *knowledge,* which I call *demonstrative,* this intuition is necessary in all the connections of the intermediate *ideas,* without which we cannot attain knowledge and certainty.

2. *Demonstrative.* The next degree of knowledge is, where the mind perceives the agreement or disagreement of any *ideas,* but not immediately. Though wherever the mind perceives the agreement or disagreement of any of its *ideas,* there be certain knowledge: yet it does not always happen, that the mind sees that agreement or disagreement, which there is between them, even where it is discoverable; and in that case, remains in ignorance, and at most, gets no farther than a probable conjecture. The reason why the mind cannot always perceive presently the agreement or disagreement of two *ideas* is, because those *ideas,* concerning whose agreement or disagreement the inquiry is made, cannot by the mind be so put together, as to show it. In this case then, when the mind cannot so bring its *ideas* together, as by their immediate comparison, and as it were juxtaposition, or application

one to another, to perceive their agreement or disagreement, it is fain, by the intervention of other *ideas* (one or more, as it happens) to discover the agreement or disagreement, which it searches; and this is that which we call *reasoning.* Thus the mind being willing to know the agreement or disagreement in bigness, between the three angles of a triangle, and two right ones, cannot by an immediate view and comparing them, do it: because the three angles of a triangle cannot be brought at once, and be compared with any other one, or two angles; and so of this the mind has no immediate, no intuitive knowledge. In this case the mind is fain to find out some other angles, to which the three angles of a triangle have an equality; and, finding those equal to two right ones, comes to know their equality to two right ones.

3. *Depends on proofs.* Those intervening *ideas,* which serve to show the agreement of any two others, are called *proofs;* and where the agreement or disagreement is by this means plainly and clearly perceived, it is called *demonstration,* it being *shown* to the understanding, and the mind made to see that it is so. A quickness in the mind to find out these intermediate *ideas,* (that shall discover the agreement or disagreement of any other,) and to apply them right, is, I suppose, that which is called *sagacity.*

4. *But not so easy. This knowledge by intervening proofs,* though it be certain, yet the evidence of it is *not* altogether *so clear* and bright, nor the assent so ready, *as* in *intuitive* knowledge. For though, in *demonstration,* the mind does at last perceive the agreement or disagreement of the *ideas* it considers; yet 'tis not without pains and attention: there must be more than one transient view to find it. A steady application and pursuit are required to this discovery: and there must be a progression by steps and degrees, before the mind can in this way arrive at certainty, and come to perceive the agreement or repugnancy between two *ideas* that need proofs and the use of reason to show it.

5. *Not without precedent doubt. Another difference between intuitive and demonstrative knowledge,* is, that though in the latter all doubt be removed, when by the intervention of the intermediate *ideas,* the agreement or disagreement is perceived; yet before the demonstration there was a doubt, which in intuitive knowledge cannot happen to the mind that has its faculty of perception left to a degree capable of distinct *ideas,* no more than it can be a doubt to the eye, (that can distinctly see white and black,) whether this ink, and this paper be all of a color. . . .

6. *Not so clear.* 'Tis true, the perception, produced by *demonstration,* is also very clear; yet it is often with a great abatement of that evident luster and full assurance, that always accompany that which I call *intuitive;* like a face reflected by several mirrors one to another. . . .

7. *Each step must have intuitive evidence.* Now, *in every step reason makes in demonstrative knowledge, there is an intuitive knowledge* of that agreement or disagreement, it seeks, with the next intermediate *idea,* which it uses as a proof: for if it were not so, that yet would need a proof. Since without the perception of such agreement or disagreement, there is no knowledge produced: if it be perceived by itself, it is intuitive knowledge: if it cannot be perceived by itself, there is need of some intervening *idea,* as a common measure to show their agreement or disagreement. By which it is plain, that every step in reasoning, that produces knowledge, has intuitive certainty; which when the mind perceives, there is no more required, but to remember it to make the agreement or disagreement of the *ideas,* concerning which we inquire, visible and certain. So that to make anything a *demonstration,* it is necessary to perceive the immediate agreement of the intervening *ideas,* whereby the agreement or disagreement of the two *ideas* under examination (whereof the one is always the first, and the other the last in the account) is found. This intuitive perception of the agreement or disagreement of the intermediate *ideas,* in each step and progression of the *demonstration,* must also be carried exactly in the mind, and a man must be sure that no part is left out; which because in long deductions, and the use of many proofs, the memory does not always so readily and exactly retain: therefore it comes to pass, that this is more imperfect than intuitive knowledge, and men embrace often falsehoods for demonstrations.

. . . .

9. *Demonstration not limited to quantity.* It has been generally taken for granted, that mathematics alone are capable of demonstrative certainty: but to have such an agreement or disagreement, as may intuitively be perceived, being, as I imagine, not the privilege of the *ideas* of *number, extension,* and *figure* alone, it may possibly be the want of due method, and application in us; and not of sufficient evidence in things, that demonstration has been thought to have so little to do in other parts knowledge, and been scarce so much as aimed at by any but mathematicians. For whatever *ideas* we have, wherein the mind can perceive the immediate agreement or disagreement that is between them, there the mind is capable of intuitive knowledge; and

where it can perceive the agreement or disagreement of any two *ideas,* by an intuitive perception of the agreement or disagreement they have with any intermediate *ideas,* there the mind is capable of demonstration, which is not limited to *ideas* of extension, figure, number, and their modes.

10. *Why it has been so thought.* The reason why it has been generally sought for, and supposed to be only in those, I imagine, has been not only the general usefulness of those sciences; but because, in comparing their equality or excess, the modes of numbers have every the least difference very clear and perceivable: and though in extension, every the least excess is not so perceptible; yet the mind has found out ways, to examine and discover demonstratively the just equality of two angles, or extensions, or figures, and both these, *i.e.* numbers and figures, can be set down, by visible and lasting marks, wherein the *ideas* under consideration are perfectly determined, which for the most part they are not, where they are marked only by names and words.

11. But in other simple *ideas,* whose modes and differences are made and counted by degrees, and not quantity, we have not so nice and accurate a distinction of their differences, as to perceive, or find ways to measure their just equality or the least differences. For those other simple *ideas,* being appearances of sensations, produced in us, by the size, figure, number, and motion of minute corpuscles singly insensible, their different degrees also depend upon the variation of some, or of all those causes; which since it cannot be observed by us in particles of matter, whereof each is too subtle to be perceived, it is impossible for us to have any exact measures of the different degrees of these simple *ideas.* For supposing the sensation or *idea* we name *whiteness,* be produced in us by a certain number of globules, which having a verticity about their own centers, strike upon the *retina* of the eye, with a certain degree of rotation, as well as progressive swiftness; it will hence easily follow, that the more the superficial parts of any body are so ordered, as to reflect the greater number of globules of light, and to give them that proper rotation, which is fit to produce this sensation of white in us, the more white will that body appear, that, from an equal space sends to the *retina* the greater number of such corpuscles, with that peculiar sort of motion. I do not say, that the nature of light consists in very small round globules, nor of whiteness, in such a texture of parts as gives a certain rotation to these globules, when it reflects them; for I am not now treating physically of light, or colors: but this, I think, I may say, that I cannot (and I would be glad anyone would make intelligible that he did) conceive how

bodies without us, can anyways affect our senses, but by the immediate contact of the sensible bodies themselves, as in tasting and feeling, or the impulse of some insensible particles coming from them, as in seeing, hearing, and smelling; by the different impulse of which parts, caused by their different size, figure, and motion, the variety of sensations is produced in us.

. . . .

13. Not knowing therefore what number of particles, nor what motion of them is fit to produce any precise degree of *whiteness,* we cannot demonstrate the certain equality of any two degrees of *whiteness,* because we have no certain standard to measure them by, nor means to distinguish every the least real difference, the only help we have being from our senses, which in this point fail us. But where the difference is so great, as to produce in the mind clearly distinct *ideas,* whose differences can be perfectly retained, there these *ideas* of colors, as we see in different kinds, as blue and red, are as capable of demonstration, as *ideas* of number and extension. What I have here said of *whiteness* and colors, I think, holds true in all secondary qualities and their modes.

14. *Sensitive knowledge of particular existence.* These two, (*viz.*) intuition and demonstration, are the degrees of our knowledge; whatever comes short of one of these, with what assurance soever embraced, is but faith, or opinion, but not knowledge, at least in all general truths. There is, indeed, another *perception* of the mind, employed about *the particular existence of finite beings* without us; which going beyond bare probability, and yet not reaching perfectly to either of the foregoing degrees of certainty, passes under the name of knowledge. There can be nothing more certain, than that the *idea* we receive from an external object is in our minds; this is intuitive knowledge. But whether there be anything more than barely that *idea* in our minds; whether we can thence certainly infer the existence of anything without us, which corresponds to that *idea,* is that, whereof some men think there may be a question made, because men may have such *ideas* in their minds, when no such thing exists, no such object affects their senses. But yet here, I think, we are provided with an evidence, that puts us past doubting: for I ask anyone, whether he be not invincibly conscious to himself of a different perception, when he looks on the sun by day, and thinks on it by night; when he actually tastes wormwood, or smells a rose, or only thinks on that savor, or odor? We as plainly find the difference there

is between any *idea* revived in our minds by our own memory, and actually coming into our minds by our senses, as we do between any two distinct *ideas.* If anyone say, a dream may do the same thing, and all these *ideas* may be produced in us, without any external objects, he may please to dream that I make him this answer, 1. That 'tis no great matter, whether I remove his scruple, or no: where all is but dream, reasoning and arguments are of no use, truth and knowledge nothing. 2. That I believe he will allow a very manifest difference between dreaming of being in the fire, and being actually in it. But yet if he be resolved to appear so skeptical, as to maintain, that what I call being actually in the fire, is nothing but a dream; and that we cannot thereby certainly know, that any such thing as fire actually exists without us: I answer, that we certainly finding, that pleasure or pain follows upon the application of certain objects to us, whose existence we perceive, or dream that we perceive, by our senses, this certainty is as great as our happiness, or misery, beyond which, we have no concernment to know, or to be. So that, I think, we may add to the two former sorts of *knowledge,* this also, of the existence of particular external objects, by that perception and consciousness we have of the actual entrance of *ideas* from them, and allow these *three degrees of knowledge,* viz. *intuitive, demonstrative, and sensitive:* in each of which, there are different degrees and ways of evidence and certainty.

Class April 9th

15. *Knowledge not always clear, where the* ideas *are so.* But since our knowledge is founded on, and employed about our *ideas* only, will it not follow from thence, that it is conformable to our *ideas;* and that where our *ideas* are clear and distinct, or obscure and confused, our knowledge will be so too? To which I answer, no: for our knowledge consisting in the perception of the agreement, or disagreement of any two *ideas,* its clearness or obscurity, consists in the clearness or obscurity of that perception, and not in the clearness or obscurity of the *ideas* themselves: *v.g.* a man that has as clear *ideas* of the angles of a triangle, and of equality to two right ones, as any mathematician in the world, may yet have but a very obscure perception of their agreement, and so have but a very obscure knowledge of it. But *ideas,* which by reason of their obscurity or otherwise, are confused, cannot produce any clear or distinct knowledge; because, as far as any *ideas* are confused, so far the mind cannot perceive clearly, whether they agree or disagree. Or to express the same thing in a way less apt to be misunderstood. He that has not determined *ideas* to the words he uses, cannot make propositions of them, of whose truth he can be certain.

CHAP. III.

Of the extent of human knowledge.

1. *First, no farther than we have* ideas. Knowledge, as has been said, lying in the perception of the agreement, or disagreement, of any of our *ideas,* it follows from hence, that,

First, no farther than we have ideas. *First,* we can have *knowledge* no farther than we have *ideas.*

2. *Secondly, no farther than we can perceive their agreement or disagreement. Secondly,* that we can have no *knowledge* farther, than we can have perception of that agreement, or disagreement: which perception being, 1. either by *intuition,* or the immediate comparing any two *ideas;* or, 2. by *reason,* examining the agreement, or disagreement of two *ideas,* by the intervention of some others: or, 3. by *sensation,* perceiving the existence of particular things. Hence it also follows,

3. *Thirdly, intuitive knowledge extends itself not to all the relations of all our* ideas. *Thirdly,* that we cannot have an *intuitive knowledge,* that shall extend itself to all our *ideas,* and all that we would know about them; because we cannot examine and perceive all the relations they have one to another by *juxta*position, or an immediate comparison one with another. Thus having the *ideas* of an obtuse, and an acute-angled triangle, both drawn from equal bases, and between parallels, I can by intuitive knowledge, perceive the one not to be the other; but cannot that way know, whether they be equal, or no; because their agreement, or disagreement in equality, can never be perceived by an immediate comparing them: the difference of figure makes their parts uncapable of an exact immediate application; and therefore there is need of some intervening qualities to measure them by, which is demonstration, or rational knowledge.

4. *Fourthly, nor demonstrative knowledge. Fourthly,* it follows also, from what is above observed, that our *rational knowledge,* cannot reach to the whole extent of our *ideas.* Because between two different *ideas* we would examine, we cannot always find such *mediums,* as we can connect one to another with an intuitive knowledge, in all the parts of the deduction; and wherever that fails, we come short of knowledge and demonstration.

5. *Fifthly, sensitive knowledge narrower than either. Fifthly, sensitive knowledge* reaching no farther than the existence of things actually present to our senses, is yet much narrower than either of the former.

6. *Sixthly, our knowledge therefore narrower than our* ideas. From all which it is evident, that *the extent of our knowledge* comes not only short of the reality of things, but even of the extent of our own *ideas.* Though our knowledge be limited to our *ideas,* and cannot exceed them either in extent, or perfection; and though these be very narrow bounds, in respect of the extent of all being, and far short of what we may justly imagine to be in some even created understandings, not tied down to the dull and narrow information, is to be received from some few, and not very acute ways of perception, such as are our senses; yet it would be well with us, if our knowledge were but as large as our *ideas,* and there were not many doubts and inquiries concerning the *ideas* we have, whereof we are not, nor I believe ever shall be in this world, resolved. Nevertheless, I do not question, but that human knowledge, under the present circumstances of our beings and constitutions may be carried much farther, than it hitherto has been, if men would sincerely, and with freedom of mind, employ all that industry and labor of thought, in improving the means of discovering truth, which they do for the coloring or support of falsehood, to maintain a system, interest, or party, they are once engaged in. But yet after all, I think I may, without injury to human perfection, be confident, that our knowledge would never reach to all we might desire to know concerning those *ideas* we have; nor be able to surmount all the difficulties, and resolve all the questions that might arise concerning any of them. We have the *ideas* of a *square,* a *circle,* and *equality;* and yet, perhaps, shall never be able to find a circle equal to a square, and certainly know that it is so. We have the *ideas* of *matter* and *thinking,* but possibly shall never be able to know, whether any mere material being thinks, or no; it being impossible for us, by the contemplation of our own *ideas,* without revelation, to discover, whether omnipotency has not given to some systems of matter fitly disposed, a power to perceive and think, or else joined and fixed to matter so disposed, a thinking immaterial substance: it being, in respect of our notions, not much more remote from our comprehension to conceive, that GOD can, if he pleases, superadd to matter a faculty of thinking, than that he should superadd to it another substance, with a faculty of thinking; since we know not wherein thinking consists, nor to what sort of substances the almighty has been pleased to give that power, which cannot be in any created being, but merely by the good pleasure and bounty of the creator. For I see no contradiction in it,

that the first eternal thinking being or omnipotent spirit should, if he pleased, give to certain systems of created senseless matter, put together as he thinks fit, some degrees of sense, perception, and thought: though, as I think, I have proved, *Bk. IV.* c. xth it is no less than a contradiction to suppose matter (which is evidently in its own nature void of sense and thought) should be that eternal first thinking being. What certainty of knowledge can anyone have that some perceptions, such as, *v.g.* pleasure and pain, should not be in some bodies themselves, after a certain manner modified and moved, as well as that they should be in an immaterial substance, upon the motion of the parts of body: body as far as we can conceive being able only to strike and affect body; and motion, according to the utmost reach of our *ideas,* being able to produce nothing but motion, so that when we allow it to produce pleasure or pain, or the *idea* of a color, or sound, we are fain to quit our reason, go beyond our *ideas,* and attribute it wholly to the good pleasure of our maker. For since we must allow he has annexed effects to motion, which we can no way conceive motion able to produce, what reason have we to conclude, that he could not order them as well to be produced in a subject we cannot conceive capable of them, as well as in a subject we cannot conceive the motion of matter can any way operate upon? I say not this, that I would any way lessen the belief of the soul's immateriality: I am not here speaking of probability, but knowledge; and I think not only, that it becomes the modesty of philosophy, not to pronounce magisterially, where we want that evidence that can produce knowledge; but also, that it is of use to us to discern how far our knowledge does reach; for the state we are at present in, not being that of vision, we must, in many things, content ourselves with faith and probability: and in the present question, about the immateriality of the soul, if our faculties cannot arrive at demonstrative certainty, we need not think it strange. All the great ends of morality and religion, are well enough secured, without philosophical proofs of the soul's immateriality; since it is evident, that he who made us at the beginning to subsist here, sensible intelligent beings, and for several years continued us in such a state, can and will restore us to the like state of sensibility in another world, and make us capable there to receive the retribution he has designed to men, according to their doings in this life. And therefore 'tis not of such mighty necessity to determine one way or t'other, as some over-zealous for, or against the immateriality of the soul, have been forward to make the world believe. Who, either on the one side, indulging too much to their thoughts immersed altogether in matter, can allow no existence to what is not material: or, who on the other side, finding not *cogitation* within the natural powers of matter, examined over and over again, by the utmost intention of mind, have the confidence to conclude, that omnipotency itself, cannot give perception and thought to a substance which has the modification of solidity. He that considers how hardly sensation is, in our thoughts, reconcilable to extended matter; or existence to anything that has no extension at all, will confess, that he is very far from certainly knowing what his soul is. 'Tis a point, which seems to me, to be put out of the reach of our knowledge: and he who will give himself leave to consider freely, and look into the dark and intricate part of each hypothesis, will scarce find his reason able to determine him fixedly for, or against the soul's materiality. Since on which side soever he views it, either as an unextended substance, or as a thinking extended matter; the difficulty to conceive either, will, whilst either alone is in his thoughts, still drive him to the contrary side. An unfair way which some men take with themselves: who, because of the inconceivableness of something they find in one, throw themselves violently into the contrary hypothesis, though altogether as unintelligible to an unbiased understanding. This serves, not only to show the weakness and the scantiness of our knowledge, but the insignificant triumph of such sort of arguments, which, drawn from our own views, may satisfy us that we can find no certainty on one side of the question; but do not at all thereby help us to truth, by running into the opposite opinion, which, on examination, will be found clogged with equal difficulties. For what safety, what advantage to anyone is it, for the avoiding the seeming absurdities, and, to him, unsurmountable rubs he meets with in one opinion, to take refuge in the contrary, which is built on something altogether as inexplicable, and as far remote from his comprehension? 'Tis past controversy, that we have in us something that thinks, our very doubts about what it is, confirm the certainty of its being, though we must content ourselves in the ignorance of what *kind* of being it is: and 'tis in vain to go about to be skeptical in this, as it is unreasonable in most other cases to be positive against the being of anything, because we cannot comprehend its nature. For I would fain know what substance exists that has not something in it, which manifestly baffles our understandings. Other spirits, who see and know the nature and inward constitution of things, how much must they exceed us in knowledge? To which if we add larger comprehension, which enables them at one glance to see the connection and agreement of very many *ideas,* and readily supplies to them the intermediate proofs, which we by single and slow steps, and long poring in the dark, hardly at last find out, and are often ready to forget one before we have hunted out another, we may guess at some part of the happiness of superior ranks of spirits, who have a quicker and more penetrating sight, as well as a larger field of knowledge. But to return to the argument in hand, our *knowledge,* I say, is not only limited to the paucity and imperfections of the *ideas* we have, and which we employ it about, but even comes short of that too: but how far it reaches let us now inquire.

7. *How far our knowledge reaches.* The affirmations or negations we make concerning the *ideas* we have, may, as I have before intimated in general, be reduced to these four sorts, *viz.* identity, coexistence, relation, and real existence. I shall examine how far our knowledge extends in each of these:

8. *First, our knowledge of identity and diversity, as far as our* ideas. *First, as to identity and diversity,* in this way of agreement, or disagreement of our *ideas, our intuitive knowledge is as far extended as our ideas* themselves: and there can be no *idea* in the mind, which it does not presently, by an intuitive knowledge, perceive to be what it is, and to be different from any other.

9. *Secondly, of coexistence a very little way. Secondly, as to* the second sort, which is *the agreement, or disagreement* of our *ideas in coexistence,* in this our knowledge is very short, though in this consists the greatest and most material part of our knowledge concerning substances. For our *ideas* of the species of substances, being, as I have showed, nothing but certain collections of simple *ideas* united in one subject, and so coexisting together: *v.g.* our *idea* of *flame* is a body hot, luminous, and moving upward, of *gold,* a body heavy to a certain degree, yellow, malleable, and fusible. These or some such complex *ideas* as these in men's minds, do these two names of the different substances, *flame* and *gold,* stand for. When we would know anything farther concerning these, or any other sort of substances, what do we inquire but what other qualities, or powers, these substances have, or have not? which is nothing else but to know, what other simple *ideas* do, or do not coexist with those that make up that complex *idea*.

10. *Because the connection between most simple* ideas *is unknown.* This, how weighty and considerable a part soever of human science, is yet very narrow, and scarce any at all. The reason whereof is, that the simple *ideas* whereof our complex *ideas* of substances are made up, are, for the most part such, as carry with them, in their own nature, no visible necessary connection, or inconsistency with any other simple *ideas,* whose coexistence with them we would inform ourselves about.

11. *Especially of secondary qualities.* The *ideas,* that our complex ones of substances are made up of, and about which our knowledge, concerning

substances, is most employed, are those of their *secondary qualities;* which depending all (as has been shown) upon the primary qualities of their minute and insensible parts; or if not upon them, upon something yet more remote from our comprehension, 'tis impossible we should know, which have a necessary union or inconsistency one with another: for not knowing the root they spring from, not knowing what size, figure, and texture of parts they are, on which depend and from which result those qualities which make our complex *idea* of *gold,* 'tis impossible we should know what other qualities result from, or are incompatible with the same constitution of the insensible parts of *gold*; and so consequently must always coexist with that complex *idea* we have of it, or else are *inconsistent* with it.

12. *Because all connection between any secondary and primary qualities is undiscoverable.* Besides this ignorance of the primary qualities of the insensible parts of bodies, on which depend all their secondary qualities, there is yet another and more incurable part of ignorance, which sets us more remote from a certain knowledge of the *coexistence,* or *incoexistence* (if I may so say) of different *ideas* in the same subject; and that is, that there is no discoverable connection between any *secondary quality, and those primary qualities* that it depends on.

13. That the size, figure and motion of one body should cause a change in the size, figure and motion of another body, is not beyond our conception; the separation of the parts of one body, upon the intrusion of another; and the change from rest to motion, upon impulse; these, and the like, seem to have some *connection* one with another. And if we knew these primary qualities of bodies, we might have reason to hope, we might be able to know a great deal more of these operations of them one upon another: but our minds not being able to discover any *connection* betwixt these primary qualities of bodies, and the sensations that are produced in us by them, we can never be able to establish certain and undoubted rules, of the consequence or *coexistence* of any secondary qualities, though we could discover the size, figure, or motion of those invisible parts, which immediately produce them. We are so far from knowing what figure, size, or motion of parts produce a yellow color, a sweet taste,or a sharp sound, that we can by no means conceive how any *size, figure, or motion* of any particles, can possibly produce in us the *idea* of any *color, taste,* or *sound* whatsoever; there is no conceivable *connection* betwixt the one and the other.

14. In vain therefore shall we endeavor to discover by our *ideas,* (the only true way of certain and universal knowledge,) what other *ideas* are to be found constantly joined with that of our complex *idea* of any substance: since we neither know the real constitution of the minute parts, on which their qualities do depend; nor did we know them, could we discover any necessary *connection* between them, and any of the *secondary qualities:* which is necessary to be done, before we can certainly know their *necessary coexistence.* So that let our complex *idea* of any species of substances, be what it will, we can hardly, from the simple *ideas* contained in it, certainly determine the *necessary coexistence* of any other quality whatsoever. Our knowledge in all these inquiries, reaches very little farther than our experience. Indeed, some few of the primary qualities have a necessary dependence, and visible connection one with another, as figure necessarily supposes extension, receiving or communicating motion by impulse, supposes solidity. But though these, and perhaps some others of our *ideas* have: yet there are so *few* of them, that have a *visible connection* one with another, that we can by intuition or demonstration, discover the coexistence of very few of the qualities are to be found united in substances: and we are left only to the assistance of our senses, to make known to us, what qualities they contain. For of all the qualities that are *coexistent* in any subject, without this dependence and evident connection of their *ideas* one with another, we cannot know certainly any two to *coexist* any farther, than experience, by our senses, informs us. Thus though we see the yellow color, and upon trial find the weight, malleableness, fusibility, and fixedness, that are united in a piece of gold; yet because no one of these *ideas* has any evident *dependence,* or necessary connection with the other, we cannot certainly know, that where any four of these are, the fifth will be there also, how highly probable soever it may be: because the highest probability, amounts not to certainty; without which, there can be no true knowledge. For this *coexistence* can be no farther known, than it is perceived; and it cannot be perceived but either in particular subjects, by the observation of our senses, or in general, by the necessary *connection* of the *ideas* themselves.

15. *Of repugnancy to coexist larger. As to incompatibility or repugnancy to coexistence,* we may know, that any subject may have of each sort of primary qualities, but one particular at once; *v.g.* each particular extension, figure, number of parts, motion, excludes all other of each kind. The like also is certain of all sensible *ideas* peculiar to each sense; for whatever of each kind

is present in any subject, excludes all other of that sort; *v.g.* no one subject can have two smells, or two colors, at the same time. . . .

16. *Of the coexistence of powers a very little way.* But *as to the powers of substances* to change the sensible qualities of other bodies, which make a great part of our inquiries about them, and is no inconsiderable branch of our knowledge; I doubt, as to these, whether *our knowledge reaches* much farther than our experience; or whether we can come to the discovery of most of these powers, and be certain that they are in any subject by the connection with any of those *ideas,* which to us make its essence. Because the active and passive powers of bodies, and their ways of operating, consisting in a texture and motion of parts, which we cannot by any means come to discover: 'tis but in very few cases, we can be able to perceive their dependence on, or repugnance to any of those *ideas,* which make our complex one of that sort of things. I have here instanced in the corpuscularian hypothesis, as that which is thought to go farthest in an intelligible explication of the qualities of bodies; and I fear the weakness of human understanding is scarce able to substitute another, which will afford us a fuller and clearer discovery of the necessary connection, and *coexistence,* of the powers, which are to be observed united in several sorts of them. This at least is certain, that whichever hypothesis be clearest and truest, (for of that it is not my business to determine,) our knowledge concerning corporeal substances, will be very little advanced by any of them, till we are made to see, what qualities and powers of bodies have a *necessary connection or repugnancy* one with another; which in the present state of philosophy, I think, we know but to a very small degree: and, I doubt, whether with those faculties we have, we shall ever be able to carry our general knowledge (I say not particular experience) in this part much farther. Experience is that, which in this part we must depend on. And it were to be wished, that it were more improved. . . .

17. *Of spirits yet narrower.* If we are at a loss in respect of the powers, and operations of bodies, I think it is easy to conclude, *we are much more in the dark in reference to spirits;* whereof we naturally have no *ideas,* but what we draw from that of our own, by reflecting on the operations of our own souls within us, as far as they can come within our observation. But how inconsiderable a rank the spirits that inhabit our bodies hold amongst those various, and possibly innumerable, kinds of nobler beings; and how far short they come of the endowments and perfections of cherubims, and

seraphims, and infinite sorts of spirits above us, is what by a transient hint, in another place, I have offered to my reader's consideration.[42]

18. *Thirdly, of other relations it is not easy to say how far. Morality capable of demonstration.* As to the third sort of our knowledge, *viz.* the *agreement or disagreement of any of our* ideas *in any other relation:* this, as it is the largest field of our knowledge, so it is hard to determine how far it may extend: because the advances that are made in this part of knowledge, depending on our sagacity, in finding intermediate *ideas,* that may show the *relations* and *habitudes* of *ideas,* whose coexistence is not considered, 'tis a hard matter to tell, when we are at an end of such discoveries; and when reason has all the helps it is capable of, for the finding of proofs, or examining the agreement or disagreement of remote *ideas.* They that are ignorant of *algebra* cannot imagine the wonders in this kind are to be done by it: and what farther improvements and helps, advantageous to other parts of knowledge, the sagacious mind of man may yet find out, 'tis not easy to determine. This at least I believe, that the *ideas* of quantity are not those alone that are capable of demonstration and knowledge; and that other, and perhaps more useful parts of contemplation, would afford us certainty, if vices, passions, and domineering interest did not oppose, or menace such endeavors.

The *idea* of a supreme being, infinite in power, goodness, and wisdom, whose workmanship we are, and on whom we depend; and the *idea* of ourselves, as understanding, rational creatures, being such as are clear in us, would, I suppose, if duly considered, and pursued, afford such foundations of our duty and rules of action, as might place *morality amongst the sciences capable of demonstration:* wherein I doubt not, but from self-evident propositions, by necessary consequences, as incontestable as those in mathematics, the measures of right and wrong might be made out, to anyone that will apply himself with the same indifferency and attention to the one, as he does to the other of these sciences. The *relation* of other *modes* may certainly be perceived, as well as those of number and extension: and I cannot see, why they should not also be capable of demonstration, if due methods were thought on to examine, or pursue their agreement or disagreement. *Where there is no property, there is no injustice,* is a proposition as certain as any demonstration in *Euclid:* for the *idea* of *property,* being a right to any thing; and the *idea* to which the name *injustice* is given, being the invasion or violation of that right; it is evident, that these *ideas* being thus

42. See III vi 12.

established, and these names annexed to them, I can as certainly know this proposition to be true, as that a triangle has three angles equal to two right ones. Again, *no government allows absolute liberty:* the *idea* of government being the establishment of society upon certain rules or laws, which require conformity to them; and the *idea* of absolute liberty being for anyone to do whatever he pleases; I am as capable of being certain of the truth of this proposition, as of any in mathematics.

19. *Two things have made moral* ideas *thought uncapable of demonstration. Their complexedness, and want of sensible representations.* That which in this respect has given the advantage to the *ideas* of quantity, and made them thought more capable of certainty and demonstration, is,

First, that they can be set down, and represented by sensible marks, which have a greater and nearer correspondence with them than any words or sounds whatsoever. Diagrams drawn on paper are copies of the *ideas* in the mind, and not liable to the uncertainty that words carry in their signification. An angle, circle, or square, drawn in lines, lies open to the view, and cannot be mistaken: it remains unchangeable, and may at leisure be considered, and examined, and the demonstration be revised, and all the parts of it may be gone over more than once, without any danger of the least change in the *ideas.* This cannot be thus done in *moral ideas,* we have no sensible marks that resemble them, whereby we can set them down; we have nothing but words to express them by; which though, when written, they remain the same, yet the *ideas* they stand for, may change in the same man; and 'tis very seldom, that they are not different in different persons.

Secondly, another thing that makes the greater difficulty in *ethics,* is, that *moral ideas* are commonly more complex than those of the figures ordinarily considered in mathematics. From whence these two inconveniencies follow. *First*, that their names are of more uncertain signification, the precise collection of simple *ideas* they stand for not being so easily agreed on, and so the sign, that is used for them in communication always, and in thinking often, does not steadily carry with it the same *idea. . . . Secondly,* from the complexedness of these moral *ideas* there follows another inconvenience, (*viz.*) that the mind cannot easily retain those precise combinations, so exactly and perfectly, as is necessary in the examination of the habitudes and correspondencies, agreements or disagreements, of several of them one with another; especially where it is to be judged of by long deductions, and the intervention of several other complex *ideas,* to show the agreement or disagreement of two remote ones.

. . . .

20. *Remedies of those difficulties.* One part of *these disadvantages,* in moral *ideas,* which has made them be thought not capable of demonstration, may in a good measure be *remedied* by definitions, setting down that collection of simple *ideas,* which every term shall stand for; and then using the terms steadily and constantly for that precise collection. . . .

21. *Fourthly, of real existence we have an intuitive knowledge of our own, demonstrative of God's, sensible of some few other things.* As to the fourth sort of our knowledge, *viz. of* the *real, actual, existence* of things, we have an intuitive knowledge of our own *existence;* and a demonstrative knowledge of the *existence* of a God; of the *existence* of anything else, we have no other but a sensitive knowledge, which extends not beyond the objects present to our senses.

22. *Our ignorance great.* Our knowledge being so narrow, as I have showed, it will, perhaps, give us some light into the present state of our minds, if we look a little into the dark side, and take a view of *our ignorance:* which being infinitely larger than our knowledge, may serve much to the quieting of disputes, and improvement of useful knowledge; if discovering how far we have clear and distinct *ideas,* we confine our thoughts within the contemplation of those things, that are within the reach of our understandings, and launch not out into that abyss of darkness (where we have not eyes to see, nor faculties to perceive anything,) out of a presumption, that nothing is beyond our comprehension. But to be satisfied of the folly of such a conceit, we need not go far. He that knows anything, knows this in the first place, that he need not seek long for instances of his ignorance. The meanest, and most obvious things that come in our way, have dark sides, that the quickest sight cannot penetrate into. The clearest, and most enlarged understandings of thinking men find themselves puzzled, and at a loss, in every particle of matter. We shall the less wonder to find it so, when we consider the *causes of our ignorance;* which, from what has been said, I suppose, will be found to be these three:

First, want of *ideas.*

Secondly, want of a discoverable connection between the *ideas* we have.

Thirdly, want of tracing, and examining our *ideas.*

23. *First, one cause of it want of* ideas, *either such as we have no conception of, or such as particularly we have not. First,* there are some things, and those not a few, that we are ignorant of for *want of ideas.*

First, all the simple *ideas* we have are confined (as I have shown) to the observation of our senses, and the operations of our own minds, that we are conscious of in ourselves. But how much these few and narrow inlets are disproportionate to the vast whole extent of all beings, will not be hard to persuade those, who are not so foolish, as to think their span the measure of all things. What other simple *ideas* 'tis possible the creatures in other parts of the universe may have, by the assistance of senses and faculties more or perfecter, than we have, or different from ours, 'tis not for us to determine. But to say, or think there are no such, because we conceive nothing of them, is no better an argument, than if a blind man should be positive in it, that there was no such thing as sight and colors, because he had no manner of *idea,* of any such thing, nor could by any means frame to himself any notions about seeing. . . .

24. *Because of their remoteness. Secondly,* another great cause of ignorance, is the *want of* ideas *we are capable of.* As the want of *ideas,* which our faculties are not able to give us, shuts us wholly from those views of things, which 'tis reasonable to think other beings, perfecter than we, have, of which we know nothing; so the want of *ideas,* I now speak of, keeps us in ignorance of things, we conceive capable of being known to us. *Bulk, figure,* and *motion,* we have *ideas* of. But though we are not without *ideas* of these primary qualities of bodies in general, yet not knowing what is the particular *bulk, figure,* and *motion,* of the greatest part of the bodies of the universe, we are ignorant of the several powers, efficacies, and ways of operation, whereby the effects, which we daily see, are produced. These are hid from us in some things, by being *too remote; and* in others, by being too *minute.* . . .

25. *Because of their minuteness.* If a great, nay far the greatest part of the several ranks of *bodies* in the universe, scape our notice by their remoteness, there are others that are no less concealed from us by their *minuteness.* These insensible corpuscles, being the active parts of matter, and the great instruments of nature, on which depend not only all their secondary qualities, but also most of their natural operations, our want of precise distinct *ideas* of their primary qualities, keeps us in an uncurable ignorance of what we desire to know about them. I doubt not but if we could discover the figure, size, texture, and motion of the minute constituent parts of any

two bodies, we should know without trial several of their operations one upon another, as we do now the properties of a square, or a triangle. Did we know the mechanical affections of the particles of *rhubarb, hemlock, opium,* and a *man,* as a watchmaker does those of a watch, whereby it performs its operations, and of a file which by rubbing on them will alter the figure of any of the wheels, we should be able to tell beforehand, that *rhubarb* will purge, *hemlock* kill, and *opium* make a man sleep; as well as a watchmaker can, that a little piece of paper laid on the balance, will keep the watch from going, till it be removed; or that some small part of it, being rubbed by a file, the machine would quite lose its motion, and the watch go no more.The dissolving of silver in *aqua fortis,* and gold in *aqua regia,* and not *vice versa,* would be then, perhaps, no more difficult to know, than it is to a smith to understand, why the turning of one key will open a lock, and not the turning of another. But whilst we are destitute of senses acute enough, to discover the minute particles of bodies, and to give us *ideas* of their mechanical affections, we must be content to be ignorant of their properties and ways of operation; nor can we be assured about them any farther, than some few trials we make, are able to reach. But whether they will succeed again another time, we cannot be certain. This hinders our certain knowledge of universal truths concerning natural bodies: and our reason carries us herein very little beyond particular matter of fact.

26. *Hence no science of bodies.* And therefore I am apt to doubt, how far soever human industry may advance useful and *experimental* philosophy *in physical things, scientifical* will still be out of our reach: because we want perfect and adequate *ideas* of those very bodies, which are nearest to us, and most under our command. Those which we have ranked into classes under names, and we think ourselves best acquainted with, we have but very imperfect, and incomplete *ideas* of. Distinct *ideas* of the several sorts of bodies, that fall under the examination of our senses, perhaps, we may have: but adequate *ideas,* I suspect, we have not of any one amongst them. And though the former of these will serve us for common use and discourse: yet whilst we want the latter, we are not capable of *scientifical knowledge;* nor shall ever be able to discover general, instructive, unquestionable truths concerning them. *Certainty* and *demonstration,* are things we must not, in these matters, pretend to. . . .

. . . .

28. *Secondly, want of a discoverable connection between* ideas *we have. Secondly,* what a small part of the substantial beings, that are in the universe,

the want of *ideas* leaves open to our knowledge, we have seen. In the next place, another cause of ignorance, of no less moment, is a want of a *discoverable connection* between those *ideas* we have. For wherever we want that, we are utterly uncapable of universal and certain knowledge; and are, as in the former case, left only to observation and experiment: which how narrow and confined it is, how far from general knowledge, we need not be told. I shall give some few instances of this cause of our ignorance and so leave it. 'Tis evident that the bulk, figure, and motion of several bodies about us, produce in us several sensations, as of colors, sounds, tastes, or smells, pleasure and pain, *&c.* These mechanical affections of bodies, having no affinity at all with those *ideas,* they produce in us, (there being no conceivable connection between any impulse of any sort of body, and any perception of a color, or smell, which we find in our minds) we can have no distinct knowledge of such operations beyond our experience; and can reason no otherwise about them, than as effects produced by the appointment of an infinitely wise agent, which perfectly surpass our comprehensions. As the *ideas* of sensible secondary qualities, which we have in our minds, can, by us, be no way deduced from bodily causes, nor any correspondence or connection be found between them and those primary qualities which (experience shows us) produce them in us; so on the other side, the operation of our minds upon our bodies is as unconceivable. How any thought should produce a motion in body is as remote from the nature of our *ideas,* as how any body should produce any thought in the mind. That it is so, if experience did not convince us, the consideration of the things themselves would never be able, in the least, to discover to us. These, and the like, though they have a constant and regular connection, in the ordinary course of things: yet that connection being not discoverable in the *ideas* themselves, which appearing to have no necessary dependence one on another, we can attribute their connection to nothing else, but the arbitrary determination of that all-wise agent, who has made them to be, and to operate as they do, in a way wholly above our weak understandings to conceive.

29. *Instances.* In some of our *ideas* there are certain relations, habitudes, and connections, so visibly included in the nature of the *ideas* themselves, that we cannot conceive them separable from them, by any power whatsoever. And in these only, we are capable of certain and universal knowledge. Thus the *idea* of a right-lined triangle necessarily carries with it an equality of its angles to two right ones. Nor can we conceive this relation, this connection of these two *ideas,* to be possibly mutable, or to depend on any arbitrary

power, which of choice made it thus, or could make it otherwise. But the coherence and continuity of the parts of matter; the production of sensation in us of colors and sounds, *&c.* by impulse and motion; nay, the original rules and communication of motion being such, wherein we can discover no natural connection with any *ideas* we have, we cannot but ascribe them to the arbitrary will and good pleasure of the wise architect. I need not, I think, here mention the resurrection of the dead, the future state of this globe of earth, and such other things, which are by everyone acknowledged to depend wholly on the determination of a free agent. The things that, as far as our observation reaches, we constantly find to proceed regularly, we may conclude, do act by a law set them; but yet by a law, that we know not: whereby, though causes work steadily, and effects constantly flow from them, yet their *connections* and *dependencies* being not discoverable in our *ideas,* we can have but an experimental knowledge of them. . . . Several effects come every day within the notice of our senses, of which we have so far *sensitive knowledge:* but the causes, manner, and certainty of their production, for the two foregoing reasons, we must be content to be ignorant of. In these we can go no farther than particular experience informs us of matter of fact, and by analogy to guess what effects the like bodies are, upon other trials, like to produce. But as to a perfect *science* of natural bodies, (not to mention spiritual beings,) we are, I think, so far from being capable of any such thing, that I conclude it lost labor to seek after it.

30. *Thirdly, want of tracing our* ideas. *Thirdly,* where we have adequate *ideas,* and where there is a certain and discoverable connection between them, yet we are often ignorant, for want of *tracing* those *ideas* which we have, or may have; and for want of finding out those intermediate *ideas,* which may show us, what habitude of agreement or disagreement they have one with another. And thus many are ignorant of mathematical truths, not out of any imperfection of their faculties, or uncertainty in the things themselves; but for want of application in acquiring, examining, and by due ways comparing those *ideas.* That which has most contributed to hinder the due *tracing* of our *ideas,* and finding out their relations, and agreements or disagreements one with another, has been, I suppose, the ill use of *words.* It is impossible that men should ever truly seek, or certainly discover the agreement or disagreement of *ideas* themselves, whilst their thoughts flutter about, or stick only in sounds of doubtful and uncertain significations. . . .

31. *Extent in respect of universality.* Hitherto we have examined the *extent* of our knowledge, in respect of the several sorts of beings that are. There is

another *extent of it, in respect of universality,* which will also deserve to be considered: and in this regard, our knowledge follows the nature of our *ideas.* If the *ideas* are abstract, whose agreement or disagreement we perceive, our knowledge is universal. For what is known of such general *ideas,* will be true of every particular thing, in whom that essence, *i.e.* that abstract *idea* is to be found: and what is once known of such *ideas,* will be perpetually, and forever true. So that as to all general knowledge, we must search and find it only in our minds, and 'tis only the examining of our own *ideas,* that furnishes us with that. Truths belonging to essences of things, (that is, to abstract *ideas*) are eternal, and are to be found out by the contemplation only of those essences: as the existence of things is to be known only from experience. But having more to say of this in the chapters, where I shall speak of general and real knowledge, this may here suffice, as to the universality of our knowledge in general.

CHAP. IV.

Of the reality of knowledge.

1. *Objection, knowledge placed in* ideas *may be all bare vision.* I doubt not but my reader, by this time, may be apt to think, that I have been all this while only building a castle in the air; and be ready to say to me, to what purpose all this stir? Knowledge, say you, is only the perception of the agreement or disagreement of our own *ideas:* but who knows what those *ideas* may be? Is there anything so extravagant, as the imaginations of men's brains? Where is the head that has no *chimeras* in it? Or if there be a sober and a wise man, what difference will there be, by your rules, between his knowledge, and that of the most extravagant fancy in the world? They both have their *ideas,* and perceive their agreement and disagreement one with another. If there be any difference between them, the advantage will be on the warm-headed man's side, as having the more *ideas,* and the more lively. And so, by your rules, he will be the more knowing. If it be true, that all knowledge lies only in the perception of the agreement or disagreement of our own *ideas,* the visions of an enthusiast, and the reasonings of a sober man, will be equally certain. 'Tis no matter how things are: so a man observe but the agreement of his own imaginations, and talk conformably, it is all truth, all certainty. Such castles in the air, will be as strong holds of truth, as the demonstra-

tions of *Euclid.* That an harpy is not a centaur, is by this way as certain knowledge, and as much a truth, as that a square is not a circle.

But *of what use is all this* fine *knowledge of men's own imaginations,* to a man that inquires after the reality of things? It matters not what men's fancies are, 'tis the knowledge of things that is only to be prized: 'tis this alone gives a value to our reasonings, and preference to one man's knowledge over another's, that it is of things as they really are, and not of dreams and fancies.

2. *Answer, not so, where* ideas *agree with things.* To which I answer, that if our knowledge of our *ideas* terminate in them, and reach no farther, where there is something farther intended, our most serious thoughts will be of little more use, than the reveries of a crazy brain; and the truths built thereon of no more weight, than the discourses of a man, who sees things clearly in a dream, and with great assurance utters them. But, I hope, before I have done, to make it evident, that this way of certainty, by the knowledge of our own *ideas,* goes a little farther than bare imagination: and, I believe it will appear, that all the certainty of general truths a man has, lies in nothing else.

3. 'Tis evident, the mind knows not things immediately, but only by the intervention of the *ideas* it has of them. *Our knowledge* therefore is *real,* only so far as there is a conformity between our *ideas* and the reality of things. But what shall be here the criterion? How shall the mind, when it perceives nothing but its own *ideas,* know that they agree with things themselves? This, though it seems not to want difficulty, yet, I think there be two sorts of *ideas,* that, we may be assured, agree with things.

4. *As, first, all simple* ideas *do. First,* the first are simple *ideas,* which since the mind, as has been showed, can by no means make to itself, must necessarily be the product of things operating on the mind in a natural way, and producing therein those perceptions which by the wisdom and will of our maker they are ordained and adapted to. From whence it follows, that *simple* ideas *are not fictions* of our fancies, but the natural and regular productions of things without us, really operating upon us; and so carry with them all the conformity which is intended; or which our state requires: for they represent to us things under those appearances which they are fitted to produce in us: whereby we are enabled to distinguish the sorts of particular substances, to discern the states they are in, and so to take them for our necessities, and apply them to our uses. . . .

5. *Secondly, all complex* ideas, *except of substances. Secondly, all our complex* ideas, *except those of substances,* being *archetypes* of the mind's own making, not intended to be the copies of anything, nor referred to the existence of anything, as to their originals, *cannot want any conformity necessary to real knowledge.* For that which is not designed to represent anything but itself, can never be capable of a wrong representation, nor mislead us from the true apprehension of anything, by its dislikeness to it: and such, excepting those of substances, are all our complex *ideas.* . . .

6. *Hence the reality of mathematical knowledge.* I doubt not but it will be easily granted, that the *knowledge* we have *of mathematical truths, is* not only certain, but *real knowledge;* and not the bare empty vision of vain insignificant *chimeras* of the brain: and yet, if we will consider, we shall find that it is only of our own *ideas.* The mathematician considers the truth and properties belonging to a rectangle, or circle, only as they are in *idea* in his own mind. For 'tis possible he never found either of them existing mathematically, i.e. precisely true, in his life. But yet the knowledge he has of any truths or properties belonging to a circle, or any other mathematical figure, are nevertheless true and certain, even of real things existing: because real things are no farther concerned, nor intended to be meant by any such propositions, than as things really agree to those *archetypes* in his mind. Is it true of the *idea* of a *triangle,* that its three angles are equal to two right ones? It is true also of a *triangle,* wherever it really exists. Whatever other figure exists, that is not exactly answerable to that *idea* of a *triangle* in his mind, is not at all concerned in that proposition. . . .

7. *And of moral.* And hence it follows, that *moral knowledge* is as *capable of real certainty,* as mathematics. . . .

8. *Existence not required to make it real.* For the attaining of knowledge and certainty it is requisite, that we have determined *ideas:* and to make our knowledge *real,* it is requisite, that the *ideas* answer their *archetypes.* Nor let it be wondered, that I place the certainty of our knowledge in the consideration of our *ideas,* with so little care and regard (as it may seem) to the real existence of things: since most of those discourses, which take up the thoughts and engage the disputes of those who pretend to make it their business to inquire after truth and certainty, will, I presume, upon examination be found to be *general propositions*, and notions in which existence is not at all concerned. All the discourses of the mathematicians about the squaring of a circle, conic sections, or any other part of mathematics,

concern not the *existence* of any of those figures: but their demonstrations, which depend on their *ideas,* are the same, whether there be any square or circle existing in the world, or no. In the same manner, the truth and certainty of *moral* discourses abstracts from the lives of men, and the existence of those virtues in the world, whereof they treat: nor are *Tully's* offices less true, because there is nobody in the world that exactly practices his rules, and lives up to that pattern of a virtuous man, which he has given us, and which existed nowhere, when he writ, but in *idea.*[43] If it be true in speculation, *i.e.* in *idea,* that *murder deserves death,* it will also be true in reality of any action that exists conformable to that *idea* of *murder.* . . .

. . . .

10. *Misnaming disturbs not the certainty of the knowledge.* One thing more we are to take notice of, that where GOD, or any other lawmaker, has defined any moral names, there they have made the essence of that species to which that name belongs; and there it is not safe to apply or use them otherwise: but in other cases 'tis bare impropriety of speech to apply them contrary to the common usage of the country. But yet even this too disturbs not the certainty of that knowledge, which is still to be had by a due contemplation and comparing of those even nicknamed *ideas.*

11. Ideas *of substances have their archetypes without us. Thirdly,* there is another sort of *complex ideas,* which being referred to *archetypes* without us, may differ from them, and so our knowledge about them, may come short of being real. Such are our *ideas* of substances. . . .

12. *So far as they agree with those, so far our knowledge concerning them is real.* I say then, that to have *ideas* of *substances,* which, by being conformable to things, may afford us real knowledge, it is not enough, as in modes, to put together such *ideas* as have no inconsistency, though they did never before so exist. *V.g.* the *ideas* of *sacrilege* or *perjury, &c.* were as real and true *ideas* before, as after the existence of any such fact. But *our ideas of substances* being supposed copies, and referred to *archetypes* without us, must still be taken from something that does or has existed; they must not consist of *ideas* put together at the pleasure of our thoughts, without any real pattern they were taken from, though we can perceive no inconsistence in such a combination. The reason whereof is, because we knowing not what real

43. Tully is Marcus Tullius Cicero (106–43 B.C.). His "offices" is his book *De Officiis* (*On Moral Obligation*).

constitution it is of substances, whereon our simple *ideas* depend, and which really is the cause of the strict union of some of them one with another, and the exclusion of others; there are very few of them, that we can be sure are, or are not inconsistent in nature, any farther than experience and sensible observation reaches. Herein therefore is founded the *reality* of our knowledge concerning *substances,* that all our complex *ideas* of them must be such, and such only, as are made up of such simple ones, as have been discovered to coexist in nature. And our *ideas* being thus true, though not, perhaps, very exact copies, are yet the subjects of *real* (as far as we have any) *knowledge* of them. Which (as has been already showed) will not be found to reach very far: but so far as it does, it will still be *real knowledge*. . . .

. . . .

18. *Recapitulation.* Wherever we perceive the agreement or disagreement of any of our *ideas* there is certain knowledge: and wherever we are sure those *ideas* agree with the reality of things, there is certain real knowledge. Of which agreement of our *ideas* with the reality of things, having here given the marks, I think I have shown wherein it is, that *certainty, real certainty,* consists. Which whatever it was to others, was, I confess, to me heretofore, one of those *desiderata* which I found great want of.

CHAP. V.
Of truth in general.

1. *What truth is.* What is *truth,* was an inquiry many ages since; and it being that which all mankind either do, or pretend to search after, it cannot but be worth our while carefully to examine wherein it consists; and so acquaint ourselves with the nature of it, as to observe how the mind distinguishes it from falsehood.

2. *A right joining, or separating of signs;* i.e. ideas *or words. Truth* then seems to me, in the proper import of the word, to signify nothing but *the joining or separating of signs, as the things signified by them, do agree or disagree one with another.* The *joining* or *separating* of signs here meant is what by another name, we call proposition. So that truth properly belongs only to proposi-

tions: whereof there are two sorts, *viz.* mental and verbal; as there are two sorts of signs commonly made use of, *viz. ideas* and words.

3. *Which make mental or verbal propositions.* To form a clear notion of *truth,* it is very necessary to consider *truth* of thought, and *truth* of words, distinctly one from another: but yet it is very difficult to treat of them asunder. Because it is unavoidable, in treating of mental propositions, to make use of words: and then the instances given of *mental propositions,* cease immediately to be barely mental, *and* become *verbal.* For a *mental proposition* being nothing but a bare consideration of the *ideas,* as they are in our minds stripped of names, they lose the nature of purely *mental propositions,* as soon as they are put into words.

4. *Mental propositions are very hard to be treated of.* And that which makes it yet *harder to treat of mental* and verbal *propositions separately,* is, that most men, if not all, in their thinking and reasonings within themselves, make use of words instead of *ideas;* at least when the subject of their meditation contains in it complex *ideas.* . . .

5. *Being nothing but the joining, or separating* ideas *without words.* But to return to the consideration of truth. We must, I say, observe two sorts of propositions, that we are capable of making.

First, mental, wherein the *ideas* in our understandings *are* without the use of words *put together, or separated* by the mind, perceiving, or judging of their agreement, or disagreement.

Secondly, verbal propositions, which *are words* the signs of our *ideas put together or separated in affirmative or negative sentences.* By which way of affirming or denying, these signs, made by sounds, are as it were put together or separated one from another. So that proposition consists in joining, or separating signs, and truth consists in the putting together, or separating those signs, according as the things, which they stand for, agree or disagree.

6. *When mental propositions contain real truth, and when verbal.* Everyone's experience will satisfy him, that the mind, either by perceiving or supposing the agreement or disagreement of any of its *ideas,* does tacitly within itself put them into a kind of proposition affirmative or negative, which I have endeavored to express by the terms *putting together* and *separating.* But this action of the mind, which is so familiar to every thinking and reasoning man, is easier to be conceived by reflecting on what passes in us, when we

affirm or deny, than to be explained by words. . . . When *ideas* are so put together, or separated in the mind, as they, or the things they stand for do agree, or not, that is, as I may call it, *mental truth.* But *truth of words* is something more, and that is the affirming or denying of words one of another, as the *ideas* they stand for agree or disagree: and this again is twofold. Either *purely verbal,* and trifling, which I shall speak of, *Chap.* viii. *or real* and instructive; which is the object of that real knowledge, which, we have spoken of already.

7. *Objection against verbal truth, that thus it may all be chimerical.* But here again will be apt to occur the same doubt about truth, that did about knowledge: and it will be objected, that if truth be nothing but the joining or separating of words in propositions, as the *ideas* they stand for agree or disagree in men's minds, the knowledge of *truth is not so valuable a thing,* as it is taken to be; nor worth the pains and time men employ in the search of it: since *by this account,* it amounts to no more than the conformity of words, to the *chimeras* of men's brains. . . .

8. *Answered, real truth is about* ideas *agreeing to things.* Though what has been said in the foregoing chapter, to distinguish real from imaginary knowledge, might suffice here, in answer to this doubt, to distinguish *real truth* from *chimerical,* or (if you please,) *barely nominal,* they depending both on the same foundation; yet it may not be amiss here again to consider, that though our words signify nothing but our *ideas,* yet being designed by them to signify things, the *truth* they contain, when put into propositions, will be only *verbal,* when they stand for *ideas* in the mind, that have not an agreement with the reality of things. And therefore truth, as well as knowledge, may well come under the distinction of *verbal* and *real;* that being only *verbal truth,* wherein terms are joined according to the agreement or disagreement of the *ideas* they stand for, without regarding whether our *ideas* are such, as really have, or are capable of having an existence in nature. But then it is they contain *real truth,* when these signs are joined, as our *ideas* agree; and when our *ideas* are such, as we know are capable of having an existence in nature: which in substances we cannot know, but by knowing that such have existed.

9. *Falsehood is the joining of names otherwise than their* ideas *agree. Truth* is the marking down in words, the agreement or disagreement of *ideas* as it is. *Falsehood* is the marking down in words, the agreement or disagreement of *ideas* otherwise than it is. And so far as these *ideas,* thus marked by sounds,

agree to their archetypes, so far only is the *truth real.* The knowledge of this truth, consists in knowing what *ideas* the words stand for, and the perception of the agreement or disagreement of those *ideas,* according as it is marked by those words.

10. *General propositions to be treated of more at large.* But because words are looked on as the great conduits of truth and knowledge, and that in conveying and receiving of truth, and commonly in reasoning about it, we make use of words and propositions, I shall more at large inquire, wherein the certainty of real truths, contained in propositions, consists, and where it is to be had; and endeavor to show in what sort of universal propositions we are capable of being *certain* of their real truth, or falsehood.

I shall begin with general propositions, as those which most employ our thoughts, and exercise our contemplation. . . .

. . . .

Chap. VI

Of universal propositions, their truth and certainty.

1. *Treating of words necessary to knowledge.* Though the examining and judging of *ideas* by themselves, their names being quite laid aside, be the best and surest way to clear and distinct knowledge: yet through the prevailing custom of using sounds for *ideas,* I think it is very seldom practiced. Everyone may observe how common it is for names to be made use of, instead of the *ideas* themselves, even when men think and reason within their own breasts; especially if the *ideas* be very complex, and made up of a great collection of simple ones. This makes *the consideration of words and propositions,* so *necessary a part of the treatise of knowledge,* that 'tis very hard to speak intelligibly of the one, without explaining the other.

2. *General truths hardly to be understood, but in verbal propositions.* All the knowledge we have, being only of particular or *general truths,* 'tis evident, that whatever may be done in the former of these, the latter, which is that

which with reason is most sought after, can never be well made known, and is very *seldom apprehended, but as conceived and expressed in words.* It is not therefore out of our way, in the examination of our knowledge, to inquire into the truth and certainty of universal propositions.

3. *Certainty twofold, of truth and of knowledge.* But that we may not be misled in this case, by that which is the danger everywhere, I mean by the doubtfulness of terms, 'tis fit to observe, that certainty is twofold; *certainty of truth,* and *certainty of knowledge. Certainty of truth* is, when words are so put together in propositions, as exactly to express the agreement or disagreement of the *ideas* they stand for, as really it is. *Certainty of knowledge* is, to perceive the agreement or disagreement of *ideas,* as expressed in any proposition. This we usually call knowing, or being certain of the truth of any proposition.

4. *No proposition can be known to be true, where the essence of each species mentioned is not known.* Now because *we cannot be certain of the truth of any general proposition, unless we know the precise bounds and extent of the species its terms stand for,* it is necessary we should know the essence of each *species,* which is that which constitutes and bounds it. This, in all simple *ideas* and modes, is not hard to do. For in these, the real and nominal essence being the same; or, which is all one, the abstract *idea,* which the general term stands for, being the sole essence and boundary, that is or can be supposed, of the *species;* there can be no doubt, how far the *species* extends, or what things are comprehended under each term: which, 'tis evident, are all, that have an exact conformity with the *idea* it stands for, and no other. But in substances, wherein a real essence, distinct from the nominal, is supposed to constitute, determine, and bound the species, the extent of the general word is very uncertain: because not knowing this real essence, we cannot know what is, or what is not of that *species,* and consequently what may, or may not with certainty be affirmed of it. And thus speaking of a *man,* or *gold,* or any other *species* of natural substances, as supposed constituted by a precise real essence, which nature regularly imparts to every individual of that kind, whereby it is made to be of that species, we cannot be certain of the truth of any affirmation or negation made of it. For *man,* or *gold,* taken in this sense, and used for *species* of things, constituted by real essences, different from the complex *idea* in the mind of the speaker, stand for we know not what: and the extent of these species, with such boundaries, are so unknown and undetermined, that it is impossible, with any certainty, to affirm, that all men are rational, or that all gold is yellow. But where the

nominal essence is kept to, as the boundary of each species, and men extend the application of any general term no farther than to the particular things, in which the complex *idea* it stands for is to be found, there they are in no danger to mistake the bounds of each *species,* nor can be in doubt, on this account, whether any proposition be true, or no. I have chose to explain this uncertainty of propositions in this scholastic way, and have made use of the terms of *essences* and *species,* on purpose to show the absurdity and inconvenience there is to think of them, as of any other sort of realities, than barely abstract *ideas* with names to them. To suppose, that the *species* of things are anything, but the sorting of them under general names, according as they agree to several abstract *ideas,* of which we make those names the signs, is to confound truth, and introduce uncertainty into all general propositions, that can be made about them. Though therefore these things might, to people not possessed with scholastic learning, be perhaps treated of, in a better and clearer way: yet those wrong notions of *essences* or *species,* having got root in most people's minds, who have received any tincture from the learning, which has prevailed in this part of the world, are to be discovered and removed, to make way for that use of words, which should convey certainty with it.

5. *This more particularly concerns substances. The names of substances* then, *whenever made to stand for species, which are supposed to be constituted by real essences,* which we know not, *are not capable to convey certainty to the understanding:* of the truth of general propositions made up of such terms we cannot be sure. The reason whereof is plain. For how can we be sure that this or that quality is in *gold,* when we know not what is or is not *gold.* Since in this way of speaking nothing is *gold,* but what partakes of an essence, which we not knowing, cannot know where it is, or is not, and so cannot be sure, that any parcel of matter in the world is or is not in this sense *gold;* being incurably ignorant, whether it has or has not that which makes anything to be called *gold, i.e.* that real essence of *gold* whereof we have no *idea* at all. This being as impossible for us to know, as it is for a blind man to tell in what flower the color of a *pansy* is, or is not to be found, whilst he has no *idea* of the color of a *pansy* at all. Or if we could (which is impossible) certainly know where a real essence, which we know not, is, *v.g.* in what parcels of matter the real essence of *gold* is, yet could we not be sure, that this or that quality could with truth be affirmed of *gold;* since it is impossible for us to know, that this or that quality or *idea* has a necessary connection with a real essence, of which we have no *idea* at all, whatever species that supposed real essence may be imagined to constitute.

6. *The truth of few universal propositions concerning substances, is to be known.* On the other side, the *names of substances,* when made use of as they should be, for the *ideas* men have in their minds, though they carry a clear and determinate signification with them, *will not* yet *serve us to make many universal propositions, of whose truth we can be certain.* Not because in this use of them we are uncertain what things are signified by them, but because the complex *ideas* they stand for, are such combinations of simple ones, as carry not with them any discoverable connection or repugnancy, but with a very few other *ideas.*

7. *Because coexistence of* ideas *in few cases to be known.* The complex *ideas,* that our names of the species of substances properly stand for, are collections of such qualities, as have been observed to coexist in an unknown *substratum* which we call *substance;* but what other qualities necessarily coexist with such combinations, we cannot certainly know, unless we can discover their natural dependence; which in their primary qualities, we can go but a very little way in; and in all their secondary qualities, we can discover no connection at all, for the reasons mentioned, *Chap.* iii. *viz.* 1. Because we know not the real constitutions of substances, on which each *secondary quality* particularly depends. 2. Did we know that, it would serve us only for experimental (not universal) knowledge; and reach with certainty no farther, than that bare instance. Because our understandings can discover no conceivable connection between any *secondary quality,* and any modification whatsoever of any of the *primary* ones. And therefore there are very few general propositions to be made concerning substances, which can carry with them *undoubted certainty.*

. . . .

9. *Instance in gold.* . . . I would gladly meet with one general affirmation, concerning any quality of *gold,* that anyone can certainly know is true. It will, no doubt, be presently objected, is not this an universal proposition, *all gold is malleable*? To which I answer, it is a very certain proposition, if *malleableness* be a part of the complex *idea* the word *gold* stands for. But then here is nothing affirmed of *gold,* but that that sound stands for an *idea* in which *malleableness* is contained: and such a sort of truth and certainty as this, it is to say *a centaur is four-footed.* But if *malleableness* makes not a part of the specific essence the name *gold* stands for, 'tis plain, *all gold is malleable,* is not a certain proposition. Because let the complex *idea* of *gold,* be made up of whichsoever of its other qualities you please, *malleableness*

will not appear to depend on that complex *idea;* nor follow from any simple one contained in it. The connection that *malleableness* has (if it has any) with those other qualities, being only by the intervention of the real constitution of its insensible parts, which, since we know not, 'tis impossible we should perceive that connection, unless we could discover that which ties them together.

10. *As far as any such coexistence can be known, so far universal propositions may be certain. But this will go but a little way.* The more, indeed, of these coexisting qualities we unite into one complex *idea,* under one name, the more precise and determinate we make the signification of that word; but never yet make it thereby more capable of *universal certainty,* in respect of other qualities, not contained in our complex *idea;* since we perceive not their connection, or dependence one on another; being ignorant both of that real constitution in which they are all founded; and also how they flow from it. . . .

11. *The qualities which make our complex* idea *of substances, depend mostly on external, remote, and unperceived causes.* Had we such *ideas* of substances, as to know what real constitutions produce those sensible qualities we find in them, and how those qualities flowed from thence, we could, by the specific *ideas* of their real essences in our own minds, more certainly find out their properties, and discover what qualities they had, or had not, than we can now by our senses: and to know the properties of *gold,* it would be no more necessary, that *gold* should exist, and that we should make experiments upon it, than it is necessary for the knowing the properties of a triangle, that a triangle should exist in any matter, the *idea* in our minds would serve for the one as well as the other. But we are so far from being admitted into the secrets of nature, that we scarce so much as ever approach the first entrance towards them. For we are wont to consider the substances we meet with, each of them, as an entire thing by itself, having all its qualities in itself, and independent of other things; overlooking, for the most part, the operations of those invisible fluids, they are encompassed with; and upon whose motions and operations depend the greatest part of those qualities which are taken notice of in them, and are made by us the inherent marks of distinction, whereby we know and denominate them. Put a piece of *gold* anywhere by itself, separate from the reach and influence of all other bodies, it will immediately lose all its color and weight, and perhaps malleableness too; which, for ought I know, would be changed into a perfect friability. . . . We are then quite out of the way, when we think, that

things contain within themselves the qualities, that appear to us in them; and we in vain search for that constitution within the body of a fly, or an elephant, upon which depend those qualities and powers we observe in them. For which, perhaps, to understand them aright, we ought to look not only beyond this our earth and atmosphere, but even beyond the sun, or remotest star our eyes have yet discovered. For how much the being and operation of particular substances in this our globe, depend on causes utterly beyond our view, is impossible for us to determine. We see and perceive some of the motions and grosser operations of things here about us; but whence the streams come that keep all these curious machines in motion and repair, how conveyed and modified, is beyond our notice and apprehension; and the great parts and wheels, as I may so say, of this stupendious structure of the universe, may, for ought we know, have such a connection and dependence in their influences and operations one upon another, that, perhaps, things in this our mansion, would put on quite another face, and cease to be what they are, if some one of the stars, or great bodies incomprehensibly remote from us, should cease to be, or move as it does. This is certain, things, however absolute and entire they seem in themselves, are but retainers to other parts of nature, for that which they are most taken notice of by us. Their observable qualities, actions, and powers, are owing to something without them; and there is not so complete and perfect a part, that we know, of nature, which does not owe the being it has, and the excellencies of it, to its neighbors; and we must not confine our thoughts within the surface of any body, but look a great deal farther, to comprehend perfectly those qualities that are in it.

12. If this be so, it is not to be wondered, that *we have very imperfect* ideas *of substances;* and that the real essences, on which depend their properties and operations, are unknown to us. We cannot discover so much as that *size, figure,* and *texture* of their minute and active parts, which is really in them; much less the different motions and impulses made in and upon them by bodies from without, upon which depends, and by which is formed the greatest and most remarkable part of those qualities we observe in them, and of which our complex *ideas* of them are made up. This consideration alone is enough to put an end to all our hopes of ever having the *ideas* of their real essences; which, whilst we want, the nominal essences, we make use of instead of them, will be able to furnish us but very sparingly with any *general knowledge,* or universal propositions capable of real *certainty*.

13. *Judgment may reach farther, but that is not knowledge.* We are not therefore to wonder, if *certainty* be to be found in very few general propositions made concerning substances: our knowledge of their qualities and properties go very seldom farther than our senses reach and inform us. Possibly inquisitive and observing men may, by strength of *judgment,* penetrate farther, and on probabilities taken from wary observation, and hints well laid together, often guess right at what experience has not yet discovered to them. But this is but guessing still; it amounts only to opinion, and has not that *certainty,* which is requisite to knowledge. For all *general knowledge* lies only in our own thoughts, and consists barely in the contemplation of our own abstract *ideas.* . . .

14. *What is requisite for our knowledge of substances.* Before we can have any tolerable knowledge of this kind, we must first know what changes the *primary qualities* of one body, do regularly produce in the *primary qualities* of another, and how. Secondly, we must know what *primary qualities* of any body, produce certain sensations or *ideas* in us. This is in truth, no less than to know all the effects of matter, under its divers modifications of bulk, figure, cohesion of parts, motion, and rest. Which, I think, everybody will allow, is utterly impossible to be known by us, without revelation. Nor if it were revealed to us, what sort of figure, bulk, and motion of corpuscles, would produce in us the sensation of a *yellow* color, and what sort of figure, bulk, and texture of parts in the superficies of any body, were fit to give such corpuscles their due motion to produce that color, would that be enough to make *universal* propositions with *certainty,* concerning the several sorts of them, unless we had faculties acute enough to perceive the precise bulk, figure, texture, and motion of bodies in those minute parts, by which they operate on our senses, so that we might by those frame our abstract *ideas* of them. I have mentioned here only *corporeal* substances, whose operations seem to lie more level to our understandings: for as to the *operations of spirits,* both their thinking and moving of bodies, we at first sight find ourselves at a loss; though perhaps, when we have applied our thoughts a little nearer to the consideration of bodies, and their operations, and examined how far our notions, even in these, reach, with any clearness, beyond sensible matter of fact, we shall be bound to confess, that even in these too, our discoveries amount to very little beyond perfect ignorance and incapacity.

. . . .

16. *Wherein lies the general certainty of propositions.* To conclude, *general propositions,* of what kind soever, are then only capable of *certainty,* when the terms used in them, stand for such *ideas,* whose agreement or disagreement, as there expressed, is capable to be discovered by us. And we are then certain of their truth or falsehood, when we perceive the *ideas* they stand for, to agree or not agree, according as they are affirmed or denied one of another. Whence we may take notice, that *general certainty* is never to be found but in our *ideas.* Whenever we go to seek it elsewhere in experiment, or observations without us, our knowledge goes not beyond particulars. 'Tis the contemplation of our own abstract *ideas,* that alone is able to afford us *general knowledge.*

CHAP. VII.

Of maxims.

1. *They are self-evident.* There are a sort of propositions, which under the name of *maxims* and *axioms,* have passed for principles of science: and because they are *self-evident,* have been supposed innate, without that anybody (that I know) ever went about to show the reason and foundation of their clearness or cogency. It may however be worthwhile, to inquire into the reason of their evidence, and see whether it be peculiar to them alone, and also examine how far they influence and govern our other knowledge.

2. *Wherein that self-evidence consists. Knowledge,* as has been shown, consists in the perception of the agreement or disagreement of *ideas:* now where that agreement or disagreement is perceived immediately by itself, without the intervention or help of any other, there our *knowledge is self-evident.* This will appear to be so to anyone, who will but consider any of those propositions, which, without any proof, he assents to at first sight: for in all of them he will find, that the reason of his assent, is from that agreement or disagreement, which the mind, by an immediate comparing them, finds in those *ideas* answering the affirmation or negation in the proposition.

3. *Self-evidence not peculiar to received axioms.* This being so, in the next place let us consider, whether this *self-evidence* be peculiar only to those propositions, which commonly pass under the name of maxims, and have

the dignity of axioms allowed them. And here 'tis plain, that several other truths, not allowed to be axioms, partake equally with them in this *self-evidence.* This we shall see, if we go over these several sorts of agreement or disagreement of *ideas,* which I have above-mentioned, *viz.* identity, relation, coexistence, and real existence; which will discover to us, that not only those few propositions, which have had the credit of *maxims,* are self-evident, but a great many, even almost an infinite number of *other propositions* are such.

4. *First, as to identity and diversity, all propositions are equally self-evident.* For, *first,* the immediate perception of the agreement or disagreement of *identity,* being founded in the mind's having distinct *ideas,* this affords us as many *self-evident* propositions, as we have distinct *ideas.* Everyone that has any knowledge at all, has, as the foundation of it, various and distinct *ideas:* and it is the first act of the mind, (without which, it can never be capable of any knowledge,) to know every one of its *ideas* by itself, and distinguish it from others. . . . It is not therefore alone to these two general propositions, *whatsoever is, is;* and *it is impossible for the same thing to be, and not to be,* that this self-evidence belongs by any peculiar right. The perception of being, or not being, belongs no more to these vague *ideas,* signified by the terms *whatsoever,* and *thing,* than it does to any other *ideas.* These two general maxims amounting to no more in short but this, that *the same is the same,* and *the same is not different,* are truths known in more particular instances, as well as in these general maxims, and known also in particular instances, before these general maxims are ever thought on, and draw all their force from the discernment of the mind employed about particular *ideas.* There is nothing more visible, than that the mind, without the help of any proof, or reflection on either of these general propositions perceives so clearly, and knows so certainly, that the *idea* of *white,* is the *idea* of white, and not the *idea* of blue; and that the *idea* of white, when it is in the mind, is there, and is not absent, that the consideration of these axioms can add nothing to the evidence or certainty of its knowledge. . . .

5. *Secondly, in coexistence we have few self-evident propositions. Secondly,* as to *coexistence,* or such a necessary connection between two *ideas,* that in the subject where one of them is supposed, there the other must necessarily be also: of such agreement, or disagreement as this, the mind has an immediate perception but in very few of them. And therefore in this sort, we have but very little intuitive knowledge; nor are there to be found very many propositions that are self-evident, though some there are; *v.g.* the *idea* of

filling a place equal to the contents of its superficies, being annexed to our *idea* of body, I think it is a self-evident proposition, *that two bodies cannot be in the same place*.

6. *Thirdly, in other relations we may have. Thirdly,* as to the *relations* of modes, mathematicians have framed many axioms concerning that one relation of equality. As *equals taken from equals, the remainder will be equals;* which, with the rest of that kind, however they are received for maxims by the mathematicians, and are unquestionable truths; yet, I think, that anyone who considers them, will not find, that they have a clearer self-evidence than these, that *one and one are equal to two;* that *if you take from the five fingers of one hand two, and from the five fingers of the other hand two, the remaining numbers will be equal.* These, and a thousand other such propositions, may be found in numbers, which, at very first hearing, force the assent, and carry with them an equal, if not greater clearness, than those mathematical axioms.

7. *Fourthly, concerning real existence we have none. Fourthly,* as to *real existence,* since that has no connection with any other of our *ideas,* but that of ourselves, and of a first being, we have in that, concerning the real existence of all other beings, not so much as demonstrative, much less a self-evident knowledge: and therefore concerning those there are no maxims.

8. *These axioms do not much influence our other knowledge.* In the next place let us consider, what *influence* these received *maxims* have, upon the other parts of our knowledge. The rules established in the schools, that all reasonings are *ex præcognitis, & præconcessis,* seem to lay the foundation of all other knowledge, in these maxims, and to suppose them to be *pra ecognita*;[44] whereby, I think, is meant these two things: first, that these axioms, are those truths that are first known to the mind; and, secondly, that upon them, the other parts of our knowledge depend.

9. *Because they are not the truths the first known. First,* that they are not the *truths first known* to the mind, is evident to experience, as we have shown in another place. *B.* I. *Ch.* ii. Who perceives not, that a child certainly knows, that a stranger is not its mother; that its sucking-bottle is not the rod, long before he knows, that *'tis impossible for the same thing to be, and not to be*? And how many truths are there about numbers, which it is obvious to observe,

44. *ex præcognita, & præconcessis,* from [principles] that are already known, or already conceded; *præcognita,* things first known, principles.

that the mind is perfectly acquainted with, and fully convinced of, before it ever thought on these general maxims, to which mathematicians, in their arguings, do sometimes refer them? . . . Thus particular *ideas* are *first* received and distinguished, and so knowledge got about them: and next to them, the less general, or specific, which are next to particular. For abstract *ideas* are not so obvious or easy to children, or the yet unexercised mind, as particular ones. If they seem so to grown men, 'tis only because by constant and familiar use they are made so. For when we nicely reflect upon them, we shall find, that general *ideas* are fictions and contrivances of the mind, that carry difficulty with them, and do not so easily offer themselves, as we are apt to imagine. For example, does it not require some pains and skill to form the *general idea* of a *triangle,* (which is yet none of the most abstract, comprehensive, and difficult,) for it must be neither oblique, nor rectangle, neither equilateral, equicrural, nor scalenon; but all and none of these at once. In effect, it is something imperfect, that cannot exist; an *idea* wherein some parts of several different and inconsistent *ideas* are put together. 'Tis true, the mind in this imperfect state, has need of such *ideas,* and makes all the haste to them it can, for the conveniency of communication, and enlargement of knowledge; to both which, it is naturally very much inclined. But yet one has reason to suspect such *ideas* are marks of our imperfection; at least, this is enough to show, that the most abstract and general *ideas,* are not those that the mind is *first* and most easily acquainted with, nor such as its earliest knowledge is conversant about.

10. *Because on them the other parts of our knowledge do not depend. Secondly,* from what has been said, it plainly follows, that these magnified *maxims,* are not the principles and *foundations* of all our other *knowledge.* For if there be a great many other truths, which have as much self-evidence as they, and a great many that we know before them, it is impossible they should be the *principles,* from which we deduce all other truths. Is it impossible to know that *one* and *two* are equal to *three,* but by virtue of this, or some such axiom, *viz. the whole is equal to all its parts taken together*? Many a one knows that *one* and *two* are equal to *three,* without having heard, or thought on that, or any other axiom, by which it might be proved; and knows it as certainly, as any other man knows, that *the whole is equal to all its parts,* or any other maxim; and all from the same reason of self-evidence; the equality of those *ideas,* being as visible and certain to him without that, or any other axiom, as with it, it needing no proof to make it perceived. Nor after the knowledge, *that the whole is equal to all its parts,* does he know that *one and two are equal to three,* better, or more certainly than he did before. . . .

11. *What use these general maxims have.* . . . To come therefore to the use that is made of *maxims.*

1. They are of use . . . in the ordinary methods of teaching sciences as far as they are advanced: but of little or none in advancing them farther.

2. They are of use in disputes, for the silencing of obstinate wranglers, and bringing those contests to some conclusion. . . .

This method of the schools, which have been thought the fountains of knowledge, introduced as I suppose the like use of these maxims, into a great part of conversation out of the schools, to stop the mouths of cavillers, whom anyone is excused from arguing any longer with, when they deny these general self-evident principles received by all reasonable men, who have once thought of them: but yet their use herein, is but to put an end to wrangling. They in truth, when urged in such cases, teach nothing: that is already done by the intermediate *ideas* made use of in the debate, whose connection may be seen without the help of those maxims, and so the truth known before the maxim is produced, and the argument brought to a first principle. . . .

12. *Maxims, if care be not taken in the use of words, may prove contradictions.* One thing farther, I think, it may not be amiss to observe concerning these general maxims, that they are so far from improving or establishing our minds in true knowledge, that if our notions be wrong, loose, or unsteady, and we resign up our thoughts to the sound of words, rather than fix them on settled determined *ideas* of things; I say, these *general maxims* will *serve* to confirm us in mistakes; and in such a way of use of words, which is most common, will *serve* to prove contradictions: *v.g.* he that with *Descartes,* shall frame in his mind an *idea* of what he calls *body,* to be nothing but extension, may easily demonstrate, that there is no *vacuum, i.e.* no space void of body, by this maxim, *what is, is.*[45] For the *idea* to which he annexes the name *body,* being bare extension, his knowledge, that space cannot be without body, is certain. For he knows his own *idea* of extension clearly and distinctly, and knows that it is *what it is,* and not another *idea,* though it be called by these three names, *extension, body, space.* Which three words standing for one and the same *idea,* may no doubt, with the same evidence and certainty, be affirmed one of another, as each of itself: and it is as certain, that whilst I use them all to stand for one and the same *idea,* this predication is as true and identical in its signification, *that space is body,* as

45. René Descartes (1596–1650), French philosopher and scientist.

this predication is true and identical, *that body is body,* both in signification and sound.

13. *Instance in* vacuum. But if another shall come, and make to himself another *idea,* different from *Descartes*'s of the thing, which yet with *Descartes* he calls by the same name *body,* and make his *idea,* which he expresses by the word *body,* to be of a thing that has both *extension* and *solidity* together, he will as easily demonstrate, that there may be a *vacuum,* or space without a body, as *Descartes* demonstrated the contrary. Because the *idea* to which he gives the name *space,* being barely the simple one of *extension;* and the *idea,* to which he gives the name *body,* being the complex *idea* of *extension* and *resistibility,* or *solidity* together in the same subject, these two *ideas* are not exactly one and the same, but in the understanding as distinct as the *ideas* of one and two, white and black, or as of *corporeity* and *humanity,* if I may use those barbarous terms: and therefore the predication of them in our minds, or in words standing for them is not identical, but the negation of them one of another; *viz.* this proposition extension or *space is not body,* is as true and evidently certain, as this maxim, *it is impossible for the same thing to be, and not to be,* can make any proposition.

14. *They prove not the existence of things without us.* But yet though both these propositions (as you see) may be equally demonstrated, *viz.* that there may be a *vacuum,* and that there cannot be a *vacuum,* by these two certain principles, (*viz.*) *what is, is,* and *the same thing cannot be, and not be:* yet neither of these principles will serve to prove to us, that any, or what bodies do exist: for that we are left to our senses, to discover to us as far as they can. Those universal and self-evident principles, being only our constant, clear, and distinct knowledge of our own *ideas,* more general or comprehensive, can assure us of nothing that passes without the mind, their certainty is founded only upon the knowledge we have of each *idea* by itself, and of its distinction from others; about which, we cannot be mistaken whilst they are in our minds, though we may, and often are mistaken, when we retain the names without the *ideas;* or use them confusedly sometimes for one, and sometimes for another *idea.* In which cases, the force of these *axioms* reaching only to the sound, and not the signification of the words, *serves* only to lead us into confusion, mistake, and error. . . .

15. *Their application dangerous about complex* ideas. But let them be of what *use* they will in verbal propositions, they cannot discover or prove to us the

least knowledge of the nature of substances, as they are found and exist without us, any farther than grounded on experience. . . .

. . . .

CHAP. VIII.

Of trifling propositions.

1. *Some propositions bring no increase to our knowledge.* Whether the maxims treated of in the foregoing chapter, be of that use to real knowledge, as is generally supposed, I leave to be considered. This, I think, may confidently be affirmed, that there are universal propositions; that though they be certainly true, yet they add no light to our understandings, bring no increase to our knowledge. Such are,

2. *As first, identical propositions. First, all purely identical propositions.* These obviously, and at first blush, appear to contain no instruction in them. For when we affirm the said term of itself, whether it be barely verbal, or whether it contains any clear and real *idea,* it shows us nothing, but what we must certainly know before, whether such a proposition be either made by, or proposed to us. . . .

3. For at this rate, any very ignorant person, who can but make a proposition, and knows what he means when he says, *aye,* or *no,* may make a million of propositions, of whose truth he may be infallibly certain, and yet not know one thing in the world thereby; *v.g.* what is a soul, is a soul; or, *a soul is a soul; a spirit is a spirit; a fetiche is a fetiche, &c.* These all being equivalent to this proposition, *viz. what is, is,* i.e. *what has existence, has existence;* or, *who has a soul, has a soul.* What is this more than trifling with words? It is but like a monkey shifting his oyster from one hand to the other; and had he had but words, might, no doubt, have said, oyster in right hand is *subject,* and oyster in left hand is *predicate:* and so might have made a self-evident proposition of oyster, *i.e. oyster is oyster;* and yet, with all this, not have been one whit the wiser, or more knowing: and that way of handling the matter, would much at one have satisfied the monkey's hunger, or a man's understanding; and they would have improved in knowledge and bulk together. . . .

. . . .

4. *Secondly, when a part of any complex* idea *is predicated of the whole. Secondly,* another sort of trifling propositions is, *when a part of the complex* idea *is predicated of the name of the whole;* a part of the definition of the word defined. Such are all propositions wherein the *genus* is predicated of the *species,* or more comprehensive of less comprehensive terms: for what information, what knowledge carries this proposition in it, *viz. lead is a metal,* to a man, who knows the complex *idea* the name *lead* stands for. All the simple *ideas* that go to the complex one signified by the term *metal,* being nothing but what he before comprehended, and signified by the name *lead.* Indeed, to a man that knows the signification of the word *metal,* and not of the word *lead,* it is a shorter way to explain the signification of the word *lead,* by saying it is a *metal,* which at once expresses several of its simple *ideas,* than to enumerate them one by one, telling him it is a body very *heavy, fusible,* and *malleable.*

5. *As part of the definition of the defined.* Alike trifling it is, *to predicate any other part of the definition of the term defined,* or to affirm any one of the simple *ideas* of a complex one, of the name of the whole complex *idea;* as *all gold is fusible.* For *fusibility* being one of the simple *ideas* that goes to the making up the complex one the sound *gold* stands for, what can it be but playing with sounds, to affirm that of the name *gold,* which is comprehended in its received signification? . . .

. . . .

7. *For this teaches but the signification of words.* Before a man makes any proposition, he is supposed to understand the terms he uses in it, or else he talks like a parrot, only making a noise by imitation, and framing certain sounds, which he has learned of others; but not, as a rational creature, using them for signs of *ideas,* which he has in his mind. The hearer also is supposed to understand the terms as the speaker uses them, or else he talks jargon, and makes an unintelligible noise. And therefore he trifles with words, who makes such a proposition, which when it is made, contains no more than one of the terms does, and which a man was supposed to know before: *v.g. a triangle has three sides,* or *saffron is yellow.* And this is no farther tolerable, than where a man goes to explain his terms, to one who is supposed or declares himself not to understand him: and then *it teaches only the signification of that word,* and the use of that sign.

8. *But no real knowledge.* We can know then the truth of two sorts of propositions, with perfect *certainty;* the one is, of those trifling propositions, which have a certainty in them, but 'tis but a *verbal certainty,* but not instructive. And, secondly, we can know the truth, and so may be *certain* in propositions, which affirm something of another, which is a necessary consequence of its precise complex *idea,* but not contained in it. As that *the external angle of all triangles, is bigger than either of the opposite internal angles;* which relation of the outward angle, to either of the opposite internal angles, making no part of the complex *idea,* signified by the name triangle, this is a real truth, and conveys with it instructive *real knowledge.*

9. *General propositions concerning substances are often trifling.* We having little or no knowledge of what combinations there be of simple *ideas* existing together in substances, but by our senses, we cannot make any universal *certain* propositions concerning them, any farther than our nominal essences lead us: which being to a very few and inconsiderable truths, in respect of those which depend on their real constitutions, the general *propositions* that are made *about substances, if they are certain, are for the most part but trifling;* and if they are instructive, are uncertain, and such as we can have no knowledge of their real truth, how much soever constant observation and analogy may assist our judgments in guessing. Hence it comes to pass, that one may often meet with very clear and coherent discourses, that amount yet to nothing. For 'tis plain, that names of substantial beings, as well as others, as far as they have relative significations affixed to them, may, with great truth, be joined negatively and affirmatively in propositions, as their relative definitions make them fit to be so joined; and propositions consisting of such terms, may, with the same clearness, be deduced one from another, as those that convey the most real truths: and all this, without any knowledge of the nature or reality of things existing without us. By this method, one may make demonstrations and undoubted propositions in words, and yet thereby advance not one jot in the knowledge of the truth of things; *v.g.* he that having learned these following words, with their ordinary mutually relative acceptations annexed to them; *v.g. substance, man, animal, form, soul, vegetative, sensitive, rational,* may make several undoubted propositions, about the soul, without knowing at all what the soul really is; and of this sort, a man may find an infinite number of propositions, reasonings, and conclusions, in books of metaphysics, school-divinity, and some sort of natural philosophy; and after all, know as little of GOD, *spirits,* or *bodies,* as he did before he set out.

. . . .

11. *Thirdly, using words variously, is trifling with them.* Though yet concerning most words used in discourses, especially argumentative and controversial, there is this more to be complained of, which is the worst sort of *trifling,* and which sets us yet farther from the certainty of knowledge we hope to attain by them, or find in them; *viz.* that most writers are so far from instructing us in the nature and knowledge of things, that they *use their words loosely* and uncertainly, and do not, by using them constantly and steadily in the same signification, make plain and clear deductions of words one from another, and make their discourses coherent and clear, (how little soever it were instructive,) which were not difficult to do, did they not find it convenient to shelter their ignorance or obstinacy, under the obscurity and perplexedness of their terms; to which, perhaps, inadvertency, and ill custom does in many men much contribute.

12. *Marks of verbal propositions, first, predication in abstract.* To conclude, *barely verbal propositions* may be known by these following *marks:*

First, all propositions, wherein two abstract terms are affirmed one of another, are barely about the signification of sounds. . . .

13. *Secondly, a part of the definition predicated of any term. Secondly, all propositions, wherein a part of the complex* idea, which any term stands for, *is predicated of that term, are only* verbal, *v.g.* to say, *that gold is a metal,* or *heavy.* And thus all propositions, wherein more comprehensive words, called *genera,* are affirmed of subordinate, or less comprehensive, called *species, or individuals,* are barely verbal.

. . . .

This, I think, I may lay down for an infallible rule, that wherever the distinct *idea* any word stands for, is not known and considered, and something not contained in the *idea,* is not affirmed, or denied of it, there our thoughts stick wholly in sounds, and are able to attain no real truth or falsehood. This, perhaps, if well heeded, might save us a great deal of useless amusement and dispute; and very much shorten our trouble, and wandering in the search of real and true knowledge.

CHAP. IX.

Of our knowledge of existence.

1. *General certain propositions concern not existence.* Hitherto we have only considered the essences of things, which being only abstract *ideas,* and thereby removed in our thoughts from particular existence, (that being the proper operation of the mind, in abstraction, to consider an *idea* under no other existence, but what it has in the understanding,) gives us no knowledge of real existence at all. Where by the way we may take notice, that *universal propositions,* of whose truth or falsehood we can have certain knowledge, concern not *existence;* and farther, that *all particular affirmations or negations,* that would not be certain if they were made general, are only concerning *existence;* they declaring only the accidental union or separation of *ideas* in things existing, which in their abstract natures, have no known necessary union or repugnancy.

2. *A threefold knowledge of existence.* But leaving the nature of propositions, and different ways of predication to be considered more at large in another place, let us proceed now to inquire concerning our knowledge of the *existence* of things, and how we come by it. I say then, that we have the knowledge of *our own existence* by intuition; of the *existence of* GOD, by demonstration; and of other things by sensation.

3. *Our knowledge of our own existence is intuitive.* As for *our own existence,* we perceive it so plainly, and so certainly, that it neither needs, nor is capable of any proof. For nothing can be more evident to us, than our own existence. *I think, I reason, I feel pleasure and pain:* can any of these be more evident to me, than my own existence? If I doubt of all other things, that very doubt makes me perceive my own *existence,* and will not suffer me to doubt of that. For if I know *I feel pain,* it is evident, I have as certain a perception of my own existence, as of the existence of the pain I feel; or if I know *I doubt,* I have as certain a perception of the existence of the thing doubting, as of that thought, which I call *doubt.* Experience then convinces us, that *we have an intuitive knowledge of our own existence,* and an internal infallible perception that we are. In every act of sensation, reasoning or thinking, we are conscious to ourselves of our own being; and, in this matter, come not short of the highest degree of *certainty.*

but this "I" is not as a thinking spiritual substance

 but as a Person, an emergent individuated consciousness

CHAP. X.

Of our knowledge of the existence of a GOD.

1. *We are capable of knowing certainly that there is a GOD.* Though GOD has given us no innate *ideas* of himself; though he has stamped no original characters on our minds, wherein we may read his being; yet having furnished us with those faculties, our minds are endowed with, he has not left himself without witness: since we have sense, perception, and reason, and cannot want a clear proof of him, as long as we carry ourselves about us. Nor can we justly complain of our ignorance in this great point, since he has so plentifully provided us with the means to discover, and know him, so far as is necessary to the end of our being, and the great concernment of our happiness. But though this be the most obvious truth that reason discovers; and though its evidence be (if I mistake not) equal to mathematical certainty: yet it requires thought and attention; and the mind must apply itself to a regular deduction of it from some part of our intuitive knowledge, or else we shall be as uncertain, and ignorant of this, as of other propositions, which are in themselves capable of clear demonstration. To show therefore that we are capable of *knowing,* i.e. *being certain that there is a* GOD, and how we may come by this certainty, I think we need go no farther than ourselves, and that undoubted knowledge we have of our own existence.

2. *Man knows that he himself is.* I think it is beyond question, that *man has a clear perception of his own being;* he knows certainly, that he exists, and that he is something. He that can doubt, whether he be anything, or no, I speak not to, no more than I would argue with pure nothing, or endeavor to convince non-entity, that it were something. If anyone pretends to be so skeptical, as to deny his own existence, (for really to doubt of it, is manifestly impossible,) let him for me enjoy his beloved happiness of being nothing, until hunger, or some other pain convince him of the contrary. This then, I think, I may take for a truth, which everyone's certain knowledge assures him of, beyond the liberty of doubting, *viz.* that he is something that actually exists.

3. *He knows also, that nothing cannot produce a being, therefore something eternal.* In the next place, man knows by an intuitive certainty, that bare *nothing can no more produce any real being, than it can be equal to two right angles.* If a man knows not that non-entity, or the absence of all being cannot be equal to two right angles, it is impossible he should know any demonstration in *Euclid.* If therefore we know there is some real being, and that non-entity cannot produce any real being, it is an evident demonstration, that from eternity there has been something; since what was not from eternity, had a beginning; and what had a beginning, must be produced by something else.

4. *That eternal being must be most powerful.* Next, it is evident, that what had its being and beginning from another, must also have all that which is in, and belongs to its being from another too. All the powers it has, must be owing to, and received from the same source. This eternal source then of all being must also be the source and original of all power; and *so this eternal being must be also the most powerful.*

5. *And most knowing.* Again, a man finds in himself *perception,* and *knowledge.* We have then got one step farther; and we are certain now, that there is not only some being, but some knowing intelligent being in the world.

There was a time then, when there was no knowing being, and when knowledge began to be; or else there has been also *a knowing being from eternity.* If it be said, there was a time when no being had any knowledge, when that eternal being was void of all understanding. I reply, that then it was impossible there should ever have been any knowledge. It being as impossible, that things wholly void of knowledge, and operating blindly, and without any perception, should produce a knowing being, as it is impossible, that a triangle should make itself three angles bigger than two right ones. For it is as repugnant to the *idea* of senseless matter, that it should put into itself sense, perception, and knowledge, as it is repugnant to the *idea* of a triangle, that it should put into itself greater angles than two right ones.

6. *And therefore GOD.* Thus from the consideration of ourselves, and what we infallibly find in our own constitutions, our reason leads us to the knowledge of this certain and evident truth, that *there is an eternal, most powerful, and most knowing being;* which whether anyone will please to call *God,* it matters not. The thing is evident, and from this *idea* duly considered, will easily be deduced all those other attributes, which we ought to

ascribe to this eternal being. If nevertheless anyone should be found so senselessly arrogant, as to suppose man alone knowing and wise, but yet the product of mere ignorance and chance; and that all the rest of the universe acted only by that blind haphazard: I shall leave with him that very rational and emphatical rebuke of *Tully,* l. 2. *de leg.* to be considered at his leisure. "What can be more sillily arrogant and misbecoming, than for a man to think that he has a mind and understanding in him, but yet in all the universe beside, there is no such thing? Or that those things, which with the utmost stretch of his reason he can scarce comprehend, should be moved and managed without any reason at all?"[46] . . .

From what has been said, it is plain to me, we have a more certain knowledge of the existence of a GOD, than of anything our senses have not immediately discovered to us. Nay, I presume I may say, that we more certainly know that there is a GOD, than that there is anything else without us. When I say we *know,* I mean there is such a knowledge within our reach, which we cannot miss, if we will but apply our minds to that, as we do to several other inquiries.

7. *Our* idea *of a most perfect being not the sole proof of a* GOD. *How far the* idea *of a most perfect being,* which a man may frame in his mind, does, or does not prove *the existence of a* GOD, I will not here examine. For in the different make of men's tempers, and application of their thoughts, some arguments prevail more on one, and some on another, for the confirmation of the same truth. But yet, I think, this I may say, that it is an ill way of establishing this truth, and silencing atheists, to lay the whole stress of so important a point, as this, upon that sole foundation: and take some men's having that *idea* of GOD in their minds, (for 'tis evident, some men have none, and some worse than none, and the most very different,) for the only proof of a deity; and out of an over-fondness of that darling invention, cashier, or at least endeavor to invalidate all other arguments, and forbid us to hearken to those proofs, as being weak, or fallacious, which our own existence, and the sensible parts of the universe, offer so clearly, and cogently to our thoughts, that I deem it impossible for a considering man to withstand them. For I judge it as certain and clear a truth, as can anywhere be delivered, that *the invisible things of* GOD *are clearly seen from the creation of the world, being understood by the things that are made, even his eternal power, and Godhead.*[47] Though our own being furnishes us, as I have shown, with an evident, and

46. Marcus Tullius Cicero (106–43 B.C.), *De legibus* (*On the laws*) II vii.

47. *the invisible things . . . are clearly seen. . . ,* Romans 1:20.

incontestable proof of a deity; and I believe nobody can avoid the cogency of it, who will but as carefully attend to it, as to any other demonstration of so many parts: yet this being so fundamental a truth, and of that consequence, that all religion and genuine morality depend thereon, I doubt not but I shall be forgiven by my reader, if I go over some parts of this argument again, and enlarge a little more upon them.

8. *Something from eternity.* There is no truth more evident, than that *something* must be *from eternity.* I never yet heard of anyone so unreasonable, or that could suppose so manifest a contradiction, as a time, wherein there was perfectly nothing. This being of all absurdities the greatest, to imagine that pure nothing, the perfect negation and absence of all beings, should ever produce any real existence.

It being then unavoidable for all rational creatures, to conclude, that something has existed from eternity; let us next see what kind of thing that must be.

9. *Two sorts of beings, cogitative and incogitative.* There are but two sorts of beings in the world, that man knows or conceives.

First, such as are purely material, without sense, perception, or thought, as the clippings of our beards, and parings of our nails.

Secondly, sensible, thinking, perceiving beings, such as we find ourselves to be, which if you please, we will hereafter call *cogitative and incogitative* beings; which to our present purpose, if for nothing else, are, perhaps, better terms, than material and immaterial.

10. *Incogitative being cannot produce a cogitative.* If then there must be something eternal, let us see what sort of being it must be. And to that, it is very obvious to reason, that it must necessarily be a *cogitative* being. For it is as impossible to conceive, that ever bare incogitative matter should produce a thinking intelligent being, as that nothing should of itself produce matter. Let us suppose any parcel of matter eternal, great or small, we shall find it, in itself, able to produce nothing. For example; let us suppose the matter of the next pebble, we meet with, eternal, closely united, and the parts firmly at rest together, if there were no other being in the world, must it not eternally remain so, a dead inactive lump? Is it possible to conceive it can add motion to itself, being purely matter, or produce anything? Matter then, by its own strength, cannot produce in itself so much as motion: the motion it has, must also be from eternity, or else be produced, and added to matter by some other being more powerful than matter; matter, as is

evident, having not power to produce motion in itself. But let us suppose motion eternal too; yet matter, *incogitative matter* and motion, whatever changes it might produce of figure and bulk, *could never produce thought:* knowledge will still be as far beyond the power of motion and matter to produce, as matter is beyond the power of *nothing,* or *non-entity* to produce. And I appeal to everyone's own thoughts, whether he cannot as easily conceive matter produced by *nothing,* as thought to be produced by pure matter, when before there was no such thing as thought, or an intelligent being existing. Divide matter into as minute parts as you will, (which we are apt to imagine a sort of spiritualizing, or making a thinking thing of it,) vary the figure and motion of it, as much as you please; a globe, cube, cone, prism, cylinder, *&c.* whose diameters are but 1000000th part of a *gry** will operate no otherwise upon other bodies of proportionable bulk, than those of an inch or foot diameter; and you may as rationally expect to produce sense, thought, and knowledge, by putting together in a certain figure and motion, gross particles of matter, as by those that are the very minutest, that do anywhere exist. They knock, impel, and resist one another, just as the greater do, and that is all they can do. So that if we will suppose nothing first, or eternal; *matter* can never begin to be: if we suppose bare matter, without motion, eternal; *motion* can never begin to be: if we suppose only matter and motion first, or eternal; *thought* can never begin to be. For it is impossible to conceive that matter either with or without motion could have originally in and from itself sense, perception, and knowledge, as is evident from hence, that then sense, perception, and knowledge must be a property eternally inseparable from matter and every particle of it. Not to add, that though our general or specific conception of matter makes us speak of it as one thing, yet really all matter is not one individual thing, neither is there any such thing existing as one material being or one single body that we know or can conceive. And therefore if matter were the eternal first cogitative being, there would not be one eternal infinite cogitative being, but an infinite number of eternal finite cogitative beings, independent one of another, of limited force, and distinct thoughts, which could never produce that order, harmony, and beauty which are to be found in nature. Since therefore whatsoever is the first eternal *being* must necessarily be cogitative; and whatsoever is first of all things, must necessarily contain in it, and actually have, at least, all the perfections that can ever

**A gry is* 1/10 *of a line, a line* 1/10 *of an inch, an inch* 1/10 *of a philosophical foot, a philosophical foot* 1/3 *of a pendulum, whose diadroms, in the latitude of* 45 *degrees, are each equal to one second of time,* or 1/60 *of a minute. I have affectedly made use of this measure here, and the parts of it, under a decimal division with names to them; because, I think, it would be of general convenience, that this should be the common measure in the commonwealth of letters.*

after exist; nor can it ever give to another any perfection that it has not, either actually in itself, or at least in a higher degree; it necessarily follows, that the first eternal being cannot be matter.

11. *Therefore there has been an eternal wisdom. If* therefore it be evident, that *something* necessarily must *exist from eternity,* 'tis also as evident, that *that something must* necessarily *be a cogitative being:* for it is as impossible, that incogitative matter should produce a cogitative being, as that nothing, or the negation of all being, should produce a positive being or matter.

12. Though this discovery of the *necessary existence of an eternal mind,* does sufficiently lead us into the knowledge of GOD; since it will hence follow, that all other knowing beings that have a beginning, must depend on him, and have no other ways of knowledge, or extent of power, than what he gives them; and therefore if he made those, he made also the less excellent pieces of this universe, all inanimate beings, whereby his *omniscience, power,* and *providence,* will be established, and all his other attributes necessarily follow: yet to clear up this a little farther, we will see what doubts can be raised against it.

13. *Whether material or no. First,* perhaps it will be said, that though it be as clear as demonstration can make it, that there must be an eternal being, and that being must also be knowing: yet it does not follow, but that thinking being may also be material. Let it be so; it equally still follows, that there is a GOD. For if there be an eternal, omniscient, omnipotent being, it is certain, that there is a GOD, whether you imagine that being to be material, or no. But herein, I suppose, lies the danger and deceit of that supposition: there being no way to avoid the demonstration, that there is an eternal knowing being, men, devoted to matter, would willingly have it granted, that this knowing being is material; and then letting slide out of their minds, or the discourse, the demonstration whereby an eternal knowing being was proved necessarily to exist, would argue all to be matter, and so deny a GOD, that is, an eternal cogitative being: whereby they are so far from establishing, that they destroy their own hypothesis. For if there can be, in their opinion, eternal matter, without any eternal cogitative being, they manifestly separate matter and thinking, and suppose no necessary connection of the one with the other, and so establish the necessity of an eternal spirit, but not of matter; since it has been proved already, that an eternal cogitative being is unavoidably to be granted. Now if thinking and matter may be separated,

the eternal existence of matter, will not follow from the eternal existence of a cogitative being, and they suppose it to no purpose.

14. *Not material, first, because every particle of matter is not cogitative*. But now let us see how they can satisfy themselves, or others, that this, *eternal thinking being* is *material*.

First, I would ask them, whether they imagine, that all matter, *every particle of matter, thinks?* This, I suppose, they will scarce say; since then there would be as many eternal thinking beings, as there are particles of matter, and so an infinity of gods. And yet if they will not allow matter as matter, that is, every particle of matter to be as well cogitative, as extended, they will have as hard a task to make out to their own reasons, a cogitative being out of incogitative particles, as an extended being, out of unextended parts, if I may so speak.

15. *Secondly, one particle alone of matter cannot be cogitative*. *Secondly*, if all matter does not think, I next ask, whether it be *only one atom that does so?* This has as many absurdities as the other; for then this atom of matter must be alone eternal, or not. If this alone be eternal, then this alone, by its powerful thought, or will, made all the rest of matter. And so we have the creation of matter by a powerful thought, which is that the materialists stick at. For if they suppose one single thinking atom, to have produced all the rest of matter, they cannot ascribe that preeminency to it upon any other account, than that of its thinking, the only supposed difference. But allow it to be by some other way, which is above our conception, it must be still creation; and these men must give up their great maxim, *ex nihilo nihil fit*.[48] If it be said, that all the rest of matter is equally eternal, as that thinking atom, it will be to say anything at pleasure, though never so absurd: for to suppose all matter eternal, and yet one small particle in knowledge and power infinitely above all the rest, is without any the least appearance of reason to frame an hypothesis. Every particle of matter, as matter, is capable of all the same figures and motions of any other; and I challenge anyone in his thoughts, to add anything else to one above another.

16. *Thirdly, a system of incogitative matter, cannot be cogitative*. *Thirdly*, if then neither one peculiar atom alone can be this eternal thinking being; nor all matter, as matter; *i.e.* every particle of matter can be it, it only remains, that it is *some certain system of matter* duly put together, that is this *thinking eternal*

48. *ex nihilo nihil fit*, nothing comes from nothing.

being. This is that, which, I imagine, is that notion, which men are aptest to have of GOD, who would have him a material being, as most readily suggested to them, by the ordinary conceit they have of themselves, and other men, which they take to be material thinking beings. But this imagination, however more natural, is no less absurd than the other: for to suppose the eternal thinking being, to be nothing else but a composition of particles of matter, each whereof is incogitative, is to ascribe all the wisdom and knowledge of that eternal being, only to the *juxta*position of parts; than which, nothing can be more absurd. For unthinking particles of matter, however put together, can have nothing thereby added to them, but a new relation of position, which 'tis impossible should give thought and knowledge to them.

17. *Whether in motion, or at rest.* But farther, this *corporeal system* either has all its parts at rest, or it is a certain motion of the parts wherein its thinking consists. If it be perfectly at rest, it is but one lump, and so can have no privileges above one atom.

If it be the motion of its parts, on which its thinking depends, all the thoughts there must be unavoidably accidental, and limited; since all the particles that by motion cause thought, being each of them in itself without any thought, cannot regulate its own motions, much less be regulated by the thought of the whole; since that thought is not the cause of motion, (for then it must be antecedent to it, and so without it,) but the consequence of it, whereby freedom, power, choice, and all rational and wise thinking or acting, will be quite taken away: so that such a thinking being will be no better nor wiser, than pure blind matter; since to resolve all into the accidental unguided motions of blind matter, or into thought depending on unguided motions of blind matter, is the same thing; not to mention the narrowness of such thoughts and knowledge, that must depend on the motion of such parts. But there needs no enumeration of any more absurdities and impossibilities in this hypothesis, (however full of them it be,) than that before-mentioned; since let this thinking system be all, or a part of the matter of the universe, it is impossible that any one particle, should either know its own, or the motion of any other particle, or the whole know the motion of every particle; and so regulate its own thoughts or motions, or indeed have any thought resulting from such motion.

18. *Matter not co-eternal with an eternal mind.* Others would have *matter* to be *eternal,* notwithstanding that they allow an eternal, cogitative, immaterial being. This, though it take not away the being of a GOD, yet since it denies

one and the first great piece of his workmanship, the creation, let us consider it a little. *Matter* must be allowed eternal: why, because you cannot conceive how it can be made out of nothing; why do you not also think yourself eternal? You will answer, perhaps, because about twenty or forty years since, you began to be. But if I ask you what that *you* is, which began then to be, you can scarce tell me. The matter whereof you are made, began not then to be: for if it did, then it is not eternal: but it began to be put together in such a fashion and frame, as makes up your body; but yet that frame of particles, is not you, it makes not that thinking thing you are; (for I have now to do with one, who allows an eternal, immaterial, thinking being, but would have unthinking matter eternal too;) therefore when did that thinking thing begin to be? If it did never begin to be, then have you always been a thinking thing from eternity; the absurdity whereof I need not confute, till I meet with one, who is so void of understanding, as to own it. If therefore you can allow a thinking thing, to be made out of nothing, (as all things that are not eternal must be,) why also can you not allow it possible, for a material being to be made out of nothing, by an equal power, but that you have the experience of the one in view, and not of the other? Though, when well considered, creation of a spirit will be found to require no less power, than the creation of matter. Nay possibly, if we would emancipate ourselves from vulgar notions, and raise our thoughts, as far as they would reach, to a closer contemplation of things, we might be able to aim at some dim and seeming conception how matter might at first be made, and begin to exist by the power of that eternal first being: but to give beginning and being to a spirit, would be found a more inconceivable effect of omnipotent power. But this being what would perhaps lead us too far from the notions, on which the philosophy now in the world is built, it would not be pardonable to deviate so far from them; or to inquire, so far as grammar itself would authorize, if the common settled opinion opposes it: especially in this place, where the received doctrine serves well enough to our present purpose, and leaves this past doubt, that the creation or beginning of any one SUBSTANCE out of nothing, being once admitted, the creation of all other, but the CREATOR himself, may, with the same ease, be supposed.

19. But you will say, is it not impossible to admit of the *making anything out of nothing,* since we cannot possibly conceive it? I answer, no: 1. because it is not reasonable to deny the power of an infinite being, because we cannot comprehend its operations. We do not deny other effects upon this ground, because we cannot possibly conceive the manner of their production. We cannot conceive how anything but impulse of body can move body; and yet

that is not a reason sufficient to make us deny it possible, against the constant experience, we have of it in ourselves, in all our voluntary motions, which are produced in us only by the free action or thought of our own minds; and are not, nor can be the effects of the impulse or determination of the motion of blind matter, in or upon our bodies; for then it could not be in our power or choice to alter it. For example: my right hand writes, whilst my left hand is still: what causes rest in one, and motion in the other? Nothing but my will, a thought of my mind; my thought only changing, the right hand rests, and the left hand moves. This is matter of fact, which cannot be denied: explain this, and make it intelligible, and then the next step will be to understand creation. For the giving a new determination to the motion of the animal spirits (which some make use of to explain voluntary motion) clears not the difficulty one jot. To alter the determination of motion, being in this case no easier nor less, than to give motion itself: since the new determination given to the animal spirits must be either immediately by thought, or by some other body put in their way by thought, which was not in their way before, and so must owe its motion to thought; either of which leaves voluntary motion as unintelligible as it was before. In the meantime, 'tis an overvaluing ourselves, to reduce all to the narrow measure of our capacities; and to conclude, all things impossible to be done, whose manner of doing exceeds our comprehension. This is to make our comprehension infinite, or GOD finite, when what he can do, is limited to what we can conceive of it. If you do not understand the operations of your own finite mind, that thinking thing within you, do not deem it strange, that you cannot comprehend the operations of that eternal infinite mind, who made and governs all things, and whom the heaven of heavens cannot contain.

CHAP. XI.

Of our knowledge of the existence of other things.

1. *Is to be had only by sensation.* The knowledge of our own being, we have by intuition. The existence of a GOD, reason clearly makes known to us, as has been shown.

The *knowledge of the existence* of any other thing, we can have only by *sensation:* for there being no necessary connection of *real existence,* with any *idea* a man has in his memory, nor of any other existence but that of GOD, with the existence of any particular man; no particular man can know the *existence* of any other being, but only when by actual operating upon him, it makes itself perceived by him. For the having the *idea* of anything in our mind, no more proves the existence of that thing, than the picture of a man evidences his being in the world, or the visions of a dream make thereby a true history.

2. *Instance whiteness of this paper.* 'Tis therefore the actual receiving of *ideas* from without, that gives us notice of the *existence* of other things, and makes us know, that something does exist at that time without us, which causes that *idea* in us, though perhaps we neither know nor consider how it does it: for it takes not from the certainty of our senses, and the *ideas* we receive by them, that we know not the manner wherein they are produced: *v.g.* whilst I write this, I have, by the paper affecting my eyes, that *idea* produced in my mind, which whatever object causes, I call *white;* by which I know, that that quality or accident (*i.e.* whose appearance before my eyes, always causes that *idea*) does really exist, and has a being without me. And of this, the greatest assurance I can possibly have, and to which my faculties can attain, is the testimony of my eyes, which are the proper and sole judges of this thing, whose testimony I have reason to rely on, as so certain, that I can no more doubt, whilst I write this, that I see white and black, and that something really exists, that causes that sensation in me, than that I write or move my hand; which is a certainty as great, as human nature is capable of, concerning the existence of anything, but a man's self alone, and of GOD.

3. *This though not so certain as demonstration, yet may be called knowledge, and proves the existence of things without us. The notice we have by our senses, of the existing of things without* us, though it be not altogether so certain, as our intuitive knowledge, or the deductions of our reason, employed about the clear abstract *ideas* of our own minds; yet it is an assurance that *deserves the name of knowledge.* If we persuade ourselves, that our faculties act and inform us right, concerning the existence of those objects that affect them, it cannot pass for an ill-grounded confidence: for I think nobody can, in earnest, be so skeptical, as to be uncertain of the existence of those things which he sees and feels. At least, he that can doubt so far, (whatever he may have with his own thoughts) will never have any controversy with me; since he can never be sure I say anything contrary to his own opinion. As to

myself, I think GOD has given me assurance enough of the existence of things without me: since by their different application, I can produce in myself both pleasure and pain, which is one great concernment of my present state. This is certain, the confidence that our faculties do not herein deceive us, is the greatest assurance we are capable of, concerning the existence of material beings. For we cannot act anything, but by our faculties; nor talk of knowledge itself, but by the help of those faculties, which are fitted to apprehend even what knowledge is. But besides the assurance we have from our senses themselves, that they do not err in the information they give us, of the existence of things without us, when they are affected by them, we are farther confirmed in this assurance, by other concurrent reasons.

4. *First, because we cannot have them but by the inlet of the senses. First,* 'tis plain, those perceptions are produced in us by exterior causes affecting our senses: because *those that want the organs of any sense, never can have the* ideas *belonging to that sense* produced in their minds. This is too evident to be doubted: and therefore we cannot but be assured, that they come in by the organs of that sense, and no other way. The organs themselves, 'tis plain, do not produce them: for then the eyes of a man in the dark, would produce colors, and his nose smell roses in the winter: but we see nobody gets the relish of a pineapple, till he goes to the *Indies,* where it is, and tastes it.

5. *Because an* idea *from actual sensation, and another from memory, are very distinct perceptions. Secondly,* because *sometimes I find, that I cannot avoid the having those* ideas *produced in my mind.* For though when my eyes are shut, or windows fast, I can at pleasure recall to my mind the *ideas* of *light,* or the *sun,* which former sensations had lodged in my memory; so I can at pleasure lay by that *idea,* and take into my view that of the *smell* of a rose, or *taste* of sugar. But if I turn my eyes at noon towards the sun, I cannot avoid the *ideas,* which the light, or sun, then produces in me. So that there is a manifest difference, between the *ideas* laid up in my memory; (over which, if they were there only, I should have constantly the same power to dispose of them, and lay them by at pleasure) and those which force themselves upon me, and I cannot avoid having. And therefore it must needs be some exterior cause, and the brisk acting of some objects without me, whose efficacy I cannot resist, that produces those *ideas* in my mind, whether I will, or no. Besides, there is nobody who does not perceive the difference in himself, between contemplating the sun, as he has the *idea* of it in his

memory, and actually looking upon it: of which two, his perception is so distinct, that few of his *ideas* are more distinguishable one from another. And therefore he has certain knowledge, that they are not both memory, or the actions of his mind, and fancies only within him; but that actual seeing has a cause without.

6. *Thirdly, pleasure or pain, which accompanies actual sensation, accompanies not the returning of those* ideas *without the external objects. Thirdly,* add to this, that *many of those* ideas *are produced in us with pain, which afterwards we remember without the least offense.* Thus the pain of heat or cold, when the *idea* of it is revived in our minds, gives us no disturbance; which, when felt, was very troublesome, and is again, when actually repeated: which is occasioned by the disorder the external object causes in our bodies, when applied to it: and we remember the pains of *hunger, thirst,* or the *headache,* without any pain at all; which would either never disturb us, or else constantly do it, as often as we thought of it, were there nothing more but *ideas* floating in our minds, and appearances entertaining our fancies, without the real existence of things affecting us from abroad. The same may be said of pleasure, accompanying several actual sensations: and though mathematical demonstration depends not upon sense, yet the examining them by diagrams, gives great credit to the evidence of our sight, and seems to give it a certainty approaching to that of the demonstration itself. For it would be very strange, that a man should allow it for an undeniable truth, that two angles of a figure, which he measures by lines and angles of a diagram, should be bigger one than the other; and yet doubt of the existence of those lines and angles, which by looking on, he makes use of to measure that by.

7. *Fourthly, our senses assist on another's testimony of the existence of outward things. Fourthly,* our *senses,* in many cases bear *witness* to the truth of each other's report, concerning the existence of sensible things without us. He that sees a *fire,* may, if he doubt whether it be anything more than a bare fancy, feel it too; and be convinced, by putting his hand in it. Which certainly could never be put into such exquisite pain, by a bare *idea* or phantom, unless that the pain be a fancy too: which yet he cannot, when the burn is well, by raising the *idea* of it, bring upon himself again.

Thus I see, whilst I write this, I can change the appearance of the paper; and by designing the letters, tell beforehand what new *idea* it shall exhibit the very next moment, by barely drawing my pen over it: which will neither appear (let me fancy as much as I will) if my hands stand still; or though I move my pen, if my eyes be shut: nor when those characters are once made on the paper, can I choose afterwards but see them as they are; that is, have the *ideas* of such letters as I have made. Whence it is manifest, that they are not barely the sport and play of my own imagination, when I find, that the characters, that were made at the pleasure of my own thoughts, do not obey them; nor yet cease to be, whenever I shall fancy it, but continue to affect my senses constantly and regularly, according to the figures I made them. To which if we will add, that the sight of those shall, from another man, draw such sounds, as I beforehand design they shall stand for, there will be little reason left to doubt, that those words, I write, do really exist without me, when they cause a long series of regular sounds to affect my ears, which could not be the effect of my imagination, nor could my memory retain them in that order.

8. *This certainty is as great as our condition needs.* But yet, if after all this, anyone will be so skeptical, as to distrust his senses, and to affirm, that all we see and hear, feel and taste, think and do, during our whole being, is but the series and deluding appearances of a long dream, whereof there is no reality; and therefore will question the existence of all things, or our knowledge of anything: I must desire him to consider, that if all be a dream, then he does but dream, that he makes the question; and so it is not much matter, that a waking man should answer him. But yet, if he pleases, he may dream that I make him this answer, that *the certainty of* things existing *in rerum natura,* when we have *the testimony of our senses* for it, is not only *as great* as our frame can attain to, but *as our condition needs.*[49] For our faculties being suited not to the full extent of being, nor to a perfect, clear, comprehensive knowledge of things free from all doubt and scruple; but to the preservation of us, in whom they are; and accommodated to the use of life: they serve to our purpose well enough, if they will but give us certain notice of those things, which are convenient or inconvenient to us. For he that sees a candle burning, and has experimented the force of its flame, by putting his finger in it, will little doubt, that this is something existing without him, which does him harm, and puts him to great pain: which is assurance enough, when no man requires greater certainty to govern his actions by, than what is as certain as his actions themselves. And if our dreamer pleases to try, whether the glowing heat of a glass furnace, be barely a wandering imagination in a drowsy man's fancy, by putting his hand into it, he may perhaps be wakened into a certainty greater than he

49. *in rerum natura,* in the nature of things.

could wish, that it is something more than bare imagination. So that this evidence is as great, as we can desire, being as certain to us, as our pleasure or pain, *i.e.* happiness or misery; beyond which we have no concernment, either of knowing or being. Such an assurance of the existence of things without us, is sufficient to direct us in the attaining the good and avoiding the evil, which is caused by them, which is the important concernment we have of being made acquainted with them.

9. *But reaches no farther than actual sensation.* In fine then, when our senses do actually convey into our understandings any *idea,* we cannot but be satisfied, that there does something at that time really exist without us, which does affect our senses, and by them give notice of itself to our apprehensive faculties, and actually produce that *idea,* which we then perceive: and we cannot so far distrust their testimony, as to doubt, that such collections of simple *ideas,* as we have observed by our senses to be united together, do really exist together. But *this knowledge extends as far as the present testimony of our senses,* employed about particular objects, that do then affect them, *and no farther.* For if I saw such a collection of simple *ideas,* as is wont to be called *man,* existing together one minute since, and am now alone, I cannot be certain, that the same man exists now, since there is no necessary connection of his existence a minute since, with his existence now: by a thousand ways he may cease to be, since I had the testimony of my senses for his existence. And if I cannot be certain, that the man I saw last today, is now in being, I can less be certain, that he is so, who has been longer removed from my senses, and I have not seen since yesterday, or since the last year: and much less can I be certain of the existence of men, that I never saw. And therefore though it be highly probable, that millions of men do now exist, yet whilst I am alone writing this, I have no unquestionable knowledge of it; though the great likelihood of it puts me past doubt, and it be reasonable for me to do several things upon the confidence, that there are men (and men also of my acquaintance, with whom I have to do) now in the world: but this is but probability, not knowledge.

10. *Folly to expect demonstration in everything.* Whereby yet we may observe, how foolish and vain a thing it is, for a man of narrow knowledge, who having reason given him to judge of the different evidence and probability of things, and to be swayed accordingly; how *vain,* I say, it is *to expect demonstration* and certainty *in things not capable of it;* and refuse assent to very rational propositions, and act contrary to very plain and clear truths, because they cannot be made out so evident, as to surmount every the least

(I will not say reason, but) pretense of doubting. He that in the ordinary affairs of life, would admit of nothing but direct plain demonstration, would be sure of nothing, in this world, but of perishing quickly. The wholesomeness of his meat or drink would not give him reason to venture on it: and I would fain know, what 'tis he could do upon such grounds, as are capable of no doubt, no objection.

11. *Past existence is known by memory.* As when our senses are actually employed about any object, we do know that it does exist; so *by our memory* we may be assured, that heretofore things, that affected our senses, have existed. And thus *we have knowledge of the past existence* of several things, whereof our senses having informed us, our memories still retain the *ideas;* and of this we are past all doubt, so long as we remember well. But this knowledge also reaches no farther than our senses have formerly assured us. Thus seeing water at this instant, 'tis an unquestionable truth to me, that water, does exist: and remembering that I saw it yesterday, it will also be always true; and as long as my memory retains it, always an undoubted proposition to me, that water did exist 10th. *July,* 1688. as it will also be equally true, that a certain number of very fine colors did exist, which, at the same time, I saw upon a bubble of that water: but being now quite out of sight both of the water and bubbles too, it is no more certainly known to me, that the water does now exist, than that the bubbles or colors therein do so; it being no more necessary that water should exist today, because it existed yesterday, than that the colors or bubbles exist today, because they existed yesterday, though it be exceedingly much more probable, because water has been observed to continue long in existence, but bubbles, and the colors on them quickly cease to be.

12. *The existence of spirits not knowable.* What *ideas* we have of spirits, and how we come by them, I have already shown. But though we have those *ideas* in our minds, and know we have them there, the having the *ideas* of spirits does not make us *know,* that any such things do exist without us, or *that there are any finite spirits,* or any other spiritual beings, but the eternal GOD. We have ground from revelation, and several other reasons, to believe with assurance, that there are such creatures: but our senses not being able to discover them, we want the means of knowing their particular existences. For we can no more know, that there are finite spirits really existing, by the *idea* we have of such beings in our minds, than by the *ideas* anyone has of fairies, or centaurs, he can come to know, that things answering those *ideas,* do really exist.

And therefore concerning the existence of finite spirits, as well as several other things, we must content ourselves with the evidence of faith; but universal certain propositions concerning this matter are beyond our reach. For however true it may be, *v.g.* that all the intelligent spirits that GOD ever created, do still exist; yet it can never make a part of our certain knowledge. These and the like propositions, we may assent to, as highly probable, but are not, I fear, in this state, capable of knowing. We are not then to put others upon demonstrating, nor ourselves upon search of universal certainty in all those matters, wherein we are not capable of any other knowledge, but what our senses give us in this or that particular.

13. *Particular propositions concerning existence are knowable.* By which it appears, that there are two sorts of *propositions.* 1. There is one sort of propositions *concerning* the *existence* of anything answerable to such an *idea:* as having the *idea* of an *elephant, phoenix, motion,* or an *angel,* in my mind, the first and natural inquiry is, whether such a thing does anywhere exist? And this knowledge is only of *particulars.* No existence of anything without us, but only of GOD, can certainly be known farther than our senses inform us. 2. There is another sort of *propositions,* wherein is expressed the agreement, or disagreement of our abstract *ideas,* and their dependence one on another. Such propositions may be *universal* and certain. So having the *idea* of GOD and myself, of fear and obedience, I cannot but be sure that GOD is to be feared and obeyed by me: and this proposition will be certain, concerning *man* in general, if I have made an abstract *idea* of such a species, whereof I am one particular. But yet this proposition, how certain soever, that men ought to fear and obey GOD, proves not to me the existence of men in the world, but will be true of all such creatures, whenever they do exist: which *certainty* of such general propositions, depends on the agreement or disagreement to be discovered in those abstract *ideas.*

14. *And general propositions concerning abstract* ideas. In the former case, our knowledge is the consequence of the existence of things producing *ideas* in our minds by our senses: in the latter, knowledge is the consequence of the *ideas* (be they what they will) that are in our minds producing there general certain propositions. Many of these are called *æternæ veritates,* and all of them indeed are so; not from being written all or any of them in the minds of all men, or that they were any of them propositions in anyone's mind, till he, having got the abstract *ideas,* joined or

separated them by affirmation or negation.[50] But wheresoever we can suppose such a creature as *man* is, endowed with such faculties, and thereby furnished with such *ideas,* as we have, we must conclude, he must needs, when he applies his thoughts to the consideration of his *ideas,* know the truth of certain propositions, that will arise from the agreement or disagreement, which he will perceive in his own *ideas.* Such propositions are therefore called *eternal truths,* not because they are eternal propositions actually formed, and antecedent to the understanding, that at any time makes them; nor because they are imprinted on the mind from any patterns, that are anywhere of them out of the mind, and existed before: but because being once made, about abstract *ideas,* so as to be true, they will, whenever they can be supposed to be made again at any time past or to come, by a mind having those *ideas,* always actually be true. For names being supposed to stand perpetually for the same *ideas;* and the same *ideas* having immutably the same habitudes one to another, propositions, concerning any abstract *ideas,* that are once true, must needs be *eternal verities.*

CHAP. XII.

Of the improvement of our knowledge.

1. *Knowledge is not from maxims.* It having been the common received opinion amongst men of letters, that *maxims* were the foundations of all knowledge; and that the sciences were each of them built upon certain *pra ecognita,* from whence the understanding was to take its rise, and by which it was to conduct itself, in its inquiries into the matters belonging to that science; the beaten road of the schools has been, to lay down in the beginning one or more general propositions, as foundations whereon to build the knowledge that was to be had of that subject.[51] These doctrines thus laid down for foundations of any science, were called *principles,* as the beginnings from which we must set out, and look no farther backwards in our inquiries, as we have already observed.

2. *(The occasion of that opinion.)* One thing, which might probably give an occasion to this way of proceeding in other sciences, was (as I suppose) the good success it seemed to have in *mathematics,* wherein men, being ob-

50. *æternæ veritates,* eternal truths.

51. *præcognita,* principles, or things first known.

served to attain a great certainty of knowledge, these sciences came by pre-eminence to be called μαθήματα, and μάθησις, learning, or things learned, thoroughly learned, as having of all others the greatest certainty, clearness, and evidence in them.[52]

3. *But from the comparing clear and distinct* ideas. But if anyone will consider, he will (I guess) find, that *the great advancement* and certainty of *real knowledge,* which men arrived to in these sciences, was not owing to the influence of these principles, nor derived from any peculiar advantage they received from two or three general maxims laid down in the beginning; but *from* the *clear, distinct, complete ideas* their thoughts were employed about, and the relation of equality and excess so clear between some of them, that they had an intuitive knowledge, and by that, a way to discover it in others, and this without the help of those *maxims.* For I ask, is it not possible for a young lad to know, that his whole body is bigger than his little finger, but by virtue of this axiom, that *the whole is bigger than a part;* nor be assured of it, till he has learned that *maxim*? . . . I desire anyone to consider, from what has been elsewhere said, which is known first and clearest by most people, the particular instance, or the general rule; and which it is that gives life and birth to the other. These general rules are but the comparing our more general and abstract *ideas,* which are the workmanship of the mind, made, and names given to them, for the easier dispatch in its reasonings, and drawing into comprehensive terms, and short rules, its various and multiplied observations. But knowledge began in the mind, and was founded on particulars; though afterwards, perhaps, no notice be taken thereof: it being natural for the mind (forward still to enlarge its knowledge) most attentively to lay up those general notions, and make the proper use of them, which is to disburden the memory of the cumbersome load of particulars. . . .

4. *Dangerous to build upon precarious principles.* But be it in the mathematics as it will, whether it be clearer, that taking an inch from a black line of two inches, and an inch from a red line of two inches, the remaining parts of the two lines will be equal, or that *if you take equals from equals, the remainder will be equals:* which, I say, of these two, is the clearer and first known, I leave to anyone to determine, it not being material to my present occasion. That which I have here to do, is to inquire, whether if it be the readiest way to knowledge, to begin with general maxims, and build upon them, it be yet

52. μαθήματα, things learned or known; μάθησις, learning.

a safe way to take the *principles,* which are laid down in any other science, as unquestionable truths; and so receive them without examination, and adhere to them, without suffering them to be doubted of, because mathematicians have been so happy, or so fair, to use none but self-evident and undeniable. If this be so, I know not what may not pass for truth in morality, what may not be introduced and proved in natural philosophy.

Let that principle of some of the old philosophers, that all is matter, and that there is nothing else, be received for certain and indubitable, and it will be easy to be seen by the writings of some that have revived it again in our days, what consequences it will lead us into. Let anyone, with *Polemo,* take the world; or with the Stoics, the *æther,* or the sun; or, with *Anaximenes,* the air, to be *God;* and what a divinity, religion, and worship must we needs have! *Nothing* can be *so dangerous, as principles* thus *taken up without questioning or examination. . . .*

5. *This is no certain way to truth.* If therefore those that pass for *principles,* are *not certain,* (which we must have some way to know, that we may be able to distinguish them from those that are doubtful,) but are only made so to us by our blind assent, we are liable to be misled by them; and instead of being guided into truth, we shall, by principles, be only confirmed in mistake and error.

6. *But to compare clear complete* ideas *under steady names.* But since the knowledge of the certainty of principles, as well as of all other truths, depends only upon the perception, we have, of the agreement, or disagreement of our *ideas, the way to improve our knowledge,* is not, I am sure, blindly, and with an implicit faith, to receive and swallow principles; but is, I think, *to* get and *fix in our minds clear, distinct, and complete* ideas, as far as they are to be had, *and annex to them proper and constant names.* And thus, perhaps, without any other principles, but barely considering those perfect *ideas,* and by *comparing them one with another,* finding their agreement, and disagreement, and their several relations and habitudes; we shall get more true and clear knowledge, by the conduct of this one rule, than by taking up principles, and thereby putting our minds into the disposal of others.

7. *The true method of advancing knowledge, is by considering our abstract* ideas. *We must* therefore, if we will proceed, as reason advises, *adapt our methods of inquiry to the nature of the* ideas *we examine,* and the truth we search after. General and certain truths, are only founded in the habitudes and relations of abstract *ideas.* A sagacious and methodical application of our thoughts,

for the finding out these relations, is the only way to discover all, that can be put, with truth and certainty concerning them, into general propositions. By what steps we are to proceed in these, is to be learned in the schools of the mathematicians, who from very plain and easy beginnings, by gentle degrees, and a continued chain of reasonings, proceed to the discovery and demonstration of truths, that appear at first sight beyond human capacity. The art of finding proofs, and the admirable methods they have invented for the singling out, and laying in order those intermediate *ideas,* that demonstratively show the equality or inequality of unapplicable quantities, is that which has carried them so far, and produced such wonderful and unexpected discoveries: but whether something like this, in respect of other *ideas,* as well as those of magnitude, may not in time be found out, I will not determine. This, I think, I may say, that if other *ideas,* that are the real, as well as nominal essences of their species, were pursued in the way familiar to mathematicians, they would carry our thoughts farther, and with greater evidence and clearness, than possibly we are apt to imagine.

8. *By which morality also may be made clearer.* This gave me the confidence to advance that conjecture, which I suggest, *Chap.* iii. viz. that *morality is capable of demonstration,* as well as mathematics. For the *ideas* that ethics are conversant about, being all real essences, and such as, I imagine, have a discoverable connection and agreement one with another; so far as we can find their habitudes and relations, so far we shall be possessed of certain, real, and general truths: and I doubt not, but if a right method were taken, a great part of morality might be made out with that clearness, that could leave, to a considering man, no more reason to doubt, than he could have to doubt of the truth of propositions in mathematics, which have been demonstrated to him.

9. *But knowledge of bodies is to be improved only by experience.* In our search after the knowledge of *substances,* our want of *ideas,* that are suitable to such a way of proceeding, obliges us to a quite different method. We advance not here, as in the other (where our abstract *ideas* are real as well as nominal essences) by contemplating our *ideas,* and considering their relations and correspondencies; that helps us very little, for the reasons, that in another place we have at large set down. By which, I think, it is evident, that substances afford matter of very little general knowledge; and the bare contemplation of their abstract *ideas,* will carry us but a very little way in the search of truth and certainty. What then are we to do for the improvement of our *knowledge in substantial beings*? Here we are to take a quite contrary

course, the want of *ideas* of their real *essences* sends us from our own thoughts, to the things themselves, as they exist. *Experience here must teach me,* what reason cannot; and 'tis by trying alone, that I can certainly know, what other qualities coexist with those of my complex *idea, v.g.* whether that *yellow, heavy, fusible* body, I call *gold,* be *malleable,* or no; which experience (which way ever it prove, in that particular body, I examine) makes me not certain, that it is so, in all, or any other *yellow, heavy, fusible* bodies, but that which I have tried. Because it is no consequence one way or t'other from my complex *idea;* the necessity or inconsistence of *malleability,* has no visible connection with the combination of that *color, weight,* and *fusibility* in any body. What I have said here of the nominal essence of *gold,* supposed to consist of a body of such a determinate *color, weight,* and *fusibility,* will hold true, if *malleableness, fixedness,* and *solubility* in *aqua regia* be added to it. Our reasonings from these *ideas* will carry us but a little way in the certain discovery of the other properties in those masses of matter, wherein all these are to be found. Because the other properties of such bodies, depending not on these, but on that unknown real essence, on which these also depend, we cannot by them discover the rest; we can go no farther than the simple *ideas* of our nominal essence will carry us, which is very little beyond themselves; and so afford us but very sparingly any certain, universal, and useful truths. . . .

10. *This may procure us convenience, not science.* I deny not, but a man accustomed to rational and regular experiments shall be able to see farther into the nature of bodies, and guess righter at their yet unknown properties, than one, that is a stranger to them: but yet, as I have said, this is but judgment and opinion, not knowledge and certainty. This *way of* getting, and *improving our knowledge in substances only by experience* and history, which is all that the weakness of our faculties in this state of *mediocrity,* which we are in in this world, can attain to, makes me suspect, that natural philosophy is not capable of being made a science. We are able, I imagine, to reach very little general knowledge concerning the species of bodies, and their several properties. Experiments and historical observations we may have, from which we may draw advantages of ease and health, and thereby increase our stock of conveniences for this life: but beyond this, I fear our talents reach not, nor are our faculties, as I guess, able to advance.

11. *We are fitted for moral knowledge, and natural improvements.* From whence it is obvious to conclude, that since our faculties are not fitted to penetrate into the internal fabric and real essences of bodies; but yet plainly discover

to us the being of a GOD, and the knowledge of ourselves, enough to lead us into a full and clear discovery of our duty, and great concernment, it will become us, as rational creatures, to employ those faculties we have about what they are most adapted to, and follow the direction of nature, where it seems to point us out the way. For 'tis rational to conclude, that our proper employment lies in those inquiries, and in that sort of knowledge, which is most suited to our natural capacities, and carries in it our greatest interest, *i.e.* the condition of our eternal estate. Hence I think I may conclude, that *morality* is *the proper science, and business of mankind in general;* (who are both concerned, and fitted to search out their *summum bonum*,) as several arts, conversant about several parts of nature, are the lot and private talent of particular men, for the common use of human life, and their own particular subsistence in this world.[53] Of what consequence the discovery of one natural body, and its properties may be to human life, the whole great continent of *America* is a convincing instance: whose ignorance in useful arts, and want of the greatest part of the conveniences of life, in a country that abounded with all sorts of natural plenty, I think, may be attributed to their ignorance, of what was to be found in a very ordinary despicable stone, I mean the mineral of *iron.* And whatever we think of our parts or improvements in this part of the world, where knowledge and plenty seem to vie with each other; yet to anyone, that will seriously reflect on it, I suppose, it will appear past doubt, that were the use of *iron* lost among us, we should in a few ages be unavoidably reduced to the wants and ignorance of the ancient savage *Americans,* whose natural endowments and provisions come no way short of those of the most flourishing and polite nations. So that he who first made known the use of that contemptible mineral, may be truly styled the father of arts, and author of plenty.

12. *But must beware of hypotheses and wrong principles.* I would *not therefore* be thought to disesteem, or *dissuade the study of nature.* I readily agree the contemplation of his works gives us occasion to admire, revere, and glorify their author: and if rightly directed, may be of greater benefit to mankind, than the monuments of exemplary charity, that have at so great charge been raised, by the founders of hospitals and almshouses. He that first invented printing; discovered the use of the compass; or made public the virtue and right use of *kin kina,* did more for the propagation of knowledge; for the supplying and increase of useful commodities; and saved more from the grave, than those who built colleges, work-houses, and hospitals. All that I

53. *summum bonum,* supreme or highest good.

would say, is, that we should not be too forwardly possessed with the opinion, or expectation of knowledge, where it is not to be had; or by ways, that will not attain it: that we should not take doubtful systems, for complete sciences, nor unintelligible notions, for scientifical demonstrations. In the knowledge of bodies, we must be content to glean, what we can, from particular experiments: since we cannot from a discovery of their real essences, grasp at a time whole sheaves; and in bundles, comprehend the nature and properties of whole species together. Where our inquiry is concerning coexistence, or repugnancy to coexist, which by contemplation of our *ideas,* we cannot discover; there experience, observation, and natural history, must give us by our senses, and by retail, an insight into corporeal substances. The knowledge of bodies we must get by our senses, warily employed in taking notice of their qualities, and operations on one another: and what we hope to know of separate spirits in this world, we must, I think, expect only from revelation. . . .

13. *The true use of hypotheses.* Not that we may not, to explain any *phænomena* of nature, make use of a probable *hypothesis* whatsoever: *hypotheses,* if they are well made, are at least great helps to the memory, and often direct us to new discoveries. But my meaning is, that we should *not take up any one too hastily,* (which the mind, that would always penetrate into the causes of things, and have principles to rest on, is very apt to do,) till we have very well examined particulars, and made several experiments, in that thing which we would explain by our hypothesis, and see whether it will agree to them all; whether our principles will carry us quite through, and not be as inconsistent with one *phænomenon* of nature, as they seem to accommodate, and explain another. And at least, that we take care, that the name of *principles* deceive us not, nor impose on us, by making us receive that for an unquestionable truth, which is really, at best, but a very doubtful conjecture, such as are most (I had almost said all) of the *hypotheses* in natural philosophy.

14. *Clear and distinct* ideas *with settled names, and the finding of those which show their agreement, or disagreement, are the ways to enlarge our knowledge.* But whether natural philosophy be capable of certainty, or no, the *ways to enlarge our knowledge,* as far as we are capable, seem to me, in short, to be these two:

First, the *first* is *to get and settle in our minds* determined *ideas* of those things, whereof we have general or specific names; at least so many of them as we would consider and improve our knowledge in, or reason about. And if they be *specific* ideas of *substances,* we should endeavor also to make them as complete as we can, whereby I mean, that we should put together as many simple *ideas,* as being constantly observed to coexist, may perfectly determine the *species:* and each of those simple ideas, which are the ingredients of our complex ones, should be clear and distinct in our minds. For it being evident, that our knowledge cannot exceed our *ideas;* as far as they are either imperfect, confused, or obscure, we cannot expect to have certain, perfect, or clear knowledge.

Secondly, the other is the art of *finding out* those *intermediate ideas,* which may show us the agreement, or repugnancy of other *ideas,* which cannot be immediately compared.

15. *Mathematics an instance of it.* That these two (and not the relying on maxims, and drawing consequences from some general propositions) are the right methods of improving our knowledge in the *ideas* of other modes besides those of quantity, the consideration of mathematical knowledge will easily inform us. Where first we shall find, that he, that has not a perfect, and clear *idea* of those angles, or figures of which he desires to know anything, is utterly thereby uncapable of any knowledge about them. Suppose but a man, not to have a perfect exact *idea* of a *right angle,* a *scalenum,* or *trapezium;* and there is nothing more certain than, that he will in vain seek any demonstration about them. Farther it is evident, that it was not the influence of those maxims, which are taken for principles in mathematics, that has led the masters of that science into those wonderful discoveries they have made. . . . They have been discovered by the thoughts other ways applied: the mind had other objects, other views before it, far different from those maxims, when it first got the knowledge of such truths in mathematics, which men well enough acquainted with those received axioms, but ignorant of their method, who first made these demonstrations, can never sufficiently admire. And who knows what methods, to enlarge our knowledge in other parts of science, may hereafter be invented, answering that of *algebra* in mathematics, which so readily finds out *ideas* of quantities to measure others by, whose equality or proportion we could otherwise very hardly, or, perhaps, never come to know?

CHAP. XIII.

Some farther considerations concerning our knowledge.

1. *Our knowledge partly necessary, partly voluntary. Our knowledge,* as in other things, so in this, has a great conformity with our sight, that it is *neither wholly necessary, nor wholly voluntary.* If our knowledge were altogether necessary, all men's knowledge would not only be alike, but every man would know all that is knowable: and if it were wholly voluntary, some men so little regard or value it, that they would have extreme little, or none at all. Men that have senses, cannot choose but receive some *ideas* by them; and if they have memory, they cannot but retain some of them; and if they have any distinguishing faculty, cannot but perceive the agreement, or disagreement of some of them one with another. . . .

2. *The application voluntary; but we know as things are, not as we please.* There is also another thing in a man's power, and that is, though he turns his eyes sometimes towards an object, yet he may choose whether he will curiously survey it, and with an intent application, endeavor to observe accurately all that is visible in it. But yet what he does see, he cannot see otherwise than he does. It depends not on his will to see that *black,* which appears *yellow;* nor to persuade himself, that what actually *scalds* him, feels *cold.* . . . Just thus is it with our understanding, all that is *voluntary* in our knowledge, is the *employing,* or withholding any of *our faculties* from this or that sort of objects, and a more, or less accurate survey of them: but they being employed, *our will has no power to determine the knowledge of the mind* one way or the other; that is done only by the objects themselves, as far as they are clearly discovered. . . .

. . . .

CHAP. XIV.
Of judgment.

1. *Our knowledge being short, we want something else.* The understanding faculties being given to man, not barely for speculation, but also for the conduct of his life, man would be at a great loss, if he had nothing to direct him, but what has the certainty of true *knowledge.* For that being very short and scanty, as we have seen, he would be often utterly in the dark, and in most of the actions of his life, perfectly at a stand, had he nothing to guide him in the absence of clear and certain knowledge. He that will not eat, till he has demonstration that it will nourish him; he that will not stir, till he infallibly knows the business he goes about will succeed; will have little else to do, but sit still and perish.

2. *What use is to be made of this twilight state.* Therefore as God has set some things in broad daylight; as he has given us some certain knowledge, though limited to a few things in comparison, probably, as a taste of what intellectual creatures are capable of, to excite in us a desire and endeavor after a better state: so in the greatest part of our concernment, he has afforded us only the twilight, as I may so say, of *probability,* suitable, I presume, to that state of mediocrity and probationership, he has been pleased to place us in here; wherein to check our over-confidence and presumption, we might by every day's experience be made sensible of our short-sightedness and liableness to error; the sense whereof might be a constant admonition to us, to spend the days of this our pilgrimage with industry and care, in the search, and following of that way, which might lead us to a state of greater perfection. It being highly rational to think, even were revelation silent in the case, that as men employ those talents, God has given them here, they shall accordingly receive their rewards at the close of the day, when their sun shall set, and night shall put an end to their labors.

3. *Judgment supplies the want of knowledge.* The faculty, which God has given man to supply the want of clear and certain knowledge, in cases where that cannot be had, is *judgment:* whereby the mind takes its *ideas* to agree, or disagree; or which is the same, any proposition to be true, or false, without perceiving a demonstrative evidence in the proofs. The mind sometimes exercises this *judgment* out of necessity, where demonstrative proofs, and

certain knowledge are not to be had; and sometimes out of laziness, unskilfulness, or haste, even where demonstrative and certain proofs are to be had. Men often stay not warily to examine the agreement or disagreement of two *ideas,* which they are desirous, or concerned to know; but either incapable of such attention, as is requisite in a long train of gradations, or impatient of delay, lightly cast their eyes on, or wholly pass by the proofs; and so without making out the demonstration, determine of the agreement or disagreement of two *ideas,* as it were by a view of them as they are at a distance, and take it to be the one or the other, as seems most likely to them upon such a loose survey. This faculty of the mind, when it is exercised immediately about things, is called *judgment;* when about truths delivered in words, is most commonly called *assent* or *dissent:* which being the most usual way, wherein the mind has occasion to employ this faculty, I shall under these terms treat of it, as least liable in our language to equivocation.

4. *Judgment is the presuming things to be so without perceiving it.* Thus the mind has two faculties, conversant about truth and falsehood.

First, knowledge, whereby it certainly perceives, and is undoubtedly satisfied of the agreement or disagreement of any *ideas.*

Secondly, judgment, which is the putting *ideas* together, or separating them from one another in the mind, when their certain agreement or disagreement is not perceived, but *presumed* to be so; which is, as the word imports, taken to be so before it certainly appears. And if it so unites, or separates them, as in reality things are, it is *right judgment.*

Chap. XV.

Of probability.

1. *Probability is the appearance of agreement upon fallible proofs.* As demonstration is the showing the agreement, or disagreement of two *ideas,* by the intervention of one or more proofs, which have a constant, immutable, and visible connection one with another: so *probability* is nothing but the appearance of such an agreement, or disagreement, by the intervention of proofs, whose connection is not constant and immutable, or at least is not perceived to be so, but is, or appears for the most part to be so, and is enough to induce the mind to *judge* the proposition to be true, or false, rather than the contrary. For example: in the demonstration of it, a man

perceives the certain immutable connection there is of equality, between the three angles of a *triangle,* and those intermediate ones, which are made use of to show their equality to two right ones: and so by an intuitive knowledge of the agreement, or disagreement of the intermediate *ideas* in each step of the progress, the whole series is continued with an evidence, which clearly shows the agreement, or disagreement, of those three angles, in equality to two right ones: and thus he has certain knowledge that it is so. But another man who never took the pains to observe the demonstration, hearing a mathematician, a man of credit, affirm the three angles of a triangle, to be equal to two right ones, *assents* to it, *i.e.* receives it for true. In which case, the foundation of his assent is the probability of the thing, the proof being such, as for the most part carries truth with it: the man, on whose testimony he receives it, not being wont to affirm anything contrary to, or besides his knowledge, especially in matters of this kind. So that that which causes his assent to this proposition, that the three angles of a triangle are equal to two right ones, that which makes him take these *ideas* to agree, without knowing them to do so, is the wonted veracity of the speaker in other cases, or his supposed veracity in this.

2. *It is to supply the want of knowledge.* Our knowledge, as has been shown, being very narrow, and we not happy enough to find certain truth in everything which we have occasion to consider; most of the propositions we think, reason, discourse, nay act upon, are such, as we cannot have undoubted knowledge of their truth: yet some of them border so near upon certainty, that we make no doubt at all about them; but *assent* to them as firmly, and act, according to that assent, as resolutely, as if they were infallibly demonstrated, and that our knowledge of them was perfect and certain. But there being degrees herein, from the very neighborhood of certainty and demonstration, quite down to improbability and unlikeliness, even to the confines of impossibility; and also degrees of *assent* from certain knowledge, and what is next it, full *assurance* and confidence, quite down to *conjecture, doubt, distrust,* and *disbelief.* I shall come now, as having (as I think) found out the bounds of human knowledge and certainty, in the next place to consider *the several degrees and grounds of probability, and assent or faith.*

3. *Being that which makes us presume things to be true, before we know them to be so. Probability* is likeliness to be true, the very notation of the word, signifying such a proposition, for which there be arguments or proofs, to make it pass or be received for true. The entertainment the mind gives this sort of propositions, is called *belief, assent,* or *opinion,* which is the admitting

or receiving any proposition for true, upon arguments or proofs that are found to persuade us to receive it as true, without certain knowledge that it is so. And herein lies the *difference between probability* and *certainty, faith* and *knowledge,* that in all the parts of knowledge, there is intuition; each immediate *idea,* each step has its visible and certain connection; in belief not so. That which makes me believe, is something extraneous to the thing I believe; something not evidently joined on both sides to, and so not manifestly showing the agreement, or disagreement of those *ideas,* that are under consideration.

4. *The grounds of probability are two; conformity with our own experience, or the testimony of others' experience. Probability* then, being to supply the defect of our knowledge, and to guide us where that fails, is always conversant about propositions, whereof we have no certainty, but only some inducements to receive them for true. The *grounds of it* are, in short, these *two* following:

First, the conformity of anything with our own knowledge, observation, and experience.

Secondly, the testimony of others, vouching their observation and experience. In the testimony of others, is to be considered, 1. The number. 2. The integrity. 3. The skill of the witnesses. 4. The design of the author, where it is a testimony out of a book cited. 5. The consistency of the parts, and circumstances of the relation. 6. Contrary testimonies.

5. *In this all the agreements* pro *and* con *ought to be examined, before we come to a judgment.* Probability wanting that intuitive evidence, which infallibly determines the understanding, and produces certain knowledge, *the mind if it will proceed rationally, ought to examine all the grounds of probability,* and see how they make more or less, *for or against* any probable proposition, before it assents to or dissents from it, and upon a due balancing the whole, reject, or receive it, with a more or less firm assent, proportionably to the preponderancy of the greater grounds of probability on one side or the other. For example:

If I myself see a man walk on the ice, it is past *probability,* 'tis knowledge: but if another tells me he saw a man in *England* in the midst of a sharp winter, walk upon water hardened with cold; this has so great conformity with what is usually observed to happen, that I am disposed by the nature of the thing itself to assent to it, unless some manifest suspicion attend the relation of that matter of fact. But if the same thing be told to one born between the tropics, who never saw nor heard of any such thing before, there the whole probability relies on testimony: and as the relators are more in number, and of more credit, and have no interest to speak contrary to the truth; so that matter of fact is like to find more or less belief. Though to a man, whose experience has always been quite contrary, and who has never heard of anything like it, the most untainted credit of a witness will scarce be able to find belief, as it happened to a Dutch ambassador, who entertaining the king of *Siam* with the particularities of *Holland,* which he was inquisitive after, amongst other things told him, that the water in his country, would sometimes, in cold weather, be so hard, that men walked upon it, and that it would bear an elephant, if he were there. To which the king replied, *hitherto I have believed the strange things you have told me, because I look upon you as a sober fair man, but now I am sure you lie.*

6. *They being capable of great variety.* Upon these grounds depends the *probability* of any proposition: and as the conformity of our knowledge, as the certainty of observations, as the frequency and constancy of experience, and the number and credibility of testimonies, do more or less agree, or disagree with it, so is any proposition in itself, more or less probable. There is another, I confess, which though by itself it be no true ground of *probability,* yet is often made use of for one, by which men most commonly regulate their assent, and upon which they pin their faith more than anything else, and, that is, *the opinion of others;* though there cannot be a more dangerous thing to rely on, nor more likely to mislead one; since there is much more falsehood and error among men, than truth and knowledge. And if the opinions and persuasions of others, whom we know and think well of, be a ground of assent, men have reason to be heathens in *Japan,* Mahumetans in *Turkey,* Papists in Spain, Protestants in *England,* and Lutherans in *Sweden.* But of this wrong ground of assent, I shall have occasion to speak more at large in another place.

CHAP. XVI.

Of the degrees of assent.

1. *Our assent ought to be regulated by the grounds of probability.* The grounds of probability, we have laid down in the foregoing chapter, as they are the foundations on which our *assent* is built; so are they also the measure whereby its several degrees are, or ought to be *regulated:* only we are to take notice, that whatever grounds of probability there may be, they yet operate

no farther on the mind, which searches after truth, and endeavors to judge right, than they appear; at least in the first judgment or search that the mind makes. I confess, in the opinions men have, and firmly stick to, in the world, their *assent* is not always from an actual view of the reasons that at first prevailed with them: it being in many cases almost impossible, and in most very hard, even for those who have very admirable memories, to retain all the proofs, which upon a due examination, made them embrace that side of the question. It suffices, that they have once with care and fairness, sifted the matter as far as they could; and that they have searched into all the particulars, that they could imagine to give any light to the question; and with the best of their skill, cast up the account upon the whole evidence: and thus having once found on which side the probability appeared to them, after as full and exact an inquiry as they can make, they lay up the conclusion in their memories, as a truth they have discovered; and for the future, they remain satisfied with the testimony of their memories, that this is the opinion, that by the proofs they have once seen of it, deserves such a *degree* of their *assent* as they afford it.

. . . .

3. *The ill consequence of the remembrance that we once saw ground for such a degree of assent, if our former judgment were not rightly made.* I cannot but own, that men's *sticking to* their *past judgment,* and adhering firmly to conclusions formerly made, is often the cause of great obstinacy in error and mistake. But the fault is not that they rely on their memories, for what they have before well judged; but because they judged before they had well examined. . . . Who almost is there, that has the leisure, patience, and means, to collect together all the proofs concerning most of the opinions he has, so as safely to conclude, that he has a clear and full view; and that there is no more to be alleged for his better information? And yet we are forced to determine ourselves on the one side or other. The conduct of our lives, and the management of our great concerns, will not bear delay: for those depend, for the most part, on the determination of our judgment in points, wherein we are not capable of certain and demonstrative knowledge, and wherein it is necessary for us to embrace the one side, or the other.

4. *The right use of it mutual charity and forbearance.* Since therefore it is unavoidable to the greatest part of men, if not all, to have several *opinions,* without certain and indubitable proofs of their truths; and it carries too great an imputation of ignorance, lightness, or folly, for men to quit and

renounce their former tenets, presently upon the offer of an argument, which they cannot immediately answer, and show the insufficiency of: it would, methinks, become all men to maintain *peace,* and the common offices of humanity, *and friendship, in the diversity of opinions,* since we cannot reasonably expect, that anyone should readily and obsequiously quit his own opinion, and embrace ours with a blind resignation to an authority, which the understanding of man acknowledges not. For however it may often mistake, it can own no other guide but reason, nor blindly submit to the will and dictates of another. If he, you would bring over to your sentiments, be one that examines before he assents, you must give him leave, at his leisure, to go over the account again, and recalling what is out of his mind, examine all the particulars, to see on which side the advantage lies: and if he will not think our arguments of weight enough to engage him anew in so much pains, 'tis but what we often do ourselves in the like case; and we should take it amiss, if others should prescribe to us what points we should study. . . . The necessity of believing, without knowledge, nay, often upon very slight grounds, in this fleeting state of action and blindness we are in, should make us more busy and careful to inform ourselves, than constrain others. At least those, who have not thoroughly examined to the bottom all their own tenets, must confess, they are unfit to prescribe to others; and are unreasonable in imposing that as truth on other men's belief, which they themselves have not searched into, nor weighed the arguments of probability, on which they should receive or reject it. . . .

5. *Probability is either of matter or fact or speculation.* But to return to the grounds of assent, and the several degrees of it, we are to take notice, that the propositions we receive upon inducements of *probability,* are *of two sorts;* either concerning some particular existence, or, as it is usually termed, matter of fact, which falling under observation, is capable of human testimony, or else concerning things, which being beyond the discovery of our senses, are not capable of any such testimony.

6. *The concurrent experience of all other men with ours, produces assurance approaching to knowledge.* Concerning the *first* of these, *viz. particular matter of fact,*

First, where any particular thing, consonant to the constant observation of ourselves and others, in the like case, comes attested by the concurrent reports of all that mention it, we receive it as easily, and build as firmly upon it, as if it were certain knowledge; and we reason and act thereupon with as little doubt, as if it were perfect demonstration. . . . This we call an argument from the nature of things themselves. For what our own and other men's constant observation has found always to be after the same manner, that we with reason conclude to be the effect of steady and regular causes, though they come not within the reach of our knowledge. Thus, that fire warmed a man, made lead fluid, and changed the color or consistency in wood or charcoal: that iron sunk in water, and swam in quicksilver: these and the like propositions about particular facts, being agreeable to our constant experience, as often as we have to do with these matters; and being generally spoke of, (when mentioned by others,) as things found constantly to be so, and therefore not so much as controverted by anybody; we are put past doubt, that a relation affirming any such thing to have been, or any predication that it will happen again in the same manner, is very true. These *probabilities* rise so near to *certainty,* that they govern our thoughts as absolutely, and influence all our actions as fully, as the most evident demonstration: and in what concerns us, we make little or no difference between them and certain knowledge: our belief thus grounded, rises to *assurance*.

7. *Unquestionable testimony and experience for the most part produce confidence. Secondly, the next degree of probability* is, when I find by my own experience, and the agreement of all others that mention it, a thing to be, for the most part, so; and that the particular instance of it is attested by many and undoubted witnesses: *v.g.* history giving us such an account of men in all ages; and my own experience, as far as I had an opportunity to observe, confirming it, that most men prefer their private advantage, to the public. If all historians that write of *Tiberius,* say that *Tiberius* did so, it is extremely probable. And in this case, our assent has a sufficient foundation to raise itself to a degree, which we may call *confidence*.

8. *Fair testimony, and the nature of the thing indifferent, produces also confident belief. Thirdly,* in things that happen indifferently, as that a bird should fly this or that way; that it should thunder on a man's right or left hand, *&c.* when any particular matter of fact is vouched by the concurrent testimony of unsuspected witnesses, there our assent is also unavoidable. Thus: that there is such a city in *Italy* as *Rome;* that about 1700 years ago, there lived in it a man, called *Julius Caesar;* that he was a general, and that he won a battle against another called *Pompey.* This, though in the nature of the thing, there be nothing for, nor against it, yet, being related by historians of credit, and contradicted by no one writer, a man cannot avoid believing it, and can

as little doubt of it, as he does of the being and actions of his own acquaintance, whereof he himself is a witness.

9. *Experiences and testimonies clashing, infinitely vary the degrees of probability.* Thus far the matter goes easy enough. Probability upon such grounds carries so much evidence with it, that it naturally determines the judgment, and leaves us as little liberty to believe, or disbelieve, as a demonstration does, whether we will know, or be ignorant. The difficulty is, when testimonies contradict common experience, and the reports of history and witnesses clash with the ordinary course of nature, or with one another; there it is, where diligence, attention, and exactness is required, to form a right judgment, and to proportion the *assent* to the different evidence and probability of the thing; which rises and falls, according as those two foundations of credibility, *viz.* common observation in like cases, and particular testimonies in that particular instance, favor or contradict it. These are liable to so great variety of contrary observations, circumstances, reports, different qualifications, tempers, designs, oversights, *&c.* of the reporters, that 'tis impossible to reduce to precise rules, the various degrees wherein men give their assent. This only may be said in general, that as the arguments and proofs, *pro* and *con,* upon due examination, nicely weighing every particular circumstance, shall to anyone appear, upon the whole matter, in a greater or less degree, to preponderate on either side, so they are fitted to produce in the mind such different entertainment, as we call *belief, conjecture, guess, doubt, wavering, distrust, disbelief,* &c.

10. *Traditional testimonies, the farther removed, the less their proof.* . . . Any testimony, the farther off it is from the original truth, the less force and proof it has. The being and existence of the thing itself, is what I call the original truth. A credible man vouching his knowledge of it, is a good proof: but if another equally credible, do witness it from his report, the testimony is weaker; and a third that attests the hearsay of an hearsay, is yet less considerable. So that *in traditional truths, each remove weakens the force of the proof:* and the more hands the tradition has successively passed through, the less strength and evidence does it receive from them. . . .

11. *Yet history is of great use.* I would not be thought here to lessen the credit and use of *history:* 'tis all the light we have in many cases; and we receive from it a great part of the useful truths we have, with a convincing evidence. I think nothing more valuable than the records of antiquity: I wish we had more of them, and more uncorrupted. But this, truth itself forces me to say,

that no *probability* can arise higher than its first original. What has no other evidence than the single testimony of one only witness, must stand or fall by his only testimony, whether good, bad or indifferent; and though cited afterwards by hundreds of others, one after another, is so far from receiving any strength thereby, that it is only the weaker. Passion, interest, inadvertency, mistake of his meaning, and a thousand odd reasons, or caprichios, men's minds are acted by, (impossible to be discovered,) may make one man quote another man's words or meaning wrong. He that has but ever so little examined the citations of writers, cannot doubt how little credit the quotations deserve, where the originals are wanting; and consequently how much less quotations of quotations can be relied on. This is certain, that what in one age was affirmed upon slight grounds, can never after come to be more valid in future ages, by being often repeated. . . .

12. *In things which sense cannot discover, analogy is the great rule of probability.* The probabilities we have hitherto mentioned, are only such as concern matter of fact, and such things as are capable of observation and testimony. There remains that other sort, *concerning* which, men entertain opinions with variety of assent, though the *things* be such, *that falling not under the reach of our senses, they are not capable of testimony.* Such are, 1. The existence, nature, and operations of finite immaterial beings, without us; as spirits, angels, devils, *&c.* Or the existence of material beings; which either for their smallness in themselves, or remoteness from us, our senses cannot take notice of; as whether there be any plants, animals, and intelligent inhabitants in the planets, and other mansions of the vast universe. 2. Concerning the manner of operation in most parts of the works of nature: wherein though we see the sensible effects, yet their causes are unknown, and we perceive not the ways and manner how they are produced. We see animals are generated, nourished, and move; the lodestone draws iron; and the parts of a candle successively melting, turn into flame, and give us both light and heat. These and the like effects we see and know: but the causes that operate, and the manner they are produced in, we can only guess, and probably conjecture. For these and the like coming not within the scrutiny of human senses cannot be examined by them, or be attested by anybody, and therefore can appear more or less probable, only as they more or less agree to truths that are established in our minds, and as they hold proportion to other parts of our knowledge and observation. *Analogy* in these matters is the only help we have, and 'tis from that alone we draw all our grounds of probability. Thus observing that the bare rubbing of two bodies violently one upon another, produces heat, and very often fire itself, we

have reason to think, that what we call heat and fire, consists in a violent agitation of the imperceptible minute parts of the burning matter: observing likewise that the different refractions of pellucid bodies produce in our eyes the different appearances of several colors; and also that the different ranging and laying the superficial parts of several bodies, as of velvet, watered silk, *&c.* does the like, we think it probable that the color and shining of bodies, is in them nothing but the different arrangement and refraction of their minute and insensible parts. Thus finding in all parts of the creation, that fall under human observation, that there is a gradual connection of one with another, without any great or discernible gaps between, in all that great variety of things we see in the world, which are so closely linked together, that, in the several ranks of beings, it is not easy to discover the bounds betwixt them, we have reason to be persuaded, that by such gentle steps things ascend upwards in degrees of perfection. 'Tis an hard matter to say where sensible and rational begin, and where insensible and irrational end: and who is there quick-sighted enough to determine precisely, which is the lowest species of living things, and which the first of those which have no life? . . . Observing, I say, such gradual and gentle descents downwards in those parts of the creation, that are beneath man, the rule of analogy may make it probable, that it is so also in things above us, and our observation; and that there are several ranks of intelligent beings, excelling us in several degrees of perfection, ascending upwards towards the infinite perfection of the creator, by gentle steps and differences, that are every one at no great distance from the next to it. This sort of probability, which is the best conduct of rational experiments, and the rise of hypothesis, has also its use and influence; and a wary reasoning from analogy leads us often into the discovery of truths, and useful productions, which would otherwise lie concealed.

13. *One case where contrary experience lessens not the testimony.* Though the common experience, and the ordinary course of things have justly a mighty influence on the minds of men, to make them give or refuse credit to anything proposed to their belief; yet there is one case, wherein the strangeness of the fact lessens not the assent to a fair testimony given of it. For where such supernatural events are suitable to ends aimed at by him, who has the power to change the course of nature, there, under such circumstances, they may be the fitter to procure belief, by how much the more they are beyond, or contrary to ordinary observation. This is the proper case of *miracles,* which well attested, do not only find credit themselves; but give it also to other truths, which need such confirmation.

14. *The bare testimony of revelation is the highest certainty.* Besides those we have hitherto mentioned, there is one sort of propositions that challenge the highest degree of our assent, upon bare testimony, whether the thing proposed, agree or disagree with common experience, and the ordinary course of things, or no. The reason whereof is, because the testimony is of such an one, as cannot deceive, nor be deceived; and that is of God himself. This carries with it a certainty beyond doubt, evidence beyond exception.[54] This is called by a peculiar name, *revelation;* and our assent to it, *faith:* which has as much certainty as our knowledge itself; and we may as well doubt of our own being, as we can, whether any revelation from GOD be true.[55] So that faith is a settled and sure principle of assent and assurance, and leaves no manner of room for doubt or hesitation. Only we must be sure, that it be a divine revelation, and that we understand it right: else we shall expose ourselves to all the extravagancy of enthusiasm, and all the error of wrong principles, if we have faith and assurance in what is not divine revelation. And therefore in those cases, our assent can be rationally no higher than the evidence of its being a revelation, and that this is the meaning of the expressions it is delivered in. If the evidence of its being a revelation, or that this is its true sense be only on probable proofs, our assent can reach no higher than an assurance or diffidence, arising from the more, or less apparent probability of the proofs. But of faith, and the precedency it ought to have before other arguments of persuasion, I shall speak more hereafter, where I treat of it, as it is ordinarily placed, in contradistinction to reason; though in truth, it be nothing else but an assent founded on the highest reason.

CHAP. XVII.

Of reason.

1. *Various significations of the word reason. The word reason* in the *English* language *has different significations:* sometimes it is taken for true, and clear principles: sometimes for clear, and fair deductions from those principles: and sometimes for the cause, and particularly the final cause. But the

54. In the fifth edition, Locke replaced the word "certainty" with "assurance."

55. In the fifth edition, Locke replaced "has as much certainty as our knowledge itself" with "as absolutely determines our minds, and as perfectly excludes all wavering as our knowledge itself".

consideration I shall have of it here, is in a signification different from all these; and that is, as it stands for a faculty in man, that faculty, whereby man is supposed to be distinguished from beasts, and wherein it is evident he much surpasses them.

2. *Wherein reasoning consists.* If general knowledge, as has been shown, consists in a perception of the agreement, or disagreement of our own *ideas;* and the knowledge of the existence of all things without us (except only of a GOD whose existence every man may certainly know and demonstrate to himself from his own existence) be had only by our senses; what room then is there for the exercise of any other faculty, but outward sense and inward perception? What need is there of reason? Very much; both for the enlargement of our knowledge, and regulating our assent: for it has to do, both in knowledge and opinion, and is necessary, and assisting to all our other intellectual faculties, and indeed contains two of them, *viz. sagacity and illation.* By the one, it finds out, and by the other, it so orders the intermediate *ideas,* as to discover what connection there is in each link of the chain, whereby the extremes are held together; and thereby, as it were, to draw into view the truth sought for, which is that which we call *illation* or *inference,* and consists in nothing but the perception of the connection there is between the *ideas,* in each step of the deduction, whereby the mind comes to see, either the certain agreement or disagreement of any two *ideas,* as in demonstration, in which it arrives at knowledge; or their probable connection, on which it gives or withholds its assent, as in opinion. Sense and intuition reach but a very little way. The greatest part of our knowledge depends upon deductions and intermediate *ideas:* and in those cases, where we are fain to substitute assent instead of knowledge, and take propositions for true, without being certain they are so, we have need to find out, examine, and compare the grounds of their probability. In both these cases, the faculty which finds out the means, and rightly applies them to discover certainty in the one, and probability in the other, is that which we call reason. For as reason perceives the necessary, and indubitable connection of all the *ideas* or proofs one to another, in each step of any demonstration that produces knowledge: so it likewise perceives the probable connection of all the *ideas* or proofs one to another, in every step of a discourse, to which it will think assent due. This is the lowest degree of that, which can be truly called reason. For where the mind does not perceive this probable connection; where it does not discern, whether there be any such connection, or no, there men's opinions are not the product of judgment, or the consequence of reason; but the effects of chance and hazard, of a mind floating at all adventures, without choice, and without direction.

3. *Its four parts.* So that we may in *reason* consider these *four degrees*; the first and highest, is the discovering, and finding out of truths; the second, the regular and methodical disposition of them, and laying them in a clear and fit order, to make their connection and force be plainly and easily perceived; the third is the perceiving their connection; and the fourth, the making a right conclusion. These several degrees may be observed in any mathematical demonstration: it being one thing to perceive the connection of each part, as the demonstration is made by another; another to perceive the dependence of the conclusion on all the parts; a third, to make out a demonstration clearly and neatly oneself, and something different from all these, to have first found out those intermediate *ideas* or proofs by which it is made.

4. *Syllogism not the great instrument of reason.* There is one thing more, which I shall desire to be considered concerning reason; and that is, whether *syllogism*, as is generally thought, be the proper instrument of it, and the usefullest way of exercising this faculty.[56] The causes I have to doubt, are these.

First, because syllogism serves our reason, but in one only of the forementioned parts of it; and that is, to show the connection of the proofs in any one instance, and no more: but in this, it is of no great use, since the

56. A syllogism is an argument with two premisses and a conclusion. According to the Aristotelian account of the syllogism, to which Locke is responding here, each constituent proposition exhibits one of four forms: *universal* and *affirmative* (as in *all human beings are mortal*), *universal* and *negative* (as in *no angel is mortal*), *particular* and *affirmative* (as in *some human beings are mortal*), or *particular* and *negative* (as in *some angels are not mortal*). The predicate of the conclusion is the *major term* of the syllogism, and the subject of the conclusion is the *minor term*. The remaining term, present in each premiss but absent from the conclusion, is the *middle term* or *medius terminus*. Syllogisms were often presented in a standard order: the *major* premiss (in which the major term appears) was listed first, followed by the *minor* premiss (in which the minor term appears) and the conclusion. For example:

Every animal is a living thing. (The major premiss, containing the major term *living thing*.)
Every human being is an animal. (The minor premiss, containing the minor term *human being*.)
Therefore every human being is a living thing. (The conclusion, in which the middle term—*animal*—does not appear.)

The forms of the three propositions (in standard order) determine the *mood* of the syllogism; the arrangement of the three terms determines its *figure*. According to the Aristotelian account, the validity of a syllogism is a matter of its mood and figure.

mind can perceive such connection where it really is, as easily, nay, perhaps, better without it.

If we will observe the actings of our own minds, we shall find, that we reason best and clearest, when we only observe the connection of the proofs, without reducing our thoughts to any rule of syllogism. And therefore we may take notice, that there are many men that reason exceeding clear and rightly, who know not how to make a syllogism. He that will look into many parts of *Asia* and *America,* will find men reason there, perhaps, as acutely as himself, who yet never heard of a syllogism, nor can reduce any one argument to those forms: and I believe scarce anyone makes syllogisms in reasoning within himself. Indeed syllogism is made use of on occasion to discover a fallacy hid in a rhetorical flourish, or cunningly wrapped up in a smooth period; and stripping an absurdity of the cover of wit, and good language, show it in its naked deformity. . . . Now if of all mankind, those who can make syllogisms are extremely few in comparison of those who cannot, and if of those few who have been taught logic, there is but a very small number, who do any more than believe that syllogisms in the allowed *modes* and *figures* do conclude right, without knowing certainly that they do so; if syllogisms must be taken for the only proper instrument of reason and means of knowledge, it will follow, that before *Aristotle* there was not one man that did or could know anything by reason; and that since the invention of syllogisms, there is not one of ten thousand that does.

But God has not been so sparing to men to make them barely two-legged creatures, and left it to *Aristotle* to make them rational, *i.e.* those few of them that he could get so to examine the grounds of syllogisms, as to see, that in above three score ways, that three propositions may be laid together, there are but about fourteen wherein one may be sure that the conclusion is right, and upon what ground it is, that in these few the conclusion is certain, and in the other not. God has been more bountiful to mankind than so. He has given them a mind that can reason without being instructed in methods of syllogizing: the understanding is not taught to reason by these rules; it has a native faculty to perceive the coherence, or incoherence of its *ideas,* and can range them right, without any such perplexing repetitions. I say not this any way to lessen *Aristotle,* whom I look on as one of the greatest men amongst the ancients; whose large views, acuteness and penetration of thought, and strength of judgment, few have equalled: and who in this very invention of forms of argumentation, wherein the conclusion may be shown to be rightly inferred, did great service against those, who were not ashamed to deny anything. And I readily own, that all right reasoning may be reduced to his forms of syllogism. But yet I think without any diminution to him I may truly say, that they are not the only, nor the best way of reasoning, for the leading of those into truth who are willing to find it, and desire to make the best use they may of their reason, for the attainment of knowledge. And he himself it is plain, found out some forms to be conclusive, and others not, not by the forms themselves but by the original way of knowledge, *i.e.* by the visible agreement of *ideas*. . . .

. . . .

To infer is nothing but by virtue of one proposition laid down as true, to draw in another as true, *i.e.* to see or suppose such a connection of the two *ideas,* of the inferred proposition. *v.g.* Let this be the proposition laid down, *men shall be punished in another world,* and from thence be inferred this other, *then men can determine themselves.* The question now is to know, whether the mind has made this inference right or no; if it has made it by finding out the intermediate *ideas,* and taking a view of the connection of them, placed in a due order, it has proceeded rationally, and made a right inference. If it has done it without such a view, it has not so much made an inference that will hold, or an inference of right reason, as shown a willingness to have it be, or be taken for such. But in neither case is it *syllogism* that discovered those *ideas,* or showed the connection of them, for they must be both found out, and the connection everywhere perceived, before they can rationally be made use of in *syllogism:* unless it can be said, that any *idea* without considering what connection it has with the two other, whose agreement should be shown by it, will do well enough in a *syllogism,* and may be taken at a venture for the *medius terminus,* to prove any conclusion. But this nobody will say, because it is by virtue of the perceived agreement of the intermediate *idea* with the extremes, that the extremes are concluded to agree, and therefore each intermediate *idea* must be such, as in the whole chain has a visible connection with those two it is placed between, or else thereby, the conclusion cannot be inferred or drawn in; for wherever any link of the chain is loose, and without connection, there the whole strength of it is lost, and it has no force to infer or draw in anything.[57] In the instance above-mentioned, what is it shows the force of the inference, and consequently the reasonableness of it, but a view of the connection of all the intermediate *ideas* that draw in the conclusion, or proposition inferred. *v.g. Men shall be punished,——God the punisher,——just punishment,——the punished guilty——could have done otherwise——freedom——self-determination,* by which chain of *ideas* thus visibly linked

57. *medius terminus,* middle term. See note 56.

together in train, *i.e.* each intermediate *idea* agreeing on each side with those two it is immediately placed between, the *ideas* of men and self-determination appear to be connected, *i.e.* this proposition, *men can determine themselves* is drawn in, or inferred from this *that they shall be punished in the other world.* For here the mind seeing the connection there is between the *idea of men's punishment in the other world,* and the *idea of God punishing,* between *God punishing,* and *the justice of the punishment;* between *justice of punishment* and *guilt,* between *guilt* and a *power to do otherwise,* between a *power to do otherwise* and *freedom,* and between *freedom* and *self-determination,* sees the connection between *men,* and *self-determination.*

Now I ask whether the connection of the extremes be not more clearly seen in this simple and natural disposition, than in the perplexed repetitions, and jumble of five or six *syllogisms.* . . . And as for the logicians themselves they see the connection of each intermediate *idea* with those it stands between (on which the force of the inference depends) as well before as after the *syllogism* is made, or else they do not see it at all. For a *syllogism* neither shows nor strengthens the connection of any two *ideas* immediately put together, but only by the connection seen in them shows what connection the extremes have one with another. But what connection the intermediate has with either of the extremes in that syllogism, that no syllogism does or can show. That the mind only does, or can perceive as they stand there in that *juxtaposition* only by its own view, to which the syllogistical form it happens to be in, gives no help or light at all; it only shows that if the intermediate *idea* agrees with those it is on both sides immediately applied to, then those two remote ones, or as they are called *extremes* do certainly agree, and therefore the immediate connection of each *idea* to that which it is applied to on each side, on which the force of the reasoning depends, is as well seen before as after the *syllogism* is made, or else he that makes the syllogism could never see it at all. This as has been already observed, is seen only by the eye or the perceptive faculty of the mind, taking a view of them laid together, in a *juxtaposition,* which view of any two it has equally, whenever they are laid together in any proposition, whether that proposition be placed as a *major,* or a *minor,* in a *syllogism* or no.

Of what use then are *syllogisms*? I answer, their chief and main use is in the schools, where men are allowed without shame to deny the agreement of *ideas,* that do manifestly agree; or out of the schools to those, who from thence have learned without shame to deny the connection of *ideas,* which even to themselves is visible. But to an ingenuous searcher after truth, who has no other aim, but to find it, there is no need of any such form, to force the allowing of the inference: the truth and reasonableness of it is better seen in ranging of the *ideas* in a simple and plain order; and hence it is, that men, in their own inquiries after truth never use *syllogisms* to convince themselves. Because, before they can put them into a *syllogism* they must see the connection, that is between the intermediate *idea*, and the two other *ideas* it is set between, and applied to, to show their agreement, and when they see that, they see whether the inference be good or no, and so *syllogism* comes too late to settle it. . . .

. . . .

Secondly, another reason that makes me doubt whether syllogism be the only proper instrument of reason in the discovery of truth, is, that of whatever use *mode* and *figure* is pretended to be in the laying open of fallacy . . . those scholastic forms of discourse, are not less liable to fallacies, than the plainer ways of argumentation: and for this I appeal to common observation, which has always found these artificial methods of reasoning more adapted to catch and entangle the mind, than to instruct and inform the understanding. And hence it is, that men even when they are baffled and silenced in this scholastic way, are seldom or never convinced, and so brought over to the conquering side; they perhaps acknowledge their adversary to be the more skillful disputant; but rest nevertheless persuaded of the truth on their side; and go away, worsted as they are, with the same opinion they brought with them, which they could not do, if this way of argumentation carried light and conviction with it, and made men see where the truth lay. And therefore syllogism has been thought more proper for the attaining victory in dispute, than for the discovery or confirmation of truth, in fair inquiries. And if it be certain, that fallacy can be couched in syllogisms, as it cannot be denied, it must be something else, and not syllogism that must discover them.

I have had experience, how ready some men are, when all the use which they have been wont to ascribe to anything is not allowed, to cry out, that I am for laying it wholly aside. But to prevent such unjust and groundless imputations, I tell them, that I am not for taking away any helps to the understanding, in the attainment of knowledge. And if men skilled in, and used to syllogisms, find them assisting to their reason in the discovery of truth, I think they ought to make use of them. All that I aim at is, that they should not ascribe more to those forms than belongs to them; and think that men have no use, or not so full a use of their reasoning faculty without them. Some eyes want spectacles to see things clearly and distinctly; but let not those that use them therefore say, nobody can see clearly without them:

those who do so, will be thought in favor of art (which perhaps they are beholding to) a little too much to depress and discredit nature. Reason by its own penetration where it is strong, and exercised usually sees, quicker and clearer without syllogism. If use of those spectacles has so dimmed its sight, that it cannot without them see consequences or inconsequences in argumentation, I am not so unreasonable as to be against the using them. Everyone knows what best fits his own sight. But let him not thence conclude all in the dark, who use not just the same helps that he finds a need of.

5. *Helps little in demonstration, less in probability.* But however it be in knowledge, I think I may truly say, it is of *far* less, or *no use* at all *in probabilities.* For the assent there, being to be determined by the preponderancy, after due weighing of all the proofs, with all circumstances on both sides, nothing is so unfit to assist the mind in that, as syllogism; which running away with one assumed probability, or one topical argument, pursues that till it has led the mind quite out of sight of the thing under consideration; and forcing it upon some remote difficulty, holds it fast there, entangled perhaps, and as it were, manacled in the chain of syllogisms, without allowing it the liberty, much less affording it the helps requisite to show on which side, all things considered, is the greater probability.

6. *Serves not to increase our knowledge, but fence with it.* But let it help us (as, perhaps may be said) in convincing men of their errors and mistakes: (and yet I would fain see the man, that was forced out of his opinion by dint of *syllogism*,) yet still it *fails our reason in* that part, which if not its highest perfection, is yet certainly its hardest task, and that which we most need its help in; and that is *the finding out of proofs, and making new discoveries.* The rules of *syllogism* serve not to furnish the mind with those intermediate *ideas,* that may show the connection of remote ones. This way of reasoning discovers no new proofs, but is the art of marshalling, and ranging the old ones we have already. The 47th. proposition of the first book of *Euclid* is very true; but the discovery of it, I think, not owing to any rules of common logic. A man knows first, and then he is able to prove syllogistically. So that *syllogism* comes after knowledge, and then a man has little or no need of it. But 'tis chiefly by the finding out those *ideas* that show the connection of distant ones, that our stock of knowledge is increased, and that useful arts and sciences are advanced. *Syllogism,* at best, is but the art of fencing with the little knowledge we have, without making any addition to it. . . .

. . . .

9. *First, reason fails us for want of* ideas. *Reason,* though it penetrates into the depths of the sea and earth, elevates our thoughts as high as the stars, and leads us through the vast spaces, and large rooms of this mighty fabric, yet it comes far short of the real extent of even corporeal being: and there are many instances wherein it *fails us:* as,

First, it perfectly fails us, *where our* ideas *fail.* It neither does, nor can extend itself farther than they do. And therefore, wherever we have no *ideas,* our reasoning stops, and we are at an end of our reckoning: and if at any time we reason about words, which do not stand for any *ideas,* 'tis only about those sounds, and nothing else.

10. *Secondly, because of obscure and imperfect* ideas. *Secondly,* our reason is often puzzled, and at a loss, *because of the obscurity, confusion, or imperfection of the* ideas *it is employed about;* and there we are involved in difficulties and contradictions. Thus, not having any perfect *idea* of the least extension of matter, nor of infinity, we are at a loss about the divisibility of matter; but having perfect, clear, and distinct *ideas* of number, our reason meets with none of those inextricable difficulties in numbers, nor finds itself involved in any contradictions about them. Thus, we having but imperfect *ideas* of the operations of our minds, and of the beginning of motion or thought how the mind produces either of them in us, and much imperfecter yet, of the operation of GOD, run into great difficulties about free created agents, which reason cannot well extricate itself out of.

11. *Thirdly, for want of intermediate* ideas. *Thirdly,* our reason is often at a stand, *because it perceives not those* ideas, *which could serve to show the certain or probable agreement, or disagreement of any other two* ideas: and in this, some men's faculties far outgo others. Till *algebra,* that great instrument and instance of human sagacity, was discovered, men, with amazement, looked on several of the demonstrations of ancient mathematicians, and could scarce forbear to think the finding several of those proofs to be something more than human.

12. *Fourthly, because of wrong principles. Fourthly,* the mind *by proceeding upon false principles* is often engaged in absurdities and difficulties, brought into straits and contradictions, without knowing how to free itself: and in that case it is in vain to implore the help of reason, unless it be to discover the falsehood, and reject the influence of those wrong principles. Reason is so

far from clearing the difficulties which the building upon false foundations brings a man into, that if he will pursue it, it entangles him the more, and engages him deeper in perplexities.

13. *Fifthly, because of doubtful terms. Fifthly,* as obscure and imperfect *ideas* often involve our reason, so, upon the same ground, do *dubious words,* and uncertain signs, *often,* in discourses and arguings, when not warily attended to, *puzzle men's reason,* and bring them to a *non-plus.* But these two latter are our fault, and not the fault of reason. But yet, the consequences of them are nevertheless obvious; and the perplexities, or errors, they fill men's minds with, are everywhere observable.

14. *Our highest degree of knowledge is intuitive, without reasoning.* Some of the *ideas* that are in the mind, are so there, that they can be, by themselves immediately compared, one with another: and in these the mind is able to perceive, that they agree or disagree as clearly, as that it has them. Thus the mind perceives, that an arch of a circle is less than the whole circle, as clearly as it does the *idea* of a circle: and this, therefore, as has been said, I call *intuitive knowledge;* which is certain, beyond all doubt, and needs no probation, nor can have any; this being the highest of all human certainty. In this consists the evidence of all those *maxims,* which nobody has any doubt about, but every man (does not, as is said, only assent to, but) knows to be true, as soon as ever they are proposed to his understanding. In the discovery of, and assent to these truths, there is no use of the discursive faculty, *no need of reasoning,* but they are known by a superior, and higher degree of evidence. And such, if I may guess at things unknown, I am apt to think, that angels have now, and the spirits of just men made perfect, shall have, in a future state, of thousands of things, which now, either wholly escape our apprehensions, or which, our short-sighted reason having got some faint glimpse of, we, in the dark, grope after.

15. *The next is demonstration by reasoning.* But though we have, here and there, a little of this clear light, some sparks of bright knowledge: yet the greatest part of our *ideas* are such, that we cannot discern their agreement, or disagreement, by an immediate comparing them. And in all these, we have *need of reasoning,* and must, by discourse and inference, make our discoveries. Now of these, there are two sorts, which I shall take the liberty to mention here again.

First, those whose agreement, or disagreement, though it cannot be seen by an immediate putting them together, yet may be examined by the intervention of other *ideas,* which can be compared with them. In this case when the agreement, or disagreement of the intermediate *idea,* on both sides with those which we would compare, is plainly discerned, there it amounts to demonstration, whereby knowledge is produced, which though it be certain, yet it is not so easy, nor altogether so clear, as *intuitive knowledge*. Because in that there is barely one simple intuition, wherein there is no room for any the least mistake or doubt: the truth is seen all perfectly at once. In demonstration, 'tis true, there is intuition too, but not altogether at once; for there must be a remembrance of the intuition of the agreement of the *medium,* or intermediate *idea,* with that we compared it with before, when we compare it with the other; and where there be many *mediums,* there the danger of the mistake is the greater. . . . But yet where the mind clearly retains the intuition it had of the agreement of any *idea* with another, and that with a third, and that with a fourth, *&c.* there the agreement of the first and the fourth is a demonstration, and produces certain knowledge, which may be called *rational knowledge,* as the other is *intuitive*.

16. *To supply the narrowness of this, we have nothing but judgment upon probable reasoning. Secondly,* there are other *ideas,* whose agreement, or disagreement, can no otherwise be judged of, but by the intervention of others, which have not a certain agreement with the extremes, but an usual or likely one: and in these it is, that the *judgment* is properly exercised, which is the acquiescing of the mind, that any *ideas* do agree, by comparing them with such probable *mediums.* This, though it never amounts to knowledge, no not to that which is the lowest degree of it: yet sometimes the intermediate *ideas* tie the extremes so firmly together, and the probability is so clear and strong, that assent as necessarily follows it, as knowledge does demonstration. . . .

. . . .

23. *Above, contrary, and according to reason.* By what has been before said of *reason,* we may be able to make some guess at the distinction of things, into those that are according to, above, and contrary to reason. 1. *According to reason* are such propositions, whose truth we can discover, by examining and tracing those *ideas* we have from *sensation* and *reflection;* and by natural deduction, find to be true, or probable. 2. *Above reason* are such propositions, whose truth or probability we cannot by reason derive from those principles. 3. *Contrary to reason* are such propositions, as are inconsistent with, or irreconcilable to our clear and distinct *ideas.* Thus the existence of

one GOD is according to reason; the existence of more than one GOD, contrary to reason; the resurrection of the dead, above reason. Above reason also may be taken in a double sense, *viz.* above probability, or above certainty: and in that large sense also, contrary to reason, is, I suppose, sometimes taken.

24. *Reason and faith not opposite.* There is another use of the word *reason,* wherein it is *opposed to faith;* which though it be in itself a very improper way of speaking, yet common use has so authorized it, that it would be folly either to oppose or hope to remedy it: only I think it may not be amiss to take notice, that however *faith* be opposed to reason, *faith* is nothing but a firm assent of the mind: which if it be regulated, as is our duty, cannot be afforded to anything, but upon good reason; and so cannot be opposite to it. He that believes, without having any reason for believing, may be in love with his own fancies; but neither seeks truth as he ought, nor pays the obedience due to his maker, who would have him use those discerning faculties he has given him, to keep him out of mistake and error. . . . For he governs his assent right, . . . who in any case or matter whatsoever, believes or disbelieves, according as reason directs him. He that does otherwise, transgresses against his own light, and misuses those faculties, which were given him to no other end, but to search and follow the clearer evidence, and greater probability. But since reason and faith are by some men opposed, we will so consider them in the following chapter.

CHAP. XVIII.

Of faith and reason, and their distinct provinces.

1. *Necessary to know their boundaries.* It has been above shown, 1. That we are of necessity ignorant, and want knowledge of all sorts, where we want *ideas.* 2. That we are ignorant, and want rational knowledge, where we want proofs. 3. That we want certain knowledge and certainty, as far as we want clear and determined specific *ideas.* 4. That we want probability to direct our assent in matters where we have neither knowledge of our own, nor testimony of other men to bottom our reason upon.

From these things thus premised, I think we may come to lay down the measures and *boundaries between faith and reason:* the want whereof, may possibly have been the cause, if not of great disorders, yet at least of great disputes, and perhaps mistakes in the world. For till it be resolved, how far we are to be guided by reason, and how far by faith, we shall in vain dispute, and endeavor to convince one another in matters of religion.

2. *Faith and reason what, as contradistinguished.* I find every sect, as far as reason will help them, make use of it gladly: and where it fails them, they cry out, *'tis matter of faith, and above reason.* And I do not see how they can argue with anyone, or ever convince a gainsayer, who makes use of the same plea, without setting down strict boundaries between *faith* and *reason;* which ought to be the first point established in all questions, where *faith* has anything to do.

Reason therefore here, as contradistinguished to *faith*, I take to be the discovery of the certainty or probability of such propositions or truths, which the mind arrives at by deductions made from such *ideas,* which it has got by the use of its natural faculties, *viz.* by sensation or reflection.

Faith, on the other side, is the assent to any proposition, not thus made out by the deductions of reason; but upon the credit of the proposer, as coming from GOD, in some extraordinary way of communication. This way of discovering truths to men we call *revelation.*

3. *No new simple idea can be conveyed by traditional revelation. First,* then, I say, that *no man inspired by GOD, can by any revelation communicate to others any new simple ideas* which they had not before from sensation or reflection. For whatsoever impressions he himself may have from the immediate hand of GOD, this revelation, if it be of new simple *ideas,* cannot be conveyed to another, either by words, or any other signs. Because words, by their immediate operation on us, cause no other *ideas,* but of their natural sounds: and 'tis by the custom of using them for signs, that they excite, and revive in our minds latent *ideas;* but yet only such *ideas,* as were there before. . . . The same holds in all other signs. . . .

. . . For our simple *ideas* then, which are the foundation, and sole matter of all our notions, and knowledge, we must depend wholly on our reason, I mean, our natural faculties; and can by no means receive them, or any of them, from *traditional revelation.* I say, *traditional revelation,* in distinction to *original revelation.* By the one, I mean that first impression, which is made immediately by GOD, on the mind of any man, to which we cannot set any bounds; and by the other, those impressions delivered over to others in words, and the ordinary ways of conveying our conceptions one to another.

4. *Traditional revelation may make us know propositions knowable also by reason, but not with the same certainty that reason does. Secondly,* I say, that *the same truths may be discovered, and conveyed down from revelation, which are discoverable to us by reason,* and by those *ideas* we naturally may have. So GOD might, by revelation, discover the truth of any proposition in *Euclid;* as well as men, by the natural use of their faculties, come to make the discovery themselves. In all things of this kind, there is little need or use of *revelation,* GOD having furnished us with natural, and surer means to arrive at the knowledge of them. For whatsoever truth we come to the clear discovery of, from the knowledge and contemplation of our own *ideas,* will always be certainer to us, than those which are conveyed to us by *traditional revelation.* For the knowledge, we have, that this *revelation* came at first from GOD, can never be so sure, as the knowledge we have from the clear and distinct perception of the agreement, or disagreement of our own *ideas, v.g.* if it were revealed some ages since, that the three angles of a triangle were equal to two right ones, I might assent to the truth of that proposition, upon the credit of the tradition, that it was revealed: but that would never amount to so great a certainty, as the knowledge of it, upon the comparing and measuring my own *ideas* of two right angles, and the three angles of a triangle. The like holds in matter of fact, knowable by our senses, *v.g.* the history of the deluge is conveyed to us by writings, which had their original from revelation: and yet nobody, I think, will say, he has as certain and clear a knowledge of the flood, as *Noah* that saw it; or that he himself would have had, had he then been alive and seen it. For he has no greater an assurance than that of his senses, that it is writ in the book supposed writ by *Moses* inspired: but he has not so great an assurance, that *Moses* writ that book, as if he had seen *Moses* write it. So that the assurance of its being a revelation, is less still than the assurance of his senses.

5. *Revelation cannot be admitted against the clear evidence of reason.* In propositions then, whose certainty is built upon the clear perception of the agreement, or disagreement of our *ideas* attained either by immediate intuition, as in self-evident propositions, or by evident deductions of reason, in demonstrations, we need not the assistance of *revelation,* as necessary to gain our assent, and introduce them into our minds. Because the natural ways of knowledge could settle them there, or had done it already, which is the greatest assurance we can possibly have of anything,

unless where GOD immediately reveals it to us: and there too our assurance can be no greater, than our knowledge is, that it is a *revelation* from GOD. But yet nothing, I think, can, under that title, shake or over-rule plain knowledge; or rationally prevail with any man, to admit it for true, in a direct contradiction to the clear evidence of his own understanding. For since no evidence of our faculties, by which we receive such *revelations,* can exceed, if equal, the certainty of our intuitive knowledge, we can never receive for a truth anything, that is directly contrary to our clear and distinct knowledge, *v.g.* the *ideas* of one body, and one place, do so clearly agree; and the mind has so evident a perception of their agreement, that we can never assent to a proposition, that affirms the same body to be in two distant places at once, however it should pretend to the authority of a divine *revelation:* since the evidence, *first,* that we deceive not ourselves in ascribing it to GOD; *secondly,* that we understand it right, can never be so great, as the evidence of our own intuitive knowledge, whereby we discern it impossible, for the same body to be in two places at once. And therefore, *no proposition can be received for divine revelation,* or obtain the assent due to all such, *if it be contradictory to our clear intuitive knowledge.* Because this would be to subvert the principles, and foundations of all knowledge, evidence, and assent whatsoever: and there would be left no difference between truth and falsehood, no measures of credible and incredible in the world, if doubtful propositions shall take place before self-evident; and what we certainly know, give way to what we may possibly be mistaken in. In propositions therefore contrary to the clear perception of the agreement or disagreement of any of our *ideas,* 'twill be in vain to urge them as matters of *faith.* . . .

6. *Traditional revelation much less.* Thus far a man has use of reason, and ought to hearken to it, even in immediate and original *revelation,* where it is supposed to be made to himself: but to all those who pretend not to immediate *revelation,* but are required to pay obedience, and to receive the truths revealed to others, which, by the tradition of writings, or word of mouth, are conveyed down to them, reason has a great deal more to do, and is that only which can induce us to receive them. For matter of faith being only divine revelation, and nothing else, *faith,* as we use the word, (called commonly, *divine faith*) has to do with no propositions, but those which are supposed to be divinely revealed. So that I do not see how those, who make revelation alone the sole object of *faith,* can say, that it is a matter of *faith,* and not of *reason,* to believe, that such or such a proposition, to be found in such or such a book, is of divine inspiration; unless it be revealed, that that

proposition, or all in that book, was communicated by divine inspiration. Without such a *revelation,* the believing, or not believing that proposition, or book, to be of divine authority, can never be matter of *faith,* but matter of reason; and such, as I must come to an assent to, only by the use of my reason, which can never require or enable me to believe that, which is contrary to itself: it being impossible for reason, ever to procure any assent to that, which to itself appears unreasonable.

In all things therefore, where we have clear evidence from our *ideas,* and those principles of knowledge, I have above-mentioned, *reason* is the proper judge; and *revelation,* though it may in consenting with it, confirm its dictates, yet cannot in such cases, invalidate its decrees: *nor can we be obliged, where we have the clear and evident sentence of reason, to quit it, for the contrary opinion, under a pretense that it is matter of faith;* which can have no authority against the plain and clear dictates of *reason.*

7. *Things above reason.* But *thirdly,* there being many things, wherein we have very imperfect notions, or none at all; and other things, of whose past, present, or future existence, by the natural use of our faculties, we can have no knowledge at all; these, as being beyond the discovery of our natural faculties, and above *reason,* are, when revealed, *the proper matter of faith.* Thus that part of the angels rebelled against GOD, and thereby lost their first happy state: and that the dead shall rise, and live again: these, and the like, being beyond the discovery of *reason* are purely matters of *faith;* with which *reason* has, directly, nothing to do.

8. *Or not contrary to reason, if revealed, are matter of faith.* But since GOD in giving us the light of *reason* has not thereby tied up his own hands from affording us, when he thinks fit, the light of *revelation* in any of those matters, wherein our natural faculties are able to give a probable determination, *revelation,* where God has been pleased to give it, *must carry it, against the probable conjectures of reason.* Because the mind, not being certain of the truth of that it does not evidently know, but only yielding to the probability that appears in it, is bound to give up its assent to such a testimony, which, it is satisfied, comes from one, who cannot err, and will not deceive. But yet, it still belongs to *reason,* to judge of the truth of its being a revelation, and of the signification of the words, wherein it is delivered. . . .

9. *Revelation in matters where reason cannot judge, or but probably, ought to be hearkened to. First,* whatever proposition is revealed, of whose truth our

mind, by its natural faculties and notions, cannot judge, that is purely *matter of faith,* and above reason.

Secondly, all propositions, whereof the mind, by the use of its natural faculties, can come to determine and judge, from naturally acquired *ideas,* are *matter of reason;* with this difference still, that in those, concerning which it has but an uncertain evidence, and so is persuaded of their truth, only upon probable grounds, which still admit a possibility of the contrary to be true, without doing violence to the certain evidence of its own knowledge, and overturning the principles of all reason, in such probable propositions, I say, an evident *revelation* ought to determine our assent even against probability. For where the principles of reason have not evidenced a proposition to be certainly true or false, there clear *revelation,* as another principle of truth, and ground of assent, may determine; and so it may be matter of *faith,* and be also above *reason.* Because *reason,* in that particular matter, being able to reach no higher than probability, *faith* gave the determination, where *reason* came short; and *revelation* discovered on which side the truth lay.

10. *In matters where reason can afford certain knowledge that is to be hearkened to.* Thus far the dominion of *faith* reaches, and that without any violence, or hindrance to *reason;* which is not injured, or disturbed, but assisted and improved, by new discoveries of truth, coming from the eternal fountain of all knowledge. Whatever GOD has revealed, is certainly true; no doubt can be made of it. This is the proper object of *faith:* but whether it be a divine revelation, or no, *reason* must judge; which can never permit the mind to reject a greater evidence to embrace what is less evident, nor allow it to entertain probability in opposition to knowledge and certainty. There can be no evidence, that any traditional revelation is of divine original, in the words we receive it, and in the sense we understand it, so clear, and so certain, as those of the principles of reason: and therefore, *nothing that is contrary to, and inconsistent with the clear and self-evident dictates of reason, has a right to be urged, or assented to, as a matter of faith, wherein reason has nothing to do.* Whatsoever is divine *revelation,* ought to over-rule all our opinions, prejudices, and interests, and has a right to be received with a full assent: such a submission as this of our *reason* to *faith,* takes not away the landmarks of knowledge: this shakes not the foundations of reason, but leaves us that use of our faculties, for which they were given us.

. . . .

CHAP. XX.

Of wrong assent or error.

1. *Causes of error.* Knowledge being to be had only of visible and certain truth, *error* is not a fault of our knowledge, but a mistake of our judgment giving assent to that, which is not true.

But if assent be grounded on likelihood, if the proper object and motive of our assent be probability, and that probability consists in what is laid down in the foregoing chapters, it will be demanded, how men come to give their assents contrary to probability. For there is nothing more common, than contrariety of opinions; nothing more obvious, than that one man wholly disbelieves what another only doubts of, and a third steadfastly believes, and firmly adheres to. The reasons whereof, though they may be very various, yet, I suppose, may all be reduced to these four:

1. *Want of proofs.*
2. *Want of ability to use them.*
3. *Want of will to use them.*
4. *Wrong measures of probability.*

2. *First, want of proofs. First,* by *want of proofs:* I do not mean, only the want of those proofs which are nowhere extant, and so are nowhere to be had; but the want even of those proofs which are in being, or might be procured. And thus men want proofs, who have not the convenience, or opportunity to make experiments and observations themselves, tending to the proof of any proposition; nor likewise the convenience to inquire into, and collect the testimonies of others: and in this state are the greatest part of mankind, who are given up to labor, and enslaved to the necessity of their mean condition; whose lives are worn out, only in the provisions for living. . . . So that a great part of mankind are, by the natural and unalterable state of things in this world, and the constitution of human affairs, unavoidably given over to invincible ignorance of those proofs, on which others build, and which are necessary to establish those opinions: the greatest part of men, having much to do to get the means of living, are not in a condition to look after those of learned and laborious inquiries.

. . . .

4. *People hindered from inquiry.* Besides those, whose improvements and informations are straitened by the narrowness of their fortunes, there are others, whose largeness of fortune would plentifully enough supply books, and other requisites for clearing of doubts, and discovering of truth: but they are *cooped in* close, *by the laws* of their countries, and the strict guards of those, whose interest it is to keep them ignorant, lest, knowing more, they should believe the less in them. These are as far, nay *farther from the liberty and opportunities of a fair inquiry,* than those poor and wretched laborers, we before spoke of. . . .

5. *Secondly, want of skill to use them. Secondly,* those who *want skill to use those evidences they have* of probabilities; who cannot carry a train of consequences in their heads, nor weigh exactly the preponderancy of contrary proofs and testimonies, making every circumstance its due allowance, may be easily misled to assent to positions that are not probable. There are some men of one, some but of two syllogisms, and no more; and others that can but advance one step farther. These cannot always discern that side on which the strongest proofs lie; cannot constantly follow that which in itself is the more probable opinion. . . .

6. *Thirdly, want of will to use them. Thirdly,* there are another sort of people that *want proofs,* not because they are out of their reach, but *because they will not use them:* who though they have riches and leisure enough, and want neither parts nor other helps, are yet never the better for them. Their hot pursuit of pleasure, or constant drudgery in business engages some men's thoughts elsewhere: laziness and oscitancy in general, or a particular aversion for books, study, and meditation keep others from any serious thoughts at all: and some out of fear, that an impartial inquiry would not favor those opinions, which best suit their prejudices, lives, and designs, content themselves without examination, to take upon trust, what they find convenient, and in fashion. Thus most men, even of those that might do otherwise, pass their lives without an acquaintance with, much less a rational assent to probabilities, they are concerned to know, though they lie so much within their view, that to be convinced of them, they need but turn their eyes that way. . . .

7. *Fourthly, wrong measures of probability. Fourthly,* there remains yet the last sort, who, even where the real probabilities appear, and are plainly laid before them, do not admit of the conviction, nor yield unto manifest reasons, but do either ἐπέχειν, suspend their assent, or give it to the less

probable opinion.[58] And to this danger are those exposed, who have taken up *wrong measures of probability,* which are,

1. *Propositions that are not in themselves certain and evident, but doubtful and false, taken up for principles.*
2. *Received hypotheses.*
3. *Predominant passions or inclinations.*
4. *Authority.*

8. *First, doubtful propositions taken for principles. First,* the first and firmest ground of probability, is the conformity anything has to our own knowledge; especially that part of our knowledge which we have embraced, and continue to look on as *principles.* These have so great an influence upon our opinions, that 'tis usually by them we judge of truth, and measure probability, to that degree, that what is inconsistent with our *principles,* is so far from passing for probable with us, that it will not be allowed possible. The reverence is born to these *principles* is so great, and their authority so paramount to all other, that the testimony not only of other men, but the evidence of our own senses are often rejected, when they offer to vouch anything contrary to these established rules. How much the doctrine of innate *principles,* and that *principles* are not to be proved or questioned, has contributed to this, I will not here examine. This I readily grant, that one truth cannot contradict another: but withal I take leave also to say, that everyone ought very carefully to beware what he admits for a *principle,* to examine it strictly, and see whether he certainly knows it to be true of itself by its own evidence, or whether he does only with assurance believe it to be so, upon the authority of others. For he has a strong bias put into his understanding, which will unavoidably misguide his assent, who has imbibed *wrong principles,* and has blindly given himself up to the authority of any opinion in itself not evidently true.

. . . .

11. *Secondly, received hypothesis. Secondly,* next to these, are men whose understandings are cast into a mold, and fashioned just to the size of a *received hypothesis.* The difference between these and the former, is, that they will admit of matter of fact, and agree with dissenters in that; but differ only in assigning of reasons, and explaining the manner of operation. These are not at that open defiance with their senses, as the former: they

58. ἐπέχειν, to suspend judgment.

can endure to hearken to their information a little more patiently; but will by no means admit of their reports, in the explanation of things; nor be prevailed on by probabilities, which would convince them, that things are not brought about just after the same manner, that they have decreed within themselves, that they are. . . .

12. *Thirdly, predominant passions. Thirdly,* probabilities, which cross men's appetites, and *prevailing passions,* run the same fate. Let never so much probability hang on one side of a covetous man's reasoning, and money on the other; it is easy to foresee which will outweigh. Earthly minds, like mud walls, resist the strongest batteries: and though, perhaps, sometimes the force of a clear argument may make some impression, yet they nevertheless stand firm, and keep out the enemy truth, that would captivate, or disturb them. . . . Not but that it is the nature of the understanding constantly to close with the more probable side, but yet a man has a power to suspend and restrain its inquiries, and not permit a full and satisfactory examination, as far as the matter in question is capable, and will bear it to be made. Until that be done, there will be always *these two ways left of evading the most apparent probabilities.*

13. *The means of evading probabilities,* 1st. *supposed fallacy. First,* that the arguments being (as for the most part they are) brought in words, *there may be a fallacy latent* in them: and the consequences being, perhaps, many in train, they may be some of them incoherent. There be very few discourses, are so short, clear and consistent, to which most men may not, with satisfaction enough to themselves, raise this doubt; and from whose *conviction* they may not, without reproach of disingenuity or unreasonableness, set themselves free with the old reply, *non persuadebis, etiamsi persuaseris; though I cannot answer, I will not yield.*

14. 2ly. *Supposed arguments for the contrary. Secondly,* manifest probabilities may be evaded, and the assent withheld upon this suggestion, that *I know not yet all that may be said on the contrary side.* And therefore though I be beaten, 'tis not necessary I should yield, not knowing what forces there are in reserve behind. This is a refuge against *conviction* so open and so wide, that it is hard to determine, when a man is quite out of the verge of it.

15. *What probabilities determine the assent.* But yet there is some end of it, and a man having carefully inquired into all the grounds of probability and unlikeliness; done his utmost to inform himself in all particulars fairly; and

cast up the sum total on both sides, may in most cases come to acknowledge, upon the whole matter, on which side the probability rests: wherein some proofs in matter of reason, being suppositions upon universal experience, are so cogent and clear; and some testimonies in matter of fact so universal, that he cannot refuse his assent. So that, I think, we may conclude, that in propositions, where though the proofs in view are of most moment, yet there are sufficient grounds, to suspect that there is either fallacy in words, or certain proofs, as considerable, to be produced on the contrary side, there assent, suspense, or dissent, are often voluntary actions: but *where* the proofs are such as make it highly probable and there is not sufficient ground to suspect, that there is either fallacy of words, (which sober and serious consideration may discover,) nor equally valid proofs yet undiscovered latent on the other side, (which also the nature of the thing may, in some cases, make plain to a considerate man,) there, I think, *a man,* who has weighed them, *can scarce refuse his assent* to the side, on which the greater probability appears. Whether it be probable, that a promiscuous jumble of printing letters should often fall into a method and order, which should stamp on paper a coherent discourse; or that a blind fortuitous concourse of atoms, not guided by an understanding agent, should frequently constitute the bodies of any species of animals: in these and the like cases, I think, nobody that considers them, can be one jot at a stand which side to take, nor at all waver in his assent. Lastly, when there can be no supposition, (the thing in its own nature indifferent, and wholly depending upon the testimony of witnesses,) that there is as fair testimony against, as for the matter of fact attested; which by inquiry, is to be learned, *v.g.* whether there was 1700 years ago such a man at *Rome* as *Julius Caesar:* in all such cases, I say, I think it is not in any rational man's power to refuse his assent; but that it necessarily follows, and closes with such probabilities. In other less clear cases, I think, it is in man's power to suspend his assent; and, perhaps, content himself with the proofs he has, if they favor the opinion that suits with his inclination, or interest, and so stop from farther search. But that a man should afford his assent to that side, on which the less probability appears to him, seems to me utterly impracticable, and as impossible, as it is to believe the same thing probable and improbable at the same time.

16. *Where it is in our power to suspend it.* As knowledge, is no more arbitrary than perception: so, I think, assent is no more in our power than knowledge. When the agreement of any two *ideas* appears to our minds, whether immediately, or by the assistance of reason, I can no more refuse to

perceive, no more avoid knowing it, than I can avoid seeing those objects, which I turn my eyes to, and look on in daylight: and what upon full examination I find the most probable, I cannot deny my assent to. But though we cannot hinder our knowledge, where the agreement is once perceived; nor our assent, where the probability manifestly appears upon due consideration of all the measures of it: yet *we can hinder both knowledge and assent, by stopping our inquiry,* and not employing our faculties in the search of any truth. If it were not so, ignorance, error, or infidelity could not in any case be a fault. Thus in some cases, we can prevent or suspend our assent: but can a man, versed in modern or ancient history, doubt whether there be such a place as *Rome,* or whether there was such a man as *Julius Caesar*? Indeed there are millions of truths, that a man is not, or may not think himself concerned to know; as whether our King *Richard* the Third was crook-backed, or no; or whether *Roger Bacon* was a mathematician, or a magician. In these and such like cases, where the assent one way or other, is of no importance to the interest of anyone, no action, no concernment of his following, or depending thereon, there 'tis not strange, that the mind should give itself up to the common opinion, or render itself to the first comer. These and the like opinions, are of so little weight and moment, that like motes in the sun, their tendencies are very rarely taken notice of. They are there, as it were, by chance, and the mind lets them float at liberty. But where the mind judges that the proposition has concernment in it; where the assent, or not assenting is thought to draw consequences of moment after it, and good or evil to depend on choosing, or refusing the right side, and the mind sets itself seriously to inquire, and examine the probability: there, I think, it is not in our choice, to take which side we please, if manifest odds appear on either. The greater probability, I think, in that case, will determine the assent: and a man can no more avoid assenting, or taking it to be true, where he perceives the greater probability, than he can avoid knowing it to be true, where he perceives the agreement or disagreement of any two *ideas*.

If this be so, the foundation of error will lie in wrong measures of probability; as the foundation of vice in wrong measures of good.

17. *Fourthly, authority. Fourthly,* the fourth and last *wrong measure of probability* I shall take notice of, and which keeps in ignorance, or error, more people than all the other together, is . . . the *giving up our assent to the common received opinions,* either of our friends, or party; neighborhood or country. How many men have no other ground for their tenets, than the supposed honesty, or learning, or number of those of the same profession?

As if honest, or bookish men could not err; or truth were to be established by the vote of the multitude: yet this with most men serves the turn. The tenet has had the attestation of reverend antiquity, it comes to me with the passport of former ages, and therefore I am secure in the reception I give it: other men have been, and are of the same opinion, (for that is all is said,) and therefore it is reasonable for me to embrace it. A man may more justifiably throw up cross and pile for his opinions, than take them up by such measures. All men are liable to error, and most men are in many points, by passion or interest, under temptation to it. If we could but see the secret motives, that influenced the men of name and learning in the world, and the leaders of parties, we should not always find, that it was the embracing of truth for its own sake, that made them espouse the doctrines, they owned and maintained. This at least is certain, there is not an opinion so absurd, which a man may not receive upon this ground. There is no error to be named, which has not had its professors: and a man shall never want crooked paths to walk in, if he thinks that he is in the right way, wherever he has the footsteps of others to follow.

18. *Men not in so many errors as is imagined.* But notwithstanding the great noise is made in the world about errors and opinions, I must do mankind that right, as to say, *there are not so many men in errors, and wrong opinions, as is commonly supposed.* Not that I think they embrace the truth; but indeed, because, concerning those doctrines they keep such a stir about, they have no thought, no opinion at all. For if anyone should a little catechize the greatest part of the partisans of most of the sects in the world, he would not find, concerning those matters they are so zealous for, that they have any opinions of their own: much less would he have reason to think, that they took them upon the examination of arguments, and appearance of probability. They are resolved to stick to a party, that education or interest has engaged them in; and there, like the common soldiers of an army, show their courage and warmth, as their leaders direct, without ever examining, or so much as knowing the cause they contend for. If a man's life shows, that he has no serious regard to religion; for what reason should we think, that he beats his head about the opinions of his church, and troubles himself to examine the grounds of this or that doctrine? 'Tis enough for him to obey his leaders, to have his hand and his tongue ready for the support of the common cause, and thereby approve himself to those, who can give him credit, preferment, or protection in that society. Thus men become professors of, and combatants for those opinions, they were never convinced of, nor proselytes to; no, nor ever had so much as floating in their heads:

and though one cannot say, there are fewer improbable or erroneous opinions in the world than there are; yet this is certain, there are fewer, that actually assent to them, and mistake them for truths, than is imagined.

CHAP. XXI.

Of the division of the sciences.

1. *Three sorts.* All that can fall within the compass of human understanding, being either, *first,* the nature of things, as they are in themselves, their relations, and their manner of operation: or, *secondly,* that which man himself ought to do, as a rational and voluntary agent, for the attainment of any end, especially happiness: or, *thirdly,* the ways and means, whereby the knowledge of both the one and the other of these, are attained and communicated: I think, *science* may be divided properly into these *three sorts.*

2. *First,* physica. *First,* the knowledge of things, as they are in their own proper beings, their constitutions, properties, and operations; whereby I mean not only matter, and body, but spirits also, which have their proper natures, constitutions, and operations as well as bodies. This in a little more enlarged sense of the word, I call φυσική, *or natural philosophy.*[59] The end of this, is bare speculative truth, and whatsoever can afford the mind of man any such, falls under this branch, whether it be God himself, angels, spirits, bodies, or any of their affections, as number, and figure, *&c.*

3. *Secondly,* practica. *Secondly,* πρακτική, the skill of right applying our own powers and actions, for the attainment of things good and useful.[60] The most considerable under this head, is *ethics,* which is the seeking out those rules, and measures of human actions, which lead to happiness, and the means to practice them. The end of this is not bare speculation, and the knowledge of truth; but right, and a conduct suitable to it.

4. *Thirdly,* σημειωτική. Thirdly, the third branch may be called σημειωτική, or *the doctrine of signs,* the most usual whereof being words, it is aptly enough termed also λογική, logic; the business whereof, is to consider the nature of signs, the mind makes use of for the understanding of things, or

59. φυσική, the science of the nature of things.

60. πρακτική, the science of practice.

conveying its knowledge to others.[61] For since the things, the mind contemplates are none of them, besides itself, present to the understanding, 'tis necessary that something else, as a sign or representation of the thing it considers, should be present to it: and these are *ideas.* And because the scene of *ideas* that makes one man's thoughts, cannot be laid open to the immediate view of another, nor laid up anywhere but in the memory, a no very sure repository: therefore to communicate our thoughts to one another, as well as record them for our own use, signs of our *ideas* are also necessary. Those which men have found most convenient, and therefore generally make use of, are articulate sounds. The consideration then of *ideas* and *words,* as the great instruments of knowledge, makes no despicable part of their contemplation, who would take a view of human knowledge in the whole extent of it. And, perhaps, if they were distinctly weighed, and duly considered, they would afford us another sort of logic and critic, than what we have been hitherto acquainted with.

5. *This is the first division of the objects of knowledge.* This seems to me *the first and most general, as well as natural division* of the objects of our understanding. For a man can employ his thoughts about nothing, but either the contemplation of *things* themselves for the discovery of truth; or about the things in his own power, which are his own *actions,* for the attainment of his own ends; or the *signs* the mind makes use of, both in the one and the other, and the right ordering of them for its clearer information. All which three, *viz. things* as they are in themselves knowable; *actions* as they depend on us, in order to happiness; and the right use of *signs* in order to knowledge, being *toto cælo* different, they seemed to me to be the three great provinces of the intellectual world, wholly separate and distinct one from another.[62]

61. σημειωτική, the science of signs; λογική, logic.

62. *toto cælo,* completely, "by the whole heavens."

The Stillingfleet Correspondence

In the concluding chapter of his *Discourse in Vindication of the Doctrine of the Trinity,* published in 1697, Edward Stillingfleet (1635–1699), who was then Bishop of Worcester, harshly criticized Locke's *Essay*. He cast Locke as a representative of a "new way of reasoning" (or, as he later called it, a "new way of ideas") that endangered Christian faith. Locke replied to Stillingfleet's criticisms in *A Letter to the Right Reverend Edward, Lord Bishop of Worcester* (1697). Stillingfleet responded with *The Bishop of Worcester's Answer to Mr. Locke's Letter* (1697). Locke then replied to Stillingfleet's answer (still in 1697), Stillingfleet answered Locke's reply (1698), and Locke ended the exchange with a reply to Stillingfleet's second answer (1699, the year of Stillingfleet's death). Though it is usually referred to as a "correspondence," the exchange between Locke and Stillingfleet was not a private correspondence but a public controversy, conducted in epistolary form.

Because they clarify some of the *Essay*'s main themes, long passages from Locke's side of the controversy were included in footnotes to the fifth (1706) edition of the *Essay*. What follows is a selection from those passages, arranged by topic, and supplemented, in some cases, by passages that were not included in the fifth edition. The text is based on volume 4 of the 1823 edition of Locke's works (for details, see the Bibliography). I have modernized the spelling and capitalization to conform to the present abridgment, and supplied bracketed references to the *Essay*.

ON THE "WAY OF IDEAS"

(i) My new way by ideas, or my way by ideas, which often occurs in your lordship's letter, is, I confess, a very large and doubtful expression; and may, in the full latitude, comprehend my whole essay: because treating in it of the understanding, which is nothing but the faculty of thinking, I could not well treat of that faculty of the mind, which consists in thinking, without considering the immediate objects of the mind in thinking, which I call ideas: and therefore in treating of the understanding, I guess it will not be thought strange, that the greatest part of my book has been taken up, in considering what these objects of the mind, in thinking, are; whence they come; what use the mind makes of them, in its several ways of thinking; and what are the outward marks whereby it signifies them to others, or records them for its own use. And this, in short, is my way by ideas, that which your lordship calls my new way by ideas: which, my lord, if it be new, it is but a new history of an old thing. For I think it will not be doubted, that men always performed the actions of thinking, reasoning, believing, and knowing, just after the same manner that they do now; though whether the same account has heretofore been given of the way how they performed these actions, or wherein they consisted, I do not know. Were I as well read as your lordship, I should have been safe from that gentle reprimand of your lordship's, for "thinking my way of ideas new, for want of looking into other men's thoughts, which appear in their books."[1]

(ii) All therefore that I can say of my book is, that it is a copy of my own mind, in its several ways of operation. And all that I can say for the publishing of it is, that I think the intellectual faculties are made, and operate alike in most men; and that some, that I showed it to before I published it, liked it so well that I was confirmed in that opinion. And therefore if it should happen, that it should not be so, but that some men should have ways of thinking, reasoning, or arriving at certainty, different from others, and above those that I find my mind to use and acquiesce in, I do not see of what use my book can be to them. I can only make it my humble request, in my own name, and in the name of those that are of my size, who find their minds work, reason, and know, in the same low way that mine does, that those men of a more happy genius would show us the way of their nobler flights; and particularly would discover to us their shorter or surer way to certainty, than by ideas, and the observing their agreement or disagreement.[2]

(iii) But you will say, that Descartes built his system of philosophy upon ideas; and so I say does your lordship too, and everyone else as much as he, that has any system of that or any other part of knowledge. For ideas are nothing but the immediate objects of our minds in thinking; and your lordship, I conclude, in building your system of any part of knowledge thinks on something: and therefore you can no more build, or have any system of knowledge without ideas, than you can think without some immediate objects of thinking. Indeed, you do not so often use the word ideas as Descartes or I have done; but using the things signified by that

1. *Works,* volume 4, pp. 134–35. This passage appeared in the fifth edition of the *Essay,* in a footnote to I i 8.

2. *Works,* volume 4, p. 139. This passage appeared in the fifth edition of the *Essay,* in a footnote to I i 8.

term as much as either of us (unless you can think without an immediate object of thinking) yours also is the way of ideas, as much as his or mine. Your condemning the way of ideas, in those general terms, which one meets with so often in your writings on this occasion, amounts at last to no more but an exception against a poor sound of three syllables, though your lordship thinks fit not to own, that you have any exception to it.[3]

(iv) Your lordship adds, "but now, it seems, nothing is intelligible but what suits with the new way of ideas." My lord, the new way of ideas, and the old way of speaking intelligibly, was always, and ever will be the same. And if I may take the liberty to declare my sense of it, herein it consists: (1.) That a man use no words but such as he makes the signs of certain determined objects of his mind in thinking, which he can make known to another. (2.) Next, that he use the same word steadily for the sign of the same immediate object of his mind in thinking. (3.) That he join those words together in propositions, according to the grammatical rules of that language he speaks in. (4.) That he unite those sentences in a coherent discourse. Thus, and thus only, I humbly conceive, anyone may preserve himself from the confines and suspicion of jargon, whether he pleases to call those immediate objects of his mind, which his words do or should stand for, ideas or no.[4]

SUBSTANCE AND THE IDEA OF SUBSTANCE

(i) These words of mine your lordship brings to prove, that I am one of "the gentlemen of this new way of reasoning, that have almost discarded substance out of the reasonable part of the world." An accusation which your lordship will pardon me, if I do not readily know what to plead to, because I do not understand what is "almost to discard substance out of the reasonable part of the world." If your lordship means by it, that I deny or doubt that there is in the world any such thing as substance, that your lordship will acquit me of, when your lordship looks again into that chapter [II xxiii], which you have cited more than once. . . .[5]

(ii) "Our idea of body, I say, is an extended, solid substance; and our idea of our souls is of a substance that thinks" [a paraphrase of II xxiii 22]. So that

3. *Works,* volume 4, p. 362. This passage was not included in the fifth edition of the *Essay.*

4. *Works,* volume 4, p. 430. This passage appeared in the fifth edition of the *Essay,* in a footnote to I i 8.

5. *Works,* volume 4, pp. 5–6. All but the first sentence of this passage was included in the fifth edition of the *Essay,* in a footnote to II xxiii 2.

as long as there is any such thing as body or spirit in the world, I have done nothing towards the discarding substance out of the reasonable part of the world. Nay, as long as there is any simple idea or sensible quality left, according to my way of arguing, substance cannot be discarded; because all simple ideas, all sensible qualities, carry with them a supposition of a substratum to exist in, and of a substance wherein they inhere: and of this that whole chapter is so full, that I challenge anyone who reads it to think I have almost, or one jot discarded substance out of the reasonable part of the world. And of this, man, horse, sun, water, iron, diamond, &c. which I have mentioned of distinct sorts of substances, will be my witnesses as long as any such thing remains in being; of which I say, "that the *ideas* of *substances* are such combinations of simple *ideas,* as are taken to represent distinct particular things subsisting by themselves; in which the supposed, or confused *idea* of substance . . . is always the first and chief" [II xii 6].

If by almost discarding substance out of the reasonable part of the world your lordship means, that I have destroyed, and almost discarded the true idea we have of it, by calling it "a substratum, a supposition of we know not what support of such qualities as are capable of producing simple ideas in us; an obscure and relative idea: that without knowing what it is, it is that which supports accidents; so that of substance we have no idea of what it is, but only a confused and obscure one, of what it does" [see II xxiii 1, 2, 3]; I must confess this, and the like I have said of our idea of substance; and should be very glad to be convinced by your lordship, or anybody else, that I have spoken too meanly of it. He that would show me a more clear and distinct idea of substance, would do me a kindness I should thank him for. But this is the best I can hitherto find, either in my own thoughts, or in the books of logicians: for their account or idea of it is, that it is "Ens," or "res per se subsistens et substans accidentibus;" which in effect is no more, but that substance is a being or thing; or, in short, something they know not what, or of which they have no clearer idea, than that it is something which supports accidents, or other simple ideas or modes, and is not supported itself as a mode or an accident.[6]

(iii) Your lordship seems to charge me with two faults: one, that I make "the general idea of substance to be framed, not by abstracting and enlarging simple ideas, but by a complication of many simple ideas together:" the

6. *Works,* volume 4, pp. 7–8. This passage appeared in the fifth edition of the *Essay,* in a footnote to II xxiii 2.

other, as if I had said, the being of substance had no other foundation but the fancies of men.

As to the first of these, I beg leave to remind your lordship, that I say in more places than one, and particularly those above quoted, where . . . I treat of abstraction and general ideas, that they are all made by abstracting; and therefore could not be understood to mean, that that of substance was made any other way; however my pen might have slipped, or the negligence of expression, where I might have something else than the general idea of substance in view, make me seem to say so.

Speaking . . . of the ideas of distinct substances, such as man, horse, gold &c. I say they are made up of certain combinations of simple ideas; which combinations are looked upon, each of them, as one simple idea, though they are many; and we call it by one name of substance, though made up of modes, from the custom of supposing a substratum, wherein that combination does subsist. . . .

But that my notion of substance in general is quite different from these, and has no such combination of simple ideas in it, is evident from the immediately following words, where I say; "the idea of pure substance in general is only a supposition of we know not what support of such qualities as are capable of producing simple ideas in us" [see II xxiii 2]. And these two I plainly distinguish all along, particularly where I say, "whatever therefore be the secret and abstract nature of substance in general, all the ideas we have of particular distinct substances are nothing but several combinations of simple ideas, coexisting in such, though unknown, cause of their union, as makes the whole subsist of itself" [see II xxiii 6].

The other thing laid to my charge, is as if I took the being of substance to be doubtful, or rendered it so by the imperfect and ill-grounded idea I have given of it. To which I beg leave to say, that I ground not the being, but the idea of substance, on our accustoming ourselves to suppose some substratum; for it is of the idea alone I speak there, and not of the being of substance. And having everywhere affirmed and built upon it, that a man is a substance; I cannot be supposed to question or doubt of the being of substance, till I can question or doubt of my own being. Further I say, "that sensation convinces us that there are solid extended substances; and reflection, that there are thinking ones." So that I think the being of substance is not shaken by what I have said: and if the idea of it should be, yet (the being of things depending not on our ideas) the being of substance would not be at all shaken by my saying, we had but an obscure imperfect idea of it, and that that idea came from our accustoming ourselves to suppose some substratum; or indeed, if I should say, we had no idea of substance at all. For a great many things may be and are granted to have a being, and be in nature, of which we have no ideas. For example; it cannot be doubted but there are distinct species of separate spirits, of which we have no distinct ideas at all: it cannot be questioned but spirits have ways of communicating their thoughts, and yet we have no idea of it at all.

The being then of substance being safe and secure, notwithstanding anything I have said, let us see whether the idea of it be not so too. Your lordship asks, with concern, "and is this all indeed that is to be said for the being" (if your lordship please, let it be the idea) "of substance, that we accustom ourselves to suppose a substratum? Is that custom grounded upon true reason, or no?" I have said, that it is grounded upon this, "that we cannot conceive how simple ideas of sensible qualities should subsist alone, and therefore we suppose them to exist in, and to be supported by, some common subject, which support we denote by the name substance" [see II xxiii 4]. Which I think is a true reason, because it is the same your lordship grounds the supposition of a substratum on, in this very page; even on "repugnancy to our conceptions, that modes and accidents should subsist by themselves." So that I have the good luck here again to agree with your lordship: and consequently conclude, I have your approbation in this, that the substratum to modes or accidents, which is our idea of substance in general, is founded in this, "that we cannot conceive how modes or accidents can subsist by themselves."[7]

(iv) All the ideas of all the sensible qualities of a cherry come into my mind by sensation; the ideas of perceiving, thinking, reasoning, knowing, &c. come into my mind by reflection: the ideas of these qualities and actions, or powers, are perceived by the mind to be by themselves inconsistent with existence; or, as your lordship well expresses it, "we find that we can have no true conception of any modes or accidents, but we must conceive a substratum or subject, wherein they are;" *i.e.* that they cannot exist or subsist of themselves. Hence the mind perceives their necessary connexion with inherence or being supported; which being a relative idea superadded to the red color in a cherry, or to thinking in a man, the mind frames the correlative idea of a support. For I never denied, that the mind could frame to itself ideas of relation, but have showed the quite contrary in my chapters about relation. But because a relation cannot be founded in nothing, or be the relation of nothing, and the thing here related as a supporter or support

7. *Works,* volume 4, pp. 16, 17–19. This passage was included in the fifth edition of the *Essay,* in a footnote to II xxiii 2.

is not represented to the mind by any clear and distinct idea; therefore the obscure, indistinct, vague idea of thing or something, is all that is left to be the positive idea, which has the relation of a support or substratum to modes or accidents; and that general indetermined idea of something, is, by the abstraction of the mind, derived also from the simple ideas of sensation and reflection: and thus the mind, from the positive, simple ideas got by sensation or reflection, comes to the general relative idea of substance; which, without the positive simple ideas, it would never have.[8]

ESSENCES, UNIVERSALS, AND GENERAL TERMS

(i) Here I must acknowledge to your lordship, that my notion of these essences differs a little from your lordship's; for I do not take them to flow from the substance in any created being, but to be in everything that internal constitution, or frame, or modification of the substance, which God in his wisdom and good pleasure thinks fit to give to every particular creature, when he gives it being: and such essences I grant there are in all things that exist.[9]

(ii) I think the real essences of things are not so much founded on, as that they are the very real constitution of things, and therefore I easily grant there is reality in them; and it was from that reality that I called them real essences.[10]

(iii) Your lordship farther adds, "And these real essences are unchangeable, *i.e.* the internal constitutions are unchangeable." Of what, I beseech your lordship, are the internal constitutions unchangeable? Not of anything that exists, but of God alone; for they may be changed all as easily by that hand that made them, as the internal frame of a watch. What then is it that is unchangeable? The internal constitution or real essence of a species: which, in plain English, is no more but this, whilst the same specific name, *v.g.* of man, horse, or tree, is annexed to, or made the sign of the same abstract, complex idea, under which I rank several individuals, it is impossible but the real constitution on which that unaltered complex idea, or nominal essence, depends, must be the same: *i.e.* in other words, where we

8. *Works,* volume 4, pp. 21–22. This passage was included in the fifth edition of the *Essay,* in a footnote to II ii 2.

9. *Works,* volume 4, p. 82. This passage was not included in the fifth edition of the *Essay.*

10. *Works,* volume 4, p. 83. This passage was not included in the fifth edition of the *Essay.*

find all the same properties, we have reason to conclude there is the same real, internal constitution, from which those properties flow.[11]

(iv) It is true, the real constitutions or essences of particular things existing, do not depend on the ideas of men, but on the will of the creator; but their being ranked into sorts, under such and such names, does depend, and wholly depend, upon the ideas of men.[12]

(v) There is an internal constitution of things, on which their properties depend. This your lordship and I are agreed of, and this we call the real essence. There are also certain complex ideas, or combinations of these properties in men's minds, to which they commonly annex specific names, or names of sorts or kinds of things. This, I believe, your lordship does not deny. These complex ideas, for want of a better name, I have called nominal essences; how properly, I will not dispute. But if anyone will help me to a better name for them, I am ready to receive it; till then I must, to express myself, use this. Now, my lord, body, life, and the power of reasoning, being not the real essence of a man, as I believe your lordship will agree: will your lordship say, that they are not enough to make the thing wherein they are found of the kind called man, and not of the kind called baboon, because the difference of these kinds is real? If this be not real enough to make the thing of one kind and not of another, I do not see how *animal rationale* can be enough to distinguish a man from a horse: for that is but the nominal, not real essence of that kind, designed by the name man. And yet, I suppose, everyone thinks it real enough, to make a real difference between that and other kinds. And if nothing will serve the turn, to make things of one kind and not of another (which, as I have showed, signifies no more but ranking of them under different specific names) but their real, unknown constitutions, which are the real essences we are speaking of, I fear it would be a long while before we should have really different kinds of substances, or distinct names for them; unless we could distinguish them by these differences, of which we have no distinct conceptions. For I think it would not be readily answered me, if I should demand, wherein lies the real difference in the internal constitution of a stag from that of a buck, which are each of them very well known to

11. *Works,* volume 4, pp. 90–91. This passage appeared in the fifth edition of the *Essay,* in a footnote to III iii 11.

12. *Works,* volume 4, p. 91. This passage appeared in the fifth edition of the *Essay,* in a footnote to III iii 11.

be of one kind, and not of the other; and nobody questions but that the kinds whereof each of them is, are really different.[13]

(vi) The difficulty to me is, to conceive an universal nature, or universal anything, to exist; which would be, in my mind, to make an universal a particular: which, to me, is impossible.[14]

(vii) General terms (as nature and person are in their ordinary use in our language) are the signs of general ideas, and general ideas exist only in the mind; but particular things (which are the foundations of these general ideas, if they are abstracted as they should be) do, or may exist conformable to those general ideas, and so fall under those general names; as he that writes this paper is a person to him, *i.e.* may be denominated a person by him to whose abstract idea of person he bears a conformity; just as what I here write is to him a book or a letter, to whose abstract idea of a book or a letter it agrees.[15]

THINKING MATTER

(i) Your lordship argues, that upon my principles it "cannot be proved that there is a spiritual substance in us." To which give me leave, with submission, to say, that I think it may be proved from my principles, and I think I have done it; and the proof in my book stands thus: first, we experiment in ourselves thinking. The idea of this action or mode of thinking is inconsistent with the idea of self-subsistence, and therefore has a necessary connection with a support or subject of inhesion: the idea of that support is what we call substance; and so from thinking experimented in us, we have a proof of a thinking substance in us, which in my sense is a spirit. Against this your lordship will argue, that by what I have said of the possibility that God may, if he pleases, superadd to matter a faculty of thinking, it can never be proved that there is a spiritual substance in us, because upon that supposition it is possible it may be a material substance that thinks in us. I grant it; but add, that the general idea of substance being the same everywhere, the modification of thinking, or the power of thinking joined to it, makes it a spirit, without considering what other modifications it has,

13. *Works,* volume 4, pp. 87–88. This passage was included in the fifth edition of the *Essay,* in a footnote to III iii 11.

14. *Works,* volume 4, p. 166. This passage was not included in the fifth edition of the *Essay.*

15. *Works,* volume 4, p. 336. This passage was not included in the fifth edition of the *Essay.*

as whether it has the modification of solidity or no. As on the other side, substance, that has the modification of solidity, is matter, whether it has the modification of thinking or no. And therefore, if your lordship means by a spiritual an immaterial substance, I grant I have not proved, nor upon my principles can it be proved, (your lordship meaning, as I think you do, demonstratively proved) that there is an immaterial substance in us that thinks. Though I presume, from what I have said about the supposition of a system of matter thinking [IV x 16] (which there demonstrates that God is immaterial) will prove it in the highest degree probable, that the thinking substance in us is immaterial. But your lordship thinks not probability enough; and by charging the want of demonstration upon my principles, that the thinking thing in us is immaterial, your lordship seems to conclude it demonstrable from principles of philosophy. That demonstration I should with joy receive from your lordship, or anyone. For though all the great ends of morality and religion are well enough secured without it, as I have shown [IV iii 6]; yet it would be a great advance of our knowledge in nature and philosophy.[16]

(ii) Your first argument I take to be this, that, according to me, the knowledge we have being by our ideas, and our idea of matter in general being a solid substance, and our idea of body a solid extended figured substance; if I admit matter to be capable of thinking, I confound the idea of matter with the idea of a spirit: to which I answer, no; no more than I confound the idea of matter with the idea of a horse, when I say that matter in general is a solid extended substance; and that a horse is a material animal, or an extended solid substance with sense and spontaneous motion.

The idea of matter is an extended solid substance; wherever there is such a substance, there is matter, and the essence of matter, whatever other qualities, not contained in that essence, it shall please God to superadd to it. For example, God creates an extended solid substance, without the superadding anything else to it, and so we may consider it at rest: to some parts of it he superadds motion, but it has still the essence of matter: other parts of it he frames into plants, with all the excellencies of vegetation, life, and beauty, which are to be found in a rose or a peach-tree, &c. above the essence of matter in general, but it is still but matter: to other parts he adds sense and spontaneous motion, and those other properties that are to be found in an elephant. Hitherto it is not doubted but the power of God may

16. *Works*, volume 4, pp. 32–33. This passage was included in the fifth edition of the *Essay*, in a footnote to IV iii 6.

go, and that the properties of a rose, a peach, or an elephant, superadded to matter, change not the properties of matter; but matter is in these things matter still. But if one venture to go on one step further, and say, God may give to matter thought, reason, and volition, as well as sense and spontaneous motion, there are men ready presently to limit the power of the omnipotent creator, and tell us he cannot do it; because it destroys the essence, "changes the essential properties of matter." To make good which assertion, they have no more to say, but that thought and reason are not included in the essence of matter. I grant it; but whatever excellency, not contained in its essence, be superadded to matter, it does not destroy the essence of matter, if it leaves it an extended solid substance; wherever that is, there is the essence of matter: and if everything of greater perfection, superadded to such a substance, destroys the essence of matter, what will become of the essence of matter in a plant, or an animal, whose properties far exceed those of a mere extended solid substance?

But it is farther urged, that we cannot conceive how matter can think. I grant it; but to argue from thence, that God therefore cannot give to matter a faculty of thinking, is to say God's omnipotency is limited to a narrow compass, because man's understanding is so; and brings down God's infinite power to the size of our capacities. If God can give no power to any parts of matter, but what men can account for from the essence of matter in general; if all such qualities and properties must destroy the essence, or change the essential properties of matter, which are to our conceptions above it, and we cannot conceive to be the natural consequence of that essence: it is plain, that the essence of matter is destroyed, and its essential properties changed in most of the sensible parts of this our system. For it is visible, that all the planets have revolutions about certain remote centers, which I would have anyone explain, or make conceivable by the bare essence or natural powers depending on the essence of matter in general, without something added to that essence, which we cannot conceive: for the moving of matter in a crooked line, or the attraction of matter by matter, is all that can be said in the case; either of which it is above our reach to derive from the essence of matter, or body in general; though one of these two must unavoidably be allowed to be superadded in this instance to the essence of matter in general. The omnipotent creator advised not with us in the making of the world, and his ways are not the less excellent, because they are past our finding out.

In the next place, the vegetable part of the creation is not doubted to be wholly material; and yet he that will look into it, will observe excellencies and operations in this part of matter, which he will not find contained in the essence of matter in general, nor be able to conceive how they can be produced by it. And will he therefore say, that the essence of matter is destroyed in them, because they have properties and operations not contained in the essential properties of matter as matter, nor explicable by the essence of matter in general?

Let us advance one step farther, and we shall, in the animal world, meet with yet greater perfections and properties, no ways explicable by the essence of matter in general. If the omnipotent creator had not superadded to the earth, which produced the irrational animals, qualities far surpassing those of the dull dead earth, out of which they were made, life, sense, and spontaneous motion, nobler qualities than were before in it, it had still remained rude senseless matter; and if to the individuals of each species he had not superadded a power of propagation, the species had perished with those individuals: but by these essences or properties of each species, superadded to the matter which they were made of, the essence or properties of matter in general were not destroyed or changed, any more than anything that was in the individuals before was destroyed or changed by the power of generation, superadded to them by the first benediction of the almighty.

In all such cases, the superinducement of greater perfections and nobler qualities destroys nothing of the essence or perfections that were there before, unless there can be showed a manifest repugnancy between them; but all the proof offered for that, is only, that we cannot conceive how matter, without such superadded perfections, can produce such effects; which is, in truth, no more than to say, matter in general, or every part of matter, as matter, has them not; but is no reason to prove that God, if he pleases, cannot superadd them to some parts of matter: unless it can be proved to be a contradiction, that God should give to some parts of matter qualities and perfections, which matter in general has not; though we cannot conceive how matter is invested with them, or how it operates by virtue of those new endowments. Nor is it to be wondered that we cannot, whilst we limit all its operations to those qualities it had before, and would explain them by the known properties of matter in general, without any such superinduced perfections. For if this be a right rule of reasoning to deny a thing to be, because we cannot conceive the manner how it comes to be; I shall desire them who use it to stick to this rule, and see what work it will make both in divinity as well as philosophy; and whether they can advance anything more in favor of skepticism.

For to keep within the present subject of the power of thinking and self-motion, bestowed by omnipotent power on some parts of matter: the objection to this is, I cannot conceive how matter should think. What is the consequence? *ergo,* God cannot give it a power to think. Let this stand for a good reason, and then proceed in other cases by the same. You cannot conceive how matter can attract matter at any distance, much less at the distance of 1,000,000 miles; *ergo,* God cannot give it such a power. You cannot conceive how matter should feel or move itself, or affect an immaterial being, or be moved by it; *ergo,* God cannot give it such powers: which is in effect to deny gravity and the revolution of the planets about the sun; to make brutes mere machines, without sense or spontaneous motion; and to allow man neither sense nor voluntary motion.

Let us apply this rule one degree farther. You cannot conceive how an extended solid substance should think, therefore God cannot make it think: can you conceive how your own soul, or any substance thinks? You find indeed, that you do think, and so do I; but I want to be told how the action of thinking is performed: this, I confess, is beyond my conception; and I would be glad anyone, who conceives it, would explain it to me. God, I find, has given me this faculty; and since I cannot but be convinced of his power in this instance, which though I every moment experiment in myself, yet I cannot conceive the manner of; what would it be less than an insolent absurdity to deny his power in other like cases only for this reason, because I cannot conceive the manner how?

To explain this matter a little farther: God has created a substance; let it be, for example, a solid extended substance: is God bound to give it, besides being, a power of action? that, I think, nobody will say. He therefore may leave it in a state of inactivity, and it will be nevertheless a substance; for action is not necessary to the being of any substance, that God does create. God has likewise created and made to exist, *de novo,* an immaterial substance, which will not lose its being of a substance, though God should bestow on it nothing more but this bare being, without giving it any activity at all. Here are now two distinct substances, the one material, the other immaterial, both in a state of perfect inactivity. Now I ask what power God can give to one of these substances (supposing them to retain the same distinct natures, that they had as substances in their state of inactivity) which he cannot give to the other? In that state, it is plain, neither of them thinks; for thinking being an action, it cannot be denied that God can put an end to any action of any created substance, without annihilating of the substance whereof it is an action: and if it be so, he can also create or give existence to such a substance, without giving that substance any action at all. Now I would ask, why omnipotency cannot give to either of these substances, which are equally in a state of perfect inactivity, the same power that it can give to the other? Let it be, for example, that of spontaneous or self-motion, which is a power that it is supposed God can give to an unsolid substance, but denied that he can give to a solid substance.

If it be asked, why they limit the omnipotency of God, in reference to the one rather than the other of these substances; all that can be said to it is, that they cannot conceive how the solid substance should ever be able to move itself. And as little, say I, are they able to conceive how a created unsolid substance should move itself; but there may be something in an immaterial substance, that you do not know. I grant it; and in a material one too: for example, gravitation of matter towards matter, and in the several proportions observable, inevitably shows, that there is something in matter that we do not understand, unless we can conceive self-motion in matter; or an inexplicable and inconceivable attraction in matter, at immense and almost incomprehensible distances: it must therefore be confessed, that there is something in solid, as well as unsolid substances, that we do not understand. But this we know, that they may each of them have their distinct beings, without any activity superadded to them, unless you will deny, that God can take from any being its power of acting, which it is probable will be thought too presumptuous for anyone to do; and, I say, it is as hard to conceive self-motion in a created immaterial, as in a material being, consider it how you will: and therefore this is no reason to deny omnipotency to be able to give a power of self-motion to a material substance, if he pleases, as well as to an immaterial; since neither of them can have it from themselves, nor can we conceive how it can be in either of them. . . .

As to self-consciousness, your lordship asks, "what is there like self-consciousness in matter?" Nothing at all in matter as matter. But that God cannot bestow on some parcels of matter a power of thinking, and with it self-consciousness, will never be proved by asking, "how is it possible to apprehend that mere body should perceive that it does perceive?" The weakness of our apprehension I grant in the case: I confess as much as you please, that we cannot conceive how a solid, no nor how an unsolid created substance thinks; but this weakness of our apprehensions reaches not the power of God, whose weakness is stronger than anything in man.[17]

(iii) Your argument from abstraction we have in this question, "if it may be in the power of matter to think, how comes it to be so impossible for such

17. *Works,* volume 4, pp. 460–65, 468. This passage was included in the fifth edition of the *Essay,* in a footnote to IV iii 6.

organized bodies as the brutes have to enlarge their ideas by abstraction?" Answ. This seems to suppose, that I place thinking with in the natural power of matter. If that be your meaning, my lord, I neither say, nor suppose, that all matter has naturally in it a faculty of thinking, but the direct contrary. But if you mean that certain parcels of matter, ordered by the divine power, as seems fit to him, may be made capable of receiving from his omnipotency the faculty of thinking; that indeed I say, and that being granted, the answer to your question is easy, since if omnipotency can give thought to any solid substance, it is not hard to conceive, that God may give that faculty in an higher or lower degree, as it pleases him, who knows what disposition of the subject is suited to such a particular way or degree of thinking.

Another argument to prove, that God cannot endue any parcel of matter with the faculty of thinking, is taken from those words of mine, where I show by what connection of ideas we may come to know, that God is an immaterial substance. They are these: "the idea of an eternal, actual knowing being, with the idea of immateriality, by the intervention of the idea of matter, and of its actual division, divisibility, and want of perception," &c. From whence your lordship thus argues: "here the want of perception is owned to be so essential to matter, that God is therefore concluded to be immaterial." Answ. Perception and knowledge in that one eternal being, where it has its source, it is visible, must be essentially inseparable from it; therefore the actual want of perception in so great part of the particular parcels of matter, is a demonstration, that the first being, from whom perception and knowledge is inseparable, is not matter. How far this makes the want of perception an essential property of matter, I will not dispute; it suffices that it shows, that perception is not an essential property of matter; and therefore matter cannot be that eternal original being, to which perception and knowledge is essential. Matter, I say, naturally is without perception; *ergo,* says your lordship, "want of perception is an essential property of matter, and God does not change the essential properties of things, their nature remaining." From whence you infer, that God cannot bestow on any parcel of matter (the nature of matter remaining) a faculty of thinking. If the rules of logic, since my days, be not changed, I may safely deny this consequence. For an argument that runs thus, "God does not, *ergo,* he cannot;" I was taught, when I came first to the university, would not hold. For I never said God did; but "that I see no contradiction in it, that he should, if he pleased, give to some systems of senseless matter a faculty of thinking:" [see IV iii 6] and I know nobody, before Descartes, that ever pretended to show that there was any contradiction in it. So that, at worst, my not being able to see in matter any such incapacity as makes it impossible for omnipotency to bestow on it a faculty of thinking, makes me opposite only to the Cartesians. For, as far as I have seen or heard, the fathers of the Christian church never pretended to demonstrate that matter was incapable to receive a power of sensation, perception, and thinking, from the hand of the omnipotent creator. Let us therefore, if you please, suppose the form of your argumentation right, and that your lordship means, God cannot: and then if your argument be good, it proves, that God could not give to Balaam's ass a power to speak to his master as he did; for the want of rational discourse being natural to that species, it is but for your lordship to call it an essential property, and then God cannot change the essential properties of things, their nature remaining: whereby it is proved, that God cannot, with all his omnipotency, give to an ass a power to speak as Balaam's did.[18]

GRAVITY AND IMPULSE

(i) What I have . . . said I take to be a full answer to all that your lordship would infer from my idea of matter, of liberty, and of identity, and from the power of abstracting. You ask, "how can my way of liberty agree with the idea that bodies can operate only by motion and impulse?" Answ. By the omnipotency of God, who can make all things agree, that involve not a contradiction. It is true, I say, "that bodies operate by impulse, and nothing else" [II viii 11, in the first three editions]. And so I thought when I writ it, and can yet conceive no other way of their operation. But I am since convinced by the judicious Mr. Newton's incomparable book, that it is too bold a presumption to limit God's power, in this point, by my narrow conceptions. The gravitation of matter towards matter, by ways inconceivable to me, is not only a demonstration that God can, if he pleases, put into bodies powers and ways of operation above what can be derived from our idea of body, or can be explained by what we know of matter, but also an unquestionable and everywhere visible instance, that he has done so. And therefore in the next edition of my book I shall take care to have that passage rectified.[19]

18. *Works*, volume 4, pp. 468–70. This passage was included in the fifth edition of the *Essay*, in a footnote to IV iii 6.

19. *Works*, volume 4, pp. 467–68. This passage was included in the fifth edition of the *Essay*, in a footnote to IV iii 6.

KNOWLEDGE AND FAITH

(i) My lord, your lordship has been pleased to find fault with my use of the new term, ideas, without telling me a better name for the immediate objects of the mind in thinking. Your lordship has also been pleased to find fault with my definition of knowledge, without doing me the favour to give me a better. For it is only about my definition of knowledge, that all this stir, concerning certainty, is made. For with me, to know, and be certain, is the same thing; what I know, that I am certain of; and what I am certain of, that I know. What reaches to knowledge, I think may be called certainty; and what comes short of certainty, I think cannot be called knowledge; as your lordship could not but observe in § 18. of c. iv. of my fourth book, which you have quoted.

My definition of knowledge, in the beginning of the fourth book of my essay, stands thus: "knowledge seems to me to be nothing but the perception of the connexion and agreement or disagreement and repugnancy of any of our ideas" [IV i 2]. This definition your lordship dislikes, and apprehends "it may be of dangerous consequence as to that article of christian faith which your lordship has endeavoured to defend." For this there is a very easy remedy: it is but for your lordship to set aside this definition of knowledge by giving us a better, and this danger is over. But your lordship chooses rather to have a controversy with my book, for having it in it, and to put me upon the defense of it.[20]

(ii) Faith stands by itself, and upon grounds of its own; nor can be removed from them, and placed on those of knowledge. Their grounds are so far from being the same, or having anything common, that when it is brought to certainty, faith is destroyed; it is knowledge then, and faith no longer.

With what assurance soever of believing, I assent to any article of faith, so that I steadfastly venture my all upon it, it is still but believing. Bring it to certainty, and it ceases to be faith. I believe, that Jesus Christ was crucified, dead and buried, rose again the third day from the dead, and ascended into heaven; let now such methods of knowledge or certainty be started, as leave men's minds more doubtful than before: let the grounds of knowledge be resolved into what anyone pleases, it touches not my faith: the foundation of that stands as sure as before, and cannot be at all shaken by it: and one may as well say, that anything that weakens the sight, or casts a mist before the eyes, endangers the hearing; as that anything which alters the nature of

20. *Works,* volume 4, p. 145. This passage was included in the fifth edition of the *Essay,* in a footnote to IV i 2.

knowledge (if that could be done) should be of dangerous consequence to an article of faith.

Whether then I am or am not mistaken, in the placing certainty in the perception of the agreement or disagreement of ideas; whether this account of knowledge be true or false, enlarges or straitens the bounds of it more than it should; faith still stands upon its own basis, which is not at all altered by it; and every article of that has just the same unmoved foundation, and the very same credibility that it had before. So that, my lord, whatever I have said about certainty, and how much soever I may be out in it; if I am mistaken, your lordship has no reason to apprehend any danger to any article of faith from thence; every one of them stands upon the same bottom it did before, out of the reach of what belongs to knowledge and certainty. And thus much out of my way of certainty by ideas; which, I hope, will satisfy your lordship, how far it is from being dangerous to any article of the Christian faith whatsoever.[21]

RESURRECTION

(i) But, my lord, before we go any farther, I crave leave humbly to represent to your lordship, that I thought you undertook to make out that my notion of ideas was inconsistent with the articles of the Christian faith. But that which your lordship instances in here, is not, that I yet know, any article of the Christian faith. The resurrection of the dead I acknowledge to be an article of the Christian faith: but that the resurrection of the same body, in your lordship's sense of the same body, is an article of the Christian faith, is what, I confess, I do not yet know.

In the New Testament (wherein, I think, are contained all the articles of the Christian faith) I find our Savior and the apostles to preach the resurrection of the dead, and the resurrection from the dead, in many places: but I do not remember any place, where the resurrection of the same body is so much as mentioned. Nay, which is very remarkable in the case, I do not remember in any place of the New Testament (where the general resurrection at the last day is spoken of) any such expression as the resurrection of the body, much less of the same body.[22]

21. *Works,* volume 4, pp. 146–47. This passage was included in the fifth edition of the *Essay,* in a footnote to IV i 2.

22. *Works,* volume 4, pp. 303–4. This passage was included in the fifth edition of the *Essay,* in a footnote to II xxvii 29.

(ii) Give me leave to say, my lord, that whatsoever is not necessary, does not thereby become inconsistent. It is not necessary to the same person, that his body should always consist of the same numerical particles; this is demonstration, because the particles of the bodies of the same persons in this life change every moment, and your lordship cannot deny it; and yet this makes it not inconsistent with God's preserving, if he thinks fit, to the same persons, bodies consisting of the same numerical particles, always from the resurrection to eternity. And so likewise, though I say anything that supposes it not necessary, that the same numerical particles, which were vitally united to the soul in his life, should be reunited to it at the resurrection, and constitute the body it shall then have; yet it is not inconsistent with this, that God may, if he pleases, give to everyone a body consisting only of such particles as were before vitally united to his soul. And thus, I think, I have cleared my book from all that inconsistency which your lordship charges on it, and would persuade the world it has with the article of the resurrection of the dead.[23]

(iii) I must not part with this article of the resurrection without returning my thanks to your lordship for making me take notice of a fault in my essay. When I writ that book, I took it for granted, as I doubt not but many others have done, that the Scripture had mentioned in express terms, "the resurrection of the body:" but upon the occasion your lordship has given me in your last letter to look a little more narrowly into what revelation has declared concerning the resurrection, and finding no such express words in the Scripture, as that "the body shall rise or be raised, or the resurrection of the body;" I shall in the next edition of it change these words of my book, "the dead bodies of men shall rise," into these of the Scripture, "the dead shall rise" [IV xviii 7, but see also IV xvii 23]. Not that I question, that the dead shall be raised with bodies: but in matters of revelation, I think it not only safest, but our duty, as far as any one delivers it for revelation, to keep close to the words of the Scripture; unless he will assume to himself the authority of one inspired, or make himself wiser than the Holy Spirit himself: if I had spoken of the resurrection in precisely Scripture terms, I had avoided giving your lordship the occasion of making here such a verbal reflection on my words; "What, not if there be an idea of identity as to the body?"[24]

23. *Works,* volume 4, pp. 332–33. This passage was included in the fifth edition of the *Essay,* in a footnote to II xxvii 29.

24. *Works,* volume 4, pp. 333–34. This passage was included in the fifth edition of the *Essay,* in a footnote to II xxvii 29.

Glossary

This glossary includes obsolete words, words used in archaic or unfamiliar senses, and Latin expressions not explained in the notes. It is based on the second edition of the *Oxford English Dictionary*.

abstruse	remote from apprehension or comprehension, recondite
acceptation	received meaning
accident	attribute, especially a non-essential one
adamant	a body of surpassing hardness
adventitious	(of an idea) derived from experience
adventures	*at all adventures*: at random, anyhow
æther	ether, the thinnest or most subtle form of matter
affection	attribute, state or mode of being
agreement	point of likeness
amour	love affair
amusement	distraction, diversion
animal spirits	volatile bodies inhabiting the nerves and blood vessels
antimony	a brittle metallic substance, bright bluish white in color
aqua fortis	"strong water," dilute nitric acid, a powerful solvent and corrosive
aqua regia	"royal water," a mixture of nitric and hydrochloric acid, able to dissolve gold
aright	rightly, justly, correctly
atom	indivisible body
barely	only, only just, not quite, hardly
bating	excepting, leaving out of account
beholden to	obliged to
bethink	think about, consider
betwixt	between, among
billet	piece of wood used for fuel
by the by	in passing
calcine	(of lime) reduce by roasting or burning
candid	free from bias, fair, impartial
caprichio	caprice, prank

catechize	examine orally and systematically
changeling	child left by fairies in exchange for another, a half-witted person
cherubim	angel
circumambient	surrounding
communication	sharing, transferring
compass	bounds, range, reach, scope
concernment	concern, importance, weight
consequent	resulting, logically coherent
consistent	(as in *hard and consistent*) firm
corporeal	bodily, material
corpuscle	particle of matter
cousin-germain	first cousin
crave	beg, ask
critic	art or action of criticism, critique
cross and pile	coin (tossed heads or tails)
cumbered	obstructed, blocked, encumbered
cups	alcoholic drink, state of intoxication
deduce	trace the course of
denominate	name, constitute
diadrom	vibration of a pendulum
differentia	distinguishing mark or characteristic, attribute by which a species is distinguished from other species in the same genus
discover	disclose
disingenuity	disingenuousness
dispatch	speed in settling something
dispose	arrange
distribution	classification
divers	several, different
draft	drawing
drill	baboon
ellipsis	ellipse
entire	whole, complete, perfect
environ	surround
equicrural	(of a triangle) having legs of equal size, isosceles
ergo	therefore
espy	spy, observe, discover

esteem value, deem, think
experiment *(verb)* experience, feel, suffer

faculty power
fain (*adj.*) content, willing, obliged (to); (*adv.*), gladly, willingly
fancy imagination
fatal fateful, having to do with destiny
feign fashion, invent, imagine, frame
fetiche fetish, amulet
feuillemorte color of a dried or faded leaf
fiction something fashioned or invented
final cause the end or purpose of an act or thing
fixedness resisting the action of heat, non-volatile
forbear abstain, refrain
forensic having to do with courts of law
forwardly readily, promptly, eagerly
freestone fine-grained sandstone or limestone, easily cut
fugitive fleeting

gainsayer one who gainsays or speaks against
genus class or kind including a number of subordinate kinds, or *species*
gimar (variant spelling of *jumart*) hybrid born of bull and mare
give off relinquish, cease, leave off
grateful pleasing
guinea gold coin (made of gold from Guinea, and used in trade with Africa)

habitude relation
het heated
historical narrative; concerning the course or career of a thing; being a systematic account of a range of phenomena

i.e. id est, that is
immaterial incorporeal
impertinent irrelevant
import *(verb)* signify
improved cultivated, enhanced, made greater, made worse

impulse the action of one body as it pushes another
inane *(noun)* empty space, the void
incommunicable incapable of being imparted or shared
indolency state neither pleasurable nor painful
ingenuous straightforward, open, honest
inhærentia inherence, existing in
in infinitum to infinity, without end
insensible imperceptible
insensibly imperceptibly, by small degrees
instance *(verb)* cite an example, illustrate or exemplify
intention meaning

jargon nonsense, gibberish
jet black

kin kina quinquina or Peruvian bark, the source of quinine

lay by lay aside, store
lest for fear that
light *(verb)* settle on

Mahumetan Muslim
manna medicinal juice derived from tree bark
mansion dwelling, apartment in a large house
mean inferior in rank, poor
mechanism machine, device that operates by impulse
molest annoy, afflict
monster something unnatural, an abnormal animal or plant
muchwhat somewhat, greatly

native inherent, innate, inborn, natural
natural person naturally deficient in intelligence
natural history aggregation of facts about a thing (especially a natural thing) or class of things
natural philosophy physical or natural science
nearly carefully, with close inspection or scrutiny
never so ever so
nicknamed misnamed
nihil nothing
non-plus state in which nothing can be done or said, perplexity

note mark, sign, indication; characteristic or distinguishing feature

oblique not right-angled
obliquity deviation from rule, fault, error
office duty, obligation
orbis magnus "great circle," the orbit of a planet (for example the earth, as in II xvii 3)
original origin
oscitancy drowsiness, inattention
otherways in another way, otherwise
ought variant spelling of *aught*
over-rule rule over
own acknowledge, admit

parasang a Persian measure of distance (of between three and four miles)
passion effect produced from without, something undergone or suffered
peculiar particular, special
pellucid transparent, clear
perfectly completely
physical having to do with the nature of things
plenitude the condition of being full or occupied
porphyry hard rock of white and red crystals embedded in a fine red mass
positive having an affirmative nature, present as opposed to absent
postern back door
pravity evil, sin, depravity
precise distinguished with precision from all others
prepossessed biased, prejudiced
privative characterized by absence, lack, or negation
profession declaration, avowal
professor one who proclaims or publicly declares
propriety fitness
pudder (variant spelling of *pother)* tumult, uproar, din, stir
purpose *(verb)* resolve to do, intend

quære it is a question (whether. . .); used to introduce a question or subject of inquiry

quickness	vigor, liveliness of perception
quicksilver	mercury
radical	fundamental
rectangle	right-angled
reflex	turned back on the mind itself
remark	observe, take notice of
resolve	free (a person) from doubt
retainer	dependent
retired	(of thoughts) private, hidden, inner
scape	escape
scarce	barely, only just, not quite
school-divinity	religious doctrines as taught in the schools
schoolman	one versed in the learning of the schools
schools	(as in *the schools*): the universities, the domain of traditional academic doctrines and methods
scruple	doubt, uncertainty, hesitation
seat	place in which a power or faculty is realized
seeming	apparent
sensible	able to be sensed; able to sense or feel
sentence	judgment
separate	(as in *separate spirits*) disembodied
seraphim	angel
series	succession or connected sequence
since	ago
sounding	investigation
species	sort or kind within a larger kind (or *genus*); appearance, image
speculative	theoretical
stay	*(verb trans.)* stop, check
stupendious	stupendous
substantia	substance
substratum	that which underlies
superficies	outer surface of a body, boundary
superinduced	brought in over and above something
texture	arrangement of corpscules within a body
thence	from there
thus much	so much

trapezium	four-sided figure with only one pair of parallel sides
ubiquity	omnipresence
uncouth	strange, unusual
unregarded	unnoticed, not attended to
use	custom, habit
uses to be	accustomed to be
velleity	quality or state of merely willing, without any effort toward action
verticity	power of turning or revolving
v.g.	verbi gratia, for example
vitally	so as to cause or produce life
vitriol	sulphate of iron or other metal
viz.	videlicet, that is to say, namely
vulgar	common, ordinary, usual
want	deficiency, lack
wherewith	with which
wherewithal	by means of which
whilst	while
withal	along with the rest, besides, as well
without	outside
wont	custom, habit
wonted	customary, accustomed, usual
wormwood	a bitter plant, used to make vermouth and absinthe, and to protect clothes from moths and fleas
wrangler	disputant, controversialist

Index

This index covers only the text of the *Essay*. The entries and references are taken from the index Locke himself created. Unmarked numbers refer to pages; numbers marked with "§" refer to sections.

Abstraction, 64 § 9
  puts a perfect distance between men and brutes, 64 § 10
  what, 274 § 1
  how, 66 § 1
Accident, 118 § 2
Actions, the best evidence of men's principles, 16 § 3
  but two sorts of, 94 § 4
  unpleasant may be made pleasant, and how, 111 § 69, 117 § 11
  cannot be the same in different places, 134 § 2
  considered as modes, or as moral, 153 § 15
Adequate ideas, 160 § 1, 2
  ideas we have not of any species of substances, 247 § 26
Agreement and disagreement of our ideas fourfold, 224 § 3–4, 225 § 5–6, 226 § 7
Algebra, 299 § 15
Alteration, 132 § 2
Analogy useful in natural philosophy, 310 § 13
Anger, 92 § 12, 14
Antipathy and sympathy whence, 174 § 7
  natural and acquired, 174 § 7
  caused sometimes by connection of ideas, 174 § 7
Assent to maxims, upon hearing and understanding the terms, 12 § 17–18
  a mark of self-evidence, 12 § 18
  not of innate, 12 § 18, 13 § 19
  is to propositions, 301 § 3
  what, 302 § 1, 303 § 3
  ought to be proportioned to the proofs, 302 § 1
  often depends on memory, 305 § 1
  dissent or suspense where voluntary, and where necessary, 332 § 15
Association of ideas, 172
  this association how made, 173 § 6
  ill effects of it, as to antipathies, 174 § 7
  errors, 174 § 9
  disorders of it sometimes cured by time, why, 174 § 13
  its ill influences as to intellectual habits, 175 § 17
Assurance, 307 § 6
Atheism in the world, 25 § 8
Atom what, 135 § 3
Authority relying on others' opinions, one great cause of error, 334 § 17
Axioms not the foundations of sciences, 264 § 1

Beings, but two sorts, 278 § 9
  the eternal being must be cogitative, 278 § 10
Belief what, 303 § 3
  to b. without reason is against our duty, 323 § 24
Blind man if made to see, would not know which a globe, which a cube by his sight, though he knew them by his touch, 58 § 8
Body: we have no more primary ideas of body than of spirit, 123 § 16

Body *(continued)*
the primary ideas of body, 123 § 17
the extension or cohesion of body as hard to be understood, as the thinking of spirit, 124 § 23, 25
moving of b. by b. as hard to be conceived as by spirit, 125 § 28
operates only by impulse, 50 § 11
what, 70 § 11
Brutes have no universal ideas, 64 § 10, 65 § 11
abstract not, 64 § 10

Capacity, 69 § 3
Capacities to know their extent useful, 5
to cure skepticism and idleness, 6
Cause, 132 § 1
and effect, 132 § 1
Certainty depends on intuition, 228 § 1
wherein it consists, 254 § 18
of truth, 258 § 3
of knowledge, 258 § 3
to be had in very few general propositions concerning substances, 263 § 13
where to be had, 264 § 16
verbal, 272 § 8
real, 272 § 8
sensible knowledge the utmost certainty we have of existence, 285 § 2
Clear and obscure ideas, 154 § 2
Complex ideas how made, 63 § 6, 66 § 1
in these the mind is more than passive, 67 § 2
ideas reducible to modes, substances, and relations, 67 § 3
Comparing ideas, 63 § 4
Compounding ideas, 63 § 6
Compulsion, 97 § 13
Confidence, 308 § 7
Confusion of ideas, grounded on a reference to names, 155 § 10, 11
Confused ideas, 155 § 4
Consciousness the same.
c. probably annexed to the same individual immaterial substance, 147 § 25
necessary to thinking, 36 § 10, 11, 38 § 19
Contemplation, 60 § 1
Corpuscularian philosophy most intelligible, 242 § 16
Creation, 132 § 2
not to be denied, because we cannot conceive the manner how, 283 § 19

Definition, why the genus is used in ds. 183 § 10
what, 188 § 6
Defining of terms would cut off a great part of disputes, 211 § 15
Demonstration, 230 § 3
not so clear as intuitive knowledge, 230 § 4, 231 § 6–7
intuitive knowledge necessary in each step of a d. 231 § 7
not limited to quantity, 231 § 9
why that has been supposed, 232 § 10
not to be expected in all cases, 289 § 10
what, 302 § 1, 321 § 15
Desire, 91 § 6
is a state of uneasiness, 101 § 31–2
is moved only by happiness, 104 § 41
how far, 104 § 43
how to be raised, 105 § 46
Dictionaries, how to be made? 221 § 25
Discerning, 63 § 1
the foundation of some general maxims, 63 § 1

Disputing; the art of d. prejudicial to knowledge, 209 § 6
Disputes, whence, 78 § 27
multiplicity of d. owing to the abuse of words, 214 § 22
Distance, 69 § 3
Distinct ideas, 155 § 4
Divisibility of matter incomprehensible, 126 § 31
Duration, 79 § 1-2
whence we get the idea of d. 79 § 3
its measure, 80 § 17
any regular periodical appearance, 80 § 19
minutes, days, years, &c. not necessary to d. 81 § 23
the measures of d. as the revolutions of the sun may be applied to d. before the sun existed, 81 § 25
how we measure d. 81 § 28
what kind of simple ideas we have of d. 83 § 9
recapitulation concerning our ideas of d. time and eternity, 82 § 32
and expansion compared, 83

Education, partly cause of unreasonableness, 172 § 3
Effect, 117 § 11
Envy, 92 § 13, 14
Error, what, 329 § 1
causes of error, 329 § 1
1. want of proofs, 329 § 2
2. want of skill to use them, 330 § 5
3. want of will to use them, 330 § 6
4. wrong measures of probability, 330 § 7
fewer men assent to errors than is supposed, 335 § 18

Essence, real and nominal, 185 § 15, 192 § 2–3
supposition of unintelligible real essences of species of no use, 186 § 17
real and nominal e. in simple ideas and modes always the same, in substances always different, 186 § 18
Essences though arbitrary, yet not at random, 190 § 7
of mixed modes, why, called notions, 191 § 12
what, 192 § 2
relates only to species, 193 § 4
real essences what, 194 § 6
we know them not, 196 § 9
nominal are made by the mind, 200 § 26
but not altogether arbitrarily, 201 § 28
different in several men, 201 § 28
nominal es. of substances, how made, 201 § 28–29
of species is the abstract idea the name stands for, 184 § 12
is of man's making, 184 § 12
but founded in the agreement of things, 184 § 13
real es. determine not our species, 184 § 13
real es. of substances not to be known, 262 § 12
Essential, what, 192 § 2, 194 § 5
nothing el. to individuals, 193 § 4
but to species, 194 § 6
essential difference what, 194 § 5
Eternal verities, 291 § 14
Eternity, in our disputes and reasonings about it, why we are apt to blunder, 156 § 15
whence we get its idea, 82 § 28
Evil, what, 104 § 42

Existence, an idea of sensation and reflection, 45 § 7
our own e. we know intuitively, 274 § 3
and cannot doubt of, 275 § 2
of created things, knowable only by our senses, 284 § 1
past e. known only by memory, 290 § 11
Expansion should be applied to space in general, 77 § 26
Experience often helps us, where we think not it does, 59 § 8
Extension, we have no distinct ideas of very great, or very little e. 156 § 16
of body incomprehensible, 124 § 23
denominations from place and e. are many of them relatives, 133 § 5, 167 § 3
and body not the same thing, 70 § 11
of body and of space how distinguished, 43 § 5, 77 § 26

Faculties of the mind are but powers, 97 § 17
Faith and opinion, as distinguished from knowledge what, 304 § 3
and knowledge their difference, 303 § 3
what, 312 § 14
not opposite to reason, 323 § 24
and reason, 323
as contradistinguished to reason what, 324 § 2
cannot convince us of anything contrary to our reason, 325 § 5, 326 § 6, 327 § 8
matter of f. is only divine revelation, 326 § 6
things above reason are only proper matters of f. 327 § 7, § 9
Falsehood, 256 § 9
Fantastical ideas, 157 § 1
Figure, 70 § 5
Figurative speech, an abuse of language, 214 § 34
Finite and infinite modes of quantity, 85 § 1
all positive ideas of quantity finite, 87 § 8
Free, how far a man is f. 98 § 21
a man not f. to will or not will, 98 § 22, 99 § 23–24
Freedom belongs only to agents, 98 § 19
wherein it consists, 100 § 27
Free will, liberty belongs not to the will, 97 § 14
wherein consists that which is called f. 105 § 47

General ideas how made 64 § 9
knowledge what, 249 § 31
propositions cannot be known to be true without knowing the essence of the species, 258 § 4
words how made, 181 § 6–8, 182 § 9
belongs only to signs, 183 § 11
Genus and species what, 182 § 9
are but Latin names for sorts, 192 § 1
is but a partial conception of what is in the species, 201 § 32
Generation, 132 § 2
God: an idea of G. not innate, 25 § 8
the existence of a G. evident and obvious to reason, 26 § 9
the notion of a G. once got is the likeliest to spread and be continued, 26 § 9, 27 § 10
ideas of G. contrary, 27 § 15
inconsistent, 28 § 15
the best notions of G. got by thought and application, 28 § 15

the being of a G. demonstrable, 275 § 1, 276 § 6
more certain than any other existence without us, 277 § 6
the idea of G. not the only proof of his existence, 277 § 7
the being of a G. the foundation of morality and divinity, 278 § 7
not material, 280 § 13, *&c.*
how we make our idea of G. 127 § 33–34
Good and evil what, 91 § 2, 104 § 42
the greater g. determines not the will, 102 § 35, 103 § 38, 104 § 44
why, 104 § 44
works on the will only by desire, 105 § 46
desire of g. how to be raised, 105 § 46–47

Happiness, what, 104 § 42
what h. men pursue, 104 § 43
Hardness, what, 43 § 4
Heat and cold, how the sensation of them both is produced by the same water at the same time, 53 § 21
Hypotheses their use, 298 § 13
ill consequences of wrong h. 331 § 11

Idea, what, 6 § 8, 48 § 8
is. their original in children, 23 § 2
none innate, 28 § 17
because not remembered, 29 § 20
are what the mind is employed about in thinking, 33 § 1
all from sensation or reflection, 33 § 2 *&c.*
their way of getting observable in children, 35 § 6
why some have more, some fewer i. 35 § 7
of reflection got late, and in some very negligently, 35 § 8
their beginning and increase in children, 39 § 23–24
their original in sensation and reflection, 39 § 24
of one sense, 41 § 1
want names, 42 § 2
of more than one sense, 44
of reflection, 44 § 1
of sensation and reflection, 45
as in the mind, and in things must be distinguished, 48 § 7
of sensation often altered by the judgment, 58 § 8
principally those of sight, 59 § 9
simple i. men agree in, 78 § 27
original, 113 § 73
all complex is. resolvable into simple, 116 § 9
what simple is. have been most modified, 117 § 10
our complex i. of God and other spirits common in everything, but infinity, 128 § 36
clear and obscure, 154 § 2
distinct and confused, 155 § 4
may be clear in one part, and obscure in another, 156 § 13
real and fantastical, 157 § 1
simple are all real, 158 § 2
and adequate, 158 § 2
what i. of mixed modes are fantastical, 159 § 4
what i. of substances are fantastical, 159 § 5
adequate and inadequate, 160 § 1
how said to be in things, 160 § 2
modes are all adequate i. 161 § 3
unless as referred to names, 161 § 5
of substances inadequate, 161 § 3
1. as referred to real essences, 162–64 § 6–7

Idea, what *(continued)*
2. as referred to a collection of simple ideas, 164 § 8
simple ideas are perfect ἔκτυπα, 165 § 12
of substances are perfect ἔκτυπα, 166 § 13
of modes are perfect archetypes, 166 § 14
true or false, 166
as bare appearances in the mind, neither true nor false, 166 § 3
as referred to other men's ideas, or to real existence, or to real essences may be true or false, 167 § 4, 5
simple i. referred to other men's i. less apt to be false, 167 § 9
complex ones in this respect more apt to be false, especially those of mixed modes, 168 § 11
simple i. referred to existence are all true, 169 § 14, 170 § 16
though not resemblances, 169 § 14
though they should be different in different men, 169 § 15
complex i. of modes are all true, 170 § 17
of substances when false, 170 § 18
when right or wrong, 171 § 26
that we are uncapable of, 246 § 23
that we cannot attain, because of their remoteness, 246 § 24
because of their minuteness, 246 § 25
simple have a real conformity to things, 251 § 4
and all others but of substances, 252 § 5
of substances different in different men, 207 § 13
our is. almost all relative, 94 § 3
particular are first in the mind, 267 § 9
general are imperfect, 267 § 9
how positive is. may be from privative causes, 47 § 4
Identical propositions teach nothing 270 § 2
identical propositions trifling, 270 § 3
Identity, not an innate idea, 24 § 3-4, 25 § 5
and diversity, 133
of a plant wherein it consists, 136 § 4
of animals, 136 § 5
of a man, 137 § 6, 8
unity of substance does not always make the same i. 137 § 7 § 7
personal i. 138 § 9
depends on the same consciousness, 138 § 10
continued existence makes i. 149 § 29
and diversity in ideas the first perception of the mind, 224 § 4
Ignorance, our i. infinitely exceeds our knowledge, 245 § 22
causes of i. 246 § 23
1. for want of ideas, 246 § 23
2. for want of a discoverable connection between the ideas we have, 247 § 28
3. for want of tracing the ideas we have, 249 § 30
Illation, what, 313 § 2
Immensity, 69 § 4
how this idea is got, 86 § 3
Immoralities, of whole nations, 18–19 § 9–10
Impenetrability, 42
Imposition of opinions unreasonable, 306 § 4

Impossibility, not an innate idea, 24 § 3
Impression on the mind what, 8 § 5
Inadequate ideas, 160 § 1
Incompatibility, how far knowable, 241 § 15
Individuationis principium, is existence, 135 § 3
Inference, what, 313 § 2, 316–17
Infinite
the idea of infinity of space or number, and of space or number i. must be distinguished, 87 § 7
our idea of i. very obscure, 87 § 8
number furnishes us with the clearest ideas of i. 88 § 9
the idea of i. a growing idea, 88 § 12
our idea of ity. has its original in sensation and reflection, 89 § 22
we have no positive idea of i. 89 § 13, 156 § 16
Infinity, how applied to God by us, 85 § 1
how we get this idea, 86 § 3
Innate moral rules to no purpose if effaceable or alterable, 21 § 20
the doctrine of i. principles of ill consequence, 22 § 24
Instant and continual change, 80 § 13–14
Intuitive knowledge, 228 § 1
admits no doubts, 230 § 5
our highest certainty, 321 § 14
Iron of what advantage to mankind, 297 § 11

Judgment,
men's wrong judgments in reference to good and evil, 111 § 57
right j. 302 § 4
one cause of wrong j. 301 § 3
wherein it consists, 322 § 16

Knowledge what, 224 § 2
how much our k. depends on our senses, 220 § 23
actual, 226 § 8
habitual, 226 § 8
habitual twofold, 226 § 9
intuitive, 228 § 1
intuitive the clearest, 229 § 1
intuitive irresistible, 229 § 1
demonstrative, 229 § 2
of general truths is all either intuitive or demonstrative, 233 § 14
of particular existences is sensitive, 233 § 14
clear ideas do not always produce clear knowledge, 234 § 15
what kind of k. we have of nature, 121 § 12
its beginning and progress, 65 § 15, § 17, 11 § 15
men's k. according to the employment of their faculties, 30 § 22
to be got only by the application of our own thought to the contemplation of things, 30 § 23
extent of human k. 235
our k. goes not beyond our ideas, 235 § 1
nor beyond the perception of their agreement or disagreement, 235 § 2
reaches not to all our ideas, 235 § 3
much less to the reality of things, 236 § 6
yet very improvable if right ways were taken, 236 § 6
of coexistence very narrow, 239–40 § 9–11
and therefore of substances very narrow, 241–42 § 14–16

Knowledge what *(continued)*
of other relations indeterminable, 243 § 18
of existence, 245 § 21
certain and universal, where to be had, 248 § 29, 264 § 16
ill use of words a great hindrance of k. 249 § 30
general, where to be got, 249 § 31
lies only in our thoughts, 263 § 13
reality of our k. 250
of mathematical truths, how real, 252 § 6
of morality real, 252 § 7
of substances, how far real, 253 § 12
what makes our k. real, 251 § 3, 252 § 8
of substances, wherein it consists, 261§ 10
what required to any tolerable k. of substances, 263 § 14
self-evident, 264 § 2
of identity and diversity, as large as our ideas, 239 § 8, 265 § 4
wherein it consists, 265 § 4
of coexistence very scanty, 265 § 5
of relations of modes not so scanty, 266 § 6
of real existence none, 266 § 7
intuitive of our own existence, 274 § 3
demonstrative of a God, 275 § 1
sensible k. is k. 285 § 3 *&c.*
improvement of k. 292
not improved by maxims, 293 § 3
why so thought, 292 § 2
k. improved only by perfecting and comparing ideas, 294 § 6, 298 § 14
and finding their relations, 294 § 7
by intermediate ideas, 299 § 14
in substances how to be improved, 295 § 9
partly necessary, partly voluntary, 300 § 1–2
why some, and so little, 301 § 2
how increased, 319 § 6

Language,
wherein it consists, 176 § 1–3
its use, 190 § 7
its imperfections, 204 § 1
double use, 204 § 1
to use no word without a clear and distinct idea annexed to it, is one remedy of the imperfections of l. 215–16 § 8–9
propriety in the use of words, another remedy, 216 § 11
making known the meaning of our words, another remedy, 217 § 12
meaning of words made known in simple ideas, by showing, 217 § 14
in mixed modes by defining, 218 § 15
in substances by showing and defining too, 219 § 19, 220 § 21
Law of nature generally allowed, 17 § 6
there is, though not innate, 20 § 13
its enforcement, 151 § 6
Learning of the schools of ill consequence, 210 § 12
Least visible, 80 § 9
Liberty, what, 95–96 § 8–11, 97 § 15
belongs not to the will, 97 § 14
to be determined by the result of our own deliberation, is no restraint of l. 105–7 § 47–50
founded in a power of suspending our particular desires, 105 § 47, 108 § 51–52
Logic has introduced obscurity into languages, 209 § 6
Love, 91 § 4

Madness,
opposition to reason deserves that name, 173 § 4
Making, 132 § 2
Man not the product of blind chance, 276 § 6
we know not his real essence, 192 § 3, 199 § 22, 200 § 27
the boundaries of the human species not determined, 200 § 27
what makes the same individual m. 145 § 21, 149 § 29
the same m. may be different persons, 145 § 21, 149 § 29
Mathematics, their methods, 294 § 7
improvement, 299 § 15
Matter incomprehensible both in its cohesion and divisibility, 124, 126
what, 211 § 15
whether in us it thinks is not to be known, 236 § 6
cannot produce motion, or anything else, 278 § 10
and motion cannot produce thought, 278 § 10
not eternal, 282 § 18
Maxims, 268–69 § 12-15
not alone self-evident, 264 § 3
are not the truths first known, 266 § 9
not the foundation of our knowledge, 267 § 10
how made, 293 § 3
wherein their evidence consists, 267 § 10, 269 § 14
their use, 268
maxims from the schools introduced into conversation, 268 § 11
the use that is made of them, 268
of dangerous use with doubtful terms, 268 § 12
when first known, 10 § 9, § 12, 11 § 14
how they gain assent, 13 § 21, 14 § 22
not in the understanding, before they are actually known, 14 § 22
Memory, 60 § 2
difference of m. 61 § 5
in remembrance, the mind sometimes active, sometimes passive, 61 § 7
its necessity, 62 § 8
defects, 62 § 8
in brutes, 62 § 10
Metaphysic, and school-divinity filled with uninstructive propositions, 272 § 9
Method used in mathematics, 294 § 7
Minutes, hours, days, not necessary to duration, 81 § 23
Miracles, the ground of assent to m. 311 § 13
Misery, what, 104 § 42
Modes, mixed m. 114 § 1
made by the mind, 115 § 2
sometimes got by the explication of their names, 115 § 3
whence a mixed mode has its unity, 116 § 4
occasion of mixed modes, 116 § 5
mixed m. their ideas, how got, 116 § 9
ms. simple and complex, 67 § 5, 67 § 4
simple m. 69 § 1
Moral good and evil, what, 151 § 5
three rules whereby men judge of m. rectitude, 151 § 7
beings how founded on simple ideas of sensation and reflection, 153 § 14–15
rules not self-evident, 16 § 4
variety of opinions concerning m. rules, whence, 17 § 5–6

Moral good and evil *(continued)*
rules if innate cannot with public allowance be transgressed, 19–20 § 11–13
Morality capable of demonstration, 218 § 16, 243 § 18, 295 § 8
the proper study of mankind, 297 § 11
of actions in their conformity to a rule, 153 § 15
discourses in m. if not clear, 'tis the fault of the speaker, 219 § 17
hindrances of demonstrative treating of m.
1. want of marks, 244 § 19
2. complexedness, 244 § 19
and mechanism hard to be reconciled, 21 § 14
Motion, voluntary inexplicable, 283 § 19

Naming of ideas, 64 § 8
Names moral established by law are not to be varied from, 253 § 10
of substances standing for real essences are not capable to convey certainty to the understanding, 259 § 5
standing for nominal essences, will make some, though not many certain propositions, 260 § 6
a particular name to every particular thing impossible, 180 § 2
and useless, 180 § 3
specific ns. are affixed to the nominal essence, 185 § 16
of simple ideas, modes, and substances, have each of them something peculiar, 187
of simple ideas and substances refer to things, 187 § 2
of simple ideas stand for both real and nominal essence, 188 § 3
of simple ideas not capable of definitions, 188 § 4
why, 188 § 7
of complex ideas may be defined, 189 § 12
of mixed modes stand for arbitrary ideas, 190 § 2
general ns. of substances stand for sorts, 192 § 1
of substances doubtful, because referred to patterns that cannot be known, or known but imperfectly, 206–7 § 11–13
of simple ideas, why least doubtful, 207 § 18
Natural philosophy not capable of science, 247 § 26, 296 § 10
yet very useful, 297 § 12
how to be improved, 298 § 12
what has hindered its improvement, 298 § 12
Necessity, 97 § 13
Negative terms, 176 § 4
names signify the absence of positive ideas, 48 § 5
Nothing, that n. cannot produce anything is demonstration, 276 § 3
Notions, 115 § 2
Number, 84
modes of n. the most distinct ideas, 84 § 3
the general measure, 85 § 8
affords the clearest idea of infinity, 89 § 13

Obstinate they are most who have least examined 306 § 3
Opinion, what, 303 § 3
how os. grow up to principles, 22 § 22, § 24, § 25
of others a wrong ground of assent, 305 § 6, 334 § 17

often taken without full proof, 306 § 3
Organs: our organs suited to our state, 121 § 12

Particles join parts or whole sentences together, 203 § 1
in them lies the beauty of well speaking, 203 § 2
they express some action or posture of the mind, 203 § 4
Passion, 117 § 11
Passions, how they lead us into error, 332 § 12
turn on pleasure and pain, 91 § 3
Perception threefold, 95 § 5
in p. the mind for the most part passive, 56 § 1
is an impression made on the mind, 57 § 3–4
in the womb, 57 § 5
difference between it and innate ideas, 57 § 6
puts the difference between the animal and vegetable kingdom, 59 § 11
belongs to all animals, 59 § 12
Person, what, 138 § 9
a forensic term, 148 § 26
the same consciousness alone makes the same p. 140 § 13, 146 § 23
the same soul without the same consciousness makes not the same p. 142 § 15 &c.
reward and punishment follow personal identity, 144 § 18
Pleasure and pain, 90 § 1, 92 § 15
join themselves to most of our ideas, 45 § 2
Power, how we come by its idea, 93 § 1
active and passive, 93 § 2
no passive power in God, no active power in matter, both active and passive in spirits, 93 § 2
our idea of active p. clearest from reflection, 94 § 4
make a great part of the ideas of substances, 120 § 7
why, 120 § 8
an idea of sensation and reflection, 46 § 8
Practical principles not innate, 15 § 1
not universally assented to, 15 § 2
are for operation, 16 § 3
not agreed, 20 § 14
Principles not to be received without strict examination, 293 § 4, 331 § 8
none innate, 7
none universally assented to, 8
how ordinarily got, 22 § 22 &c.
are to be examined, 23 § 27
not innate if the ideas they are made up of, are not innate, 23 § 1
Privative terms, 176 § 4
Probability, what, 302 § 1, 303 § 3
the grounds of p. 304 § 4
in matter of fact, 307 § 6
how we are to judge in ps. 304 § 5
difficulties in ps. 309 § 9
grounds of p. in speculation, 310 § 12
wrong measures of p. 330 § 7
how evaded by prejudiced minds, 332 § 13–14
Proofs, 230 § 3
Properties of specific essences not known, 198 § 19
of things very numerous, 165 § 10
Propositions identical teach nothing, 270 § 2
generical teach nothing, 271 § 4, 273 § 13

Propositions *(continued)*
wherein a part of the definition is predicated of the subject teach nothing, 271 § 5
but the signification of that word, 271 § 7
concerning substances generally either trifling or uncertain, 272 § 9
merely verbal how to be known, 273 § 12
abstract terms predicated one of another produce merely verbal ps. 273 § 12
or part of a complex idea predicated of the whole, 273 § 13
universal ps. concern not existence, 274 § 1
what ps. concern existence, 274 § 1
certain ps. concerning existence are particular, concerning abstract ideas may be general, 291 § 13
mental, 255 § 3, 255 § 5
verbal, 255 § 3, 255 § 5
mental hard to be treated, 255 § 3, 4
Punishment, what, 151 § 5
and reward follow consciousness, 144 § 18, 148 § 26
an unconscious drunkard, why punished, 146 § 22

Quality: secondary qs. their connection or inconsistence unknown, 239 § 11
of substances scarce knowable, but by experience, 241 § 14, 242 § 16
of spiritual substances less than of corporeal, 242 § 17
secondary have no conceivable connection with the primary that produce them, 240 § 12–13, 247 § 28
of substances depend on remote causes, 261 § 11
not to be known by descriptions, 220 § 21
secondary how far capable of demonstration, 232 § 11, 233 § 13
what, 48 § 8
how said to be in things, 160 § 2
secondary would be other, if we could discover the minute parts of bodies, 121 § 11
primary qs. 49 § 9
how they produce ideas in us, 50 § 12
secondary qs. 50–51 § 13–15
primary qs. resemble our ideas, secondary not, 51 § 15–16 *&c.*
three sorts of qs. in bodies, 54 § 23
i.e. primary, secondary immediately perceivable, and secondary mediately perceivable, 56 § 26
secondary qs. are bare powers, 54–55 § 23–25
secondary qs. have no discernable connection with the first, 55 § 25
Quotations, how little to be relied on, 310 § 11

Real ideas, 157
Reason, its various significations, 312 § 1
what, 313 § 2
four parts of r. 314
where r. fails us, 320–21 § 9, 10, 11, 12, 13
necessary in all but intuition, 321 § 15
according to, contrary to, above r. 322 § 23
as contradistinguished to faith, what, 324 § 2
helps us not to the knowledge of innate truths, 9

general ideas, general terms, and reason usually grow together, 11 § 15
Recollection, 90 § 1
Reflection, 34 § 4
Related, 130 § 1
Relation, 68 § 7, 129
natural, 150 § 2
instituted, 150 § 3
moral, 151 § 4
numerous, 154 § 17
without correlative terms not so commonly observed, 130 § 2
different from the things related, 130 § 4
all things capable of r. 131 § 7
the idea of the r. often clearer than of the things related, 131 § 8
all terminate in simple ideas of sensation and reflection, 131 § 9
Relative, 130 § 1
some r. terms taken for external denominations, 130 § 2
some for absolute, 130 § 3
many words though absolute are rs. 133 § 6
Remembrance what, 29 § 20, 61 § 7
Restraint, 97 § 13
Revelation, an unquestionable ground of assent, 312 § 14
traditional r. cannot convey any new simple ideas, 324 § 3
not so sure as our reason or senses, 325 § 4
in things of reason no need of r. 325 § 5
cannot over-rule our clear knowledge, 325 § 5, 328 § 10
must over-rule probabilities of reason, 327 § 8-9
Reward, what, 151 § 5
Rhetoric, an art of deceiving, 214 § 34
Sagacity, 230 § 3
Same, whether substance, mode, or concrete, 149 § 28
Schools wherein faulty, 209 § 6
Science divided into a consideration of nature, of operation, and of signs, 336
no s. of natural bodies, 249 § 29
Self, what makes it, 143 § 17, 144 § 20, 146–47 § 23–25
Self-evident propositions, where to be had, 264 *&c.*
Sensation, 33 § 3
distinguishable from other perceptions, 233 § 14
explained, 53
what, 90 § 1 (*Chap.* xix)
Senses, why we cannot conceive other qualities than the objects of our ss. 40 § 3
cannot be affected but by contact, 232 § 11
much quicker would not be useful to us, 121 § 12
our organs of s. suited to our state, 121 § 12
Sensible knowledge is as certain as we need, 288 § 8
goes not beyond the present act, 289 § 9
Simple ideas, 40 § 1
not made by the mind, 40 § 2
power of the mind over them, 66 § 1
the materials of all our knowledge, 46 § 10
all positive, 47 § 1
very different from their causes, 47 § 2–3
Skeptical. Nobody so s. as to doubt his own existence, 275 § 2
Solidity, 42 § 1
inseparable from body, 42 § 1
by it body fills space, 43 § 2

Solidity *(continued)*
this idea got by touch, 42 § 1
how distinguished from space, 43 § 3
from hardness, 43 § 4
Something from eternity demonstrated, 276 § 3, 278 § 8
Soul thinks not always, 36 § 9 *&c.*
not in sound sleep, 36 § 11 *&c.*
its immateriality we know not, 236 § 6
religion not concerned in the ss. immateriality, 237 § 6
our ignorance about it, 149 § 27
Space, its idea got by sight and touch, 69 § 2
its modifications, 69 § 4
not body, 70 § 11–12
its parts inseparable, 71 § 13
immovable, 72 § 14
whether body or spirit, 72 § 16
whether substance or accident, 72 § 17
infinite, 74 § 21
ideas of s. and body distinct, 76 § 23, 77 § 26
Species of substances are determined by the nominal essence, 195 § 7, § 8
not by the real essence, 198 § 18, 200 § 25
more s. of creatures above than below us, 196 § 12
of creatures very gradual, 196 § 12
what is necessary to the making of s. by real essences, 197 § 14
of animals and plants cannot be distinguished by propagation, 199 § 23
is but a partial conception of what is in the individuals, 201 § 32
man makes the s. or sorts, 202 § 36
but the foundation of it is in the similitude found in things, 202 § 36
Speech, its end, 178 § 2
Spirits, the existence of s. not knowable, 290 § 12
operation of s. on bodies not conceivable, 248 § 28
what knowledge they have of bodies, 220 § 23
we have as clear a notion of the substance of s. as of body, 119 § 5
our ideas of s. 122 § 15
as clear as that of body, 124 § 22
primary ideas belonging to s. 123 § 18
move, 123 § 19-20
ideas of s. and body compared, 125 § 30
the existence of s. as easy to be admitted as that of bodies, 126 § 32
Substance, 117 § 1
s. no idea of it, 29 § 18
not very knowable, 239 § 11 *&c.*
our certainty concerning them reaches but a little way, 260 § 7, 261 § 10
in ss. we must rectify the signification of their names by the things more than by definitions, 221 § 24
their ideas single or collective, 68 § 6
we have no distinct idea of s. 72 § 18, 73 § 19
we have no idea of pure s. 118 § 2
our ideas of the sorts of ss. 118 § 3, 119 § 4, 120 § 6
observables in our ideas of ss. 128 § 37
collective ideas of ss. 129
they are single ideas, 129 § 2

the ideas of ss. have in the mind a double reference, 162 § 6
the properties of ss. numerous, and not at all to be known, 165 § 9–10
the perfectest ideas of ss. 120 § 7
three sorts of ideas make our complex one of ss. 120 § 9
Succession, an idea got chiefly from the train of our ideas, 46 § 9
Syllogism, no help to reasoning. 314 § 4
the use of s. 314 § 4
inconveniencies of s. 317 § 4
of no use in probabilities, 319 § 5
helps not to new discoveries, 319 § 6
connections and inferences seen better without than with syllogism, 316–17

Testimony, how it lessens its force, 309 § 10
Thinking.
modes of t. 90 § 1
men's ordinary way of t. 255 § 4
an operation of the soul, 36 § 10
Time, what, 80 § 17
denominations from t. are relatives, 133 § 3
Toleration necessary in our state of knowledge, 306 § 4
Tradition the older the less credible, 309 § 10
Trifling propositions, 270
discourses, 272 § 9, 273 § 11
Truth, what, 254 § 2, 255 § 5, 256 § 9
of thought, 255 § 3, § 6
of words, 255 § 3
verbal and real, 256 § 8–9
metaphysical, 166 § 2
general seldom apprehended but in words, 257 § 2
in what it consists, 171 § 19

Understanding, what, 95 § 5
like a dark room, 65 § 17
when rightly used, 6
is the power of thinking, 44 § 2
three sorts of perception in the u. 95 § 5
wholly passive in the reception of simple ideas, 39 § 25
Uneasiness alone determines the will to a new action, 100 § 29, 101 § 31, § 33 *&c.*
why it determines the will, 103 § 36–37
causes of it, 111 *&c.* § 57 *&c.*
Unity, an idea both of sensation and reflection, 45 § 7
suggested by everything, 84 § 1
Universality is only in signs, 183 § 11
Universals how made, 64 § 9

Vacuum possible, 74 § 21
motion proves a v. 75 § 22
Variety in men's pursuits accounted for, 109 § 54 *&c.*
Vice lies in wrong measures of good, 334 § 16
Virtue,
what in its common application, 152 § 10
Volition, what, 95 § 5, 97 § 15
better known by reflection than words, 101 § 30
Voluntary, what, 95 § 5, 96 § 11

What is is, is not universally assented to, 8 § 4
Whole and part not innate ideas, 25 § 6
Will, what, 95 § 5, 97 § 15, 100 § 29
what determines the w. 100 § 29
often confounded with desire, 101 § 30
is conversant only about our own actions, 101 § 30

Will, what *(continued)*
is determined by the greatest present removable uneasiness, 104 § 40
is the power of volition, 44 § 2
Words, an ill use of ws. one great hindrance of knowledge, 249 § 30
abuse of ws. 208
sects introduce ws. without signification, 208 § 2
the schools have coined multitudes of insignificant ws. 208 § 2
and rendered others obscure, 209 § 6
often used without signification, 208 § 3
inconstancy in their use an abuse of words, 209 § 5
obscurity an abuse of ws. 209 § 6
taking them for things an abuse of words, 210 § 14
who most liable to this abuse of ws. 210 § 14
making them stand for real essences, which we know not, is an abuse of ws. 212 § 17
the supposition of their certain evident signification, an abuse of ws. 214 § 22
the meaning of ws. is made known in simple ideas by showing, 217 § 14
in mixed modes by defining, 218 § 15
in substances by showing and defining too, 219 § 19, 220 § 21–22,
the ill consequence of learning ws. first, and their meaning afterwards, 221 § 24
are to be used constantly in the same sense, 222 § 26
or else to be explained, where the context determines it not, 223 § 27
how made general, 176 § 3
signifying insensible things, derived from names of sensible ideas, 177 § 5
have no natural signification, 178 § 1
but by imposition, 180 § 8
stand immediately for the ideas of the speaker, 178 § 1–2
yet with a double reference.
1. to the ideas in the hearer's mind, 178 § 4
2. to the reality of things, 179 § 5
often used without signification, 179 § 7
most general, 180 § 1
why some ws. of one language cannot be translated into those of another, 190 § 8
why I have been so large on words, 191 § 16
new ws. or in new significations are cautiously to be used, 202 § 51
civil use of ws. 204 § 3
philosophical use of words, 204 § 3
miss their end, when they excite not in the hearer, the same idea is in the mind of the speaker, 205 § 4
what words are most doubtful, and why, 205 § 5
what unintelligible, 205 § 5
are fitted to the use of common life, 150 § 2
the supposition of their certain evident signification, an abuse of ws. 214 § 22
Worship not an innate idea, 25 § 7